Sabine Baring-Gould

Legends of the Patriarchs and Prophets and Other Old Testament Characters from Various Sources

Sabine Baring-Gould

Legends of the Patriarchs and Prophets and Other Old Testament Characters from Various Sources

ISBN/EAN: 9783337155759

Printed in Europe, USA, Canada, Australia, Japan

Cover: Foto ©Lupo / pixelio.de

More available books at **www.hansebooks.com**

LEGENDS

OF THE

PATRIARCHS AND PROPHETS

AND OTHER

OLD TESTAMENT CHARACTERS

FROM VARIOUS SOURCES

BY THE

REV. S. BARING-GOULD, M.A.

Author of " Curious Myths of the Middle Ages," " The Origin and Development of Religious Belief," " In Exitu Israel," etc.

NEW YORK:
AMERICAN BOOK EXCHANGE,
764 BROADWAY.
1881.

PREFACE.

AN incredible number of legends exists connected with the personages whose history is given in the Old Testament. The collection now presented to the public must by no means be considered as exhaustive. The compiler has been obliged to limit himself as to the number, it being quite impossible to insert all. He trusts that few of peculiar interest have been omitted.

The Mussulman traditions are nearly all derived from the Talmudic writers, just as the history of Christ in the Koran is taken from the Apocryphal Gospels. The Koran follows the "Sepher Hajaschar" (Book of the Just) far more closely than the canonical Scriptures; and the "Sepher Hajaschar" is a storehouse of the Rabbinic tradition on the subject of the Patriarchs from Adam to Joshua.

The Jewish traditions are of various value. Some can be traced to their origin without fail. One class is derived from Persia, as, for instance, those of Asmodeus, the name of the demon being taken, along with his story, from Iranian sources. Another class springs from the Cabbalists, who, by permutation of the letters of a name, formed the nuclei, so to speak, from which legends spread.

Another class, again, is due to the Rabbinic commentators, who, unable to allow for poetical periphrasis, insisted on literal interpretations, and then coined fables to explain them. Thus the saying of David, "*Thou hast heard me from among the horns of the unicorns*," which signified that David was assisted by God in trouble, was taken quite literally by the Rabbis, and a story was invented to explain it.

Another class, again, is no doubt due to the exaggeration of Oriental imagery, just as that previously mentioned is due to the deficiency of the poetic fancy in certain Rabbis. Thus, imagination and defect of imagination, each contributed to add to the store.

But when we have swept all these classes aside, there remains a residuum, small, no doubt, of genuine tradition. To this class, if I am not mistaken, belong the account of Lamech and his wives, and the story of the sacrifice of Isaac. In the latter instance, the type comes out far clearer in the Talmudic tradition that in the canonical Scriptures; and this can hardly have been the result of Jewish interpolation, knowing, as they did, that Christians pointed triumphantly to this type.

With regard to Jewish traditions, it is unfortunate that both Eisenmenger and Bartolocci, who collected many of them, were so prejudiced, so moved with violent animosity against the Rabbinic writers, that they preserved only the grotesque, absurd, and indecent legends, and wholly passed over those—and there are many of them—which are redolent of poetry, and which contain an element of truth.

A certain curious interest attaches to these legends —at least, I think so; and, should they find favor with the public, this volume will be followed by another series on the legends connected with the New Testament characters.

The author is not aware of any existing collection of these legends, except that of M. Colin de Plancy, "Legendes de l'Ancien Testament," Paris, 1861 ; but he has found this work of little or no use to him in composing his volume, as M. de Plancy gives no reference to authorities; and also, because nearly the whole of the contents are taken from D'Herbelot's " Bibliothèque Orientale " and Migne's " Dictionnaire des Apocryphes.'

It will be necessary to add a few words on certain works largely quoted in the following pages.

1. Dr. G. Weil's " Biblische Legende der Muselmänner," Frankfurt a. M., 1845, is derived from three Arabic MS. works—" *Chamis*," by Husein Ibn Mohammed Ibn Alhasan Addiarbekri ; " *Dsachirat Alulun wanatidjat Alfuhum*," by Ahmed Ibn zein Alabidin Albekri; and " *Kissat Alanbija*," by Mohammed Ibn Ahmed Alkissai.

2. The Chronicle of Abou-djafar Mohammed Tabari was translated into Persian by Abou Ali Mohammed

Belami, who added sundry traditions circulating in Persia ; and has been rendered into French, in part, by M. Hermann Zolenberg, for the Oriental Translation Fund, Paris, 1867.

3. The "Sepher Hajaschar," or Book of Jasher (Yaschar), is quoted from the translation by Le Chevalier P. L. B. Drach, inserted in Migne's "Dictionnaire des Apocryphes."

4. Eisenmenger, "Neuentdektes Judenthum," 2 vols. 8vo, Königsburg, 1711, contains a great many Rabbinic traditions collected from sources inaccessible to most persons.

5. Bartolocci, "Bibliotheca Magna Rabbinica," 4 vols. fol., Rome, 1675-93, is a very valuable storehouse of information, but sadly disfigured by prejudice.

CONTENTS.

1*

CONTENTS.

XXI.

XXII.

XXIII.

XXV.

XXVI.

XXVII.

XXXIII.

XXIX.

XXXVII

LEGENDS OF THE

PATRIARCHS AND PROPHETS.

I.

THE FALL OF THE ANGELS.

IN the beginning, before the creation of heaven and earth, God made the angels; free intelligences and free wills; out of His love He made them, that they might be eternally happy. And that their happiness might be complete, He gave them the perfection of a created nature; that is, He gave them freedom.

But happiness is only attained by the free will agreeing in its freedom to accord with the will of God. Some of the angels by an act of free will obeyed the will of God, and in such obedience found perfect happiness; other angels by an act of free will rebelled against the will of God, and in such disobedience found misery.

Such is the catholic theory of the fall of the angels.

Historically, it is represented as a war in heaven. *"And there was war in heaven: Michael and his angels fought against the dragon; and the dragon fought and his angels, and prevailed not; neither was their place found any more in heaven. And the great dragon was cast out, that old serpent, called the Devil, and Satan, which deceiveth the whole world; he was cast out into the earth, and his angels were cast out with him."* [1] The reason of the revolt was that Satan desired to be as great as God. *" Thou hast said in thine heart, I will ascend into heaven, I will exalt my throne above the stars of God; I will sit also upon the mount of the congregation in the sides of the north; I will ascend above the heights of the clouds; I will be like the Most High."* [2]

[1] Rev. xii. 7–9.

[2] Isaiah xiv. 13, 14.

The war ended in the fall of Satan and those whom he had led into apostasy; and to this fall are referred the words of Christ, "*I saw Satan like lightning fall from heaven.*"[1]

Fabricius, in his collections of the apocryphal writings of the Old Testament, has preserved the song of triumph which the Archangel Michael sang on obtaining the victory. This is a portion of it :—

"Glory to our God! Praise to His holy Name! He is our God; glory be to Him! He is our Lord! His be the triumph! He has stretched forth His right hand; He has manifested His power, He has cast down our adversaries. They are mad who resist Him; they are accursed who depart from His commandments! He knoweth all things, and cannot err. His will is sovereignly just, and all that He wills is good, all that He advises is holy. Supreme Intelligence cannot be deceived; Perfect Being cannot will what is evil. Nothing is above that which is supreme, nothing is better than that which is perfect. None is worthy beside Him but him whom He has made worthy. He must be loved above all things and adored as the eternal King. You have abandoned your God, you have revolted against Him, you have desired to be gods; you have fallen from your high estates, you have gone down like a fallen stone. Acknowledge that God is great, that His works are perfect, and that His judgments are just. Glory be to God through ages of ages, praises of joy for all His works!" This song of the Archangel is said to have been revealed to S. Amadeus.[2]

According to the Talmudists, Satan, whose proper name is Sammael, was one of the Seraphim, with six wings.[3] He was not driven out of heaven till after he had led Adam and Eve into sin; then Sammael and his host were precipitated out of the place of bliss, with God's curse to weigh them down. In the struggle between Michael and Sammael, the falling Seraph caught the wings of Michael and tried to drag him down with him, but God saved him, whence Michael derives his name (the Rescued). This is what the Rabbi Bechai says in his commentary on the Five Books of Moses.[4]

---

[1] Luke x. 18.

[2] Fabricius (J. A.), Codex Pseudepigraphus Vet. Test. Hamb., 1722, p. 21.

[3] Jalkut Rubeni, 3, sub. tit. Sammael.

[4] Fol. 139, col. 1: see Eisenmenger, i. p. 831.

According to a Talmudic authority, the apostate angels having fallen in a heap, God laid his little finger on them and consumed them.[1]

Sammael was the regent of the planet Mars, and this he rules still, and therefore it is that those born under the influence of that star are lovers of war and given to strife.[2]

He was chief among the angels of God, and now he is prince among devils.[3] His name is derived from Simmé, which means to blind and deceive. He stands on the *left* side of men. He goes by various names ; such as the Old Serpent, the Unclean Spirit, Satan, Leviathan, and sometimes also Asael. In his fall he spat in his hatred against God, and his spittle stained the moon, and thus it is that the moon has on it spots.

After his fall, Satan took to himself four wives, Lilith and Naama the daughter of Lamech and sister of Tubal-Cain, Igereth and Machalath. Each became the mother of a great host of devils, and each rules with her host over a season of the year ; and at the change of seasons there is a great gath ering of devils about their mothers. Lilith is followed by four hundred and seventy-eight legions of devils, for that number is comprised in her name (לילית—478). According to some, Lilith is identical with Eve. She rules over Damascus, Naama over Tyre, Igereth over Malta and Rhodes, and Machalath over Crete.[4]

Many traditions date the existence of angels and demons from a remote period before the creation of the world, but some connect the fall of Satan and his host with the creation of man.

Abou-Djafar-Mohammed Tabari says that when God made Adam, He bade all the angels worship him as their king and superior, as says the Koran, " All the angels adored Adam " (xv. 30), but that Satan or Eblis answered God, " I will not adore Adam, for he is made of earth and I of fire, therefore I am better than he " (vii. 11), and that God thereupon cursed Eblis and gave him the form of a devil, because of his pride, vain confidence, and disobedience.[5]

Abulfeda says, " After God had made man He thus ad-dressed the angels. 'When I have breathed a portion of my

---

[1] Jalkut Rubeni, in Eisenmenger, i. p. 307.
[2] Eisenmenger, i. p. 104. [3] Ibid., i. p. 820. [4] Ibid., ii. 416, 420, 421.
[5] Chronique de Tabari. Paris, 1867, i. c. xxvii.

spirit into him, bow before him and adore.'   After He had inspired Adam with His spirit, all the angels of every degree adored him, except Eblis ; he, through pride and envy, scorned to do this, and disobeyed God.   Then God cursed him, and he cut him off from all hope in divine mercy, and He called him Scheithanan redjiman (Satan devoted to misery), and He cast him out who had been before an angel of the earth, and keeper of terrestrial things, and a guardian of Paradise." [1]

But the general opinion seems to have been that the fall of the angels preceded the creation of man.   Ibn-Ezra dates it on the second day of creation, others on the first day when God "*divided the light from the darkness.*"   Manasseh Ben Israel says that God has placed the devils in the clouds, that they might torment the wicked with thunder and lightnings, and showers of hail and tempests of wind, and that this took place on the second day, when the firmaments were divided.

As the fall of Satan took place through his aspiration to be God, so it is closely connected with the origin of idolatry and false worship ; for now that Satan is cast out of heaven, he still seeks to exalt himself into the place of God, and therefore leads men from the worship of the true God into demonolatry.   Thus the gods of the heathens were regarded by the first Christians as devils aspiring to receive that worship from men on earth which they sought and failed to obtain in heaven. Thus St. Paul tells the Corinthians that "*the Gentiles sacrifice to devils.*" [2]   The temptation of Christ can only be fully understood when we bear in mind that pride and craving for worship is the prime source of Satan's actions.   "*All these will I give thee,*" he said to Christ, "*if Thou wilt fall down and worship me.*"   It was a second attempt of Satan to set himself above the Most High.

Among the heathen, traditions of the Angelic apostasy and war have remained.

The Indian story is as follows :—

At the head of the apostate spirits is Mahisasura, or the great Asur ; he and those who followed him were once good, but before the creation of the world they refused obedience to Brahma, wherefore they were cast down by the assistance of Schiva into the abyss of Onderah. [3]   Mahisasura is also repre-

---

[1] Abulfeda, Hist. Ante-Islamica.   Lipsiæ, 1831, p. 13.
[2] 1 Cor. x. 20.   [3] Majer, Mythologische Lexicon, Th. i. p. 231.

sented as the great serpent Vrita, against which Indra fought, and which after a desperate struggle he overcame.

The Persian tradition is that Ahriman, the chief of the rebels, is not by nature evil. He was not created evil by the Eternal One, but he became evil by revolting against his will; and the ancient books of the Parsees assert that at the last day Ahriman will return to obedience, and having been purified by fire, will regain the place among the heavenly beings which he lost. In this war the Izeds fought against the Divs, headed by Ahriman, and flung the conquered into Douzahk or hell.

The Norse story is that Loki, the spirit of evil, is one of the gods, and sat with them at their table till he declared himself their enemy, when he with his vile progeny, the wolf and the serpent, were cast out. The wolf is bound, Thorr constrains the serpent, and Loki is chained under the mountains, and a serpent distils poison on his breast; when he tosses in agony, the earth quakes.

In Egypt, Typhon was brother of Osiris, but he revolted against him.

Maximus of Tyre, and Apollonius of Rhodes, following Orpheus, speak of the war of the gods against the angels who rebelled under their chief Ophion, or the Serpent, and Pherecydes, according to Origen, sang of this event as having taken place in pre-historic times; so that the knowledge of it could only have reached man by revelation. He described the two armies face to face,—one commanded by Saturn, the supreme Creator; the other by Ophioneus, the old Dragon, and the defeat of the latter and its expulsion from the realms of bliss to Ogenos, the regions of annihilation.[1] The story of the Titans is connected with this. They were the sons of Uranus (heaven) and Ge (earth), and dwelt originally in heaven, whence they are called Uranidæ. They were twelve in number. Uranus threw out of heaven his other sons, the Hecatoncheires and the Cyclopes, and precipitated them into Tartarus. Whereupon Ge persuaded her sons, the Titans, to rise up against their father, and liberate their brethren. They did as their mother bade them, deposed Uranus, and placed on his throne their brother Cronus, who immediately re-imprisoned the Cyclopes. But Zeus with his brothers fought against the reigning Titans, cast them out of heaven, and enthroned

―――――――
[1] Orig. adv. Cels. vi. 42.

himself on the seat of Cronus ; and the Titans he enchained in the abyss under Tartarus.

This is simply the same story told over twice, and formed into a dynasty. Chronos Titan is the same as the Arabic Scheitan, the Erse Teitin, the Time-god, and the Biblical Satan, or Lucifer, the Son of the Morning.

Amongst the Battas of Sumatra exists a myth to this effect : Batara Guru, the supreme God, from whose daughter Putiarla Buran all mankind are descended, cast the mountain Bakkara out of heaven upon the head of the serpent, his foe, and made the home of his son Layanga-layaad-mandi on the top of this mountain. From this summit the son descended that he might bind the hands or feet of the serpent, as it shook its head and made the earth rock.

Connected with the fall of Satan is his lameness. The devil is represented in art and in legion as limping on one foot ; this was occasioned by his having broken his leg in his fall.

Hephæstus, who pursued Athene and attempted to outrage divine Wisdom, was precipitated from heaven into the fire-island Lemnos, and was lamed thereby. Hermes cut the hamstring out of Typhon, therewith to string his lyre. The Norse god Loki lusted after Freya, and was lamed therefor. Wieland the smith (Völundr), who ventured to do violence to Beodohild, was lamed, and was known thereby. Phaethon, daring to drive his father's chariot of the sun, was cast out and thrown to earth.

The natives of the Caroline Islands relate that one of the inferior gods, named Merogrog, was driven by the other gods out of heaven, and he took with him a spark of fire which he gave to men.[1] This myth resembles that of Prometheus, " the contriver, full of gall and bitterness, who sinned against the gods by bestowing their honors on creatures of a day, the thief of fire," as Hermes calls him. He reappears as Tohil among the Quiches, the giver of fire, hated, yet adored.

The Northern Californians say that the supreme God once created invisible spirits, of whom one portion revolted against him, headed by a spirit named War or Touparan, and that the Great Spirit having overcome him, drove him from the plains of heaven, and confined him along with his comrades in a cavern, where he is guarded by whales.[2]

---

[1] Lettres Edifiantes, viii. p. 420.

[2] Bibliothèque Univ. de Genève, 1827 ; D'Anselme, i. p, 228.

The Egyptian Typhon, already alluded to, did not belong. to Egypt alone, but also to Phœnicia and Asia Minor, and thence the story passed into Greece, where it took root, and has been preserved to us as the attack of the hundred-headed dragon against the heaven-god Zeus. Typhon desired to obtain supremacy over gods and men, and, in order to win for himself this sovereignty, he fought against the gods ; but he was defeated, bound, and precipitated into Tartarus, or, according to another version, was buried under the flaming mountains.

According to a tradition of the Salivas, a people of New Granada, a serpent slew the nations, descended from God, who inhabited the region of the Orinoco, but a son of the God Puru fought him and overcame him, and bade him depart with his curse, and never to enter his house again, and, say these Salivas, from the flesh of the serpent sprang the Caribees, their great foes, as maggots from putrid meat.[1]

But these stories might be infinitely extended. How far they refer to a tradition common to the human race, and how far they relate to the strife between summer and winter, sun and storm-cloud, I do not pretend to decide. It is one of those vexed questions which it is impossible to determine.

II.

ADAM.

I. THE CREATION OF MAN.

CERTAIN of the angels having fallen, God made men, that they might take their vacated places.

According to the most authoritative Mussulman traditions, Adam was created on Friday afternoon at the Assr-hour, or about three o'clock. The four archangels—Gabriel, Michael, Israfiel, and Asrael—were required to bring earth from the four quarters of the world, that therefrom God might fashion man. His head and breast were made of clay from Mecca and Medina, from the spot where later were the Holy Kaaba and the tomb of Mohammed. Although still lifeless, his beauty amazed the angels who had flocked to the gates of

---

[1] Hist. Naturelle de l'Orinoque, par Tos. Gumilla. Avignon, 1751, t. i. p. 172.

Paradise.   But Eblis, envious of the beauty of Adam's as yet inanimate form, said to the angels : "How can you admire a creature made of earth?   From such material nothing but fragility and feebleness can come."   However, most of the angels praised God for what he had done.

The body of Adam was so great, that if he stood up his head would reach into the seventh heaven. But he was not as yet endowed with a living soul.   The soul had been made a thousand years before, and had been steeped all that while in the sea of light which flowed from Allah.   God now ordered the soul to enter the body.   It showed some indisposition to obey ; thereupon God exclaimed : "Quicken Adam against your will, and, as a penalty for your disobedience, you shall leave the body sorely against your will."   Then God blew the spirit against Adam with such force that it entered his nose, and ran up into his head, and as soon as it reached his eyes Adam opened them, and saw the throne of God with the inscription upon it : "There is no God but God, and Mohammed is His prophet."   Then the soul ran into his ears, and Adam heard the song of the angels ; thereupon his tongue was unloosed, for by this time the soul had reached it, and he said, "Praise be to Thee, my Creator, one and only!" And God answered him : "For this purpose are you made. You and your successors must pray to me, and you will find mercy and loving-kindness at my hands."   Then the soul penetrated all the members, reaching last of all the feet of Adam, which receiving strength, he sprang up, and stood upon the earth.   But when he stood upright he was obliged to close his eyes, for the light of God's throne shining directly into them blinded them.   "What light is this?" he asked, as he covered his eyes with one hand, and indicated the throne with the other.   "It is the light of a prophet," God answered, "who will spring from thee in later ages.   By mine honor I swear, for him alone have I created the world. In heaven he bears the name of the much lauded, and on earth he will be called Mohammed.   Through him all men will be led out of error into the way of truth."

God then called all created animals before Adam, and told him their names and their natures.   Then He called up all the angels, and bade them bow before Adam, the man whom He had made.   Israfiel obeyed first, and God gave to him in recompense the custody of the Book of Fate ; the other angels obeyed in order ; only Eblis refused, in the pride of his heart, saying, "Why shall I, who am made of fire, bend before him who is made of earth?" Therefore he was cast out of the angel choirs, and was forbidden admission through the gates of Paradise. Adam also was led out of Paradise, and he preached to the angels, who stood before him in ten thousand ranks, a sermon on the power, majesty, and goodness of God, and he showed such learning and knowledge—for he could name each beast in seventy languages—that the angels were amazed at his knowledge, which excelled their own. As a reward for having preached this sermon, God sent Adam a bunch of grapes out of Paradise by the hands of Gabriel.[1]

In the Midrash, the Rabbinical story is as follows : "When God wished to make man, He consulted with the angels, and said to them, We will make a man in our image. Then they said, What is man, that you regard him, and what is his nature? He answered, His knowledge excels yours. Then He placed all kinds of beasts before them, wild beasts and fowls of the air, and asked them their names, but they knew them not. And after Adam was made, He led them before him, and He asked Adam their names, and he replied at once, This is an ox, that is an ass, this is a horse, that is a camel, and so forth."[2]

The story told by Tabari is somewhat different.

When God would make Adam, He ordered Gabriel to bring Him a handful of every sort of clay, black, white, red, yellow, blue, and every other kind.[3] Gabriel went to the middle of the earth to the place where now is Kaaba. He wished to stoop and take the clay, but the earth said to him, "O Gabriel, what doest thou?" And Gabriel answered, "I am fetching a little clay, dust, and stone, that thereof God may make a Lord for thee." Then the earth swore by God, "Thou shalt take of me neither clay nor dust nor stone ; what if of the creatures made from me some should arise who would do evil upon the earth, and shed innocent blood?" Gabriel withdrew, respecting the oath, and took no earth ; and he said to God, "Thou knowest what the earth said to me."

---

[1] Weil, Biblische Legenden der Muselmänner. Frankfort, 1845, pp. 12–16.

[2] Geiger, Was hat Mohammed aus d. Judenthum aufgenommen? p. 99.

[3] So also Abulfeda, Hist. Ante-Islamica, ed. Fleischer. Lipsiæ, 1831 p. 13.

Then God sent Michael and bade him fetch a little mud. But when Michael arrived, the earth swore the same oath.

And Michael respected the oath and withdrew.

Then God sent Azrael, the angel of death. He came, and the earth swore the same oath; but he did not retire, but answered and said, "I must obey the command of God in spite of thine oath."

And the angel of death stooped, and took from forty ells below the earth clay of every sort, as we have said, and therefrom God made Adam.

No one in the world had seen a form like that of Adam. Hâreth or Satan went to look at him. Adam had lain stretched in the same place for the space of about forty years. No one thought of him or knew what sort of a thing he was. Hâreth coming up to him, saw him stretched from east to west, of huge size and as dry as dry palm leaves. Then Hâreth pushed Adam, and the dry earth rattled. Hâreth was astonished. He examined the form more attentively, and he found that it was hollow. Then he went to the mouth and crept in at it, and crept out again and let the angels know the doubt that was in his breast, for he said, "This creature is nothing, its inside is empty, and a hollow thing can easily be broken. Now that God has made him, He has given him the empire of the world, but I will fight against him and drive him from the earth as I drove out the Jins. What is your advice?"

The angels answered, "O Hâreth, if we overcame the Jins it was in obedience to God's command. Now that God has created this thing, if He orders us to submit to it, we must do so." Now when Hâreth saw that the angels thought otherwise, he changed his discourse and said, "You speak the truth, I agree with you, but I wanted to prove you."

When God gave the soul to Adam, it entered his throat and passed down into his bosom and belly, and wherever it passed, the earth, the clay, the dust, and the black mud became bones, nerves, veins, flesh, skin, and the like. And when his soul entered his head, Adam sneezed, and said, "Praise be to God." And when he turned his head, he saw Paradise and all its delights; and when the soul entered his belly, he wanted to eat, so he tried to rise and get some food, but the soul had not yet reached his extremities, which were as yet mere clay, so Gabriel said: "O Adam, don't be in a hurry."[1]

[1] Tabari, i. c. xxvi.

Then follows the story of Eblis refusing to adore Adam. According to another version of the Mussulman story, the soul showed such repugnance to enter the body, that the angel Gabriel took a flageolet, and sitting down near the head of the inanimate Adam, played such exquisite melodies that the soul descended to listen, and in a moment of ecstasy entered the feet, which began immediately to move. Thereupon the soul was given command by Allah not to leave the body again till special permission was given it by the Most High.[1]

In the Talmud we are told that the Rabbi Meir says that the dust from which Adam was made was gathered from all parts of the earth: the Rabbi Hoshea says that the body of the first man was made of dust from Babel; the head, of earth from the land of Israel, and the rest of his limbs from the soil of other countries: but the Rabbi Acha adds that his hinder quarters were fashioned out of clay from Acre.[2] When Adam was made, some of the dust remained over; of that God made locusts.[3]

A Rabbinical tale is to this effect. God was interrupted by the Sabbath in the midst of creating fauns and satyrs, after He had made man, and was obliged to postpone their completion till the Sunday, consequently these creatures are misshapen. A Talmudic account of the way in which were spent the hours of the day in which Adam was made, is sufficiently curious.

At the first hour, God gathered the dust of the earth; in the second, He formed the embryo; in the third, the limbs were extended; in the fourth, the soul was given; at the fifth hour Adam stood upright; at the sixth, Adam named the animals. Having done this, God asked him, " And I, what is my name? "

Adam replied—" Jehovah."

At the seventh hour, Adam married Eve; at the eighth, Cain and his sister were born; at the ninth, they were forbidden to eat of the tree; at the tenth hour Adam fell; at the eleventh he was banished from Eden; and at the twelfth, he felt the sweat and pain of toil.[4]

[1] Colin de Plancy, p. 55.
[2] Eisenmenger, Neuentdecktes Judenthum. Königsberg, 1711, i. pp. 364-5.
[3] Bochart, Hierozoica, p. 2, l. 8, fol. 486.
[4] Tract Sanhedrim, f. 38.

In the Apocryphal Little Genesis, we are told that Adam did not disobey God till the expiration of the seventh year, and that he was not punished till forty-five days after.   It adds, that before the Fall, Adam conversed familiarly with the animals, but that by the Fall they lost the faculty of speech.

God, say the Rabbis, made Adam so tall that his head touched the sky ; and the tree of life, planted in the midst of the garden of Eden, was so broad at the base that it would take a good walker five years to march round it, and Adam's proportions accorded with those of the tree.   The angels murmured, and told God that there were two sovereigns, one in heaven and one on earth.   Thereupon God placed his hand on the head of Adam and reduced him to a thousand cubits.[1]

To the question, How big was Adam ? the Talmud replies, He was made so tall that he stood with his head in heaven, till God pressed him down at the Fall.   Rabbi Jehuda says, that as he lay stretched on the earth he covered it completely ;[2] but the book Sepher Gilgulim says (fol. 20, col. 4), that when he was made, his head and throat were in Paradise, and his body in the earth.   To judge how long he was, says the same book, understand that his body stretched from one end of the earth to the other, and it takes a man five hundred years to walk that distance.[3]   And when Adam was created, all the beasts of earth fell down before him and desired to worship him, but he said to them, "You have come to worship me, but come and let us clothe ourselves with power and glory, and let us take Him to be king over us who has created us ; for a people chooses a king, but the king does not appoint himself monarch arbitrarily."   Therefore Adam chose God to be king of all the world, and the beasts, fowls, and fishes gladly consented thereto.[4]   But the sun, seeing Adam, was filled with fear and became dark ; and the angels quaked and were dismayed, and prayed to God to remove from them this mighty being whom He had made.   Then God cast a deep sleep on Adam, and the sun and the angels looked on him lying helpless in his slumber, and they plucked up courage and feared him no more.   The book Sepher Chasidim, however, says, that the angels seeing Adam so great and with his face shining above the brightness of the sun, bowed before him, and said,

---

[1] Jalkut Schimoni, f. 6.　　　　[3] Tract Hagida, f. 12.
[2] Eisenmenger, i. p. 367.　　　　[4] Ibid., 368.

' Holy, holy, holy!" Whereupon God cast a sleep upon him and cut off great pieces of his flesh to reduce him to smaller proportions. And when Adam woke he saw bits of flesh strewed all round him, like shavings in a carpenter's shop, and he exclaimed, " O God ! how hast Thou robbed me ? " but God answered, " Take these gobbets of flesh and carry them into all lands and drop them everywhere, and strew dust on them ; and wherever they are laid, that land will I give to thy posterity to inherit."[1]

Many are the origins attributed to man in the various creeds of ancient and modern heathendom. Sometimes he is spoken of as having been made out of water, but more generally it is of earth that he has been made, or from which he has been spontaneously born. The Peruvians believed that the world was peopled by four men and four women, brothers and sisters, who emerged from the caves near Cuzco. Among the North American Indians the earth is regarded as the universal mother. Men came into existence in her womb, and crept out of it by climbing up the roots of the trees which hung from the vault in which they were conceived and matured ; or, mounting a deer, the animal brought them into daylight ; or, groping in darkness, they tore their way out with their nails.[2]

The Egyptian philosophers pretended that man was made of the mud of the Nile.[3] In Aristophanes,[4] man is spoken of as $\pi\lambda\acute{\alpha}\delta\mu\alpha\tau\alpha$ $\pi\eta\lambda o\tilde{v}$. Among some of the Chinese it is believed that man was thus formed :—" The book Fong-zen-tong says: When the earth and heaven were made, there was not as yet man or peoples   Then Niu-hoa moulded yellow earth, and of that made man. That is the true origin of men."[5]

And the ancient Chaldeans supposed man was made by the mixing of the blood of Belus with the soil.[6]

2. THE PRE-ADAMITES.

In 1655, Isaac de la Peyreira, a converted Jew, published a curious treatise on the Pre-Adamites. Arguing upon Ro-

<hr>

[1] Eisenmenger, i. p. 369.

[2] Müller, Amerikanische Urreligionen ; Basle, 1855. Atherne Jones, North American Traditions, i. p. 210, etc. Heckewelder's Indian Nations, etc.

[3] Fourmont Anciens Peuples, i. lib. ii. p. 10.   [4] Aves, 666.

[5] Mémoires des Chinois, i. p. 105.

[6] Berosus, in Cory's Ancient Fragments, p. 26.

mans v. 12–14, he contended that there were two creations of man ; that recorded in the first chapter of Genesis and that described in the second chapter being distinct.   The first race he supposed to have peopled the whole world, but that it was bad, and therefore Adam had been created with a spiritual soul, and that from Adam the Jewish race was descended, whereas the Gentile nations issued from the loins of the Pre-Adamites.   Consequently the original sin of Adam weighed only on his descendants, and Peyreira supposed that it was his race alone which perished, with the exception of Noah and his family, in the Deluge, which Peyreira contends was partial. This book was condemned and burnt in Paris by the hands of the executioner, and the author, who had taken refuge in Brussels, was there condemned by the ecclesiastical authorities. He appealed to Rome, whither he journeyed, and he was received with favor by Alexander VII., before whom he abjured Calvinism, which he had professed.

He died at the age of 82, at Aubervilliers, near Paris, and Moreri wrote the following epigrammatic epitaph for him :—

> " La Peyrère ici gît, ce bon Israélite,
>   Huguenot, catholique, enfin pré-Adamite.
>   Quatre religions lui plurent à la fois ;
>   Et son indifférence était si peu commune,
>   Qu'après quatre-vingts ans qu'il eut à faire un choix,
>   Le bon homme partit et n'en choisit aucune."

The Oriental book Huschenk-Nameh gives a fuller history of the Pre-Adamites.   Before Adam was created, says this book, there were in the isle Muscham, one of the Maldives, men with flat heads, and for this reason they were called by the Persians, Nim-ser.   They were governed by a king named Dambac.

When Adam, expelled the earthly Paradise, established himself in the Isle of Ceylon, the flat-heads submitted to him. After his death they guarded his tomb by day, and the lions relieved guard by night, to protect his body against the Divs.

III.

EVE.[1]

THAT man was created double, *i. e.* both male and female, is and has been a common opinion. One Rabbinical interpretation of the text, " And God created man in His own image, male-female created He them," is that Adam and Eve were formed back to back, united at the shoulders, and were hewn asunder with a hatchet ; but of this more presently. The Rabbis say that when Eve had to be drawn out of the side of Adam she was not extracted by the head, lest she should be vain ; nor by the eyes, lest they should be wanton ; nor by the mouth, lest she should be given to gossiping ; nor by the ears, lest she should be an eavesdropper ; nor by the hands, lest she should be meddlesome ; nor by the feet, lest she should be a gadabout ; nor by the heart, lest she should be jealous ; but she was drawn forth by the side : yet, notwithstanding all these precautions, she has every fault specially guarded against.[2]

They also say that, for the marriage-feast of Adam and Eve, God made a table of precious stone, and each gem was a hundred ells long and sixty ells wide, and the table was covered with costly dishes.[3]

The Mussulman tradition is, that Adam having eaten the bunch of grapes given him as a reward for having preached to the angels, fell asleep ; and whilst he slept, God took from his left side a woman whom He called Hava, because she was extracted from one living (Hai), and He laid her beside Adam. She resembled him exactly, except that her features were more delicate, her hair longer and divided into seven.hundred locks, her form more slender, her eyes softer, and her voice sweeter than Adam's. In the mean time Adam had been dreaming

---

[1] It is unfortunate that I have already written on the myths relating to the formation of Eve in "Curiosities of Olden Times." I would therefore have omitted a chapter which must repeat what has been already published, but that by so doing I should leave this work imperfect. However, there is much in this chapter which was not in the article referred to.

[2] Rabboth, fol. 20 b.   [3] Eisenmenger, i. 830.

that a wife had been given to him ; and when he woke, great was his delight to find his dream turned into a reality. He put forth his hand to take that of Hava, but she withdrew hers, answering his words of love with, " God is my master, and I cannot give my hand to thee without His permission ; and, moreover, it is not proper for a man to take a wife without making her a wedding present."

Adam thereupon sent the angel Gabriel to ask God's permission to take to him Hava as his wife. Gabriel returned with the answer that she had been created to be his helpmate, and that he was to treat her with gentleness and love. For a present he must pray twenty times for Mohammed and for the prophets, who, in due season, were to be born of him. Ridhwan, the porter of Paradise, then brought to Adam the winged horse Meimun, and to Eve a light-footed she-camel. Gabriel helped them to mount and led them into Paradise, where they were greeted by all the angels and beasts with the words : " Hail, father and mother of Mohammed ! "

In the midst of Paradise was a green silk tent spread for them, supported on gold pillars, and in the tent was a throne upon which Adam and Hava were seated. Then they were bathed in one of the rivers of Paradise and brought before the presence of God, who bade them dwell in Paradise. " I have prepared you this garden for your home ; in it you shall be protected from cold and heat, from hunger and thirst. Enjoy all that meets your eye, only of one fruit taste not. Beware how you break my command, and arm yourself against the subtlety of your foe, Eblis ; he envies you, and stands by you seeking to destroy you, for through you was he cast out."

Tabari says that Adam was brought single into Paradise, through which he roamed eating from the fruit trees, and a deep sleep fell upon him, during which Eve was created from his left side. And when Adam opened his eyes, he saw her, and asked her who she was, and she replied, " I am thy wife ; God created me out of thee and for thee, that thy heart might find repose." The angels said to Adam : " What thing is this ? What is her name ? Why is she made ? " Adam replied, " This is Eve." Adam remained five hundred years in Paradise. It was on a Friday that Adam entered Eden.[2]

The inhabitants of Madagascar have a strange myth touch-

---

[1] Weil, pp. 17, 18.   [2] Tabari, i. c. xxvi.

ing the origin of woman. They say that the first man was created of the dust of the earth, and was placed in a garden, where he was subject to none of the ills which now affect mortality; he was also free from all bodily appetites, and though surrounded by delicious fruit and limpid streams, yet felt no desire to taste of the fruit or to quaff the water. The Creator had, moreover, strictly forbidden him either to eat or to drink. The great enemy, however, came to him, and painted to him in glowing colors the sweetness of the apple, the lusciousness of the date, and the succulence of the orange.

In vain: the first man remembered the command laid upon him by his Maker. Then the fiend assumed the appearance of an effulgent spirit, and pretended to be a messenger from Heaven commanding him to eat and drink. The man at once obeyed. Shortly after, a pimple appeared on his leg; the spot enlarged to a tumor, which increased in size and caused him considerable annoyance. At the end of six months it burst, and there emerged from the limb a beautiful girl.

The father of all living was sorely perplexed what to make of his acquisition, when a messenger from heaven appeared, and told him to let her run about the garden till she was of a marriageable age, and then to take her to himself as his wife. He obeyed. He called her Bahouna, and she became the mother of all races of men.

The notion of the first man having been of both sexes till the separation, was very common. He was said to have been male on the right side and female on the left, and that one half of him was removed to constitute Eve, but that the complete man consists of both sexes.

Eugubinus among Christian commentators, the Rabbis Samuel, Manasseh Ben-Israel, and Maimonides among the Jews, have given the weight of their opinion to support this interpretation. The Rabbi Jeremiah Ben-Eleazer, on the authority of the text " *Thou hast fashioned me behind and before* " (Ps. cxxxix. 4), argued that Adam had two faces, one male and the other female, and that he was of both sexes.[1]

The Rabbi Samuel Ben-Nahaman held that the first man was created double, with a woman at his back, and that God cut them apart.[2] " Adam," said other Rabbis, " had two faces

---

[1] Talmud, Tract Berachoth, f. 61 ; Bartolocci Bibl. Rabbin., iv. p. 66.
[2] Bartolocci, Bibl. Rabbin., iv. p. 67.

and one tail, and from the beginning he was both male and female, male on one side, female on the other ; but afterwards the parts were separated." [1]

The Talmudists assert that God cut off Adam's tail and thereof formed Eve. [2]

With this latter fable agrees the ludicrous myth of the Kikapoo Indians, related in my "Curiosities of Olden Times."

In Aristophanes' speech in the Symposium of Plato, a myth is given, that in the beginning there was a race of men of which every member was double, having two heads, four legs and four arms, and each of both sexes.   This race, says he, was filled with pride, and it attempted to scale heaven.   The Gods desired at once to reduce their might and punish their temerity, but did not wish to destroy the human race ; consequently at the advice of Zeus, each androgyne was hewn assunder, so as to leave to each half two arms and a pair of legs, one head and a single sex.

An Indian tradition is to this effect.   Whilst Brahma the creator was engaged in the production of beings, he saw Kaya (body) divide itself into two parts, of which each part was of a different sex, and thence sprang the whole human race. [3]

According to another much more explicit version, Viradi, the first man, finding his solitude intolerable, fell into the deepest sorrow ; and, yearning for a companion, his nature developed into two sexes united in one.   Then he separated into two individuals, but found in that separation unhappiness, for he was conscious of his imperfection ; then he reunited the existence of the two portions and was happy, and from that reunion the world was peopled. [4]

In Persia, Meschia and Meschiane, the first man and the first woman, were said to have formed originally but one body ; but they were cut apart, and from this voluntary reunion all men are sprung. [5]

The idea so prevalent that man without woman, or woman without man, is an imperfect being, was the cause of the great repugnance with which the Jews and other nations of the East regarded celibacy.   The Rabbi Eliezer, commenting on the text "He called their name Adam" (Gen. v. 2), laid down

<hr>

[1] Bartolocci, Bibl. Rabbin., iii. p. 395.
[2] Ibid., p. 396 ; Eisenmenger, t. i. p. 365
[3] Bhagavat, iii. 12, 51.
[4] Colebrooke Miscell. Essays, p. i. 64.   [5] Bundehesch, p. 377.

that he who has not a wife is not a man, for man is the recomposition of male and female into one.[1]

Bramah, says an Indian legend, being charged with the production of the human race, felt himself a prey to violent pains, till his sides opened, and from one flank emerged a boy and from the other a girl.   In China, the story is told that the Goddess Amida sweated male children out of her right arm-pit, and female children from her left arm-pit, and these children peopled the earth.[1]

Vishnu, according to an Indian fable, gave birth to Dharma by his right side, and to Adharma by his left side, and through Adharma death entered the world.[3]   Another story is to the effect, that the right arm of Vena gave birth to Pritu, the master of the earth, and the left arm to the Virgin Archis, who became the bride of Pritu.[4]

Pygmalion, says the classic story, which is really a Phœnician myth of creation, made woman of marble or ivory, and Aphrodite, in answer to his prayers, endowed the statue with life.   "Often does Pygmalion apply his hands to the work. One while he addresses it in soft terms, at another he brings it presents that are agreeable to maidens, as shells and smooth pebbles, and little birds, and flowers of a thousand hues, and lilies, and painted balls, and tears of the Heliades, that have distilled from the trees.   He decks her limbs, too, with clothing, and puts a long necklace on her neck.   Smooth pendants hang from her ears, and bows from her breast.   All things are becoming to her."[5]

But Hesiod gives a widely different account of the creation of woman.   According to him, she was sent in mockery by Zeus to be a scourge to man :—

> "The Sire who rules the earth and sways the pole
> Had spoken ; laughter filled his secret soul :
> He bade the crippled god his hest obey,
> And mould with tempering water plastic clay ;
> With human nerve and human voice invest
> The limbs elastic, and the breathing breast ;
> Fair as the blooming goddesses above,
> A virgin likeness with the looks of love.
> He bade Minerva teach the skill that sheds
> A thousand colors in the glittering threads ;

[1] Bartolocci, Bibl. Rabbin., iv. p. 463.
[2] Mendez Pinto, Voyages, ii. p. 178.   [3] Bhagavat, iii. 12, 25.
[4] Ibid., iv. 15, 27.   [5] Ovid, Metamorph., x. 7.

> He called the magic of love's golden queen
> To breathe around a witchery of mien,
> And eager passion's never-sated flame,
> And cares of dress that prey upon the frame ;
> Bade Hermes last endue, with craft refined
> Of treacherous manners, and a shameless mind." [1]

That Eve was Adam's second wife was a common Rabbinic speculation ; certain of the commentators on Genesis having adopted this view to account for the double account of the creation of woman in the sacred text,—first in Genesis i. 27, and secondly in Genesis ii. 18 ; and they say that Adam's first wife was named Lilith, but she was expelled from Eden, and after her expulsion Eve was created.

Abraham Ecchellensis gives the following account of Lilith, and her doings :—"There are some who do not regard spectres as simple devils, but suppose them to be of a mixed nature, part demoniacal, part human, and to have had their origin from Lilith, Adam's first wife, by Eblis, the prince of the devils. This fable has been transmitted to the Arabs from Jewish sources, by some converts of Mahomet from Cabbalism and Rabbinism, who have transferred all the Jewish fooleries to the Arabs. They gave to Adam a wife, formed of clay, along with Adam, and called her Lilith ; resting on the Scripture, '*male and female created He them :*' [2] but when this woman, on account of her simultaneous creation with him, became proud and a vexation to her husband, God expelled her from Paradise, and then said, '*It is not good that the man should be alone ; I will make him a help meet for him.*' [3] And this they confirm by the words of Adam when he saw the woman fashioned from his rib, '*This is now bone of my bone, and flesh of my flesh,*' [4] which is as much as to say, Now God has given me a wife and companion, suitable to me, taken from my bone and flesh, but the other wife he gave me was not of my bone and flesh, and therefore was not a suitable companion and wife for me.

"But Lilith, after she was expelled from Paradise, is said to have married the Devil, by whom she had children, who are called Jins. These were endued with six qualities, of which they share three with men, and three with devils. Like men, they generate in their own likeness, eat food, and die. Like

---

[1] Hesiod, Works and Days, 61–79.
[2] Gen. i. 27.   [3] Ibid., ii. 18.   [4] Ibid., 23.

devils, they are winged, and they fly where they list with great velocity; they are invisible, and they can pass through solid substances without injuring them. This race of Jins is supposed to be less noxious to men, and indeed to live in some familiarity and friendship with them, as in part sharers of their nature. The author of the history and acts of Alexander of Macedon relates, that in a certain region of India, on certain hours of the day, the young Jins assume a human form, and appear openly and play games with the native children of human parents quite familiarly." [1]

It must not be supposed that women, as they are now, are at all comparable to Eve in her pristine beauty; on this point the Talmud says: " All women in respect of Sarah are like monkeys in respect of men. But Sarah can no more be compared to Eve than can a monkey be compared with a man. In like manner it may be said, if any comparison could be drawn between Eve and Adam, she stood to him in the same relation of beauty as does a monkey to a man; but if you were to compare Adam with God, Adam would be the monkey, and God the man." [2]

Literary ladies may point to the primal mother as the first authoress; for a Gospel of Eve existed in the times of S. Epiphanius, who mentions it as being in repute among the Gnostics. [3] And the Mussulmans attribute to her a volume of Prophecies which were written at her dictation by the Angel Raphael. [4]

All ladies will be glad to learn that there is a tradition, Manichean, it is true, and anathematized by S. Clement, which nevertheless contains a large element of truth; it is to this effect, that Adam, when made, was like a beast, coarse, rude, and inanimate, but that from Eve he received his upright position, his polish, and his spirituality. [5]

---

[1] Abraham Ecchellensis, Hist. Arabum, p. 268.
[2] Talmud, Tract. Bava Bathra.   [3] S. Epiphan. Hæres., xxvi.
[4] Tho. Bangius, Cœlum Orientis, p. 103.
[5] S. Clementi Recog., c. iv.

IV.

THE FALL OF MAN.

WHAT was the tree of which our first parents were forbidden to eat ?   In Midrash, f. 7, the Rabbi Mayer says it was a wheat-tree ; the Rabbi Jehuda, that it was a grape-vine ; the Rabbi Aba, that it was a Paradise-apple ; the Rabbi Josse, that it was a fig-tree : therefore it was that, when driven out of Paradise, they used its leaves for a covering.

The Persian story, adopted by the Arabs, is that the forbidden fruit was wheat, and that it grew on a tree whose trunk resembled gold and its branches silver.   Each branch bore five shining ears, and each ear contained five grains as big as the eggs of an ostrich, as fragrant as musk, and as sweet as honey.   The people of Southern America suppose it was the banana, whose fibres form the cross, and they say that thus, in it, Adam discovered the mystery of the Redemption.   The inhabitants of the island of St. Vincent think it was the tobacco plant.   But, according to an Iroquois legend, the great mother of the human race lost heaven for a pot of bears' grease.[1]   The story is as follows :—The first men living alone were,

> " By the viewless winds,
> Blown with resistless violence round about
> The pendant world."

Fearing the extinction of their race, and having learnt that a woman dwelt somewhere in the heavens, they deputed one of their number to seek her out.   This messenger of mankind was borne to the skies on the wings of assembled birds ; and then watched at the foot of a tree till the woman came forth to draw water from a neighboring well.   On her approach he addressed her, offered her bears' fat, and then seduced her.   The Deity perceiving her shame, in his anger thrust her out of heaven.   The tortoise received her on his back ; and from the depths of the sea the fish brought clay, and thus gradually built up an island on which the universal mother brought forth her first twins.

---

[1] Lafitau, Mœurs des Sauvages Amériquaines, i. p. 93.

According to the traditions of the Lamaic faith, the first men lived to the age of sixty thousand years.[1] They were invisibly nourished, and were able to raise themselves at will to the heavens. In this age of the world the transmigration of souls was universal,—all men were twice born ; and in this age it was that the thousand gods settled themselves in heaven. In an unlucky hour the earth produced a honey-sweet substance : one of the men lusted after it, tasted and gave to his companions ; the consequence was, that the men lost the power of rising from off the earth, their size, and their wisdom, and were obliged to satisfy themselves with food produced by the soil.

The Nepaul account of the beginning of sin is as follows : " Originally," says one of the Tantras, " the earth was uninhabited. In those times the inhabitants of Abhaswara, one of the heavenly mansions, used frequently to visit the earth, and thence speedily return. It happened at length that when a few of these beings, who though half male, half female, through the innocence of their minds had never noticed their distinction of sex, came as usual to the earth, Adi Buddha suddenly created in them so violent a longing to eat, that they ate some of the earth, which had the taste of almonds ; and by eating it they lost their power of flying back to heaven, and so they remained on the earth. They were now constrained to eat the fruits of the earth for sustenance."[2]

According to the Cinghalese, the Brahmas inhabited the higher regions of the air, where they enjoyed perfect happiness. " But it came to pass that one of them beholding the earth said to himself, What thing is this ? and with one of his fingers having touched the earth, he put it to the tip of his tongue, and perceived the same to be deliciously sweet ; from that time all the Brahmas ate of the sweet earth for the space of sixty thousand years. In the mean time, having coveted in their hearts the enjoyment of this earth, they began to say to one another, This part is mine and that is thine ; and so fixing boundaries to their respective shares, divided the earth between them. On account of the Brahmas having been guilty of covetousness, the earth lost its sweetness, and then brought forth a kind of mushroom," which the Brahmas also coveted and divided, and of which they were also deprived ; and thus they proceeded from food to food, till their nature was changed, and from

---

[1] Pallas, Reise, i. p. 334.   [2] Hodgson, Buddhism, p. 63.

spirits they became men, imbibed wicked ideas, and lost their ancient glory.[1]

According to the Chinese, man is part spirit, part animal. The spirit follows the laws of Heaven, as a disciple his master ; the animal, on the other hand, is the slave of sense.   At his origin, man obeyed the heavens ; his first state was one of innocence and happiness ; he knew neither disease nor death ; he was by instinct wholly good and spiritual.   But the immoderate desire to be wise, or, according to Lao-tsee, to eat, was the ruin of mankind.[2]

According to the Persian faith, the father of man had heaven for his destiny, but he must be humble of heart, pure of thought, of word and of deed, not invoking the Divs : and such in the beginning were the thoughts and acts of our first parents.

First they said, " it is Ormuzd (God) who has given the water, the earth, the trees, and the beasts of the field, and the stars, the moon, the sun, and all things pure."   But Ahriman (Satan) arose, and rushed upon their thoughts and said to them, "It is Ahriman who has given these things to you."   Thus Ahriman deceived them, and to the end will deceive. To this lie they gave credence and became Darvands, and their souls were condemned till the great resurrection of the body.   During thirty days they feasted and covered themselves with black garments.   After thirty days they went to the chase ; and they found a white goat, and with their lips they drew off her milk, and drank her milk and were glad.   " We have tasted nothing like to this milk," said our first parents, Meschia and Meschiane ; " the milk we have drunk was pleasant to the taste," but it was an evil thing to their bodies.

"Then the Div, the liar, grown more bold, presented himself a second time, and brought with him fruit of which they ate ; and of a hundred excellences they before possessed, they now retained not one.   And after thirty days and nights they found a white and fat sheep, and they cut off its left ear ; and they fired a tree, and with their breath raised the fire to a flame ; and they burned part of the branches of that tree, then of the tree khorma, and afterwards of the myrtle ; and they roasted the sheep, and divided it into three portions : and of the two

[1] Upham, Sacred Books of Ceylon, iii. 156.
[2] Mémoires Chinois, i. p. 107.

which they did not eat, one was carried to heaven by the bird Kehrkas.

"Afterwards they feasted on the flesh of a dog, and they clothed themselves in its skin. They gave themselves up to the chase, and with the furs of wild beasts they covered their bodies.

"And Meschia and Meschiane digged a hole in the earth, and they found iron, and the iron they beat with a stone; and they made for themselves an axe, and they struck at the roots of a tree, and they felled the tree and arranged its branches into a hut; and to God they gave no thanks; and the Divs took heart.

"And Meschia and Meschiane became enemies, and struck and wounded each other and separated; then from out of the place of darkness the chief of the Divs was heard to cry aloud: O man, worship the Divs! And the Div of Hate sat upon his throne. And Meschia approached and drew milk from the bull, and sprinkled it towards the north, and the Divs became strong. But during fifty winters, Meschia and Meschiane lived apart; and after that time they met, and Meschiane bare twins."[1]

The story told by the Mussulmans is as follows:—

Adam and Eve lived for five hundred years in Paradise before they ate of the tree and fell; for Eblis was outside, and could not enter the gates to deceive them.

For five hundred years Eblis sought admission, but the angel Ridhwan warned him off with his flaming sword.

One day the peacock came through the gates of Paradise. This bird, with the feathers of emeralds and pearls, was not only the most beautiful creature God had made, but it had also been endowed with a sweet and clear voice, wherewith it daily sang the praises of God in the highways of Eden.

This beautiful bird, thought Eblis, when he saw it, is surely vain, and will listen to the voice of flattery.

Thereupon he addressed it as a stranger, beyond the hearing of Ridhwan. "Most beautiful of all birds, do you belong to the denizens of Paradise?"

"Certainly," answered the peacock. "And who are you who look from side to side in fear and trembling?"

---

[1] Bundehesch in Windischmann: Zoroastrische Studien. Berlin, 1863, p. 82; and tr. A. du Perron, ii. pp. 77–80.

"I belong to the Cherubim who praise God night and day, and I have slipped out of their ranks without being observed, that I might take a glimpse of the Paradise, God has prepared for the saints. Will you hide me under your feathers, and show me the garden?"

"How shall I do that which may draw down on me God's disfavor?" asked the peacock.

"Magnificent creature! take me with you. I will teach you three words which will save you from sickness, old age, and death."

"Must then the dwellers in Paradise die?"

"All, without exception, who know not these three words."

"Is this the truth?"

"By God the Almighty it is so."

The peacock believed the oath, for it could not suppose that a creature would swear a false oath by its Creator. But, as it feared that Ridhwan would search it on its return through the gates, it hesitated to take Eblis with it, but promised to send the cunning serpent out, who would certainly devise a means of introducing Eblis into the garden.

The serpent was formerly queen of all creatures. She had a head like rubies, and eyes like emeralds. Her height was that of a camel, and the most beautiful colors adorned her skin, and her hair and face were those of a beautiful maiden. She was fragrant as musk and amber; her food was saffron; sweet hymns of praise were uttered by her melodious tongues; she slept by the waters of the heavenly river Kaulhar; she had been created a thousand years before man, and was Eve's favorite companion.

This beautiful and wise creature, thought the peacock, will desire more even than myself to possess perpetual youth and health, and will gladly admit the cherub for the sake of hearing the three words. The bird was not mistaken; as soon as it had told the story, the serpent exclaimed: "What! shall I grow old and die? Shall my beautiful face become wrinkled, my eyes close, and my body dissolve into dust? Never! rather will I brave Ridhwan's anger and introduce the cherub."

The serpent accordingly glided out of the gates of Paradise, and bade Eblis tell her what he had told the peacock.

"How shall I bring you unobserved into Paradise?" asked the serpent.

"I will make myself so small that I can sit in the nick between your front teeth," answered the fallen angel.[1]

"But how then can I answer when Ridhwan addresses me?"

"Fear not. I will whisper holy names, at which Ridhwan will keep silence."

The serpent thereupon opened her mouth, Eblis flew in and seated himself between her teeth, and by so doing poisoned them for all eternity.

When she had passed Ridhwan in security, the serpent opened her mouth and asked Eblis to take her with him to the highest heaven, where she might behold the majesty of God.

Eblis answered that he was not ready to leave yet, but that he desired to speak to Adam out of her mouth, and to this she consented, fearing Ridhwan, and greatly desiring to hear and learn the three salutary words. Having reached Eve's tent, Eblis uttered a deep sigh—it was the first that had been heard in Eden, and it was caused by envy.

"Why are you so disquieted, gentle serpent?" asked Eve.

"I am troubled for Adam's future," answered the evil spirit, affecting the voice of the serpent.

"What! have we not all that can be desired in this garden of God?"

"That is true; but the noblest fruit of the garden, the only one securing to you perfect happiness, is denied to your lips."

"Have we not abundance of fruit of every color and flavor—only one is forbidden?"

"And if you knew why that one is forbidden, you would find little pleasure in tasting the others."

"Do you know?"

"I do, and for that reason am I so cast down. This fruit alone gives eternal youth and health, whereas all the others give weakness, disease, old age and death, which is the cessation of life with all its joys."

"Why, dearest serpent, did you never tell me this before? Whence know you these things?"

"An angel told me this as I lay under the forbidden tree."

"I must also see him," said Eve, leaving her tent and going towards the tree.

---

[1] So also Abulfeda, Hist. Ante-Islamica, p. 13.

At this moment Eblis flew out of the serpent's mouth, and stood in human form beneath the tree.

"Who art thou, wondrous being, the like of whom I have not seen before?" asked Eve.

"I am a man who have become an angel."

"And how didst thou become an angel?"

"By eating of this fruit," answered the tempter,—"this fruit which is denied us through the envy of God. I dared to break His command as I grew old and feeble, and my eyes waxed dim, my ears dull, and my teeth fell out, so that I could neither speak plainly nor enjoy my food ; my hands shook, my feet tottered, my head was bent upon my breast, my back was bowed, and I became so hideous that all the beasts of the garden fled from me in fear. Then I sighed for death, and hoping to find it in the fruit of this tree, I ate, and lo ! instantly I was young again ; though a thousand years had elapsed since I was made, they had fled with all their traces, and I enjoy perpetual health and youth and beauty."

"Do you speak the truth?" asked Eve.

"I swear by God who made me."

Eve believed this oath, and broke a branch from the wheat-tree.

Before the Fall, wheat grew to a tree with leaves like emeralds. The ears were red as rubies and the grains white as snow, sweet as honey, and fragrant as musk. Eve ate one of the grains and found it more delicious than any thing she had hitherto tasted, so she gave a second grain to Adam. Adam resisted at first, according to some authorities for a whole hour, but an hour in Paradise was eighty years of our earthly reckoning. But when he saw that Eve remained well and cheerful, he yielded to her persuasions, and ate of the second grain which Eve had offered him daily, three times a day, during the hour of eighty years. Thereupon all Adam's heaven-given raiment fell from him, his crown slipped off his head, his rings dropped from his fingers, his silken garments glided like water from his shoulders, and he and Eve were naked and unadorned, and their fallen garments reproached them with the words, "Great is your misfortune ; long will be your sorrows ; we were created to adorn those who serve God ; farewell till the resurrection !"

The throne recoiled from them and exclaimed, "Depart from me, ye disobedient ones !" The horse Meimun, which

Adam sought to mount, plunged and refused to allow him to touch it, saying, " How hast thou kept God's covenant ? " All the inhabitants of Paradise turned their backs on the pair, and prayed God to remove the man and the woman from the midst of them.

God himself addressed Adam with a voice of thunder, saying, " Did not I forbid thee to touch of this fruit, and caution thee against the subtlety of thy foe, Eblis ? " Adam and Eve tried to fly these reproaches, but the branches of the tree Talh caught Adam, and Eve entangled herself in her long hair.

" From the wrath of God there is no escape," cried a voice from the tree Talh ; " obey the commandment of God."

" Depart from Paradise," then spake God, " thou Adam, thy wife, and the animals which led you into sin. The earth shall be your abode ; in the sweat of thy brow shalt thou find food ; the produce of earth shall cause envy and contention ; Eve (Hava) shall be afflicted with a variety of strange affections, and shall bring forth offspring in pain. The peacock shall lose its melodious voice, and the serpent its feet ; dark and noisome shall be the den in which the serpent shall dwell, dust shall be its meat, and its destruction shall be a meritorious work. Eblis shall be cast into the torments of hell."

Our parents were then driven out of Paradise, and one leaf alone was given to each, wherewith to hide their nakedness. Adam was expelled through the gate of Repentance, that he might know that through it alone could Paradise be regained ; Eve was banished through the gate of grace ; the peacock and the serpent through that of Wrath, and Eblis through the gate of Damnation. Adam fell into the island Serendib (Ceylon), Eve at Jedda, the Serpent into the desert of Sahara, the Peacock into Persia, and Eblis into the river Eila.[1]

Tabari says that when the forbidden wheat had entered the belly of Adam and Eve, all the skin came off, except from the ends of the fingers. Now this skin had been pink and horny, so that they had been invulnerable in Paradise, and they were left naked and with a tender skin which could easily be lacerated ; but as often as Adam and Eve looked on their fingernails, they remembered what skin they had worn in Eden.[2]

Tabari also says that four trees pitying the shame of Adam and Eve, the Peacock, and the Serpent, in being driven naked out of Paradise, bowed their branches and gave each a leaf.

[1] Weil, pp. 19–28.   [2] Tabari, i. p. 80.

Certain Rabbis say that Adam ate only on compulsion, that he refused, but Eve " took of the tree,"—that is, broke a branch and " gave it him," with the stick.

According to the Talmudic book, Emek Hammelech (f. 23, col. 3), Eve, on eating the fruit, felt in herself the poison of Jezer hara, or Original sin, and resolved that Adam should not be without it also ; she made him eat and then forced the fruit on the animals, that they might all, without exception, fall under the same condemnation, and become subject to death. But the bird Chol—that is, the Phœnix—would not be deceived, but flew away and would not eat. And now the Phœnix, says the Rabbi Joden after the Rabbi Simeon, lives a thousand years, then shrivels up till it is the size of an egg, and then from himself he emerges young and beautiful again.

We have seen what are the Asiatic myths relating to Adam and Eve ; let us now turn to Africa. In Egypt it was related that Osiris lived with Isis his sister and wife in Nysa, or Paradise, which was situated in Arabia. This Paradise was an island, surrounded by the stream Triton, but it was also a steep mountain that could only be reached on one side. It was adorned with beautiful flowers and trees laden with pleasant fruits, watered by sweet streams, and in it dwelt the deathless ones.

There Osiris found the vine, and Isis the wheat, to become the food and drink of men. There they built a golden temple, and lived in supreme happiness till the desire came on Osiris to discover the water of Immortality, in seeking which he left Nysa, and was in the end slain by Typhon.[1]

The following is a very curious negro tradition, taken down by Dr. Tutschek from a native in Tumale, near the centre of Africa.

Til (God) made men and bade them live together in peace and happiness, labor five days, and keep the sixth as a festival. They were forbidden to hurt the beasts or reptiles. They themselves were deathless, but the animals suffered death. The frog was accursed by God, because when He was making the animals it hopped over his foot. Then God ordered the men to build mountains : they did so, but they soon forgot God's commands, killed the beasts and quarrelled with one another. Wherefore Til (God) sent fire and destroyed them,

---

[1] Diod. Sicul., 14 et seq.

but saved one of the race, named Musikdegen, alive. Then Til began to re-create beings. He stood before a wood and called, Ombo Abnatum Dgu ! and there came out a gazelle and licked His feet. So He said, stand up, Gazelle ! and when it stood up, its beast-form disappeared, and it was a beautiful maiden, and He called her Mariam. He blessed her, and she bore four children, a white pair and a black pair. When they were grown up, God ordered them to marry, the white together and the black together. In Dai, the story goes that Til cut out both Mariam's knee-caps, and of each He made a pair of children. Those which were white He sent north ; those which were black He gave possession of the land where they were born.

God then made the animals subject to death, but the men He made were immortal. But the new created men became disobedient, as had the first creatures ; and the frog complained to Him of His injustice in having made the harmless animals subject to death, but guilty man deathless. " Thou art right," answered Til, and He cast on the men He had made, old age, sickness, and death.[1]

The Fantis relate that they are not in the same condition as that in which they were made, for their first parents had been placed in a lofty and more suitable country, but God drave them into an inferior habitation, that they might learn humility. On the Gold Coast the reason of the Fall is said to have been that the first men were offered the choice of gold or of wisdom, and they chose the former.[2]

In Ashantee the story is thus told. In the beginning, God created three white and three black men and women, and gave them the choice between good and evil. A great calabash was placed on the earth, as also a sealed paper, and God gave the black men the first choice. They took the calabash, thinking it contained every thing, and in it were only a lump of gold, a bar of iron, and some other metals. The white men took the sealed paper, in which they learned every thing. So God left the black men in the bush and took the white men to the sea, and He taught them how to build ships and go into another land. This fall from God caused the black men to worship the subsidiary Fetishes instead of Him.[3]

---

[1] Ausland für Nov. 4, 1847.

[2] W. Smith, Nouveau Voyage de Guinée. Paris, 1751, ii. p. 176.

[3] Bowdler, Mission from Cape Coast to Ashantee. London, 1819, p. 344.

In Greenland "the first man is said to have been Kallak. He came out of the earth, but his wife issued from his thumb, and from them all generations of men have sprung. To him many attribute the origin of all things. The woman brought death into the world, in that she said, Let us die to make room for our successors." [1]

The tradition of the Dog-rib Indians near the Polar Sea, as related by Sir J. Franklin in his account of his expedition of 1825-27, is that the first man was called Tschäpiwih. He found the earth filled with abundance of all good things. He begat children and he gave to them two sorts of fruit, one white and the other black, and he bade them eat the white, but eschew the black. And having given them this command, he left them and went a long journey to fetch the sun to enlighten the world. During his absence they ate only of the white fruit, and then the father made a second journey to fetch the moon, leaving them well provided with fruit. But after a while they forgot his command, and consumed the black fruit. On his return he was angry, and cursed the ground that it should thenceforth produce only the black fruit, and that with it should come in sickness and death.

Dr. Hunter, in his " Memoirs of Captivity amongst the Indians," says that the Delawares believe that in the beginning the Red men had short tails, but they blasphemed the Great Spirit, and in punishment for their sin their tails were cut off and transformed into women, to be their perpetual worry. The same story is told by Mr. Atherne Jones, as heard by him among the Kikapoos.

The ancient Mexicans had a myth of Xolotl, making out of a man's bone the primeval mother in the heavenly Paradise; and he called the woman he had made Cihuacouhatl, which means " The woman with the serpent," or Quilatzli, which means "The woman of our flesh." She was the mother of twins, and is represented in a Mexican hieroglyph as speaking with the serpent, whilst behind her stand the twins, whose different characters are represented by different colors, one of whom is represented slaying the other.[2] Xolotl, who made her out of a bone, was cast out of heaven and became the first man. That the Mexicans had other traditions, now lost, touch-

---

[1] Cranz, Historie von Grönland. Leipzig, 1770, i. p. 262.
[2] Humboldt, Pittoreske Ansichten d. Cordilleren ; Plate xiii. and explanation, ii. pp. 41, 42.

ing this matter is probable, for they had a form of baptism for children in which they prayed that those baptized might be washed from " the original sin committed before the founding of the world."   And this had to do, in all probability, with a legend akin to that of the Iroquois, who told of the primeval mother falling, and then of the earth being built up to receive her, when precipitated out of heaven.

The Caribs of South America relate that Luoguo, the first man and god, created the earth and the sea, and made the earth as fair as the beautiful garden in the heaven where dwell the gods.   Luoguo dwelt among the men he had made for some while.   He drew the men out of his navel and out of his thigh which he cut open.. One of the first men was Racumon, who was transformed into a great serpent with a human head, and he lived twined round a great Cabatas tree and ate of its fruit, and gave to those who passed by.   Then the Caribs lived to a great age, and never waxed old or died.   Afterwards they found a garden planted with manioc, and on that they fed. But they became wicked, and a flood came and swept them away.[1]

In the South Sea Islands we find other traditions of the Fall.   In Alea, one of the Caroline Islands, the tale runs thus :—

" The sister of Eliulap the first man, who was also a god, felt herself in labor, so she descended to earth and there brought forth three children.   To her astonishment she found the earth barren ; therefore by her mighty word, she clothed it with herbage and peopled it with beasts and birds.   And the world became very beautiful, and her sons were happy and did not feel sickness or death, but at the close of every month fell into a slumber from which they awoke renewed in strength and beauty.   But Erigeres, the bad spirit, envied this happiness, so he came to the world and introduced into it pain, age, and death."[2]

With the Jewish additions to the story given in Genesis, we shall conclude.

The godless Sammael had made an alliance with all the chiefs of his hosts against the Lord, because that the holy and ever blessed Lord had said to Adam and Eve, " *Have dominion over the fish of the sea*," etc. ; and he said, " How can I make

---

[1] De la Borde, Reise zu den Caraiben.   Nümb. 1782, i. pp. 380-5.
[2] Allg. Hist. der Reisen, xviii. p. 395.

man to sin and drive him out ? "   Then he went down to earth with all his host, and he sought for a companion like to himself; he chose the serpent, which was in size like a camel, and he seated himself on its back and rode up to the woman, and said to her, " *Hath God said, Ye shall not eat of every tree of the garden ?* "   And he thought, " I will ask more presently." Then she answered, " He has only forbidden me the fruit of the Tree of Knowlege which is in the midst of the garden. And He said, ' In the day thou touchest it thou shalt die.' " She added two words ; God did not say any thing to her about touching it, and she spoke of the fruit, whereas God said the Tree.

Then the godless one, Sammael, went up to the tree and touched it.   But the tree cried out, " *Let not the foot of pride come against me, and let not the hand of the ungodly cast me down !*   Touch me not, thou godless one ! "

Then Sammael called to the woman, and said, " See, I have touched the tree and am not dead.   Do you also touch it and try."   But when Eve drew near to the tree she saw the Angel of Death waiting sword in hand, and she said in her heart, " Perhaps I am to die, and then God will create another wife for Adam ; that shall not be, he must die too."   So she gave him of the fruit.   And when he took it and bit, his teeth were blunted, and thus it is that the back teeth of men are no longer sharp.[1]

V.

ADAM AND EVE AFTER THE FALL.

WHEN Adam reached the earth, the Eagle said to the Whale, with whom it had hitherto lived in the closest intimacy, " Now we must part, for there is no safety for us animals since man has come amongst us.   The deepest abysses of ocean must be thy refuge, and thou must protect thyself with cunning from the great foe who has entered the earth.   I must soar high above the clouds, and there find a place of escape from him who is destined to be my pursuer till death." [2]

According to certain cabbalistic Rabbis, Adam, when cast out of Eden, was precipitated into Gehenna, but he escaped

[1] Eisenmenger, i. pp. 827–9.[2] Weil. p. 28.

therefrom to earth, by repeating and pronouncing properly the mystic word Laverererareri.[1]   In the Talmud it is related that when Adam heard the words of God, " *Thou shalt eat the herb of the field* " (Gen. iii. 18), he trembled in all his limbs, and exclaimed, " O Lord of all the world !   I and my beast, the Ass, shall have to eat out of the same manger ! "   But God said to him, because he trembled, " Thou shalt eat bread in the sweat of thy brow." [2]

Learned Rabbis assert that the angel Raphael had instructed Adam in all kinds of knowledge out of a book, and this book contained mighty mysteries which the highest angels could not fathom, and knew not ; and before the Fall the angels used to assemble in crowds, and listen to Adam instructing them in hidden wisdom.   In that book were seventy-two parts and six hundred and seventy writings, and all this was known ; but from the middle of the book to the end were the one thousand five hundred hidden secrets of Wisdom, and these Adam began to reveal to the angels till he was arrested by the angel Haddarniel.   This book Adam preserved and read in daily ; but when he had sinned, it fled out of his hands and flew away, and he went into the river Gihon up to his neck, and the water washed the glory wherewith he had shone in Paradise from off his body.   But God was merciful, and He restored to him the book by the hands of Raphael, and he left it to his son Seth, and Enoch and Abraham read in this book.[3]

Along with the book Adam retained the rod which God had created at the close of the Sabbath, between sun and sun ; *i. e.* between nightfall and daybreak, so says the Rabbi Levi. Adam left it to Enoch, and Enoch gave it to Noah, and Noah gave it to Shem, and Shem to Abraham, and Abraham delivered it to Isaac, and Isaac gave it to Jacob ; Jacob brought the staff with him to Egypt, and gave it to his son Joseph.   Now when Joseph died, his house was plundered by the Egyptians, and all his effects were taken into Pharaoh's house.   Jethro was a mighty magician, and when he saw the staff of Adam and read the writing thereon, he went forth into Edom and planted it in his garden.   And Jethro would allow none to touch it ; but when he saw Moses he said, " This is he who will deliver Israel out of Egypt."   Wherefore he gave him his daughter Zip-

---

[1] Basnage, Histoire des Juifs.   La Haye, iii. p. 391.
[2] Tract. Avod., f. 1. col. 3 ; also Tract. Pesachim, f. 118, col. 1.
[3] Eisenmenger, i. pp. 376, 377.

3

porah and the staff. But the book Midrash Vajoscha relates this rather differently, in the words of Moses himself: "After I had become great I went out, and seeing an Egyptian ill-treat a Hebrew man of my brethren, I slew him and buried him in the sand. But when Pharoah heard this he sought to slay me, and brought a sharp sword the like of which was not in the world; and therewith I was ten times smitten on my neck. But the Holy God wrought a miracle, for my neck became as hard as a marble pillar, so that the sword had no power over me. And I was forty years old when I fled out of Egypt; and I came to Jethro's house and stood by the well and found Zipporah his daughter; and when I saw her, I was pleased with her, and asked her to marry me. Then she related to me her father's custom, and it was this. 'My father proves every suitor for my hand by a tree which is in his garden; and when he comes to the tree, the tree clasps him in its branches.' Then I asked her where such a tree was, and she answered me, 'This is the staff which God created on the eve of the Sabbath, which was handed down from Adam to Joseph; but Jethro saw the staff at the plundering of Joseph's house, and he took it away with him from Pharaoh's palace and brought it here. This is the staff on which is cut the Schem hammphorasch and the ten plagues that are in store for Egypt, and these are indicated by ten letters on the staff, and they stand thus: *dam*, blood; *zephardeim*, frogs; *kinnim*, lice; *arof*, various insects; *defer*, murrain; *schechim*, blain; *barad*, hail; *arbeh*, locusts; *choschech*, darkness; and *bechor*, first born:—these will be the plagues of Egypt. This staff was for many days and years in my father's house, till he one day took it in his hand and stuck it into the earth in the garden; and then it sprouted and bloomed and brought forth almonds, and when he saw that, he proved every one who sought one of his daughters by that tree.'" These are the words of the Book Midrash Vajoscha, and thereby may be seen that the staff of Adam was of almond wood; but Yalkut Chadasch, under the title "Adam," says that the staff was of the wood of the Tree of the Knowledge of Good and Evil.[1]

When Adam and Eve were driven out of the garden, says the Talmud, they wandered disconsolate over the face of the earth. And the sun began to decline, and they looked with

---

[1] Eisenmenger, i. pp. 377–80.

fear at the diminution of the light, and felt a horror like death steal over their hearts.

And the light of heaven grew paler, and the wretched ones clasped one another in an agony of despair.

Then all grew dark.

And the luckless ones fell on the earth, silent, and thought that God had withdrawn from them the light for ever ; and they spent the night in tears.

But a beam of light began to rise over the eastern hills, after many hours of darkness, and the clouds blushed crimson, and the golden sun came back, and dried the tears of Adam and Eve ; and then they greeted it with cries of gladness, and said, "*Heaviness may endure for a night, but joy cometh in the morning;* this is a law that God has laid upon nature." [1]

Among the Manichean myths prevalent among the Albigenses, was one preserved to us by the troubadour Pierre de Saint-Cloud. When Adam was driven out of Paradise, God in mercy gave him a miraculous rod, which possessed creative powers, so that he had only to strike the sea with it and it would forthwith produce the beast he might require.

Adam struck the sea, and there rose from it the sheep ; then Eve took the staff and smote the water, and from it sprang the wolf, which fell on the sheep and carried it off into the wood. Then Adam took back the staff, and with it called forth the dog to hunt the wolf and recover the sheep.

According to the Mussulman tradition, Adam's beard grew after he had fallen, and it was the result of his excessive grief and penitence : how this affected his chin is not explained, the fact only is thus boldly stated. He was sorely abashed at his beard, but a voice from heaven called to him, saying, " The beard is man's ornament on earth ; it distinguishes him from the feeble woman." Adam shed so many tears that all birds and beasts drank of them, and flowing into the earth they produced the fragrant plants and gum-bearing trees, for they were still endued with the strength and virtue of the food of Paradise.

But the tears of Eve were transformed into pearls where they dribbled into the sea, and into beautiful flowers where they sank into the soil.

Both wailed so loud that Eve's cry reached Adam on the West wind, and Adam's cry was borne to Eve on the wings of

[1] Talmud, Avoda Sara, fol. 8 a, and in Levy, Parabeln, p. 300.

the East wind.   And when Eve heard the well-known voice she clasped her hands above her head, and women to this day thus testify their sorrow; and Adam, when the voice of the weeping of Eve sounded in his ears, put his right hand beneath his beard,—thus do men to this day give evidence of their mourning.   And the tears pouring out of Adam's eyes formed the two rivers Tigris and Euphrates.   All nature wept with him; every bird and beast hastened to him to mingle their tears with his, but the locust was the first to arrive, for it was made of the superfluous earth which had been gathered for the creation of Adam.   There are seven thousand kinds of locusts or grasshoppers, of all colors and sizes, up to the dimensions of an eagle; and they have a king to whom God addresses His commands when He would punish a rebellious nation such as that of Egypt.   The black character imprinted on the locust's wing is Hebrew, and it signifies, "God is One; He overcometh the mighty; the locusts are a portion of His army which He sends against the wicked."   As all nature thus wailed and lamented, from the invisible insect to the angel who upholds the world, God sent Gabriel with the words which were in after-time to save Jonah in the whale's belly, "There is no God but Thou; pardon me for Mohammed's sake, that great and last prophet, whose name is engraved on Thy throne."

When Adam had uttered these words with penitent heart, the gates of heaven opened, and Gabriel cried out, "God has accepted thy penitence, Adam! pray to him alone, He will give thee what thou desirest, even the return to Paradise, after a certain time."

Adam prayed, "Lord, protect me from the further malice of my enemy Eblis."

"Speak the word, There is no God but God; that wounds him like a poisoned arrow."

"Lord, will not the meat and drink provided by this earth lead me into sin?"

"Drink water, and eat only clean beasts which have been slain in the name of Allah, and build mosques where you dwell, so will Eblis have no power over you."

"But if he torment me at night with evil thoughts and dreams?"

"Then rise from thy couch and pray."

"Lord, how shall I be able to distinguish between good and evil?"

"My guidance will be with thee; and two angels will dwell in thy heart, who shall warn thee against evil and encourage thee to good."

"Lord, assure me Thy grace against sin."

"That can only be obtained by good works. But this I promise thee, evil shall be punished one-fold, good shall be rewarded tenfold."

In the meanwhile the angel Michael had been sent to Eve to announce to her God's mercy. When Eve saw him, she exclaimed, "O great and almighty Archangel of God, with what weapon shall I, poor frail creature, fight against sin?"

"God," answered the Angel, "has given me for thee, the most potent weapon of modesty; that, as man is armed with faith, so mayest thou be armed with shamefacedness, therewith to conquer thy passions."

"And what will protect me against the strength of man, so much more robust and vigorous than I, in mind and in body?"

"Love and compassion," answered Michael. "I have placed these in the deepest recesses of his heart, as mighty advocates within him to plead for thee."

"And will God give me no further gift?"

"For the pangs of maternity thou shalt feel, this shall be thine, death in child-bearing shall be reckoned in heaven as a death of martyrdom." [1]

Eblis, seeing the mercy shown to Adam and Eve, ventured to entreat God's grace for himself, and obtained that he should not be enchained in the place of torment till the day of the general Resurrection, and that he should exercise sovereignty over the wicked and all those who should reject God's word in this life.

"And where shall I dwell till the consummation of all things?" he asked of Allah.

"In ruined buildings, and in tombs, and in dens and caves of the mountains."

"And what shall be my nourishment?"

"All beasts slain in the name of false gods and idols."

"And how shall I slake my thirst?"

"In wine and other spirituous liquors."

---

[1] It is a popular superstition among the lower orders in England that a woman who dies in childbirth, even if she be unmarried, cannot be lost.

"And how shall I occupy myself in hours of idleness?"

"In music, dancing, and song."

"What is the word of my sentence?"

"The curse of God till the Judgment-day."

"And how shall I fight against those men who have received Thy revelation, and are protected by the two angels?"

"Thy offspring shall be more numerous than theirs: to every man born into this world, there will be born seven evil spirits, who, however, will be powerless to injure true Believers."

God then made a covenant with Adam's successors; He rubbed Adam's back, and lo! from out of his back crawled all generations of men that were to be born, about the size of ants, and they ranged themselves on the left and on the right. At the head of those on the right stood Mohammed, then the other prophets and the faithful, distinguished from those on the left by their white and dazzling splendor. Those on the left were headed by Kabil (Cain).

God then acquainted Adam with the names and fate of all his posterity; and when the recital arrived at David, to whom God had allotted only thirty years, Adam asked God, "How many years are accorded to me?"

Allah replied, "One thousand."

Then said Adam, "I make a present to David of seventy years out of my life." God consented; and knowing the shortness of Adam's memory, at all events in matters concerning himself inconveniently, He made the angels bring a formal document of resignation engrossed on parchment, and required Adam to subscribe thereto his name, and Michael and Gabriel to countersign it as witnesses.

A very similar tradition was held by the Jews, for in Midrash Jalkut (fol. 12) it is said: God showed Adam all future generations of men, with their captains, learned and literary men. Then he saw that David was provided with only three hours of life, and he said, "Lord and Creator of the world, is this unalterable?" "Such was my first intention," was the reply.

"How many years have I to live?"

"A thousand."

"And is there such a thing known in heaven as making presents?"

"Most certainly."

"Then I present seventy years of my life to David."

And what did Adam next perform? He drew up a legal document of transfer, and sealed it with his own seal, and God and Metatron did likewise.

To return to the Mussulman legend.

When all the posterity of Adam were assembled, God exclaimed to them, " Acknowledge that I am the only God, and that Mohammed is my prophet." The company on the right eagerly made this acknowledgment; those, however, on the left long hesitated,—some said only the former portion of the sentence, and others did not open their mouths.

" The disobedient," said Allah to Adam, " shall, if they remain obstinate, be cast into hell, but the true believers shall be received into Paradise."

" So be it," replied Adam. And thus shall it be at the end of the world.

After the covenant, Allah rubbed Adam's back once more, and all his little posterity retreated into it again.

When now God withdrew His presence from Adam's sight for the remainder of our first parents' life, Adam uttered such a loud and bitter cry that the whole earth quaked.

The All-merciful was filled with compassion, and bade him follow a cloud which would conduct him to a spot where he would be directly opposite His throne, and there he was to build a temple.

" Go about this temple," said Allah, " and I am as near to you as the angels who surround my throne." Adam, who was still the size that God had created him, easily strode from Ceylon to Mecca after the cloud, which stood over the place where he was to build. On Mount Arafa, near Mecca, to his great delight, he found Eve again, and from this circumstance the mountain takes its name (from Arafa, to recognize, to know again). They both began to build, and erected a temple having four doors—one was called Adam's door, another Abraham's door, the third Ishmael's door, and the fourth Mohammed's door. The plan of the temple was furnished by Gabriel, who also contributed a precious stone, but this stone afterwards, through the sin of men, turned black. This black stone is the most sacred Kaaba, and it was originally an angel, whose duty it had been to guard the Wheat-Tree of the knowledge of good and evil, and to warn off Adam should he approach it. But though his inattention the design of God was frustrated, and in punishment he was transformed into a stone, and he will not be released from his transformation till the Last Day.

Gabriel taught Adam also all the ceremonies of the great pilgrimage.

Adam now returned with his wife to India, and lived there till he died, but every year he made a pilgrimage to Mecca, till he lost his primitive size, and retained only the height of sixty eels.

The cause of his diminution in height was his horror and dismay at the murder of Abel, which made him shrink into himself, and he was never afterwards able to stretch himself out again to his pristine dimensions.[1]

The Book of the Penitence of Adam is a curious apocryphal work of Syriac origin ; I give an outline of its contents.

God planted, on the third day, the Terrestrial Paradise ; it is bounded on the east by the ocean in which, at the Last Day, the elect will wash away all those sins which have not as yet been purged away by repentance.

On leaving this garden of delights, Adam turned to take of it one last look. He saw that the Tree which had caused his fall was cursed and had withered away.

He was much surprised when night overtook him, for in Paradise he had not known darkness. As he went along his way, shedding tears, he overtook the serpent gliding over the ground, and licking the dust. That serpent he had last seen on four feet, very beautiful, with the hair of a young maiden, enamelled with brilliant colors. Now it was vile, hideous, and grovelling. The beasts which, before the Fall, had coveted its society, fled from it now with loathing.

Filled with rage at the sight of Adam and Eve, to whom it attributed its present degradation, the serpent flew at them and prostrated them. Thereupon God removed from it its sole remaining possession—the gift of speech, and it was left only its hiss of rage and shame.

Adam soon felt exhaustion, heat, fear and pain ;—afflictions he had not known in Eden. As the shadows of night fell, an intense horror overwhelmed the guilty pair ; they trembled in every limb and cried to God. The Almighty, in compassion, consoled them by announcing to them that day would return after twelve hours of night. They were relieved by this prom-ise, and they spent the first night in prayer.

But Satan, who never lost sight of them, fearing lest their

[1] Weil, pp. 29-38.

prayers should wholly appease the divine justice, assembled his host of evil angels, surrounded himself with a brilliant light, and stood at the entrance of the cave where the banished ones prayed. He hoped that Adam would mistake him for God, and prostrate himself before him.

But Adam said to Eve : "Observe this great light and this multitude of spirits. If it were God who sent them, they would enter and tell us their message." Adam did not know then that Satan cannot approach those who pray. Then Adam addressed himself to God and said, "O my God! is there another God but Thou, who can create angels and send them to us? Lord, deign to instruct us!"

Then a heavenly angel entered the cavern and said, "Adam, fear not those whom you see ; it is Satan and his host. He sought to seduce you again to your fall."

Having thus spoken, the angel fell upon Satan and tore from off him his disguise, and exposed him in his hideous nakedness to Adam and Eve. And to console them for this trial, God sent Adam gold rings, incense and myrrh, and said to him, "Preserve these things, and they will give you at night light and fragrance ; and when I shall come down on earth to save you, clothed in human flesh, kings shall bring me these three tokens."

It is because of this present that the cavern into which Adam and Eve retreated has been called the Treasure-cave.

Adam and Eve, greatly cheered, blessed the Lord, and thanked him for his goodness, and resolved to continue their repentance.

A short time after they committed a fault. Satan presented himself to them under the form of an angel of light, and announced that he was commissioned by the Most High to lead them to the brink of the River of the Water of Life, into which they were to plunge and wash away their sin.

They believed, and followed him by a strange road, and he led them to the edge of a precipice, down which he endeavored to fling them ; for, he thought, were he to destroy the man and the woman, he would be supreme in the world God had made. But the Almighty rescued Adam and Eve, and drave Satan from them.

To punish themselves for their involuntary fault, Adam and Eve separated, so as not to see one another, and resolve to spend forty days up to their necks in the sea.

3*

Before parting, Adam said to his wife, " Remain in the water here, and do not quit it till I return, and spend your time in praying the Lord to pardon us."

Now, whilst they were undergoing this penance, Satan cast about how he might bring to naught our first parents, and he sought them but could not find them, till on the thirty-fifth day of their penance he perceived the two heads above the water ; then he knew at once what was their intention, and he resolved to frustrate it. So he took upon him the form of an angel of Heaven, and flew over the sea singing praises to God ; and when he came to the place where Eve was, he cried, " Joy, joy to thee ! God is with thee, and he has sent me to bring thee to Adam to announce to him that he has found favor with the Most High."

Eve instantly scrambled out of the water, and followed Satan to Adam, and the Evil One placed her before her husband, and vanished. When Adam saw his wife, he was filled with dismay, and beat his breast and wept. When she told him why she was there, he knew that the great Enemy had been again at his work of deception, and he fell into despair. But a voice from Heaven bade him return with Eve to the Treasure-cave.

Hunger, thirst, cold, and prayer had completely exhausted the pair, and Adam cried to the Lord, " O God, my Creator ! Thou hast given me reason and an enlightened heart. When Thou didst forbid me to eat of the fruit of the Tree, Eve was not yet made, and she did not hear Thy command ; in Eden we hungered not, nor felt thirst or pain or fatigue. All this have we lost. And now we dare not touch the fruit of the trees or drink of water without Thy command. Our bodies are exhausted, our strength is gone ; grant us wherewith to satisfy our hunger, and to quench our thirst."

God ordered the Cherubim who kept the gate of Eden, to carry to Adam two figs from the tree under which our first parents had concealed themselves after the Fall.

" Take," said the Cherubim, presenting the figs to them, " take the fruit of the tree whose leaves covered your shame."

" Oh ! " cried Adam, " may God grant us some of the fruit of the Tree of Life."

But God answered, " I will give unto you this fruit and living water, to you and to your descendants, on that day that I shall descend into the abode of death and shall break the gates of iron in sunder, to bring you forth into my garden of pleasures. That which you ask of Me shall take place at the expiration of five long days and a half (*i. e.* 5,500 years), after that my blood has flowed upon thy head, O Adam, upon Golgotha."

Adam and Eve took the figs, which were very heavy, for the fruits of the earthly paradise were much larger than the fruit of this outer world in which we live. And when they were about to enter into the Cave of Treasures, they saw there a great fire ; this mightily astonished them, for as yet they had not seen fire except in the flaming sword of the Cherub. Now this fire which surprised them was the work of Satan ; he had collected branches and had fired them in the hope of burning down the cavern and driving Adam to despair.

The fire lasted till the morrow ; Satan, without showing himself, keeping it supplied with fresh fuel. Adam and Eve did not venture to approach, but recommended themselves to God ; and the Evil One, finding that his plan had failed, let the fire die out and departed.

Adam and Eve slept the following night at the foot of a mountain near their lost Eden. Satan beholding them, said, " God has made a compact with Adam, whom he desires to save, but I will slay him, and the earth shall be mine."

He therefore summoned his attendant angels, and they dislodged a huge rock from the mountain and hurled it upon the sleepers. But as this mass was bounding down the flank of the mountain, and was in mid-air in one of its leaps, God arrested it above the heads of the sleepers, and it sheltered them from the dews of night.

Adam and Eve awoke greatly troubled by their dreams, and they asked of God garments to cover their naked bodies, for they suffered from the scorching sun by day, and the frost by night. God replied, " Go to the shore of the sea ; you will there find the skins of sheep which have been devoured by lions: of them make to yourselves raiment."

Satan heard the words of God, and he outran our first parents, that he might secure the skins and destroyed them, in the hopes that Adam and Eve, finding no hides, would doubt God and think that he had failed in His word. But God fastened Satan in his naked hideousness beside the skins, immovable, till Adam and Eve arrived, when he addressed them in these terms : " Behold him who has seduced you ; see what has become of his beauty. After having made you such promises, he was about to rob you of these hides." Adam and Eve took the skins and made of them garments. A few days after, God said to them, " Go to the west till you arrive at a black land ; there you will find food." They obeyed, and they saw corn full ripe, and God inspired Adam with knowledge how to make bread. But not having sickles they tore the corn up by the roots, and having made a rick of it, they slept, expecting to thrash it out and grind it on the morrow. But Satan fired this rick and reduced their harvest to ashes.

Whilst they wept and lamented, Satan came to them as an angel, and said, " This is the work of your Enemy the Fiend, but God has sent me to bring you into a field where you will find better corn."

They followed him, nothing doubting, and he led them for eight days, and they fainted with exhaustion and were foot-sore. Then he left them in an unknown land ; but God was their protector, He brought them back to their harvest and restored their rick of corn, and they made bread and offered to God the first sacrifice.[1]

But enough of this apocryphal work, which contains a string of absurd tricks played by Satan on our first parents, which are invariably defeated by God ; of these the specimens given above are sufficient.

A curious legend exists among the Sclavonic nations by which the existence of elves is accounted for. It is said that Adam had by his wife Eve, thirty sons and thirty daughters. God asked him, one day, the number of his children. Adam was ashamed of having so many girls, so he answered, " Thirty sons and twenty-seven daughters." But from the eye of God nothing can be concealed, and He took from among Adam's daughters the three fairest, and He made them Willis, or elves ; they were good and holy, and therefore did not perish in the Deluge, but entered with Noah into the ark and were saved.

The story of Adam's penitence, as told by Tabari, is as follows :—

The moment that Adam fell out of Paradise and touched the ground on the mountains in the centre of Ceylon, he understood in all its magnitude the greatness of his loss and his

---

[1] Dillman, Das Adambuch des Morgenlandes; Göttingen, 1853. This book is not to be confounded with the Testament of Adam.

sin. He remained stupefied with his face on the earth, and
did not raise it, but allowed his tears to flow upon and soak
into the soil. For a hundred years he remained in this position, and his tears formed a stream which rolled down the
mountain, which still flows from Adam's Peak in the island
of Ceylon, and gives their virtue to the healing plants and
fragrant trees which there flourish, and are exported for medicinal purposes.

When a hundred years had elapsed, God had compassión
on Adam, and sent Gabriel to him, who said, "God salutes
thee, O Adam! and He bids me say to thee, Did I not create
thee out of the earth by My will? Did I not give thee Paradise to be thine abode? Why these tears and sighs?"

Adam replied, "How shall I not weep, and how shall I
abstain from sighing? Have I not lost the protection of God,
and have I not disobeyed His will?"

Gabriel said, "Do not afflict thyself. Recite the words I
shall teach thee, and God will grant thee repentance which He
will accept," as it is written in the Koran, "Adam learnt of
His Lord words; and the Lord returned to Him, for He is
merciful, and He returns." Adam recited these words, and in
the joy he felt at the prospect of finding mercy, he wept, and
his joyous tears watered the earth, and from them sprang up
the narcissus and the ox-eye.

Then said Adam to Gabriel, "What shall I now do?"

And Gabriel gave to Adam wheat-grains from out of Paradise, the fruit of the Forbidden Tree, and he bade him sow it,
and he said, "This shall be thy food in future."

Afterwards, Gabriel taught Adam to draw iron out of the
rock and to make instruments of husbandry. And all that
Adam sowed sprang up in the self-same hour that it was sown,
for the blessing of God was upon it. And Adam reaped and
thrashed and winnowed. Then Gabriel bade him take two
stones from the mountain, and he taught him with them to
grind the corn; and when he had made flour, he said to the
angel, "Shall I eat now?" But Gabriel answered, "Not so;"
and he showed him how to build an oven of iron. It was
from this oven that the water of the deluge at Koufa flowed.
He taught him also to make dough and to bake.

But Adam was hungry, and he said, "Let me eat now," and
the angel stayed him, and answered, "Tarry till the bread be
cold and stale," but he would not, but ate. Therefore he

suffered from pain in his belly. Next, Gabriel by the command of Allah brought out of Eden the ox and fruit ; of these latter there were ten kinds whose exterior was edible, but whose insides were useless to eat, such as the apricot, the peach and the date. And there were three that could not be eaten anyhow. Then he brought ten more whose insides and outsides might be eaten, such as the grape, the fig, and the apple. Said Gabriel to Adam, " Sow these," and he sowed them. These are the trees that the angel brought out of Paradise.

Now Adam was all alone on the peak in the midst of Ceylon, and his head was in the first heaven. The sun burnt him, so that all his hair fell off ; and God, in compassion, bade Gabriel pass his wing over Adam's head, and Adam thereupon shrank to the height of sixty cubits. And then he could no longer hear the voices of the angels in heaven, and he was sore distressed.

Then God said to him, " I have made this world thy prison, but I send to thee out of heaven a house of rubies, in order that thou mayest enter in and walk round it, and therein find repose for thy heart."

Thereupon out of heaven descended " the visited house," and it was placed where now stands the temple of Mecca. The black stone which is there was originally white and shining. It was placed in the ruby house. Whosoever looked in that direction from ten parasangs off, could see the light of that house shining like a fire up to the heaven, and in the midst of that red light shone the white stone like a star.

Afterwards, Gabriel conducted Adam to that house that he might go in procession round it. All the places where his foot was planted became verdant oases, with rivers of water and many flowers and trees, but all the tract between was barren.

Gabriel taught Adam how to make the pilgrimage ; and if any one now goes there without knowing the ceremonies, he needs a guide.

Then Adam met with Eve again, and they rejoiced together ; and she went back with him to Ceylon. Now at that time there was in the world no other pair than Adam and Eve, and no other house than the mansion of rubies.

Now Eblis had made his prayer to Allah that he might be allowed to live till Israfiel should sound the last trumpet.

And he asked this, because those who are alive when that trumpet sounds, shall not die any more, for Death will be brought in, in the shape of a sheep, and will be slaughtered; and when Death is slaughtered, no one will be able to die.

And God said, "I give thee the time till all creatures must die"

Then Eblis said, "Just as Thou didst turn me out of the right way, so shall I pervert those whom Thou hast made" Satan went to man and said to him, "God has driven me out of Paradise, never to return there, and He has taken from me the sovereignty of this world to give it to thee. Why should we not be friends and associate together, and I can advise thee on thy concerns?"

And Adam thought to himself, "I must be the companion of this one, but I will make use of him." So he suffered him to be his comrade.

The first act of treachery he did was this.

Every child Adam had by Eve died when born. Eve became pregnant for the fourth time, and Eblis said to Adam, "I believe this child will be good-looking and will live."

"I am of the same opinion," answered Adam.

"If my prophecy turns out right," said the Evil One, "give the child to me."

"I will give it," said Adam.

Now the child, when born, was very fair to look upon, and Adam, though he repented of his rash promise, did not venture to break his word; so he gave the child to Eblis, that is to say, he named it Abd-el-Hareth, or Servant of Hareth, instead of Abd-Allah, Servant of God. And after living two years it died.[1]

Thus Satan became an associate in the affairs of man.

But others tell the conclusion of the story somewhat differently. They say that the child Abd-el-Hareth became the progenitor of the whole race of Satyrs, nightmares, and hobgoblins.

Maimonides says that the Sabians attribute to Adam the introduction of the worship of the moon, on which account they call him the prophet or apostle of the moon.[2]

A large number of books are attributed to Adam. The

---

[1] Tabari, i., capp. xxviii. xxix.
[2] In More Nevochim, quoted by Fabricius, i. p. 5.

passage in Genesis, *This is the Book of the generations of Adam,*[1] led many to suppose that Moses quoted from a book written by our first parent. That such an apocryphal book did exist in after-times, appears from the fact of Pope Gelasius in his decrees rejecting it as spurious. He speaks of it as " the book which is called the Book of the generations of Adam or Geneseos." And the Rabbis say that this book was written by Adam, after he had seen all his posterity brought out before him, as already related. And this book, they say, Adam gave to Enoch.[2]

Beside this, there existed an Apocalypse of Adam, which is mentioned by S. Epiphanius, who quotes a passage from it, in which Adam describes the Tree of Life, which produced twelve kinds of fruit every year.[3] And George Syncellus, in his Chronicle, extracts a portion of an apocryphal Life of Adam.

Amongst the Revelations of S. Amadeus are found two psalms, which, in vision, he heard had been composed by Adam. One was on the production of Eve, the other is a hymn of repentance, a joint composition of the two outcasts. It runs as follows :—

Adam.—" Adonai, my Lord God, have mercy upon me for Thy great goodness, and according to the multitude of Thy mercies do away my transgressions. I am bowed down with trouble, Thy waves and storms have gone over me. Deliver me, O God, and save me from the flood of many waters. Hear my words, O Heavens, and all ye that dwell in them. May the angels bear up all my thoughts and words to Thee, and may the celestial virtues declare them. May the Lord bend His compassionate ear to my lowly petition. May He hear my prayer, and let the cry of my heart reach Him. Thou, O God, art the true and most brilliant light; all other lights are mingled with darkness. Thou art the sun that knowest no down-setting, that dwellest in inaccessible light. Thou art the end to which all flesh come. Thou art the only satisfaction of all the blessed."

Eve.—" Adonai, Lord God, have mercy upon me for Thy great goodness, and for the multitude of Thy mercies do away my transgressions. Thou before all things didst create the immovable heaven as a holy and exalted home, and Thou didst adorn it with angel spirits, to whom Thou didst in goodness

---

[1] Gen v. i.   [2] Fabricius, i. p. 11.   [3] Adv. Hæresi, c. 5.

declare thy purposes. They were the bright morning stars who sang to Thee through ages of ages. Thou didst form the movable heaven and Thou didst set in it the watery clouds. Those waters are under the immovable heaven, and are above all that live and move. Thou didst create the light; the beauteous sun, the moon with the five planets didst Thou place in the midst, and didst fix the signs and constellations. Thou didst produce four elements, and didst kindle all with Thy wisdom."

Adam.—" Adonai, Lord God, have mercy upon me for Thy great goodness, and for the multitude of Thy mercies do away my transgressions. Thou hast cast out the proud and rebel dragon with Thy mighty arm. Thou hast put down the mighty from their seat and hast exalted the humble and meek. Thou hast filled the hungry with good things, and the rich Thou hast sent empty away. Thou didst fashion me in Thine own image of the dust of earth, and destine me, mortal, to be immortal; and me, frail, to endure. Thou didst lead me into the place of life and joy, and didst surround me with all good things; Thou didst put all things under my feet, and didst reveal to me Thy great name, Adonai. Thou didst give me Eve, to be a help meet for me, whom Thou didst draw from my side."

Adam.—" Adonai, Lord and God, have mercy upon me for Thy great goodness, and for the multitude of Thy mercies do away my transgressions; for Thou hast made me the head of all men. Thou hast inspired me and my consort with Thy wisdom, and hast given us a free will and placed our lot in our own hands. But thou hast given us precepts and laws, and hast placed life and death before us that we might keep Thy commandments, and in keeping them find life; but if we keep them not, we shall die. Lucifer, the envious one, saw and envied. He fought against us and prevailed. Conquered by angels, he conquered man, and subjugated all his race. I have sinned. I am he who have committed iniquity. If I had refused in my free will, neither Eve nor the Enemy could have obtained my destruction But being in honor I had no understanding and I lost my dignity. I am like to the cattle, the horse, and the mule, which have no understanding."

Eve.—" Adonai, Lord and God, have mercy upon me for Thy great goodness, and for the multitude of Thy mercies do away mine offences. Great is our God, and great is His mercy; His goodness is unmeasured. He will supply the remedy to our sin, that if we will to rise, we may be able to arise; He has appointed His Son, the glorifier of all, and our Redeemer; and He has appointed the Holy Mother to be our mediatrix, in whose image He has built me, Eve, the mother of all flesh. He has fashioned the Mother after the likeness of her daughter. He has made the father after the image and likeness of His Son; and He will blot out our transgressions for His merits, if we yield our wills thereto, and receive His sacraments. He will receive a free-will offering, and He will not despise a contrite heart. To those going towards Him, He will fly with welcome, He will pardon their offences and will crown them with glory."

Adam.—" Adonai, Lord and God, have mercy upon me for Thy great goodness, and for the multitude of Thy mercies do away mine offences. O God, great is the abundance of Thy sweetness. Blessed are all they that hope in Thee. After the darkness Thou bringest in the light; and pain is converted into joy. Thou repayest a thousand for a hundred, and for a thousand thou givest ten thousand. For the least things, Thou rewardest with the greatest things; and for temporal joys, Thou givest those that are eternal. Blessed are they that keep Thy statutes, and bend their necks to Thy yoke. They shall dwell in Thy Tabernacle and rest upon Thy holy hill. They shall be denizens of Thy courts with Thee, whose roots shine above gold and precious stones. Blessed are they who believe in the triune God, and will to know His ways. We all sing, Glory to the Father, and to the Son, and to the Holy Ghost, and we magnify our God. As in the beginning the angels sang, so shall we now and ever, and in ages of ages. Amen."[1]

Manasseh Ben-Israel has preserved a prophecy of Adam, that the world is to last seven thousand years. He says this secret was handed down from Adam to Enoch, and from Enoch to Noah, and from Noah to Shem.[2]

At Hebron is a cave, " which," says an old traveller. " Christians and Turks point out as having been the place where Adam and Eve bewailed their sins for a hundred years. This spot is towards the west, in a valley, about a hundred paces from the Damascene field; it is a dark grotto, not very

[1] Eusebius Nierembergius, De Origine S. Scripturæ. Lugd., 1641.
[2] Fabricius, i. p. 33.

long or broad, very low, in a hard rock, and not apparently artificial, but natural. This valley is called *La valle dè Lagrime*, the Vale of Tears, as they shed such copious tears over their transgressions." [1]

Abu Mohammed Mustapha Ben-Alschit Hasen, in his Universal History, says that Adam's garment of fig-leaves, in which he went out of Eden, was left by him, when he fell, on Adam's Peak in Ceylon. There it dried to dust, and the dust was scattered by the wind over the island, and from this sprang the odoriferous plants which grow there. [2]

Adam is said to have not gone altogether empty-handed out of Paradise. Hottinger, in his Oriental History, quoting Jewish authorities, says : " Adam having gone into the land of Babel, took with him many wonderful things, amongst others a tree with flowers, leaves and branches of gold, also a stone tree, also the leaves of a tree so strong that they were inconsumable in fire, and so large as to be able to shelter under them ten thousand men of the stature of Adam ; and he carried about with him two of these leaves, of which one would shelter two men or clothe them." [3] Of these trees we read in the Gemara that the Rabbi Canaan asked of the Rabbi Simon, son of Assa, who had gone to see them, whether this was true. He was told in reply that it was so, and that at the time of the Captivity the Jews had seated themselves under these trees, and in their shadow had found consolation.

But Palestine seems also to have possessed some of the trees of Adam's planting, for Jacob Vitriacus in his Jewish History says : " There are in that land wonderful trees, which for their pre-excellence are called Apples of Paradise, bearing oblong fruit, very sweet and unctuous, having a most delicious savor, bearing in one cluster more than a hundred compressed berries. The leaves of this tree are a cubit long and half a cubit wide. There are three other trees producing beautiful apples or citrons, in which the bite of a man's teeth is naturally manifest, wherefore they are called Adam's Apples." [4] Hottinger says that at Tripoli grows a tree called Almaus, or Adam's apple, with a green head, and leaves like outspread fingers, no branches, but only leaves, and with a fruit like a bean-pod, of

---

[1] Ferdinand de Troilo, Orientale Itinerario. Dresd., 1667, p. 323.
[2] Selden, De Synedriis, ii. p. 452.
[3] Hottinger, Historia Orientalis, lib. i. c. 8.
[4] Jacobus Vitriacus, Hist. Hierosol., c. lxxxv.

delicious flavor, and an odor of roses. Buntingius, in his Itinerary, describes an Adam's apple which he tasted at Alexandria, and he said the taste was like pears, and the clusters of prodigious size, with twenty in each cluster, like magnificent bunches of grapes. But the most remarkable fact about them was that, if one of the fruit were cut with a knife, the figure of a crucifix was found to be contained in it.[1] And this tree was supposed to have been the forbidden tree, and the fruit to have thus brought hope as it also brought death to the eater. Nider, "In Formicario," also relates that this fruit, thus marked with the form of the Crucified, grows in Granada.[2]

"At Beyrut, of which S. Nicodemus was the first bishop," writes the Friar, Ignatius von Rheinfelden, "I saw a wonderful fruit which is called by the Arabs, Mauza, and by the Christians Adam's fig. This fruit grows upon a trunk in clusters of fifty or more, and hangs down towards the ground on account of its weight. The fruit is in shape something like a cucumber, and is a span long, yellow, and tasting something like figs. The Christians of those parts say it is the fruit of which Adam and Eve ate in Paradise, and they argue thus : first, there are no apples in those parts ; secondly, S. Jerome translated the word in the Bible, Mauza ; thirdly, if the fruit be cut, within it is seen the figure of a crucifix, and they conclude thereby that the first parents were showed by this figure how their sin would be atoned ; fourthly, the leaves being three ells long and half an ell wide, were admirably adapted to make skirts of, when Adam and Eve were conscious of their nakedness. And Holy Scripture says nothing of apples, but says merely—fruit. But whether this was the fruit or not, I leave others to decide."[3]

Adam is said by the Easterns to have received from Raphael a magic ring, which became his symbol, and which he handed down to his descendants selected to know and read mysteries. This was no other than the " crux ansata," or handled cross, so common on Egyptian monuments as the hieroglyph of Life out of death. The circle symbolized the apple, and thus the Carthusian emblem, which bears the motto " Stat crux dum volvitur orbis," is in reality the mystic symbol of Adam. "Which," says the Arabic philosopher, Ibn-ephi, " Mizraim re-

---

[1] As King Charles's Oak may be seen in the fern-root.
[2] Fabricius, i. p. 84.
[3] Neue Ierosolymitanische Pilgerfahrt. Würtzburg, 1667, p. 47

ceived from Ham, and Ham from Noah, and Noah from Enoch, and Enoch from Seth, and Seth from Adam, and Adam from the angel Raphael. Ham wrought with it great marvels, and Hermes received it from him and placed it amongst the hieroglyphics. But this character signifies the progress and motion of the Spirit of the world, and it was a magic seal, kept secret among their mysteries, and a ring constraining demons." [1]

VI.

CAIN AND ABEL.

AFTER that the child given to Satan died, says Tabari, Adam had another son, and he called him Seth, and Seth was prophet in the room of his father, after the death of Adam.

Adam had many more children ; every time that Eve bore, she bare twins, whereof one was male, the other female, and the twins were given to one another as husband and wife.

Now Adam sought to give to Abel the twin sister of Cain, when she was old enough to be married, but Cain (Kabil, in Arabic) was dissatisfied.[2] Adam said to the brothers, Cain and Abel, " Go, my sons, and sacrifice to the Lord ; and he whose sacrifice is accepted, shall have the young girl. Take each of you offerings in your hand and go, sacrifice to the Lord, and he shall decide."

Abel was a shepherd, and he took the fattest of the sheep, and bore it to the place of sacrifice ; but Cain, who was a tiller of the soil, took a sheaf of corn, the poorest he could find, and placed it on the altar. Then fire descended from heaven and consumed the offering of Abel, so that not even the cinders remained ; but the sheaf of Cain was left untouched.

Adam gave the maiden to Abel, and Cain was sore vexed.

One day, Abel was asleep on a mountain. Cain took a stone and crushed his head. Then he threw the corpse on his back, and carried it about, not knowing what to do with it ; but he saw two crows fighting, and one killed the other ;

---

[1] Stephanus Le Moyne, Notæ ad Varia Sacra, p. 863.

[2] Abulfeda, p. 15. In the Apocryphal book, The Combat of Adam (Dillman, Das Christliche Adambuch des Morgenlandes ; Göttingen, 1853), the same reason for hostility is given. In that account, Satan appears to Cain and prompts him to every act of wickedness.

then the crow that survived dug a hole in the earth with his beak, and buried the dead bird.   Cain said, " I have not the sense of this bird.   I too will lay my brother in the ground." And he did so.

When Adam learned the death of his son, he set out in search of Cain, but could not find him ; then he recited the following lines :—

" Every city is alike, each mortal man is vile,
  The face of earth has desert grown, the sky has ceased to smile,
  Every flower has lost its hue, and every gem is dim.
  Alas ! my son, my son is dead ; the brown earth swallows him !
  We one have had in midst of us whom death has not yet found,
  No peace for him, no rest for him, treading the blood-drenched
    ground." [1]

This is how the story is told in the Midrash : [2] Cain and Abel could not agree, for, what one had, the other wanted ; then Abel devised a scheme that they should make a division of property, and thus remove the possibility of contention. The proposition pleased Cain.   So Cain took the earth, and all that is stationary, and Abel took all that is movable.

But the envy which lay in the heart of Cain gave him no rest.   One day he said to his brother, " Remove thy foot, thou standest on my property: the plain is mine."

Then Abel ran upon the hills, but Cain cried, " Away, the hills are mine ! "   Then he climbed the mountains, but still Cain followed him, calling, " Away! the stony mountains are mine."

In the Book of Jasher the cause of quarrel is differently stated.   One day the flock of Abel ran over the ground Cain had been ploughing ; Cain rushed furiously upon him and bade him leave the spot.   " Not," said Abel, " till you have paid me for the skins of my sheep and wool of their fleeces used for your clothing."   Then Cain took the coulter from his plough, and with it slew his brother. [3]

The Targum of Jerusalem says, the subject of contention was that Cain denied a Judgment to come and Eternal Life ; and Abel argued for both. [4]   The Rabbi Menachem, however, asserts that the point on which they strove was whether a word was written *zizit* or *zizis* in the Parascha. [5]

<hr>

[1] Tabari, i. c. xxx.   [2] Jalkut, fol. 11 a.   [3] Yaschar. p. 1089.
[4] Targums, ed. Etheridge, London, 1862, i. p. 172.
[5] Eisenmenger, i. p. 320.

" And when they were in the field together, the brothers quarrelled, saying. ' Let us divide the world.' One said, ' The earth you stand on is my soil.' The other said, ' You are standing on my earth.' One said, ' The Holy Temple shall stand on my lot ;' the other said, ' It shall stand on my lot.' So they quarrelled. Now there were born with Abel two daughters, his sisters. Then said Cain, ' I will take the one I choose, I am the eldest ;' Abel said, ' They were born with me, and I will have them both to wife.' And when they fought, Abel flung Cain down and was above him ; and he lay on Cain. Then Cain said to Abel, ' Are we not both sons of one father ; why wilt thou kill me ? ' And Abel had compassion, and let Cain get up. And so Cain fell on him and killed him. From this we learn not to render good to the evil, for, because Abel showed mercy to Cain, Cain took advantage of it to slay Abel." [1]

S. Methodius the Younger refers to this tradition. He says : " Be it known that Adam and Eve when they left Paradise were virgins. But the third year after the expulsion from Eden, they had Cain, their first-born, and his sister Calmana ; and after this, next year, they had Abel and his sister Deborah. But in the three hundredth year of Adam's life, Cain slew his brother, and Adam and Eve wailed over him a hundred years." [2]

Eutychius, Patriarch of Alexandria, says, " When Adam and Eve rebelled against God, He expelled them from Paradise at the ninth hour on Friday to a certain mountain in India, and He bade them produce children to increase and multiply upon the earth. Adam and Eve therefore became parents, first of a boy named Cain, and of a girl named Azrun, who were twins ; then of another boy named Abel, and of a twin sister named Owain, or in Greek Laphura.

" Now, when the children were grown up, Adam said to Eve, ' Let Cain marry Owain, who was born with Abel, and let Abel have Azrun, who was born with Cain.' But Cain said to his mother, ' I will marry my own twin sister, and Abel shall marry his.' For Azrun was prettier than Owain. But when Adam heard this, he said, ' It is contrary to the precept that thou shouldst marry thy twin sister.'

---

[1] Liber Zenorena, quoted by Fabricius, i. p. 108.
[2] S. Methodius, jun., Revelationes, c. 3.

"Now Cain was a tiller of the ground, but Abel was a pastor of sheep. Adam said to them, 'Take of the fruits of the earth, and of the young of the sheep, and ascend the top of this holy mountain, and offer there the best and choicest to God.' Abel offered of the best and fattest of the first-born of the flock. Now as they were ascending the summit of the mountain, Satan put it into the head of Cain to kill his brother, so as to get Azrun. For that reason his oblation was not accepted by God. Therefore he was the more inflamed with rage against Abel, and as they were going down the mount, he rushed upon him and beat him about the head with a stone and killed him. Adam and Eve bewailed Abel a hundred years with the greatest grief. . . . And God cast out Cain whilst he was still unmarried into the land of Nod. But Cain carried off with him his sister Azrun."[1]

The Rabbi Zadok said, "This was the reason why Cain slew Abel. His twin sister and wife was not at all good-looking. Then he said, 'I will kill my brother Abel, and carry off his wife.'"[2]

Gregory Abulfaraj gives this account of the strife : "According to the opinion of Mar Theodosius, thirty years after he was expelled from Paradise, Adam knew his wife Eve, and she bore twins, Cain and his sister Climia ; and after thirty more years she bore Abel and his twin sister Lebuda. Then, seventy years after when Adam wanted to marry one of the brothers with the twin sister of the other, Cain refused, asking to have his own twin sister."[3]

The Pseudo-Athanasius says, "Up to this time no man had died so that Cain should know how to kill. The devil instructed him in this in a dream."[4]

Leonhard Marius on Genesis iv. says, "As to what instrument Cain used, Scripture is silent. Chrysostom calls it a sword ; Prudentius, a spade ; Irenæus, an axe ; Isidore says simply, steel ; but artists generally paint a club, and Abulensis thinks he was killed with stones." Reuchlin thinks, as iron was not discovered till the times of Tubal-cain, the weapon must have been made of wood, and he points out how much more this completes the type of Christ.[5]

Cain and Abel had been born and had lived with Adam

---

[1] Eutychius, Patriarcha Alex., Annales.   [2] Pirke R. Eliezer, c. xxi.
[3] Historia Dynastiarum, ed. Pocock ; Oxon. 1663, p. 4.
[4] Ad Antiochum, quæst. 56.   [5] Fabricius, i. p. 112.

in the land of Adamah ; but after Cain slew his brother, he was cast out into the land Erez, and wherever he went, swords sounded and flashed as though thirsting to smite him. And he fled that land and came to Acra, where he had children, and his descendants who live there to this day have two heads.[1]

Before Cain slew his brother, says the Targum of Jerusalem, the earth brought forth fruits as the fruits of Eden ; but from the day that blood was spilt upon it, thistles and thorns sprang up ; for the face of earth grew sad, its joy was gone, the stain was on its brow.

Abel's offering had been of the fattest of his sheep, the Targum adds, but Cain offered flax.[2]

Abel's offering, say certain Rabbis, was not perfect ; for he offered the chief part to God, but the remainder he dedicated to the Devil ; and Cain offered the chief part to Satan, and only the remainder to God.[3]

The Rabbi Johanan said, Cain exclaimed when accused by God of the murder, "My iniquity is greater than I can bear," and this is supposed to mean, "My iniquity is too great to be atoned for, except by my brother rising from the earth and slaying me." What did the Holy One then ? He took one letter of the twenty-two which are in the Law, and He wrote it on the arm of Cain, as it is written, "He put a mark upon him."[4]

After Abel was slain, the dog which had kept his sheep guarded his body, says the Midrash. Adam and Eve sat beside it and wept, and knew not what to do. Then said a raven whose friend was dead, " I will teach Adam a lesson," and he dug a hole in the soil and laid his friend there and covered him up. And when Adam saw this, he said to Eve, " We will do the same with Abel." God rewarded the raven for this by promising that none should ever injure his young, that he should always have meat in abundance, and that his prayer for rain should be immediately answered.[5]

But the Rabbi Johanan taught that Cain buried his brother to hide what he had done from the eye of God, not knowing that God can see even the most secret things.[6]

According to some Rabbis, all good souls are derived from

[1] Eisenmenger, i. p. 462. [2] Targum, i. p. 173.
[3] Jalkut Cadasch, fol. 6, col. i. [4] Pirke R. Eliezer, c. xxi.
[5] Ibid. [6] Ibid.

Abel and all bad souls from Cain. Cain's soul was derived from Satan, his body alone was from Eve ; for the Evil Spirit Sammael, according to some, Satan, according to others, deceived Eve, and thus Cain was the son of the Evil One.[1] All the children of Cain also became demons of darkness and nightmares, and therefore it is, say the Cabbalists, that there is no mention in Genesis of the death of any of Cain's offspring.[2]

When Cain had slain his brother, we are told in Scripture that he fled. Certain Rabbis give the reason :—He feared lest Satan should kill him : now Satan has no power over any one whose face he does not see, thus he had none over Lot's wife till she turned her face towards Sodom, and he could see it ; and Cain fled, to keep his face from being seen by the Evil One, and thus give him an opportunity of taking his life.[3]

With regard to the mark put upon Cain, there is great diverging of opinion. Some say that his tongue turned white ; others, that he was given a peculiar dress ; others, that his face became black ; but the most prevalent opinion is that he became covered with hair, and a horn grew in the midst of his forehead.

The Little Genesis says, Cain was born when Adam was aged seventy, and Abel when he was seventy-seven.

The book of the penitence of Adam gives us some curious details. When Cain had killed his brother, he was filled with terror, for he saw the earth quivering. He cast the body into a hole and covered it with dust, but the earth threw the body out. Then he dug another hole and heaped earth on his brother's corpse, but again the earth rejected it.

When God appeared before him, Cain trembled in all his limbs, and God said to him, "Thou tremblest and art in fear ; this shall be thy sign." And from that moment he quaked with a perpetual ague.

The Rabbis give another mark as having been placed on Cain. They say that a horn grew out of the midst of his forehead. He was killed by a son of Lamech, who, being shortsighted, mistook him for a wild beast ; but in the Little Genesis it is said that he was killed by the fall of his house, in the year 930, the same day that Adam died. According to the same authority, Adam and Eve bewailed Abel twenty-eight years.

---

[1] Eisenmenger, ii. p. 8.   [2] Ibid., p. 428   [3] Ibid., p. 455.

The Talmud relates the following beautiful incident.

God had cursed Cain, and he was doomed to a bitter punishment ; but moved, at last, by Cain's contrition, he placed on his brow the symbol of pardon.

Adam met Cain, and looked with wonder on the seal or token, and asked,—

" How hast thou turned away the wrath of the Almighty ? "

" By confession of sin and repentance," answered the fratricide.

" Woe is me ! " cried Adam, smiting his brow ; " is the virtue of repentance so great, and I knew it not ! And by repentance I might have altered my lot ! " [1]

Tabari says that Cain was the first worshipper of fire. Eblis (Satan) appeared to him and told him that the reason of the acceptance of Abel's sacrifice was, that he had invoked the fire that fell on it and consumed it ; Cain had not done this, and therefore fire had not come down on his oblation. Cain believed this, and adored fire, and taught his children to do the same. [2]

Cain, says Josephus, having wandered over the earth with his wife, settled in the land of Nod. But his punishment, so far from proving of advantage to him, proved only a stimulus to his violence and passion ; and he increased his wealth by rapine, and he encouraged his children and friends to live by robbery and in luxury. He also corrupted the primitive simplicity in which men lived, by the introduction amongst them of weights and measures, by placing boundaries, and walling cities. [3]

John Malala says the same : " Cain was a tiller of the ground till he committed the crime of slaying his brother ; after that, he lived by violence, his hand being against every man, and he invented and taught men the use of weights, measures, and boundaries." [4]

The passage in Genesis " *Whosoever slayeth Cain, vengeance shall be taken on him sevenfold,*" [5] has been variously interpreted. Cosmas Indopleustes renders it thus, " Whosoever slayeth Cain will discharge seven vengeances ; " that is, he will deliver him from those calamities to which he is subject when living. [6]

---

[1] Tract. Avoda Sara. [2] Tabari, i. c. xix.
[3] Antiq. Judæ., lib. i. c. 2.
[4] Excerpta Chronologica, p. 2. [5] Gen. iv. 15.
[6] Cosmas Indopleustes, Cosmographia, lib. v.

But Malala renders it otherwise; he says it is to be thus understood: "Every murderer shall die for his sin, but thou who didst commit the first homicide, and art therefore the originator of this crime, shalt be punished sevenfold; that is, thou shalt undergo seven punishments." For Cain had committed seven crimes. First, he was guilty of envy; then, of treachery; thirdly, of murder; fourthly, of killing his brother; fifthly, this was the first murder ever committed; sixthly, he grieved his parents; and seventhly, Cain lied to God. Thus the sin of Cain was sevenfold; therefore sevenfold was his punishment. First, the earth was accursed on his account; secondly, he was sentenced to labor; thirdly, the earth was forbidden from yielding to him her strength; fourthly, he was to become timid and conscience-stricken; fifthly, he was to be a vagabond on the earth; sixthly, he was to be cast out from God's presence; seventhly, a mark was to be placed upon him.

The Mussulmans say that the penitence of Cain, whom they call Kabil, was not sincere. He was filled with remorse, but it was mingled with envy and hatred, because he was regarded with disfavor by the rest of the sons of Adam.

Near Damascus is shown a place at the foot of a mountain where Cain slew Abel.[1]

The legends of the death of Cain will be found under the title of Lamech.

" Half a mile from the gates of Hebron," says the Capuchin Friar, Ignatius von Rheinfelden, in his Pilgrimage to Jerusalem, " begins the valley of Mamre, in which Abraham saw the three angels; the *Campus Damascenus* lies toward the west; there, Adam was created; and the spot is pointed out where Cain killed his brother Abel. The earth there is red, and may be moulded like wax."[2] Salmeron says the same, " Adam was made of the earth or dust of the *Campus Damascenus.*" And St. Jerome on Ezekiel, chap. xvii., says: " Damascus is the place where Abel was slain by his brother Cain; for which cause the spot is called Damascus, that is, Blood-drinking." This Damascus near Hebron is not to be confused with the city Damascus.

---

[1] D'Herbelot, Bibliothèque Orientale, *sub voce* Cabil, i. p. 438.

[2] Neue Ierosolymitanische Pilgerfahrt. Von P. F. Ignat. von Rheinfelden. Würtzburg, 1667. P. ii. p. 8.

VII.

THE DEATH OF ADAM.[1]

ACCORDING to a Mussulman tradition, Adam was consoled for the loss of Abel by the discovery of how to make wheat-bread. The story is as follows :—

The angel Gabriel was sent out of Paradise to give him the rest of the wheat-grains Eve had plucked from the forbidden tree, together with two oxen, and various instruments of husbandry. Hitherto he had fed on roots and berries, and had known nothing of sowing grain; acting under Gabriel's directions, he ploughed the land, but the plough stuck, and Adam impatiently smote one of the oxen, and it spoke to him and said, "Wherefore hast thou.smitten me?"

Adam replied, "Because thou dost not draw the plough."

"Adam!" said the ox, "when thou wast rebellious, did God smite thee thus?"

"O God!" cried Adam to the Almighty, "is every beast to reproach me, and recall to me my sin?"

Then God heard his cry, and withdrew from beasts the power of speech, lest they should cast their sin in the teeth of men.

But as the blow was still arrested, Adam dug into the soil, and found that the iron had been caught by the body of his son Abel.

When the wheat was sprung up, Gabriel gave Adam fire from hell, which however he had previously washed seventy times in the sea, or it would have consumed the earth and all things thereon. In the beginning, wheat-grains were the size of ostrich eggs, but under Edris (Enoch) they were no bigger than goose eggs; under Elias they were the size of hen's eggs; under Christ, when the Jews sought to slay him, they were no larger than grapes; it was in the time of Uzeir (Esdras) that they diminished to their present proportions.

After Adam and Eve had been instructed in all that appertained to agriculture, Gabriel brought them a lamb and showed Adam how to slay it in the name of God, how to shear off the wool, and skin the sheep. Eve was instructed in the art of spinning and weaving by the angel, and she made of the wool, first a veil for herself, and then a shirt for her husband.

The first pair brought up their grandsons and great grandsons, to the number of 40,000 according to some, and 70,000 according to others, and taught them all that they had learned of the angel.

After the death of Abel, and after Cain had been slain by the avenging angel, Eve bore a third son, named Seth, who became the father of the race of the prophets.

Finally, when Adam had reached his nine hundred and thirtieth year, the Angel of Death appeared under the form of a goat, and ran between his legs.

Adam recoiled with horror, and exclaimed, " God has given me one thousand years ; wherefore comest thou now ? "

" What ! " exclaimed the Angel of Death, " hast thou not given seventy years of thy life to the prophet David ? "

Adam stoutly denied that he had done so. Then the Angel of Death drew the document of transfer from out of his beard, and presented it to Adam, who could no longer refuse to go.

His son Seth washed and buried him, after that the angel Gabriel, or, according to some accounts, Allah himself, had blessed him : Eve died a year later.

Learned men are not agreed as to the place of their burial ; some traditions name India, others the Mount Kubais, and others again, Jerusalem—God alone knows ! [1]

Tabari says that Adam made Seth his testamentary executor.

" When Adam was dead, Gabriel instructed Seth how to bury him, and brought him the winding sheet out of heaven. And Gabriel said to Seth, 'Thou art sole executor of thy father, therefore it is thy office to perform the religious functions.' Then Seth recited over Adam thirty *Tebirs.* Four of these *Tebirs* were the legal prayers, the others were supererogatory, and were designed to exalt the virtues of Adam. Some say that Adam was buried near Mecca, on Mount Abui-Kubais." [2]

According to the apocryphal " Life of Adam and Eve," Adam before his death called to his bedside all his sons and daughters, and they numbered fifteen thousand males, and females unnumbered. Adam is said to have been the author of several psalms ; amongst others Psalm civ., *Benedic anima*

---

[1] Weil, pp. 40–3.   [2] Tabari, i. c., xxxiii.

mea, and Psalm cxxxix., *Domine probasti;* as may be gathered from the 14th, 15th, and 16th verses : *" My bones are not hid from thee: though I was made secretly, and fashioned beneath in the earth.   Thine eyes did see my substance, yet being imperfect; and in Thy book were all my members written; which day by day were fashioned, when as yet there was none of them."*

The Arabs say that when Adam dictated his last will and testament, the angel Gabriel descended from heaven to receive it, accompanied by sixty-two millions of angels, each provided with clean white sheets of parchment and pens, and that the will was sealed by Gabriel.[1]

Tradition is not agreed as to the place of Adam's burial. Khaithemah says that Adam was buried near Mecca on Mount Abu-Kubais.   But the ancient Persians assert that he was buried in Ceylon, where his sepulchre was guarded by lions at the time of the war of the giants.[2]

But the most generally received tradition is this :—

The body of Adam was taken by Noah into the ark, and when the ark rested on Ararat, Noah and his sons removed the body from it, and they followed an angel who led them to the place where the first father was to lie.   Shem or Melchizedek —for they are one, as we shall see presently—being consecrated by God to the priesthood, performed the religious rites; and buried Adam at the centre of the earth, which is Jerusalem; but, say some, he was buried by Shem along with Eve, in the cave of Machpelah, in Hebron.   But others relate that Noah on leaving the ark distributed the bones of Adam among his sons, and that he gave the head to Shem, who buried it in Jerusalem.   Some, taking this mystically, suppose that by this is meant the sin and punishment of Adam, which was transmitted to all the sons of Noah, but that to Shem was given the head, the Messiah who was to regenerate the world.[3]   S. Basil of Seleucia says : " According to Jewish traditions, the skull of Adam was found there (*i. e.,* on Golgotha), and this, they say, Solomon knew by his great wisdom.   And because it was the place of Adam's skull, therefore the hill was called Golgotha, or Calvary."[4]

With this a great concourse of Fathers agree ; whose testi-

---

[1] Colin de Plancy, p. 78.   [2] Herbelot, i. p. 95.
[3] Moses bar Cepha.   Commentarius de Paradiso, P. i. c. 14.   Fabricius, i. p. 75.
[4] S. Basil Seleuc. Orat. xxxviii.

mony has been laboriously collected by Gretser in his famous and curious book "De Cruce." And this tradition has become a favorite subject for artists, who, in their paintings or sculptures, represent the skull of Adam at the foot of the Cross of Christ.

The apocryphal "Testament of Adam" still exists.

The tomb of Eve is shown at Jedda. "On entering the great gate of the cemetery, one observes on the left a little wall three feet high, forming a square of ten to twelve feet. There lies the head of our first mother. In the middle of the cemetery is a sort of cupola, where reposes the navel of her body; and at the other extremity, near the door of egress, is another little wall also three feet high, forming a lozenge-shaped enclosure: there are her feet. In this place is a large piece of cloth, whereon the faithful deposit their offerings, which serve for the maintenance of a constant burning of perfumes over the midst of her body. The distance between her head and feet is four hundred feet. How we have shrunk since the creation!"[1]

The bones of Adam and Eve, says Tabari, were taken by Noah into the ark with him, and were reburied by him.

This article may be fitly concluded with the epitaph of Adam, composed by Gabriel Alvarez, and published by him in his "Historia Ecclesiæ Antediluvianæ," Madrid, 1713.

"Here lies, reduced to a pinch of dust, he who, from a pinch of
dust, was formed to govern the earth,
ADAM,
The son of None, the father of All, the stepfather of All
and of himself.
Having never wailed as a child, he spent his life in weeping
the result of penitence.
Powerful, Wise, Immortal, Just,
he sold for the price of disobedience, power, wisdom, justice,
immortality.
Having abused the privilege of Free-will, which weapon
he had received for the preservation of Knowledge and Grace,
by one stroke he struck with death himself and all the human race.
The Omnipotent Judge
who in His Justice took from him Righteousness, by His Mercy
restored it to him whole again:
by whose goodness it has fallen out, that we may
call that crime happy, which obtained such and so great
A Redeemer.
Thenceforth Free-will, which he in happiness used to

---

[1] Lettre de H. A. D., Consul de France en Abyssinie, 1841.

bring forth Misery, is used in Misery to bring forth
Happiness.
For if we, partakers of his pernicious inheritance, partake
also of his penitential example, and lend our ears
to salutary counsels,
Then we (who by our Free-will could lose ourselves) can be saved
by the grace of the Redeemer, and the co-operation of our
Free-will.
The First Adam Lived to Die ;
The Second Adam Died to Live.
Go, and imitate the penitence of the First Adam ;
Go, and celebrate the Goodness of the Second Adam.

VIII.

SETH.

WHEN Seth had ascended the throne of his father, says
Tabari, he was the greatest of the sons of Adam.   Every year
he made the pilgrimage to the Kaaba, and he ruled the world
with equity, and every thing flourished during his reign.   At
the age of fifty he had a son ; he called his name Enoch, and
named him his executor.   He died at the age of nine hundred.[1]

Seth and the other sons of Adam waged perpetual war
against the Dives, or giants, the sons of Kabil, or Cain.

Rocail was another son of Adam, born next after Seth.

He possessed, says the Tahmurath Nâmeh, the most wonderful knowledge in all mysteries.   He had a genius so quick
and piercing, that he seemed to be rather an angel than a
man.

Surkrag, a great giant, son of Cain, commanded in the
mountains of Kaf, which encompass the centre of the earth.
This giant asked Seth to send him Rocail, his brother, to assist him in governing his subjects.   Seth consented, and Rocail became the vizier or prime minister of Surkrag, in the
mountains of Kaf.

After having governed many centuries, and knowing, by
divine revelation, that the time of his death drew nigh, he thus
addressed Surkrag: " I am about to depart hence and enter
on another existence, but before I leave, I wish to bequeath
to you some famous work, which shall perpetuate my name
into remote ages."

[1] Tabari, i. c. xxxiv.

4*

Thercupon Rocail erected an enormous sepulchre, adorned with statues of various metals, made by talismanic art, which moved, and spake, and acted like living men.[1]

According to the Rabbinic traditions, Seth was one of the thirteen who came circumcised into the world. The rest were Adam, Enoch, Noah, Shem, Terah, Jacob, Joseph, Moses, Samuel, David, Isaiah, and Jeremiah.[2] The book Schene Luch'th says that the soul of righteous Abel passed into the body of Seth, and afterwards this same soul passed into Moses; thus the law, which was known to Adam and in which Abel had been instructed, was not new to Moses.[3]

The Little Genesis says, that Seth was instructed by the angels in what was to take place in the world; how its iniquity was to grow, and a flood was to overwhelm it; and how the Messiah would come and restore all things. Seth was remarkable for the majesty and beauty of his appearance, as he had inherited much of the loveliness of unfallen man. He married his sister Azur, or, according to others, Noræa or Horæa.

Suidas under the heading ' $\Sigma\eta\delta$,' says : " Seth was the son of Adam : of this it is said, the sons of God went in unto the daughters of men ; that is to say, the sons of Seth went in unto the daughters of Cain. For in that age Seth was called God, because he had discovered Hebrew letters, and the names of the stars ; but especially on account of his great piety, so that he was the first to bear the name of God.

Theodoret thus refers to the verse,—"*And to Seth, to him also there was born a son; and he called his name Enos; then began men to call upon the name of the Lord,*" or as our marginal reading is, "*then began men to call themselves by the name of the Lord:*" " Aquila interpreted it thus, 'then Seth began to be called by the name of the Lord.' These words intimate his piety, which deserved that he should receive the sacred name ; and he was called God by his acquaintance, and his children were termed the sons of God, just as we are called Christians after Christ."[4]

The origin of this tradition seems to be the fact that Seth was the name of an ancient Egyptian deity, at first regarded as the giver of light and civilization, but afterwards identified with

---

[1] D'Herbelot, i. p. 125, s. v. Rocail.
[2] Midrash Tillim, fol. 10, col. 2.
[3] Eisenmenger, i. p. 645.   [4] Theodoret, Quæst. in Gen. xlvii.

Typhon by the Egyptians, who considered Seth to be the chief god of the Hyksos or shepherd kings ; and in their hatred of these oppressors, the name of Seth was everywhere obliterated on their monuments, and he was regarded as one with the great adversary, Typhon ; and was represented as an ass, or with an ass's head.[1]

Abulfaraj, in his history, says that Seth discovered letters, and that, desirous to recover the Blessed Life, he and his sons went to Mount Hermon, where they served God in piety and continence, and associated not with the people of the land, nor took to themselves wives ; wherefore they were called the sons of God.[2]

Flavius Josephus relates that after the things that were to take place had been revealed to Seth,—how the earth was to be destroyed, first with water and then with fire,—lest those things which he had discovered should perish from the memory of his posterity, he set up two pillars, one of brick, the other of stone, and he wrote thereon all the science he had acquired, hoping that, in the event of the brick pillar perishing by the rain, the stone would endure.[3]

Freculphus adds that Jubal assisted the sons of Seth in engraving on the columns all that was known of the conduct and order of the heavens, and all the arts then known.[4]

The stone pillar was to be seen, in the time of Josephus, in Syria.

Anastasius of Sinai says that, when God created Adam after His image and likeness, He breathed into him grace, and illumination, and a ray of the Holy Spirit. But when he sinned, this glory left him, and his face became clouded. Then he became the father of Cain and Abel. But afterwards it is said in Scripture, " *He begat a son in his own likeness, after his image ; and called his name Seth ;* " which is not said of Cain and Abel ; and this means that Seth was begotten in the likeness of unfallen man and after the image of Adam in Paradise ; and he called his name Seth, that is, by interpretation, Resurrection, because in him he saw the resurrection of his departed beauty, and wisdom and glory, and radiance of

[1] Plutarch, Isis and Osiris, ed. Parthey; pp. 72, 88, and notes pp. 183 238.
[2] Abulfaraj, Hist. Dynast., ed. Pocock, p. 5.
[3] Joseph. Antiq. Judaic., lib. i. c. 2.
[4] Freculphus, Chron. lib. i. c. 12.

the Holy Spirit.   And all those then living, when they saw
how the face of Seth shone with divine light, and heard him
speak with divine wisdom, said he is God; therefore his sons
were commonly called the sons of God.[1]

As Seth was an ancient Egyptian Sun-god, the origin of
the myth of his shining face can be ascertained without difficulty.

To Seth were attributed several apocryphal writings.

IX.

CAINAN SON OF ENOS.

" *And Seth lived an hundred and five years, and begat Enos:
and Seth lived after he begat Enos eight hundred and seven years,
and begat sons and daughters: and all the days of Seth were
nine hundred and twelve years: and he died.   And Enos lived
ninety years, and begat Cainan.*"[2]

Alexander wrote many epistles to Aristotle, his preceptor,
in which he narrated what had befallen him in India.   Amongst
other things he wrote : " After I had entered the Persian region, which is a province of India, I arrived at some islands
of the sea, and there I found men, like women, who feed on
raw fish, and spake a language very like Greek ; they said to
me that there was in the island the sepulchre of a most ancient king, who was called Cainan, son of Enos, and who
ruled the whole world, and taught men all kinds of knowledge,
and had demons and all kinds of evil spirits under his control.
He, by his wisdom, understood that the ever-blessed God
would bring in a flood in the times of Noah; wherefore he
engraved all that was to take place on stone tables, which
exist there to this day, and are written in Hebrew characters.
He wrote therein that the ocean would, in that age, overflow
a third part of the world, which took place in the lifetime of
Enos, the son of Seth, who was the son of Adam, our first
parent.

"In the same island, Cainan built a most extensive city,
surrounded with walls ; and a great marble citadel, in which

[1] Anastasius Sinaita, $O\delta\eta\gamma\delta\varsigma$. ed. Gretser, Ingolst. 1606, p. 269.
[2] Gen. v. 6—9.

he treasured jewels and pearls, and gold and silver in great abundance.

" Moreover, he erected a tower, very lofty, over a sepulchre for himself, to serve as his monument. This tower can be approached by no man ; for it was built by astronomical art under the seven planets, and with magical skill, so that every one who draws near the wall is struck down with sudden death." [1]

X.

ENOCH.

I. THE TRANSLATION OF ENOCH.

ENOCH, or Edris,[2] as he is called by the Arabs, was born in Hindostan, but he lived in Yemen. He was a prophet. In his days men worshipped fire, being deceived by Eblis. When God sent Enoch to his brethren to turn them from their false worship, they would not believe him.

Idolatry began in the times of Jared, son of Mahalaleel, and it spread to such an extent that, when Noah was born, there were not eighty persons who worshipped the true, and living, and only God. Jared fought Satan, the prince of demons, and captured him, and led him about in chains wherever he went.

Enoch knew how to sew, and was an accomplished tailor. He was the first to put pen to paper ; he wrote many books. He had in his possession the books of Adam, and for ten years, instead of sleeping, he spent the night in reading them.

He instructed men in the art of making garments ; Enoch showed them how to cut out the skins to the proper shape, and to sew them together ; and how to make shoes to protect their feet.

And then, when the people had derived this great blessing from him, they were ready to listen to his books ; and he read

---

[1] Pseudo Josephus Gorionides ; ed. Clariss. Breithauptius, lib. ii. c. 16, p. 131.

[2] I give the Arabic legend. The account in Jasher is different. Enoch retired from the world, and showed himself only at rare intervals, when he gave advice to all who came to hear his wisdom. He was taken up to heaven in a whirlwind, in a chariot with horses of fire. (Yaschar, pp 1094–1096.)

to them the books of Adam, and endeavored thereby to bring them back to the knowledge of the true God.

When he had spent many years in prayer, the Angel of Death desired to make a compact of friendship with him. He took on him a human form and approached him, saying, "I am the Angel of Death, and I desire thy friendship. On account of thy great piety, thou mayest make me a request which I shall accomplish."

Enoch answered, "I desire that thou shouldst take my soul."

The angel replied, "I have not come to thee for this purpose; thy time is not yet arrived at its appointed close."

Then Enoch said, "It is well; but take my soul away for a little space, and then return it to my body, if God so wills."

The angel said, "I cannot do this without God's consent." But he presented the supplication of Enoch before Allah, and God, knowing what was the design of Enoch, granted the prayer.

Then Azrael bore away the soul of Enoch, and at the same instant the Eternal One restored it to him. After this, Enoch continued to praise and pray to God; and the Angel of Death became his friend, and often came to visit him.

Years passed, and Enoch said one day to the angel, "Oh, my friend! I have yet a request to make."

Azrael answered, "If I can grant it, I will do so readily."

Enoch said, "I would see Hell, for I have undergone death, and I know its sensations. I would know now the torments of the lost."

But the angel answered, "This I cannot grant without permission from the Almighty."

God heard the prayer of Enoch, and He suffered Azrael to accomplish what the prophet had desired. Then the Angel of Death bore away Enoch, and showed him the seven stages of Hell, and all the torments inflicted there on sinners: after that he replaced him where he was before.

After some while had elapsed, Enoch again addressed Azrael, and said, "I have another request to make."

The angel answered, "Say on."

Then said Enoch, "I desire to see the Paradise of God, as I have seen Hell."

Azrael replied, "I cannot grant thy petition without the consent of God."

But the All-Merciful, when he heard the request of his servant consented that it should be even as he desired. So the angel bore Enoch into Paradise. And when they had reached the gates, the keeper, Ridhwan, refused to open, saying to Enoch, " Thou art a man, and no man can enter Paradise who has not tasted death."

Then Enoch replied, " I also have tasted death ; the soul that I have will dwell eternally with me ; God has resuscitated me from death."

Ridhwan, however, said, " I cannot do this thing and admit thee without the order of God."

Then the order arrived from Allah, and the angel of the gate refused no more ; so Enoch entered ; but before Enoch and Azrael passed the gates, Ridwan said to the prophet, " Go in, and behold Paradise, but be speedy and leave it again, for thou mayest not dwell there till after the Resurrection."

Enoch replied, " Be it so ;" and he went in and viewed Paradise, and came out, as he had promised ; and as he passed the threshold of the door he turned and said to the angel, " Oh, Ridhwan ! I have left something in there ; suffer me to run and fetch it."

But Ridhwan refused ; and a dispute arose between them.

Enoch said, " I am a prophet ; and God has sent me thirty books, and I have written them all, and I have never revolted against God. In those books that God sent me, I was promised Paradise. If it be necessary that I should have undergone death I have undergone it. If it be necessary that I should have seen Hell, I have seen it. Now I am come to Paradise, and that is my home ; God has promised it to me, and now that I have entered I will leave it no more."

The dispute waxed hot, but it was terminated by the order of God, who bade Ridhwan open the gate and re-admit Enoch into Paradise, where he still dwells.[1]

2. THE BOOK OF ENOCH.

The Book of Enoch, quoted by S. Jude in his Epistle, and alluded to by Origen, S. Augustine, S. Clement of Alexandria, and others of the Fathers, must not be passed over.

The original book appears from internal evidence to have

---

[1] Tabari, i. c. xxxv.

been written about the year 110 B. C.[1] But we have not the
work as then written ; it has suffered from numerous interpola-
tions, and it is difficult always to distinguish the original text
from the additions.

The book is frequently quoted in the apocryphal "Testament of the Twelve Patriachs," which is regarded as canonical
by the Armenian Church, but the references are for the most
part not to be found in the text. It was largely used by some
of the early Christian writers, either with acknowledgment or
without. The monk George Syncellus, in the eighth century,
extracted portions to compose his Chronography. This fragment in Syncellus was all that was known of the book in the
West till the last century. The Jews, though remembering the
work, had lost it in Hebrew ; but it was alluded to by the
Rabbis down to the thirteenth century, and it is referred to in
the Book Sohar, though the writer may not have read the book
of Enoch. Bruce, the African traveller, was the first to bring
it to Europe from Abyssinia in two MSS., in the year 1773.
Much attention was not, however, paid to it till 1800, when
De Sacy in his " Magasin Encyclopédique," under the title
" Notice sur le Livre d'Enoch," gave some account of the work.
In 1801, Professor Laurence gave to the public an English
translation, accompanied by some critical remarks. Since
then, the book has been carefully and exegetically examined.
The version we now have is Ethiopic.

The Book of Enoch consists of five divisions, or books,
together with a Prolegomena and an Epilegomena.

After the introduction (caps. 1–5), which describes the
work as the revelation of the seer Enoch concerning the future judgment and its consequences, with warnings to the elect
as to the signs ; the *First* part (caps. 6-16) opens with an account of the fall of the Angels, their union with the daughters
of men, and the generation of the giants. Connected with
this, and divided from it by no superscription or sign of change
of subject, is an account of a journey made by Enoch, in the
company of the angels, over the earth and through the lower
circles of heaven, during which he is instructed in various mysteries hidden from the knowledge of men, and a great deal of
this wondrous information is communicated to the reader.

---

[1] Dillman, Das Buch Enock ; Leipzig, 1853. Ewald, in his "Geschichte der Volks Israel" (iii. 2, pp. 397–401), attributes it to the year
130. B. C.

This description of a journey, which is itself divided into two parts, unquestionably belongs to the original book, and the historical portion, narrating the procreation of the Giants, is an interpolation.

The *Second* portion of the book (caps. 37–71), with its own special superscription and introduction, is called "The Second History of Wisdom." It continues the history of the voyage. The first portion contained the description of the mysterious places and things in the earth and in the lower heaven ; the second portion contains an account of the mysteries of the highest heaven, the angel-world, the founding of the kingdom of the Messias, and the signs of His coming.

The close of this portion contains prophecies of Noah's Flood, and accounts of the fall of the Angels, their evil life and their punishment. The whole account of the Flood, which comes in without rhyme or reason, is also a manifest interpolation.

The *Third* portion (caps. 72–82) also under its own heading, is on "The Revolution of the Lights of Heaven," and describes the motions of the planets, the duration of the seasons, and the number of the days of the months, and the great winds of heaven. With this part the voyage of Enoch closes.

The *Fourth* part (caps. 83–91), which has no superscription, but which is generally designated as " The Book of the Dream History," contains the visions shown Enoch in his youth, which, in a series of pictures, gives the history of the world till the end of time. This part closes with some words of advice from Enoch to his sons.

The *Fifth* and last part (caps. 92–105) is " The Book of Exhortation," addressed by Enoch to his family against sin in all its forms, under all its disguises, and concludes with an account of certain presages which should announce the birth of Noah.

The Talmudic writers taught that Enoch at his translation became a chief angel, and that his name became Metatron. In the Chaldee version of Jonathan on the words of Genesis v. 24, it is said, " And Enoch served before the Lord in truth, and was not among the inhabitants of the earth, for he was translated above into the firmament, through the word of the Lord ; and He called him by the namê of Metatron (the great writer)." And in Rabbi Menachem's Commentary on the Five Books of Moses, it is written, " The Rabbi Ishmael relates that he spoke to the Metatron, and he asked him why he was named with the name of his Creator and with seventy names, and why he was greater than any prince, and higher than any angel, and dearer than any servant, and more honored than all the host and more excellent in greatness, in power, and dominion than all the mighty ones. Then he answered and said, ' Because I was Enoch, son of Jared. This is what the holy, ever-blessed God wrought,—when the races of the Flood (*i. e.*, the sinners who lived at the time when the Flood came) sinned, and did unrighteously in their works, and had said to God, " Depart from us,"—He took me from that untoward generation into the highest heaven, that I might be a witness against that generation. And after the ever-blessed God had removed me that I should stand before the throne of his Majesty, and before the wheels of His chariot, and accomplish the requirements of the Most High, then my flesh became flame, and my arteries fire, and my bones juniper ashes, and the light of my eyelids became the flashing of lightning, and my eyeballs torches of fire, and the hair of my head was a flame, and all my limbs were fiery, burning wings, and my body became burning fire ; and by my right hand flames were cleft asunder ; and from my left hand burnt fiery torches ; but around me blew a wind, and storm, and tempest ; and before and behind me was the voice of a mighty earthquake.'"

The Rabbi Ishmael gives further particulars which are enshrined in the great Jalkut Rubeni.[1]

The Rabbi Ishmael, according to this book, received in addition these particulars from the lips of Enoch. He was carried to heaven in a chariot of fire by horses of fire ; and when he entered into the presence of God, the Sacred Beasts, the Seraphim, the Osannim, the Cherubim, the wheels of the chariot, and all the fiery ministers recoiled five thousand three hundred and eighty miles at the smell of him, and cried aloud " What a stink is come among us from one born of a woman ! Why is one who has eaten of white wheat admitted into heaven?"

Then the Almighty answered and said, " My servants, Cherubim and Seraphim, do not be grieved, for all my sons have rejected my sovereignty and adore idols, this man alone excepted ; and in reward I exalt him to principality over the angels in heaven." When Enoch heard this he was glad, for

---

[1] Fol. 26, col. 2.

he had been a simple shoemaker on earth; but this had he done, at every stitch he had said, "The name of God and His Majesty be praised."

The height of Enoch when a chief angel was very great. It would take a man five hundred years to walk from his heel to the crown of his head. And the ladder which Jacob saw in vision was the ladder of Metatron.[1] The same authority, above quoted, the Rabbi Ishmael, is reported to have had the exact measure of Enoch from his own lips; it was seven hundred thousand times thousand miles in length and in breadth.[2]

The account in the Targum of Palestine is simply this. "Enoch served in the truth before the Lord; and behold, he was not with the sojourners of the earth; for he was withdrawn, and he ascended to the firmament by the Word before the Lord, and his name was called Metatron, the Great Saphra."[3]

Whether the Annakos, or Nannakos of whom Suidas wrote, is to be identified with Enoch, I do not venture to decide. Suidas says that Nannak was an aged king before Deucalion (Noah), and that, foreseeing the Deluge, he called all his subjects together into the temple to pray the gods with many tears to remit the evil.[4] And Stephanos, the Byzantine lexicographer, says that Annakos lived at Iconium in Phrygia, and that to weep for Annak, became a proverb.

XI.

THE GIANTS.

THE Giants, say the Cabbalists, arose thus.

Aza and Azael, two angels of God, complained to the Most High at the creation of man, and said, "Why hast Thou made man who will anger Thee?"

But God answered, "And you, O angels, if you were in the lower world, you too, would sin." And He sent them on earth, and then they fell, as says the Book of Genesis, "*And it came to pass that the sons of God saw the daughters of men that they were fair, and they took them wives of all which they chose.*" After they had sinned, they were given bodies of flesh; for an

---

[1] Jalkut Rubeni, fol. 27, col. 4.   [2] Ibid., fol. 107, col. i.
[3] Targums, ed. Etheridge, i. p. 175.
[4] Suidas, Lexic. s. v. Nannacos.

angel who spends seven days on earth becomes opaque and substantial. And when they had been clothed with flesh and with a corrupt nature, then they spake the word " Shem hamphorasch," and sought to regain their former place, but could not ; and were cast out into mountains, there to dwell. From these angels descend the sons of the giants and the Anakim, and from their seed also spring the devils.[1] The Rabbi Eliezer says that the giants sprang from the union of the angels with the daughters of Cain, who walked about in immodest clothing and cast their eyes around with bold glances. And the book Zeenaureena, in the Parascha Chykkath, says that Og sprang from this connection, and that Sammael, the angel, was the parent of Og, but that Sihon was the son of the same angel who deceived the wife of Ham when she was about to enter the ark.[2]

The account in the Book of Enoch is as follows :—

" Hear and fear not, Enoch, thou righteous man, and writer of righteousness, come hither and hear my words : Go speak unto the Watchers of Heaven, and say unto them, Ye shall pray for men and not men for you. Why have ye forsaken the high and holy and eternal heaven, and have joined yourselves to women, and polluted yourselves with the daughters of men, and have taken to you wives, and have become the fathers of a giant race? Ye who were spiritual, holy, and enjoying eternal life, have corrupted yourselves with women, and have become parents of children with flesh and blood ; lusting after the blood of men, ye have brought forth flesh and blood, like those who are mortal and perishable. Because men die, therefore did I give unto them wives, that they might have sons, and perpetuate their generation. But ye are spiritual and in the enjoyment of eternal life. Therefore give I not to you wives, for heaven is the abode of the spirits. And now the giants, who are born of flesh and blood, shall become evil spirits, and their dwelling shall be on the earth. Bad beings shall proceed from them. Because they have been generated from above, from the holy Watchers have they received their origin, therefore shall they be evil spirits on the earth, and evil spirits shall they be called. And the spirits of the giants, which mount upon the clouds, will fail and be cast down, and do violence, and cause ruin on the earth and injury ; they shall not eat, they shall not thirst, and they shall be invisible."[3]

<hr>

[1] Nischmath Chajim, fol. 116, col. i.   [2] Eisenmenger, i. p. 380.
[3] Das Buch Henoch, von Dillmann, Leipz. 1853, c. xv. p. 9.

Among the Oriental Christians it is said, that Adam having related to the children of Seth the delights of Paradise, several of them desired to recover the lost possession. They retired to Mount Hermon and dwelt there in the fear of the Lord ; living in great austerity, in hope that their penitence would recover Eden. But the Canaanites dwelt round them on all sides, and the sons of Seth becoming tired of celibacy. took the daughters of the Canaanites to wife, and to them were born the giants.[1]

Others say that the posterity of the patriarch Seth were those called the " Sons of God," because they lived on Mount Hermon in familiar discourse with the angels. On this mountain they fed only on the fruit of the earth, and their sole oath was " By the blood of Abel." [2]

Among the giants was Surkrag, of whom we have already related a few particulars. He was not of the race of men, nor of the posterity of Adam. According to the Mussulman account he was commander of the armies of Soliman Tchaghi, who reigned over the earth before the time of Gian ben Gian, who succeeded him and reigned seven thousand years. The whole earth was then in the power of the Jins. Gian ben Gian erected the pyramids of Egypt.

Surkrag obeyed God, and followed the true religion, and would not suffer his subject Jins to insult or maltreat the descendants of Adam. He reigned on Mount Kaf, and allied himself, according to Persian authorities, with Kaïumarth, the first king of the world, whom some Persian writers identify with Adam, but others suppose to be the son of Mahalaleel, and cotemporary with Enoch. Ferdusi, the author of the Schah-Nâmeh, speaks of him as the first who wore a crown and sat on a throne, and imposed a tribute on his subjects. He says that this monarch lived a thousand years, and reigned five hundred and fifty years. He was the first to teach men to build houses.

But if Kaïumarth was the first man to reign, he was the first also to weary of it ; for he abdicated his sovereignty and retired into his former abode, a cave, after having surrendered his authority to his son Siamek. Siamek having been killed, Kaïumarth re-ascended his throne to revenge his death. After

[1] Abulfaraj, p. 6.
[1] Eutych. Patriarcha Alex., Annales ab Orbe Condito, Arabice et Lat., ed. Selden ; London, 1642, i. p. 19.

having recovered the body of his son, he buried him with great honors, and kindled over his grave a great fire, which was kept perpetually burning, and this originated the worship of fire among the people of Iran.

Kaïumarth overcame the giant Semendoun, who had a hundred arms ; his son, Huschenk, also overcame a giant who had three heads, mounted on an animal with twelve legs. This animal, namad Rakhsche, was found by him in the Dog Isle, or the New Continent, and was born of the union of a crocodile and an hippopotamus, and it fed on the flesh of serpents.   Having mastered this beast, Huschenk overcame the Mahisers, which have heads of fish and are of great ferocity. After having extended his conquests to the extremities of the earth, Huschenk was crushed to death by a mass of rock which the giants, his mortal enemies, hurled against him.[1]

According to Tabari, Huschenk was the son of Kaïumarth, who was the son of Mahalaleel.   He was the first man to cut down trees and to make boards, and fashion them into doors to close the entrance to houses.   He also discovered many precious stones, such as the topaz and jacinth.   He reigned four hundred years.[2]

He was succeeded by Tahmourath, who taught men to saddle and bridle horses ; he was also the first man to write in Persian characters ; he figures as a great hero in Iranian fable. According to the story in Persia, he was carried by the Simorg to the mountain of Kaf. Now the Simorg is a wondrous bird, speaking all languages, and eminently religious.

According to the Kaherman Nàmeh, the bird Simorg, being asked its age, replied, " This world has been seven times peopled, and seven times made void of living beings.   The generation of Adam, in which we now are, will last seven thousand years, which form a cycle, and I have seen twelve of these revolutions.   How many more I shall see is unknown to me."

The same book informs us that the Simorg was a great friend of the race of Adam, and a great enemy to the demons and Jins.   He knew Adam personally, and had done obeisance to him, and enjoyed the same religion as our first fathers.   He foretold to Tahmourath all that was to take place

---

[1] D'Herbelot, s. v. Surkrag and Kaïumarth
[2] Tabari, c. xxxvii.

in the world, and plucking from his bosom some feathers, he presented them to him, and from that time all great captains and men of war wear feather crests.

Tahmourath having been transported by the bird to the mountains of Kaf, he assisted the Peris, who were at war with the Jins.   Argenk, the giant, finding that the Peris were gaining the mastery, with the assistance of Tahmourath, sent an embassy desiring peace ; but the ambassador, Imlain, abandoned the party of the Jins and assisted Tahmourath to obtain complete mastery in the mountains of Kaf, and to overcome not only the giant Argenk, but also Demrusch, a far more terrible monster.   Demrusch lived in a cavern guarding a vast treasure, which he had amassed in Persia and India.   He had also carried off the Peri Mergian.   Tahmourath slew Demrusch and released Mergian.

According to the Persian story, Tahmourath was the first to cultivate rice, and to nourish silk-worms in the province of Tabristan.[1]

To return to Tabari.

Djemschid was the brother of Tahmourath ; he was the first man to forge arms, and he is probably to be identified with Tubal-cain.   He introduced also the use of pigments, and he discovered pearls, and also to dig for lime, vermilion, and quicksilver; he likewise compounded scents, and cultivated flowers.   He divided all men into four classes,—soldiers, scribes, agriculturists, and artisans.   At the head of all he placed the learned, that they might guide the affairs of men, and set them their tasks and instruct them in what they were to do.

Then Djemschid asked the wise men, " What must a king do to secure his throne ? "

They answered, " He must reign in equity."

Consequently, Djemschid instituted justice ; and he sat the first day of every month with his wise men, and ministered righteous judgments.   For seven hundred years he continued this practice ; and in all that time no rebellion broke out, no afflictions troubled him, nor was his reign in any way menaced.

One day, whilst Djemschid was taking his siesta alone in his chamber, Eblis entered by the window, and Djemschid asked, " Who art thou ? "   Now he thought he was one of those who

---

[1] D'Herbelot, s. v. Tahmourath.

waited without till he should come forth to administer justice.
Eblis entered into conversation with Djemschid, and said, " I
am an angel, and I have descended from heaven to give thee
counsel."

" What counsel dost thou offer ? " asked the king.

Eblis replied, " Tell me, who thou art ? "

He answered, " I am one of the sons of Adam."

" Thou mistakest," said the Evil One : " thou art not a man.
Consider, since thou hast reigned, has any thing failed thee ?
Hast thou suffered any affliction, any loss, any revolt ? If thou
wert a son of Adam, sorrow would be thy lot. Nay, verily, thou
art a god ! "

" And what sign canst thou show me of my divinity ? "

" I am an angel. Mortal man cannot behold an angel, and
live."

Then he vanished. Djemschid fell into the snare of pride.

Next day he caused a great fire to be lighted, and he called
together all men and said to them, " I am a god, worship me ;
I created heaven above and earth beneath ; and those that refuse to adore me shall be consumed in the fire."

Then from fear of him many obeyed ; and the same hour
revolt broke out.

There was a man named Beyourasp who stirred up the people, and led a great army against Djemschid, and overcame him,
and took from him his kingdom, and sawed the king asunder
from the head to the feet.'

XII.

LAMECH.

*" Methusael begat Lamech. And Lamech took unto him two
wives : the name of one was Adah, and the name of the other Zillah. And Adah bare Jabal : he was the father of such as dwell
in tents, and of such as have cattle. And his brother's name was
Jubal : he was the father of all such as handle the harp and organ. And Zillah, she also bare Tubal-cain, an instructor of every artificer in brass and iron : and the sister of Tubal-cain was
Naamah. And Lamech said unto his wives, Adah and Zillah,
Hear my voice ; ye wives of Lamech, hearken unto my speech :
for I have slain a man to my wounding, and a young man to my*

<hr>

' Tabari, caps. xxxix. xl.

hurt. If Cain shall be avenged sevenfold, truly Lamech seventy-fold." [1]

The speech of Lamech points to a tradition unrecorded in the Sacred Text, with which the Israelites were probably well acquainted, and which therefore did not need repetition ; or else, there has been a paragraph dropped out of the original text. The speech is sufficiently mysterious to raise our curiosity. Whom had Lamech slain ? and why should Lamech be avenged ?

The Targums throw no light on the passage, merely paraphrasing it, without supplying the key to the speech of Lamech. [2] But Rabbinic tradition is unanimous on its signification. The book Jasher says that in those days men did not love to have children, therefore they gave their wives drink to make them sterile. Zillah had taken this drink, and she was barren till in her old age she bare Tubal-cain and Naamah. Now Lamech became blind in his old age, and he was led about by the boy Tubal-cain. Tubal-cain saw Cain in the distance, and supposing from the horn on his forehead that he was a beast, he said to his father, " Span thy brow and shoot ! " Then the old man discharged his arrow, and Cain fell dead.

But when he ascertained that he had slain his great ancestor, he smote his hands together, and in so doing, by accident struck his son and killed him. Therefore his wives were wroth and would have no communication with him. But he appeased them with the words recorded in Genesis. [3] The same story is told in the book of the " Combat with Adam."

Some Jewish writers adopt a tradition that Tubal-cain was not slain, but was severely injured by his father ; according to some, he was lamed. Connecting this tradition with his name, a striking analogy springs up between him and the Vulcan of classic antiquity, and the Völundr of Norse mythology. Both were lame, both were forgers of iron, and the names Vulcan and Völundr bear some affinity to Tubal-cain ; for cutting off Tu, we have Balcain or Vulcan. A very learned and exhaustive monograph on Völundr has been written by MM. Depping and Michel. [4]

---

[1] Gen. iv. 18–24.　　　[2] Targums, ed. Etheridge, i. p. 173.

[3] Yaschar, tr. Drach, p. 1092 ; the same in Midrash Jalkut, c. 3b, Midrash, Par. Berœchith, fol. 2 ; Rabbi Raschi on Genesis ; etc., etc.

[4] Véland le Forgeron ; Paris, 1833. There is an English translation by Wright.

Tubal is said by Tabari to have discovered the art of fer
menting the juice of the grape, as well as that of music.   Eblis
deceived the young man, who was full of gayety, and taught him
many things, amongst others how to make wine.   Tubal took
grapes and crushed them, and made must, and let it grow bitter.   Then he took it and put it in a glass jug.   He made
flutes, lutes, cymbals, and drums.   When he began to drink the
wine he had made, he jumped and danced.   All the sons of
Cain looked on, and, pleased with his merriment, they also
drank and played on the instruments Tubal had made.[1]

Naamah, the sister of Tubal-cain, became the wife of the
devil Schomron, by whom she became the mother of Asmodeus.[2]

XIII.

METHUSELAH.

It is related that an angel appeared to Methuselah, who
was then aged five hundred years, and lived in the open air,
and advised him to build a house.   The Patriarch asked how
long he had to live.   " About five hundred years more," answered the angel.   " Then," said Methuselah, " it is not worth
taking the trouble for so short a time." [3]

"Methuselah," says the Midrash, " was a thoroughly righteous man.   Every word that fell from his lips was superlative-
ly perfect, exhausting the praises of the Lord.   He had learnt
nine hundred chapters of the Mischna.   At his death a frightful thunder was heard, and all beasts burst into tears.   He
was mourned seven days by men, and therefore the outbreak
of the Flood was postponed till the morning was over." [4]

Eusebius says, " He lived longer than all who had preceded him.   He, according to all editions (of the LXX.), lived
fifteen years after the Deluge, but where he was preserved
through it is uncertain." [5]

But the general opinion of the Jews follows the Midrash.
The Rabbi Solomon says, he died seven days before the Flood ;
and the Pirke of Rabbi Eliezer and the Jalkut confirm this

---

[1] Tabari, i. c. xxi.   [2] Eisenmenger, ii. p. 416.
[3] Colin de Plancy, p. 102.
[4] Midrash, fol. 12 ; so also Targum of Palestine, Etheridge, i. p. 179.
[5] Chron. Græc., ed. Scaliger, Lugd. Batav. 1606, p. 4.

opinion. He is said to have pronounced three hundred and thirty parables to the honor of the Most High. But the origin of this is to be traced to the Cabbalists, who say that, by transposition of the letters of his name, the anagram " He who prophesied in parables " can be read.[1]

He had a sword inscribed with the Schem hammphorasch (the Incommunicable Name), and with it he succeeded in slaying a thousand devils.[2]

XIV.

NOAH.

THE earth being filled with violence, God resolved on its destruction, but Noah, the just, He purposed to save alive.

On the words of Genesis, " *All flesh had corrupted his way upon the earth*," the Rabbi Johanan taught that not only was the race of men utterly demoralized, but also all the races of animals.[3]

Noah and his family, and one pair of all the beasts of earth, were to be saved in the ark, but of every clean beast seven were to enter in. Falsehood hastened to the ark and asked to be admitted; Noah refused. " I admit the animals only in pairs," said he.

Then Falsehood went away in wrath, and met Injustice, who said—

" Why art thou so sad? "

" I have been refused admittance into the ark, for I am single," said Falsehood ; " be thou my companion."

" See, now," answered Injustice, " I take no companionship without prospect of gain."

" Fear not," said Falsehood, " I will spread the toils and thou shalt have the booty."

So they went together to the ark, and Noah was unable to refuse them admission. And when the Flood was passed and the beasts went forth out of the ark, Falsehood said angrily, " I have done my work and have caused evil, but thou hast all the plunder ; share with me."

---

[1] Fabricius, i. p. 225. [2] Eisenmenger, i. p. 651.
[3] Talmud, Tractat. Sanhedrin, fol. 108, col. 1. So also the Book Yaschar, p. 1097.

"Thou fool!" answered Injustice, "dost thou forget the agreement? Thine it is to spread the net, mine alone to take the spoil."[1]

At the time of the Deluge the giants were not all drowned, for Og planted his foot upon the fountains of the great deep, and with his hands stopped the windows of heaven, or the water would have risen over his head. The Rabbi Eliezer[2] said that the giants exclaimed, when the Flood broke out, "If all the waters of the earth be gathered together, they will only reach our waists ; but if the fountains of the great deep be broken up, we must stamp them down again." And this they did, but God made the waters boiling hot, and it scalded them so that their flesh was boiled and fell off their bones.[3] But what became of Og in the Deluge we learn from the Talmud.[4] He went into the water along with a rhinoceros[5] beside the ark, and clung to it ; now the water round the ark was cold, but all the rest was boiling hot. Thus he was saved alive, whereas the other giants perished.

According to another authority, Og climbed on the roof of the ark ; and on Noah attempting to dislodge him, he swore that, if allowed to remain there, he and his posterity would be the slaves of the sons of Noah. Thereupon the patriarch yielded. He bored a hole in the side of the vessel, and passed through it every day the food necessary for the giant's consumption.[6]

It is asserted by some Rabbinic writers that the Deluge did not overflow the land of Israel, but was partial ; some say the Holy Land was alone left dry, and a rhinoceros had taken refuge on it and so escaped being drowned. But others say that the land of Israel was submerged, though all agree that the rhinoceros survived without having entered the ark. And they explain the escape of the rhinoceros in this manner. Its head was taken into the ark, and it swam behind the vessel. Now the rhinoceros is a very large animal, and could not be admitted into the ark lest it should swamp it. The Rabbi Jannai says, he saw a young rhinoceros of a day old, and it was as big as Mount Tabor ; and Tabor's dimensions are forty miles. Its

---

[1] Jalkut, Genesis, fol. 14a.
[2] Jalkut Shimoni, Job. fol. 121, col. 2.
[3] Eisenmenger, i.. p. 385. The Targum of Palestine says the water was hot (i. p. 179).
[4] Tractat. Sevachim, fol. 113, col. 2.
[5] Or, a unicorn ; the Hebrew word is Reém.   [6] Midrash, fol. 14.

neck was three miles long, and its head half a mile. It dropped dung, and the dung choked up Jordan. Other commentators object that the head was too large to be admitted into the ark, and suppose that only the tip of its nose was received. But as the ark swayed on the waters, Noah tied the horn of the rhinoceros to the side of the vessel, lest the beast's nose should slip off in a lurch of the ark, and so the creature perish.

All this is from the Talmud.

Let us now turn to some of the Mussulman legends of Noah. His history is briefly related in the Koran, in the chapter entitled " Hud."

" Noah built the ark with our assistance and that of the angels, following the knowledge we revealed to him, and we said to him: Speak no more in behalf of the sinners ; they shall all be drowned.

" Whilst Noah was building his ark, all those who passed by mocked him ; but he said to them : Though you rail at me now, the time will come when I shall rail at you ; for you will learn to your cost, Who it is that punishes the wicked in this world, and reserves for them a further punishment in the world to come."

In the annals of Eutychius of Alexandria, who wrote in Egypt in the tenth century, and who probably quoted from apocryphal documents now perished, we read that, before the Flood broke out, Noah made a bell of plane wood, about five feet high, which he sounded every day, morning, noon, and evening. When any one asked him why he did so, he replied, " To warn you that God will send a deluge to destroy you all."

Eutychius adds some further particulars.

" Before they entered the ark," says he, " Noah and his sons went to the cave of Elcanuz, where lay the bodies of Adam, Seth, Cainan, Mahalaleel, Jared, Methuselah, and Lamech. He kissed his dead ancestors, and bore off the body of Adam together with precious oblations. Shem bore gold ; Ham took myrrh ; and Japheth incense. Having gone forth, as they descended the Holy Mount they lifted their eyes to Paradise, which crowned it, and said, with tears, ' Farewell ! Holy Paradise, farewell ! ' and they kissed the stones and embraced the trees of the Holy Mount." [1]

---

[1] Eutych, Patriarcha Alex., ed. Selden, i. p. 36.

Ibn Abbas, one of the commentators on the Koran, adds, that Noah being in doubt as to the shape he was to give to the ark, God revealed to him that it was to be modelled on the plan of a bird's belly, and that it was to be constructed of teak wood. Noah planted the tree, and in twenty years it grew to such a size that out of it he was able to build the entire ark.[1]

To return to the Koran.

" When the time prescribed for the punishment of men was arrived, and the oven began to boil and vomit, we said to Noah : Take and bring into the ark two couples of every kind of animal, male and female, with all your family, except him who has been condemned by your mouth, and receive the faithful, and even the unbelievers ; but few only will enter."

The interpreters of the Koran say that the ark was built in two years. They give it the dimensions mentioned in Genesis : —three stages, that on the top for the birds, the middle one for the men and the provisions, whilst the beasts occupied the hold. The sign of the outburst of the Flood was that water flowed out of the burning oven of Noah's wife. Then all the veins and arteries of the earth broke and spirted out water. He who was excluded was Canaan, the son of Ham, whom he had cursed. But Abulfeda says that it was Jam, a fourth son of Noah, who was excluded from the ark.[2] The Persians say that Ham incurred his father's malediction as well, and, for that, he and his posterity became black and were enslaved ; but that Noah, grieved for his son's progeny, prayed God to have mercy on them, and God made the slave to be loved and cherished by his master.

The Koran says, " Noah having entered the ark with his wife (Noema, daughter of Enoch, according to the Yaschar , Noria, according to the Gnostics ; Vesta, according to the Cabbalists), and his three sons, Shem, Ham, and Japheth, and their wives, the three daughters of Eliakim, son of Methuselah, he said to those who dwell on the earth, ' Embark in the name of the Lord.'

" And whilst he thus spake, the ark advanced or halted, according to his order, in the name of God."

But the Yaschar says that the ungodly dwellers on the earth, finding the Flood rising, hastened in such crowds to the

---

[1] Tabari, p. 108.   [2] Abulfeda, p. 17.

ark, that they would have overfilled it, had not the lions and other animals within defended the entrance and repulsed them.[1]

According to some Oriental traditions, Noah embarked at Koufah; according to others, near where Babylon was afterwards erected; but some say in India; and some affirm that in the six months during which the Deluge lasted, the ark made the circuit of the world.[2]

Noah, seeing that his grandson Canaan was not on board, called to him, and said, "Embark, my child, and do not remain among the ungodly."

But Canaan replied, "I will ascend the mountains, and shall be safe there."

"Nothing can save thee to-day but the mercy of God," said Noah.

Whilst thus speaking, a wave rushed between them and submerged Canaan.

After forty days, the ark swam from one end of the earth to the other, over the highest mountains. Over Mount Kubeis, chosen by God in which to preserve the sacred black stone of the Kaaba, the ark revolved seven times.[3]

Tabari says that Noah had four sons, and that of these Canaan was the youngest, and that the three elder believed in his mission, but his wife and Canaan laughed at his predictions. The animals that were brought into the ark were collected and wafted to it by the wind. When the ass was about to enter, Eblis (Satan) caught hold of its tail. The ass came on slowly; Noah was impatient, and exclaimed, "You cursed one, come in quick."

When Eblis was within, Noah saw him, and said, "What right have you in here?"

"I have entered at your invitation," answered the Evil One. "You said, 'Cursed one, come in;' I am the accursed one."

When six months had passed, the ark rested on the surface of the water above Djondi,[4] and the rain ceased to fall, and God said to the earth, "Suck in the water;" and to the sky, "Withhold thy rains." The water abated; and the ark lodged on the top of the mountain.

"There left the ark two sorts of animals which had not entered it—the pig and the cat. These animals did not exist

---

[1] Yaschar, p. 1100.
[3] Weil, p. 45.
[2] Colin de Plancy, p. 110.
[4] Ararat.

before the Deluge, and God created them in the ark because it was full of filth and human excrements, which caused a great stench. The persons in the ark, not being able to endure any longer the smell, complained to Noah. Then Noah passed his hand down the back of the elephant, and it evacuated the pig. The pig ate all the dung which was in the ark, and the stench was no more.

"Some time after the rats gave great annoyance. They ate the food, and befouled what they did not eat. Then the voyagers went to Noah, and said to him, You delivered us in our former difficulty, but now we are plagued with rats, which gnaw our garments, eat our victuals, and cover every thing with their filth. Then Noah passed his hand down the back of the lion, who sneezed, and the cat leaped out of its nose. And the cat ate the rats.

"When Noah had left the ark, he passed forty days on the mountain, till all the water had subsided into the sea. All the briny water that is there is what remains from the Flood.

"Noah said to the raven, Go and place your foot on the earth and see what is the depth of the water. The raven departed; but, having found a carcase, it remained to devour it, and did not return. Noah was provoked, and he cursed the raven, saying, May God make thee contemptible among men and let carrion be thy food!

"After that Noah sent forth the dove. The dove departed, and, without tarrying, put her feet in the water. The water of the Flood scalded and pickled the legs of the dove. It was hot and briny, and feathers would not grow on her legs any more, and the skin scaled off. Now, doves which have red and featherless legs are of the sort that Noah sent forth. The dove returning showed her legs to Noah, who said, May God render thee well-pleasing to men! For that reason the dove is dear to men's hearts."[1]

Another version of the story is this. Noah blessed the dove, and since then she has borne a neck-ring of green feathers; but the raven, on the other hand, he cursed, that its flight should be crooked, and never direct like that of other birds.[2] This is also a Jewish legend.[3]

After that, Noah descended the mountain along with the eighty persons who had been saved with him, and he found

---

[1] Tabari, c. xli.   [2] Weil, p. 45.   [3] Midrash, fol. 15.

that not a house was left standing on the face of the earth. Noah built a town consisting of eighty houses,—a house apiece for all who had been saved with him.[1]

Fabricius, in his collection of apocrypha of the Old Testament, has published the prayer that Noah offered daily in the ark, beside the body of Adam, which he bore with him, to bury it on Golgotha.

"O Lord, Thou art excellent in truth, and nothing is great beside Thee; look upon us in mercy; deliver us from this deluge of water for the sake of the pangs of Adam, the first man whom Thou didst make; for the sake of the blood of Abel, the holy one; for the sake of just Seth, in whom Thou didst delight; number us not amongst those who have broken Thy commandments, but cover us with Thy protection, for Thou art our deliverer, and to Thee alone are due the praises uttered by the works of Thy hands from all eternity." And all the children of Noah responded, "Amen, O Lord."[2]

Noah is said to have left the ark on the tenth day of the first month of the Mussulman year, and to have instituted the fast which the Mahommedans observe on that day, to thank God for his deliverance.

According to the Book of Enoch, the water of the Flood was transformed by God into fire, which will consume the world and the ungodly, at the consummation of all things.[3]

The Targum of Palestine says that the dove plucked the leaf she brought to Noah from off a tree on the Mount of Olives.[4]

The Book Jasher supplies an omission in Genesis. In Genesis it is said of Lamech, on the birth of Noah, "*He called his name Noah; saying, This same shall comfort us concerning our work and toil of our hands, because of the ground which the Lord hath cursed;*"[5] but Noah signifies *rest*, not *comfort*. The Book Jasher says that the Methuselah called the child Noah, *rest*, because the land rested from the curse; but Lamech called him Menahem, *comfort*, for the reason given in the text of Genesis. The sacred writer has given one name with the signification of the other.[6]

---

[1] Tabari, p. 113.   [2] Fabricus, i. pp. 74, 243.
[3] Ed. Dillmann, c. 67.   [4] Ed. Etheridge, i. p. 182.   [5] Gen. v. 20.
[6] In the Midrash Rabba, this want of connection between the name and the signification is remarked upon, and Solomon Jarki in his commentary says that, for the meaning assigned, the name ought to have been, not Noah, but Menahem.

5*

XV.

HEATHEN LEGENDS OF THE DELUGE.

ARARAT has borne this name for three thousand years. We read in the Book of Genesis that "*the ark rested, in the seventh month, on the seventeenth day of the month, upon the mountains of Ararat.*" In passages of the Old Testament, as in Isaiah xxxvii. 38 and 2 Kings xix. 37, mention is made of a land, in Jeremiah li. 27 of a kingdom, of Ararat ; and we are likewise informed by Moses of Chorene, the first authority among Armenian writers, that an entire country bore this name after an ancient Armenian king, Arai the Fair, who lived about 1750 years before Christ. He fell in a bloody battle with the Babylonians on a plain in Armenia, called after him Arai-Arat, the Fall of Arai.

Before this event the country bore the name of Amasia, from its sovereign, Amassis, the sixth in descent from Japheth, who gave the name of Massis to the mountain. This is still the only name by which it is known to the Armenians ; for, though it is called Ararat in the Armenian edition of the Old Testament, yet the people call it Massis, and know no other name for it. The Mussulmans call it Agridagh, the strong mountain. The name by which it is known to the Persians is Kuhi-Nuh, the mountain of Noah, or Saad-dagh, the Blessed Mountain.[1]

But tradition is not at one as to the peak on which the ark rested, or from which Noah descended, as we shall presently see. Ararat is 17,210 feet in altitude above the sea, and 14,320 feet above the plain of the Araxes. On the north-eastern slope of the mountain, even from a distance, may be seen a deep, gloomy chasm, which gives the appearance as if the mountain had been rent asunder at the top : this was probably at some remote period the volcanic vent, for the mountain is composed of tufa, scoria, and erupted matter. It shoots up in one rigid crest, and then sweeps down towards

---

[1] Buttmann, Ueber der Mythus d. Sûndfluth, Berlin, 1819 ; Lûken Die Traditionen des Menschengeschlechts, Munster, 1856 ; Bryant, Of the Deluge in Ancient Mythology, London, 1775, etc.

Little Ararat, the second summit, which stands 13,000 feet above the sea.[1]

The people of the neighborhood point to a step on the mountain side, covered with perpetual snow and glacier, and where, say they, the ark rested; and to a town near Ararat named Naktschiwan, or "the first outgoing" of Noah from the ark. This etymological interpretation is probably as questionable as that of Ararat given by Moses of Chorene; it is true the city is ancient, for it was severely injured by an earthquake in the reign of Astyages the Median, in the sixth century before Christ. It is called Naxuana by Josephus,[2] and he says it was so called because there Noah first descended from the ark, and that remains of the ark were there to be seen carefully preserved. And there, says the Armenian historian Vartan, is also the tomb of Noah. Nicolas of Damascus, in his History of Syria, Berosus the ancient Babylonian writer and other heathen historians, tell a similar tale; and we learn that relics of the ark were distributed thence, and were regarded with the utmost reverence, as amulets.

Nicolas of Damascus, who wrote in the reign of Augustus, says, "There is beyond the Minyadian land a great mountain in Armenia, Baris by name (perhaps for Masis), on which, as the tradition says, some one sailing over it in an ark, lodged on the topmost peak. The remains of the wood continued to exist long. Perhaps this may be the same as he of whom Moses, the Jewish historian, has written."[3]

The story quoted by Eusebius from an ancient writer named Molo, gives a form of the Syrian tradition. "After the Deluge, the man who with his sons escaped the flood, went out of Armenia, after he had been driven out of his inheritance by the violence of the natives. He came thence into the mountains of Syria, which were then uninhabited."[4] And with this agrees a curious allusion in Lucian, who was himself a Syrian. He says that there was in Syria, in the city Hierapolis, a religious festival, and a very ancient temple, connected "with the popular story of Deucalion the Scythian, who lived at the time of the great Deluge." It is curious that he should give to the Syrian Noah the Greek name, and that he should speak of him as not a native, but as coming from the East, from Scy-

---

[1] Parrot, Journey to Ararat, English Trans. Lond. 1845.
[2] Joseph. Antiq., i. 3; see also Ptolem. Geogr. vi. 2.
[3] Joseph. Antiq., i. 4.   [4] Euseb. Præp. Evang. ix. 19.

thia. He says: "Of this Deucalion have I heard in Greece, what the Greeks relate. The story is this: The present race of men is not the first, for that perished. This is the second race which sprang from Deucalion, and was very numerous. The earlier generation was very evil, and violated the Divine law. They neither kept oaths nor showed hospitality; they took not the stranger in, nor protected him when he sought protection; therefore a terrible destruction fell upon them. Much water gushed out of the earth, great rains poured down, and the sea rose and overwhelmed the earth. Deucalion alone of all men was preserved to another generation on account of his wisdom and piety. He was thus saved. He went into a great ark which he had built, along with his wife and children. Then came to him, pair by pair, cows, horses, lions, serpents, and all kinds of animals which are nourished on earth, and he took them all in. They did not hurt him, for Zeus ordained a great friendship amongst them. So they all sailed in the ark as long as the flood lasted. This is the Greek story of Deucalion.

"But very wonderful is the confirmation of the history as it is related in Hierapolis. In the neighborhood of that city a great chasm opened which engulphed all the waters of the Flood. Thereupon Deucalion erected altars, and dedicated a temple to Here (Atergatis) over the chasm. I have seen this; it is very small: whether it was once large but has since become smaller, I cannot say; but I saw that it was small. For the confirmation of the history the following takes place: twice in the year the sea-water is brought into the temple. Not only do the priests bear it, but all Syria and Arabia, and many from beyond Euphrates, come and carry water. They pour it out in the temple; then it runs down into the chasm, and, though it may be very small, it takes in all the water poured into it. This they do, say they, because Deucalion instituted this rite as a memorial of his deliverance, and of the mercy of God."[1]

Equally fully has the Babylonian tradition reached us from the Chaldee history of the old priest of Bel, Berosus (B. C. 260). The Chaldees had placed ten kings at the head of this mystic history, which answer to the ten generations in Genesis before the Flood. The last of these patriarchs was called Xisuthrus, who is the same as the Biblical Noah. Berosus relates the

---

[1] Lucian, De Dea Syra, c. 12, 13.

story of the Deluge thus : " Under the reign of Xisuthrus there was a great flood. Kronos (*i. e.*, Bel) appeared to Xisuthrus in a dream, and warned him that all men would be destroyed by a deluge on the 15th of the month Dæsios, and he commanded him to write down all the learning and science of men, and to hide it in the sun-city Siparis, and then to build a ship and to enter it along with his family and relatives and nearest friends, and to take into it with him food and drink, and beasts and winged fowl. When he was asked whither he was about to sail, he was bidden reply : To the gods, to pray them that men may prosper. He obeyed ; and made an ark five stadia long and two wide, laid in what was commanded, and sailed with his wife and child and relatives. When the flood abated, Xisuthrus sent out a bird which, as it found no food nor ground on which to perch, returned to the ship. After a day, he sent out another bird ; this came back with mud on its feet. The third bird he sent out did not return. So Xisuthrus knew that the land appeared, and he broke a hole in the ship and saw that the ship was stranded on a mountain ; so he disembarked with his wife and daughter and steersman ; and when he had adored the earth, raised an altar, and offered to the gods, he vanished. Those who remained in the ship also went out, when they saw that Xisuthrus did not return, to seek Xisuthrus, and they called him by name. But Xisuthrus appeared again no more, only his voice was heard bidding them fear God, and telling them that he had taken to dwell with the gods, because he was pious. The same honor was accorded to his wife and daughter and to the steersman." This refers to their being set in the sky as constellations : Xisuthrus as the water-bearer, the virgin, and steersman still occupy their places there. " He bade them," continues Berosus, " return to Babylon, and, as Fate decreed, take his writings out of Siparis, and from them instruct men. The place where they found themselves was Armenia. Some fragments of the ship remain on the mountains of the Kordyæans in Armenia, and some take away particles and use them as amulets." [1]

Eusebius has preserved a fragment of another Babylonian writer, Abydenos, which gives the same story precisely. [2]

Another Chaldee tradition preserved by Cassian is that,

---

[1] Georg. Syncellus, Chronographia, p. 29, B., ed. Bonn ; or Cory's Ancient Fragments, p. 26 et seq.

[2] Præp. Evang. ix. 12 ; see also S. Cyril contra Julian, i.

before the Flood, Ham concealed in the ground treaties of witchcraft and alchemy, and that, when the water abated, he recovered them.[1]   According to Berosus also, Xisuthrus had three sons,—Zerovanos, Titan, and Japetosthes.   Zerovanos is the same as Zoroaster.

From Phrygia also come to us traces of a Diluvian tradition.   A number of coins of Apamea, a city of Phrygia, between the rivers Mæander and Marsyas, of the period of Septimius Severus and the following emperors, possibly bear reference to this event.[2]   One, a coin of Philip, bears on the reverse something like a box, containing a man and woman ; on the panel of the box, under the man, is written "Noe," the dove is bringing the olive branch, and the raven is seated on the edge of the box above the head of the female figure.   The same two persons are also represented on dry land, with the right hand uplifted in the attitude of prayer.   Another coin with the same subject, on the reverse has, inscribed on the ark, *NHTΩN.*

To elucidate these coins, reference is made to a passage in the Sibylline Oracles to this effect : " In Phyrgia lies steep, to be seen from afar, a mountain, named Ararat. . . . Therefrom streams the river Marsyas ; but on its crest rested the ark (*κιβωτό·*) when the rain abated."[3]   As the ancient name of Apamea seems to have been Kibotos, it is not unlikely that the Sibylline writer mixed together in those lines the Mosaic and the Phrygian traditions.

It must, however, be admitted that it is quite as probable that the box represents a temple, and the two figures tutelary deities, and that the " Noe " is a contraction for " Neocoros," the most important title assumed by Greek cities, and often recorded on their coins.

The ancient Persian account in the Bundehesch is this :— " Taschter (the spirit ruling the waters) found water for thirty days and thirty nights upon the earth.   Every water-drop was as big as a bowl.   The earth was covered with water the height of a man.   All idolaters on earth died through the rain ; it penetrated all openings.   Afterwards a wind from heaven divided the water and carried it away in clouds, as souls bear

---

[1] Bochart, Geogr. Sacra, p. 231.
[2] Ekhel, Doctrina Numm. Vet. iii. p. 132 et seq. ; see also Bryant's New System of Ancient Mythology, Lond. 1775, i. note 3.
[3] Orac. Sibvll, i. v. 260, 265–7.   Ed. Fiedlieb.

bodies; then Ormuzd collected all the water together and placed it as a boundary to the earth, and thus was the great ocean formed."[1]

The ancient Indian tradition is, "that in the reign of the sun-born monarch Satyavrata, the whole earth was drowned, and the whole human race destroyed by a flood, except the pious prince himself, the seven Rishis and their several wives." This general *pralaya*, or destruction, is the subject of the first Purana, or sacred poem; and the story is concisely told in the eighth book of the Bhagavata, from which the following is an abridged extract:—"The demon Hayagriva having purloined the Vedas from Brahma while he was reposing, the whole race of man became corrupt, except the seven Rishis and Satyavrata. This prince was performing his ablutions in the river Critamala, when Vishnu appeared to him in the shape of a small fish, and after several augmentations of bulk in different waters, was placed by Satyavrata in the ocean, when he thus addressed his amazed votary:—'In seven days all creatures who have offended me shall be destroyed by a deluge; but thou shalt be secured in a capacious vessel miraculously formed. Take, therefore, all kinds of medicinal herbs and esculent grain for food, and together with the seven holy men, your respective wives, and pairs of all animals, enter the ark without fear; then shalt thou know God face to face, and all thy questions shall be answered.' Saying this, he disappeared; and, after seven days, the ocean began to overflow the coasts, and the earth to be flooded by constant showers, when Satyavrata, meditating on the Deity, saw a large vessel moving on the waters: he entered it, having in all respects conformed to the instructions of Vishnu, who, in the form of a large fish, suffered the vessel to be tied with a great sea-serpent, as with a cable, to his measureless horn. When the deluge had ceased, Vishnu slew the demon and recovered the Vedas, and instructed Satyavrata in divine knowledge."[2]

The Mahabharata says that the boat containing Manu and his seven companions rested on Mount Naubhandanam, the highest peak of the Himalayas; and the name Naubhandanam signifies "ships stranding."[3]

---

[1] Bundehesch, 7.

[2] On the Chronology of the Hindus, by Sir W. Jones; Asiatic Researches, ii. pp. 116–7.

[3] Bopp, Die Sündfluth; Berlin, 1829, p. 9.

The Greek traditions are not early, and were probably borrowed from Semitic sources. We have seen the story told by Lucian in his book " De Dea Syra," but in his " Timon " he follows the more authentic Greek legend, and makes Deucalion escape in a little skiff (consequently without the animals), and land on Mount Lycoris.

We have also the same catastrophe somewhat differently related by Ovid. The world he represents " as confederate in crime," and doomed therefore to just punishment. Jupiter sends down rain from heaven, and rivers and seas gushing forth from their caves gather over the earth's surface, and sweep mankind away. Deucalion and his wife alone, borne in a little skiff, are stranded on the top of Parnassus. By degrees, the waters subside : the only surviving pair inquire of the gods how they may again people the desert earth. They are ordered, with veiled heads, to throw behind them the bones of their great mother. Half doubtful as to the meaning of the oracle, they throw behind them stones, which are immediately changed into men and women, and the earth spontaneously produces the rest of the animal creation. [1]

Apollodorus relates the matter thus :—" When Zeus determined to destroy the brazen race, Deucalion, by the advice of Prometheus, made a great ark, λάρναξ, and put into it all necessary things, and entered it with Pyrrha. Zeus then, pouring down heavy rains from heaven, overwhelmed the greater part of Greece, so that all men perished except a few who fled to the highest mountains. He floated nine days and nights in the sea of waters, and at last stopped on Mount Parnassus. Then Zeus sent Hermes to ask him what he wished, and he solicited that mankind might be made again. Zeus bade him throw stones over his head, from which men should come, and said that those cast by Pyrrha should be turned into women."

Stephanus of Byzantium says that the tradition was that after the surface of the earth became dry, Zeus ordered Prometheus and Athene to make images of clay in the form of men ; and when they were dry, he called the winds and made them breathe into each, and rendered them vital : and thus the earth after the Flood was repeopled. [2] Diodorus says, " In the Deluge, which happened in the time of Deucalion, almost all flesh died." [3]

[1] Ovid. Metam. i. 240 et seq.   [2] Steph. Bryzant., s. voce *Ἰκόνιον*.
[3] Diod. Sicul. lib. i.

The Chinese begin their dynasties with Jao, the last of the old race, whose words are thus recorded in the Schu-Kiug:— "The mighty waters of the flood spread themselves out, and overflowed, and drowned every thing. The mountains disappeared in the deep, and the hills were buried beneath them. The foaming billows seemed to threaten heaven. All people were drowned."[1] An ancient inscription, which the Chinese attribute to Yu, the third patriarch after the Flood, and which at least dates from before Christ, refers to this event:—"The illustrious Emperor Jao said, sighing, 'Companions and counsellors! The great and little territories up to the mountain's peak, the homes of birds, and wild beasts, were overflowed far and wide. Long had I forgotten my home; now I rest upon the mountain top of Jo-lu. . . . The trouble is over, and the misfortune is at an end; the streams of the south flow, clothes and food are before us. The world is at rest, and the flying rain cannot again destroy us.'"[2]

In one of the writings of the disciples of Tao-tse, the tradition takes a fuller form. Kung-Kung, a bad spirit, enraged at having been overcome in war, gave such a blow against one of the pillars of the sky with his head that he broke it; and the vault of heaven fell in, and a tremendous flood overwhelmed the earth. But Niu-Noa overcame the water with wood, and made a boat to save himself, which could go far; and he polished a stone of five colors—the rainbow—and therewith he fastened the heavens, and lifted them up on a tortoise shell. Then he killed the black dragon Kong-Kong, and choked the holes in heaven with the ashes of a pumpkin.[3] In the story of Jao there is also a faint trace of his connection with the rainbow, for he is said to have eyebrows colored and shaped like rainbows.[4]

The Kamskadales say, "that in the remote ages when their great ancestor and God, Kutka, lived in Kamschatka, there was a mighty deluge. Many men were drowned therein, but some tried to save themselves in boats, but the waves overwhelmed them. Those who were saved were rescued on great rafts made of trees bound together, to which they retreated, taking food and their property with them. And that they might not drift out to sea, they anchored themselves with great stones,

---

[1] Mém. concernant les Chinois, i. p. 157.
[2] Klaproth, Inschrift, des Yu; Halle, 1811, p. 29.
[3] Mém. concernant les Chinois, ix. p. 383.
[4] Mart. Martinii, Hist. Sin. p. 26.

which they tied to the edges and let down into the water. And when the flood abated, they rested on the top of a high mountain."[1]

A Lapp tradition is that God once submerged the world, saving only one brother and sister alive, whom He placed on Mount Passeware. When the water disappeared, the children separated to wander over the earth, and see whether they alone remained alive. They met after three years, and then separated again, for they recognized one another as brother and sister. After three years they met, but turned their backs on one another once more for the same reason. Again they met after the lapse of three years, and again they parted ; but when they met again, after three years' further absence, they no longer recognized each other, and so they took one another in marriage ; and of them all generations of men are come.[2]

Among the Kelts, the Deluge formed a prominent feature, and the ark was connected with their most sacred religious rites.

A Welsh legend is this :—"One of the most dreadful of events was the outbreak of Llyn Llion, the sea of seas, which overwhelmed the world and drowned all men except Dwyan and Dwyvach, who escaped in a bare boat and colonized Britain. This ship was one of the three masterpieces of Hu, and was built by the heavenly lord, Reivion ; and it received into it a pair of every kind of beasts when the Llyn Llion burst forth." Reivion is the same as Hu Cadarn, the discoverer of the vine ; and it is said of him that " he built the ark laden with fruit, and it was stayed up in the water, and carried forward by serpents ; " and of the rainbow it was said, that the Woman of the silver wheel, Arianrhod, to control the wizards of night and evil spirits of tempest, and out of love to the Britons, " wove the stream of the rainbow,—a stream which drives the storm from the earth, and makes its former destruction stay far from it, throughout the world's circle."[3]

The Norse legend in the younger Edda is, " Bör's sons (Odin, Vilj, and Ve) slew the giant Ymir ; and when he fell, so much blood (in poetic phraseology Ymir's blood signified water) ran out of the wounds, that the whole race of the giants

---

[1] Steller, Beschreibung v. Kamschatka ; Frankf. 1744, p. 273.

[2] Serres, Kosmoganie des Moses, übersetzt von F. X. Stech, p. 149.

[3] Davies, Mythology of the British Druids, London, 1809 ; and Celtic Researches, London, 1844 : curious works on the Arkite worship and arditions of the Kelts.

was drowned in it, except one, who with his family escaped; this one was called Bergelmr. He got into a boat along with his wife, and was thus saved."[1]

The Lithuanian myth was this:—When Pramzimas, the most high God, looked out of his heavenly house upon the world through a window, he saw that it was filled with violence. Then he sent Wind and Water to devastate the earth, and this they did for twenty days and nights. Pramzimas looked on, and as he looked on, he ate nuts at his window, and threw the shells down. One shell fell on the top of a mountain, and some men, women, and beasts scrambled into it and were saved alive, while all the rest of the inhabitants of the world were drowned. When the flood drained away, the pairs in the nut-shell left it, and were scattered over the earth. Only one aged couple remained, and they complained; then God sent them the rainbow to console them, and bade them jump over the bones of the earth. They jumped nine times, and nine pairs of living human beings started to life, and founded the nine races of Lithuanian blood.[2]

Among the negroes of Africa, traditions are faint, or have been little sought after and collected. The Jumala negroes say that once when the earth was full of cruelty and wickedness, the good Til destroyed it with fire, and that one man alone was saved alive, named Musikdgen, *i. e.*, the mountain chief, because he was found without blame.

In America the crop of traditions is abundant.

The Kolosches, living in Russian America, say that the first dweller on the earth was Kitkhughia-si, and that he resolved to destroy all his children who sinned against him. Thereupon he brought a flood over the land, and all perished save a few who escaped in boats to the tops of mountains, where, say they, the remains of the boats, and the ropes which fastened them, remained to be seen.[3]

Among the Dog-rib Indians, Sir John Franklin found the story much more complete; and as this tribe lives near the Polar Sea, far from any mission stations, it is scarcely possible that the story can have been derived from Christian teachers.

[1] The prose Edda; Mallet, Northern Antiq., ed. Bohn, p. 404.
[2] Grimm, Deutsche Mythol.; Göttingen, 1854, p. 545.
[3] The same story precisely, is told by the closely allied race of the Chippewas; Atherne-Jones, Traditions of the North American Indians, London, 1830, ii. p. 9 et seq.

They say that Tschäpiwih, their great ancestor, lived on a track between two seas. He built a weir, and caught fish in such abundance that they choked the water-course, and the water overflowed the earth. Tschäpiwih with his family entered his canoe, and took with him all kinds of beasts and birds. The land was covered for many days ; at last Tschäpiwih could bear it no longer, so he sent out the beaver to look for the earth. But the beaver was drowned. Then he sent out the muskrat, which had some difficulty in returning, but it had mud on its paws. Tschäpiwih was glad to see the earth, and moulded it between his fingers, till it became an island on the surface of the water, on which he could land.[1]

The Pacullies, on the west coast of New Georgia, say that at the Deluge one man and one woman were saved by escaping into a cave ; and they add that when the earth was drowned, a water rat dived for it and brought it to the surface again.[2]

A Caddoque tradition is, that Sakechah was a great hunter. One night he saw in vision the Master of Life, who spoke to the dreamer in these words :—

"The world is getting very wicked, Sakechah."

"I know it," answered the hunter.

"I hear no longer the voices of men supplicating me for favors ; they no longer thank me for what I send them. I must sweep, wash, and purify the earth ; I must destroy all living creatures from off the face of it."

Then Sakechah said, "What have I done, Master of Life, that I should be involved in this general destruction ?"

The Master answered, "No, Sakechah, thou hast been a good servant ; I will except thee from the general doom. Go now, cut thee a hemlock, knock off the cones, and bring them, together with the trunk and leaves, to the bottom of the hill Wecheganawan. Burn them in a fire made of the dry branches of the oak, kindled with the straw of wild rice. When the heap is reduced to ashes, take the ashes and strew them in a circle round the hill. Nothing need be gathered within the circle, for the living creatures will of themselves retreat to it for safety ; but when this is done, take the trunk of the hemlock, and strike it into the earth at the spot where the large tuft of grass is growing on the barren hill. There lies the great fountain of water ; and when the staff is struck into the earth

<hr>

[1] Lütke, Voyage autour du Monde, i. p. 189.
[2] Braunschweig, Die alten Amerik. Denkmäler ; Berlin, 1840, p. 18.

the fountain shall burst forth, and the earth be swept and washed and purified by the great deluge that shall overwhelm it. Sakechah and his family shall alone, of all the inhabitants of the earth, be saved; and the creatures he assembles around him on the hill Wecheganawan be alone those exempted from the all-sweeping destruction."

The hunter obeyed. He took the staff and stuck it deep into the earth at the place indicated, and the great fountain was broken up, and the waters burst forth in a mighty volume. Slowly the element began to creep over the earth, while the hunter and his family looked on. Now the low grounds appeared but as they appear in the season of showers; here a little water, and there a little water; soon they became one vast sheet. Now a little hill sank from view, then the tops of trees disappeared; again a tall hill hid its head. At length the waves rose so high that Sakechah could see nothing more; he stood as it were in a well. The waters were piled up on every side of him, restrained from harming him, or his, or the beasts that had clustered around him, by the magic belt of hemlock ashes.

"Sakechah!" said the Master of Life, "when the moon is exactly over thy head, she will draw the waters to the hill. She is angry with me because I scourged a comet. I cannot prevent her revenge unless I destroy her, and that I may not do, as she is my wife. Therefore bid every living creature that is on the hill take off the nail from the little finger of his right hand, if a man; if a bird, or beast, of the right foot or claw. When each has done this, bid him blow in the hollow of the nail with the right eye shut, saying these words, ' Nail become a canoe, and save me from the wrath of the moon.' The nail will become a large canoe, and in this canoe will its owner be safe."

The Great Spirit was obeyed, and shortly every creature was floating in a boat on the surface of the water. And, lest they should be dispersed, Sakechah bound them together by thongs of buffalo-hide.

They continued floating for a long time, till at last Sakechak said, " This will not do—we must have land. Go," said he to a raven that sat in his canoe near him, " fetch me a little earth from the bottom of the abyss. I will send a female, because women are quicker and more searching than men."

The raven, proud of the praise bestowed on her sex, left her tail feathers at home, and dived into the abyss. She was gone a long time, but, notwithstanding her being a woman, she returned baffled of her object. Whereupon Sakechah said to the otter, " My little man, I will send you to the bottom, and see if your industry and perseverance will enable you to accomplish what has been left undone by the wit and cunning of the raven." So the otter departed upon his dangerous expedition. He accomplished his object. When he again appeared on the earth, he held in his paw a lump of black mud. This he gave into the hands of Sakechah ; and the Great Master bade him divide the lump into five portions ; that which came out of the middle of the lump he was commanded to mould into a cake and to cast into the water: he did so, and it became dry land, on which he could disembark ; and the earth thus formed was repeopled from his time. No matter whether the men of the earth be red or white, all are descended from Sakechah.[1]

The Iroquois tell a very similar story, differing from the above in merely a few trivial particulars. According to the tradition of the Knistineaux on the Upper Missouri, all men perished in the Deluge except one woman, who caught the leg of a bird which carried her to the top of a rock, where she was confined of twins, of whom the earth was peopled.[2]

The Appalachian tribe in Florida is a relic of a more ancient nation than the North American Indian tribes. They relate that the lake Theomi burst its bounds, and overflowed the earth, and stood above the top of the highest mountains, saving only the peak Oldamy, on which stood a temple to the sun. Those men who had succeeded in reaching this temple were saved, but all the rest perished.[3]

According to the Cherokees, a dog foresaw the destruction that was coming on the earth. It went every day to the bank of a river and howled ; and when its master rebuked it, it revealed to him what was about to take place. The man therefore built a boat and entered it with his family, and he alone of all mankind was saved.[4]

If we turn to Central America, we find that there also traditions of the Flood abounded.

[1] Atherne Jones, Traditions of the North American Indians, ii. 21–33.
[2] Catlin, Letters and Notes on the Manners, etc., of the N. American Indians ; London, 1841.
[3] Mayer, Mytholog. Taschenbuch ; Weimar, 1811, p. 245.
[4] Schoolcraft, Notes on the Iroquois ; New York, 1847, p. 358

The ancient inhabitants of Mexico related the event as follows :—

There was a great deluge which destroyed all men and beasts, save Coxcox and his wife Chichequetzal, who escaped in a cyprus trunk and landed on Mount Colhuacan, where they became parents of many children, who, however, were all dumb. Then appeared a dove, which seated itself on a high tree, and taught them language. But as none of them understood the speech of the other, they separated and dispersed over the world. Fifteen heads of families, however, had the good fortune to speak the same language. These lived together in the same place, but at last they moved, and after 104 years of wandering they settled in Aztlan. Thence they journeyed to Chiapultepeque, and then returned to the Mount Colhuacan and settled in Mexico.[1]

There was a story of similar description connected with the ancient city of Cholula in the modern province of Puebla. " Before the great flood in the year 4,008 after the creation of the world, the land Anaknac (Mexico) was peopled with giants. All those who did not perish, with the exception of seven, escaped into holes, and were transformed into fish. When the deluge was over, one of these giants, Xelhuaz by name, the builder, went to Cholula, and built a pyramid on Mount Tlalok, to commemorate his having been saved thereon along with his six brothers." [2]

The inhabitants of Mechoacan related that, on account of the iniquity of men, a flood was sent to sweep them all away ; but a priest, named Tezbi, along with his wife and children, were saved in a box of wood into which they had entered along with all kinds of seeds and animals. After some time Tezbi, wearying of his confinement, sent forth the vulture, which however did not return to him ; then he sent forth other birds, but they did not come back ; finally, he sent out the Colibri, which returned with a branch in its beak.[3] And of this event they had paintings in their temples which they showed to the white men who arrived amongst them.

---

[1] Müller, Geschichte des Amerikanischen Urreligionem, Basle, 1855, p. 515 ; Lüken, Die Traditionem des Menschengeschlechts, p. 223.

[2] Humboldt, Anh. des Cordilleren, i. p. 42.

[3] Antonio de Herrera, Hist. general de los Hecos, etc. ; Madrid, 1601, iii. c. 10.

The Indians in Cuba told a similar story, so did those at St. Domingo and the Antilles.[1]

Nor is South America without a rich crop of similar legends, Humboldt says, " This belief (in a deluge) is not found merely among the Tamanaks, but is a portion of a whole system of historical traditions of which the scattered accounts are to be gathered from the Maipures of the Great Cataract, the Indians of Rio-Crevato, which pours into the Cauca, and almost from all the races in the Upper Orinoko."[2]

This is the tradition of the Tamanaks. " At the time of our ancestors the whole earth was overflowed. Then two persons alone were saved, a man and a woman, who remained on Mount Tamanaku, which is not far from the Cucivero river, where our ancestors formerly dwelt. They lamented sore over the loss of their friends and relations, and as they wandered sadly about the mountain they heard a voice which told them to cast the kernels of the nuts of the *Palma Mauritia* backwards over their shoulders. They did so, and out of the nuts cast by the woman rose females, and out of those cast by the man sprang males."[3]

The Peruvians related that their first king and founder of their nation, Manco Capak, along with his wife Mama Ocllo, after the great deluge left their land, and came from the holy island in the lake Titicaca, on which the sun cast its first beam when the flood drained away.[4]

A Brazilian legend is that the Evil Spirit Arbomoku, and the spirits of the air, made a compact together to destroy mankind. The former opened all the fountains of the earth, the latter poured the clouds upon the ground and inundated it, so that only one mountain-top appeared above the water, and on that took refuge two persons, a brother and a sister, from whom all the new generations sprang.[5]

---

[1] Compare Lüken and Müller.

[2] Humboldt, Reise in die Aequinoctial Gegenden, iii. pp. 406–7.

[3] Nachrichten aus dem Lande Guiana, v. Salvator Gili ; Hamb. 1785 pp. 440–1, quoted by Lüken.

[4] Garcilasso de la Vega, Hist. des Yncas ; Amst., i. pp. 73 and 326.

[5] Ausland, Jan. 1845, No. 1.

XVI.

THE PLANTING OF THE VINE.

BOWED under his toil, dripping with perspiration, stood the patriarch Noah, laboring to break the hard clods. All at once Satan appeared and said to him,—

"What new undertaking have you in hand? What new fruit do you expect to extract from these clods?"

"I plant the grape," answered the patriarch.

"The grape! proud plant, most precious fruit! joy and delight to men! Your labor is great; will you allow me to assist you? Let us share the labor of producing the vine."

The patriarch in a fit of exhaustion consented.

Satan hastened, got a lamb, slaughtered it, and poured its blood over the clods of earth. "Thence shall it come," said Satan, "that those who taste of the juice of the grape, shall be soft-spirited and gentle as this lamb."

But Noah sighed; Satan continued his work; he caught a lion, slew that, and poured the blood upon the soil prepared for the plant. "Thence shall it come," said he, "that those who taste the juice of the grape shall be strong and courageous as the lion."

Noah shuddered. Satan continued his work; he seized a pig and slaughtered it, and drenched the soil with its blood. "Thence shall it come," said he, "that those who drink of the juice of the grape in excess, shall be filthy, degraded, and bestial as the swine."[1]

The Mussulman tradition is somewhat similar.

"When Ham had planted the vine, Satan watered it with the blood of a peacock. When it thrust forth leaves, he sprinkled it with the blood of an ape; when it formed grapes, he drenched it with the blood of a lion; when the grapes were ripe, he watered it with the blood of a swine.

"The vine, watered by the blood of these four animals, has assumed these characters. The first glass of wine makes a man animated, his vivacity great, his color is heightened. In this condition he is like the peacock. When the fumes of the liquor rise into his head, he is gay, leaps and gambols as an

---

[1] Jalkut, Genesis, fol. 16 a.

6

ape. Drunkenness takes possession of him, he is like a furious lion. When it is at its height, he is like the swine ; he
falls and grovels on the ground, stretches himself out, and
goes to sleep." [1]

Mohammed, to justify his forbidding his disciples to drink
wine, cites the history of the two angels, Arot and Harot.

"God," says he, "charged them with a commission on the
earth. A young lady invited them to dinner, and they found
the wine so good that they got drunk. They then remarked
that their hostess was beautiful, and they were filled with love
which they declared to her. This lady, who was prudent, replied that she would only listen to their protestations when she
knew the words by which they were enabled to ascend to
heaven. When she had learned these words, she mounted to
the throne of God, who, as a reward for her virtue, transformed
her into a shining star (the Morning Star), and condemned the
two drunken angels to await the day of judgment, suspended
by their heels in the well of Babel, near Bagdad, which Mussulman pilgrims visit."

According to Tabari,[2] Ham, for having laughed at his father's drunkenness, was cursed by Noah, that his skin should
become black, as well as all the fruits which were to grow in
the land he should inhabit, and thus the purple grape arose.
It was the white grape that Ham transplanted, but it black-
ened in his hands.

Abulfaraj relates that after the Deluge, Noah divided the
habitable world between his sons. He gave to Ham the
country of the Black, to Shem that of the Brown, and to Japheth that of the Red.[3] Noah also, he continues, said to his
son Shem, "When I am dead, take the bier of our father Adam
from the ark, and, together with your son Melchizedek, who
is a priest of the Most High, go with the body of Adam whither
an angel shall guide you."

This they did ; and an angel directed them to mount Breital-
makdes (Jerusalem), where they deposited the bier on a certain hill, and instantly it sank out of their sight into the ground.
Then Shem returned to his home, but not so Melchizedek,
who remained to guard the body of Adam : and he built there
a city called Jerusalem, and he was called Melek Salim, the
King of Peace, and there he spent the rest of his life in the

---

[1] Colin de Plancy, p. 121.   [2] Tabari, i. c. xli.
[3] Hist. Dynastiarum, ed. Pocock ; Oxon., 1663, p. 9.

worship of God ; he touched not women, nor shed blood, but offered to God oblations of bread and wine.[1]

Eutychius, the Egyptian patriarch of Alexandria, in his Annals, which are rife with Oriental traditions, gives a fuller account of the same incident.

When Noah was near his death, he bade Shem take the body of Adam, and go with Melchizedek, son of Peleg, whither the angel of the Lord should lead. "And," said he, "thou shalt enjoin on Melchizedek to fix his habitation there, to take to him no wife, and to spend his life in acts of devotion, for God has chosen him to preserve His true worship. He shall build himself no house, nor shall he shed blood of beast, or bird, or any animal ; nor shall he offer there any oblation save bread and wine ; and let the skins of lions be his only vesture ; he shall remain alone there ; he shall not clip his hair, or pare his nails ; for he is a priest of the Most High. The angel of God shall go before you, till ye come to the place where ye shall bury the body of Adam, and know that that place is the middle of the world." Now Noah died on Wednesday, at the second hour, in the second month of Ayar, which is the same as Bashnes, in the nine hundred and fiftieth year of his age. And this year Shem was aged forty-five. The sons of Noah buried him, and bewailed him forty days.[2]

The wife of Noah is said by some to have been called Bath-Enos, or the daughter of Enos ; but the Rabbi Gedaliah says her name was Noema ; others say it was Tethiri, or Tithœa, the nurse of men, as Eve was the mother of men. The Gnostics called her Noria. She is, however, generally supposed by the Rabbis to have been Naamah, the sister of Tubal-cain.[3] But Eutychius, of Alexandria, says she was called Haical, and was the daughter of Namus, son of Enoch ; and that the wives of Shem, Ham, and Japheth were the three daughters of Methuselah. Shem's wife was named Salith ; the wife of Ham, Nahlath ; and the wife of Japheth, Arisivah.[4]

The nurse of Noah was an important personage, and must not be forgotten. She was named Sambethe, and was the first Sibyl. Suidas, the grammarian, says, "The Chaldee Sibyl, named Sambethi by the Hebrews, and identified with

---

[1] Hist. Dynastiarum, ed. Pocock ; Oxon., 1663, p. 10.
[2] Eutychius, Patr. Alex., Annal., t. i. p. 44.
[3] Bereschith Rabba, fol. 22, col. 4.
[4] Eutych. Annal., ed. Selden, i. p. 35.

the Persian Sibyl, was of the race of Noah. She foretold those things which were to befall Alexander of Macedon. She also predicted the coming of the Lord Christ, and many other things, through divine inspiration."[1]

XVII.

THE SONS OF NOAH.

HAM, the accursed, the third son of Noah, was the inventor or the preserver of magic. As we have already seen, he buried the books of magic which existed in the world, before the Deluge swept over the globe ; and when it abated he exhumed them. Cerco d'Ascoli, in the fourth chapter of his " Commentary on the Sphere of Sacrabosco," declares that he had seen a book of magic which had been composed by Ham, " which contained the elements and practice of necromancy." Certain it is that apocryphal books of alchemy and conjuration of spirits existed in the Middle Ages, which purported to have been composed by Ham.

Ham was turned black, according to the Talmud, because he did not maintain himself in perfect continence whilst in the ark ;[2] other authorities say his skin became sooty in consequence of his scoffing at his father's drunkenness ; and Japheth, for having smiled, says the Mussulman lost the gift of prophecy from his family.[3]

Berosus supposed that Ham was the same as Zoroaster.

Japheth, according to Khondemir, was given by his father all the land to the east and north of Ararat ; he was the progenitor of the Turks, the Sclaves, of Gog and Magog, says Tabari. Before he started with his family to people these countries, Noah gave him a stone, on which was written the great name of God. The Turks say that, by means of this stone, Noah was able to guide the course of the ark without sail or oars. The Turks have similar stones, which, they pretend, came by a process of generation from the parental stone given to Japheth.[4] He is said by the Mussulmans to have had eleven male children : Sin or Tchin, the father of the Chinese ; Scklab, the ancestor of the Sclavonian races ; Manschug or Magog, the

<hr>

[1] Suidas, Lexic. s. v. $\Sigma i\beta v\lambda\lambda\alpha$,[2] Tract. Sanhedrin, fol. 108, col. 2.
[3] Tabari, i. p. 115.   [4] Colin de Plancy, p. 224.

parent of the Scythians and Kalmuks ; Gomari, the father of the Franks ; Turk and Khalos, the ancestors of the Turks ; Khozaz, from whom the Khozarans trace their pedigree ; Rus, father of the Russians ; Souffan, Ghoy, and Tarag, from whom the Turcomans derive.

Ilak, son of Turk, discovered the use of salt by having let fall a piece of meat he was eating on the ground covered with saline deposit.

Of Shem the Rabbis have somewhat to say. "I have found in the Midrash that the Rabbi Johanan, son of Nuri, said : ' The holy, ever-blessed God took Shem, son of Noah, and consecrated him priest of the Most High, that he should minister before Him : and He let his Majesty dwell with Him, and He gave him the name Melchizedek, a priest of the Most High God, king of Salem. His brother Japheth learnt the law of him in his school, till Abraham came, who learnt it in the school of Shem. For this Abraham obtained, praying to God that his Majesty should remain and dwell in the house of Shem, wherefore it was said of him, *Thou art a priest forever after the order of Melchizedek.*' " [1]

Shem learned his knowledge from the Book of Wisdom which Raphael, the holy angel, gave to Adam ; but Shem's instructor was the angel Jophiel.[2]

The Rabbi Gerson writes in his book called "Sepher geliloth erez Israel," that having travelled through the lands of Og, king of Bashan, he saw there a grave which measured eighty ells, and it was indicated to him as the sepulchre of Shem.[3] A curious tradition that Shem, Ham, and Japheth fell asleep in a cave, and woke up at the Nativity of Christ, and that they were themselves the three wise men who came to adore Him, shall be mentioned more fully when we treat of the legends connected with the New Testament characters.

Shem is said to have received the priesthood instead of Noah, because Noah was bitten by the lion as he was leaving the ark, and, being suffused with blood, became incapable of receiving the priesthood.

Shem is believed to have written many books, and apocryphal writings of his exist.

[1] Eisenmenger, i. pp. 318–9   [2] Ibid., p. 376.   [3] Ibid., p. 395.

XVIII.

RELICS OF THE ARK.

WE have already seen that Berosus relates how in his time portions of the ark were removed, and used as amulets. Josephus says that remains of the ark were to be seen at his day upon Ararat; and Nicolas of Damascus reports the same. S. Epiphanius writes: " The wood of the ark of Noah is shown to this day in the Kardæn (Koord) country." [1] And he is followed by a host of fathers. El Macin, in his History of the Saracens, relates that the Emperor Heraclius visited the relics after he had conquered the Persians, in the city of Thenia, at the roots of Ararat. Haithon, the Armenian, declares that upon the snows of Ararat a black speck is visible at all times: this is Noah's ark. [2] Benjamin of Tudela, in his Itinerary, says that all the wood was carried away by the Caliph Omar, in A. D. 640, and was placed by him in a temple or mosque he erected in an island formed by the Tigris. One of the beams is shown in the Lateran at Rome. In 1670, Johann Jansenius Strauss ascended to a hermit's cell on the side of Ararat, to bind up the cœnobite's leg which was broken. The hermit's cell, said Strauss, was five days' journey up the mountain, athwart three clouds, and above a region of intolerable cold, in a calm warm atmosphere. From the account of the hermit, Herr Strauss learnt that the old man had dwelt there twenty-five years, and that he had felt there neither rain nor winds. On the top of the mountain, fifteen Italian miles from the cell, through the clear air, was distinguishable the great vessel grounded in the snow. The hermit had reached it, and of one of its planks had cut a cross, which he exhibited to the German traveller.

In the town of Chenna, in Arabia Felix, says the traveller Prévoux, is a large building, said to have been erected by Noah; and a large piece of wood is exhibited through an iron grating, which is said to have formed a portion of his ark. There is also to be seen at Chenna a well, said to have been dug by the patriarch Jacob, of which the water is icy cold.

The Armenians say that a certain monk, Jacob, once as-

---

[1] Adv. Hæres., lib. i.   [2] De Tartaris, c. 9.

cended Ararat, and carried off a fragment of the ark, which he made afterwards into a cross, and this is preserved amongst the sacred relics of Etchmiadzin. When the Persian king, Abassus the great, sent to inquire about the ark, the monks replied that it was in vain for him to attempt to reach it, on account of the precipices and glaciers, and innumerable difficulties of the way.[1]

XIX.

CERTAIN DESCENDANTS OF HAM.

WE shall follow certain Mussulman traditions for what follows. Ad, son of Amalek, therefore grandson of Ham, established himself in Arabia, where he became chief of the tribe of the Adites. He fell into idolatry. He had two sons named Schedad and Scheded, who reigned over numerous subjects —one for two hundred and fifty, the other for three hundred years. They built a superb city, where houses were of sumptuous magnificence; the like of this city was never seen before, nor will be seen again. This city vanished when the tribe of the Adites was exterminated; as we shall relate when we give the legends attaching to Heber. The commentators of the Koran tell marvels of this wondrous city.

Under the Khalifate of Moawiyah, first of the Ommiades, an Arab of the desert, named Kolabah, going in quest of his camel in the plain of Aden, lighted on the gate of a beautiful city. He went in, but, being filled with fear, he did not remain there more time than sufficed for him to collect some of the stones of the street, and then he returned.

His neighbors, to whom he relates his adventure, repeated it to the Khalif, who ordered Kolabah to be brought before him. The Arab related frankly what he had seen, but Moawiyah would not give credence to the marvellous tale, till he had consulted his learned men, and especially the illustrious Al-Akhbar, who assured him that the story of the poor Arab was worthy of all trust, for the city he had seen was none other than that built by Schedad, son of Ad, in the land of the Adites in which Aden is situated; and that, as the pride of this prince knew no bounds, God had sent His angel to destroy

[1] Reliquiæ Arcæ Noæ, in Fabricius, i. art. 33.

all the inhabitants, and conceal their splendid city from the eyes of men, to be revealed only at intervals, that the memory of God's judgment might not fade out of men's minds.

Schedad had a son named Dhohak, of whom strange tales are told. He knew magic, and gained the sovereignty over the entire universe; and he kept his subjects in terror by excessive cruelty. In the Caherman-Nâmeh it is related that the Devil, satisfied with his proceedings, offered him his services gratuitously, and they were cheerfully accepted. The ferocity of the tyrant increased, he skinned men alive, impaled and crucified them on the slightest charges.

After having served him five years, the Evil One thus addressed him: "Sire! for many years I have been thy faithful attendant, neither have I received of thee any recompense. Now I beseech of thee one favor—that I may kiss thy shoulders."

This favor was readily granted. Dhohak himself plucked off his mantle to facilitate the kiss.

But no sooner had the Devil applied his lips to the two shoulders of the tyrant, than two serpents, which could not be plucked off, fastened there and began to gnaw his flesh.

Tabari says that the king bore on his shoulders two frightful ulcers or cancers, resembling serpents' heads, sent him by God as a punishment for his crimes. These cancers caused him such acute agony, that he shrieked night and day. No one was able to provide a remedy or to abate the torment.

One night when he was asleep, some one appeared to him in a dream, and said, "If you desire your ulcers to give less pain, apply to them human brains."

Next day, Dhohak awoke and ordered two men to be brought before him; he slew them, cut open their skulls, extracted the brains and applied them to his cancers. The relief was instantaneous, and Dhohak felt, for the first time for many days, some hours of repose.

After this, every day two men were killed to form poultices for his ulcers. During the two hundred latter years of the life of Dhohak, the prisons were emptied to satisfy his requirement for fresh brains; and when no more criminals could be procured, it was made a tribute for his kingdom to render to him two men, each day, to be immolated to soothe his pain.

Now there was at Ispahan a blacksmith, named Kaveh, who had two beautiful sons, whom he loved more dearly than his own life. One day they were seized, carried before the king, and his shoulders were poulticed with their brains.

Kaveh was at work at his anvil when the news of the slaying of his sons reached him. He deserted his anvil; and uttering a piercing cry, he rushed into the streets, with his leathern apron before him, bitterly lamenting his loss, and calling for vengeance on the monarch. The people crowded about him, they plucked off his leather apron, and converted it into a standard.

The crowd gathered as it advanced. From every street men flowed to join the army, and shortly the blacksmith found himself at the head of a hundred thousand men.

They marched to Demavend, where was the palace of the tyrant. And Kaveh, before attacking it, thus addressed his soldiers, "I am not one to lead you against a king; you need a king to make war against a king."

"Well," said his followers, "we elect you to be our king.'

" I am but a simple blacksmith, and am not fit to rule," answered Kaveh, "but there is a royal prince named Afridoun, the son of Djemschid, who is fled from the cruelty of Dhohak: choose him."

They agreed. The prince was found and invested with the sovereignty; then a battle was fought, and Dhohak's army was routed, and the tyrant was slain.

When Afridoun mounted the throne, he named Kaveh governor of Ispahan. And when Kaveh was dead, the king asked his children to give him their father's leathern apron. Then, having obtained it, he placed it among his treasures, and whenever he went to battle he attached the smith's apron to a tall staff, and marched under that banner against his enemies.

In after years, this leathern apron was studded with precious stones, till Omar, despising it, ordered the old piece of leather to be burnt; but Yezdeguerd had already robbed it of its gems.[1]

Afridoun exercised the sovereignty during two hundred years. He was the first to study astronomy, and he founded the science of medicine. He was the first king to ride on an elephant. He had three sons, Tur, Salm, and Irad. He loved the third son, Irad, more than the two elder, and he gave him the sovereignty over Irad, Mosul, Koufa, Bagdad.

---

[1] Tabari, i. c. xlii. xliii.

After the death of Afridoun, Tur and Salm marched against Irad, defeated him and killed him, saying : " Our father has divided his inheritance unjustly. He has given to Irad the best portion, the centre of the world ; as for us, we are cast out to its extremities."

On the death of Tur and Salm, the crown left this family, and passed to a king named Cush, who was of the sons of Ham, the son of Noah. Cush reigned forty years. After him Canaan ascended the throne. Cush and Canaan worshipped idols. It is said that Nimrod was the son Canaan. When Canaan died, Nimrod succeeded him. Nimrod had a vizir named Azar (Terah), son of Nahor, son of Sarough (Serug), who was sixth in generation from Noah. This Azar was the father of Abraham, the friend of God.

From the time of the Deluge to the time of Abraham was three thousand years. During that period, there was no prophet save Hud (Eber), who was sent to the Adites, and Saleh, who was sent to the Thamudites.

We shall relate the history of Hud and of Saleh, and then return to that of Nimrod.[1]

XX.

SERUG.

" *And Eber lived four and thirty years, and begat Peleg.*
" *And Peleg lived thirty years, and begat Reu. And Reu lived two and thirty years, and begat Serug. And Serug lived thirty years, and begat Nahor.*"[2]

Serug is said to have discovered the art of coining gold and silver money. In his days men erected many idols, into which demons entered and wrought great signs by them. Samiri was king of the Chaldees, and he discovered weights and measures and how to weave silk, and also how to dye fabrics. He is related to have had three eyes and two horns.

At the same time Apiphanus was king of Egypt. He built a ship, and in it made practical descents upon the neighboring people living on the shores of the Mediterranean Sea. He was succeeded by Pharaoh, son of Saner, and the kings after him assumed his name as their title.[3]

[1] Tabari, i. c. xliii.　　　　　　　[2] Gen. xi. 16, 18, 20, 22.
[3] Abulfaraj, Hist. Dynastiarum, p. 12.

Nahor was the son of Serug. In the twenty-fifth year of his life, Job the Just, underwent his trial, according to the opinion of Arudha the Canaanite. At that time Armun, king of Canaan, built the two cities Sodom and Gomorrah, and called them after the names of his two sons; but Zoar he named after his mother. At the same time, Murk or Murph, king of Palestine, built Damascus.[1]

XXI.

THE PROPHET EBER.

" Unto Shem, the father of all the children of Eber, the brother of Japheth the elder, even to him were children born.

" The children of Shem;—Elam, and Asshur, and Arphaxad and Lud and Aram.

" And the children of Aram ;—Uz, and Hul, and Gether, and Mash.

" And Arphaxad begat Salah; and Salah begat Eber."[2]

According to some Mussulman writers, Oudh (Lud), the son of Shem, had a son named Ad ; but, according to others, Ad was the son of Aram, son of Shem.

The tribes of Ad and Thamud lived near one another in the desert of Hedjaz, in the south of Arabia. The land of the people of Ad was nearer Mecca than the valley of Hidjr, and the valley of Hidjr is situated at the extremity of the desert on the road to Syria.

Never in all the world were there such great and mighty men as the Adites. Each of them was twelve cubits high, and they were so strong that if any of them stamped on the ground he sank up to his knees.

The Adites raised great monuments in the land which they inhabited. Wherever these Cyclopean edifices exist, they are called by the Arabs the constructions of the Adites.

God ordered the prophet Hud (Eber) to go to the Adites and preach to them the One true God, and turn them from idolatry. But the Adites would not hearken to his words, and when he offered them the promises of God, they said, " What better dwellings can He give us than those which we have

---

[1] Abulfaraj, Hist. Dynastiarum, p. 13. [2] Gen. x. 21–24.

made ?"   And when he spoke to them of God's threatenings, they mocked and said, "Who can resist us who are so strong?"

For fifty years did the prophet Hud speak to the Adites, and their reply to his exhortations is preserved in the Koran, "O Hud, you produce no evidence of what you advance ; we will not abandon our gods because of your preaching. We mistrust your mission. We believe that one of our gods bears a hatred against you."

Hud replied, "I take God to witness, and you also be witnesses, that I am innocent of your polytheism."[1]

The words of the Adites, "We believe that one of our gods bears a hatred against thee," signified that they believed one of . their gods had driven him mad.

During the fifty years that Hud's mission lasted, the Adites believed neither in God nor in the prophet, with the exception of a very few, who believed in secret.

At the end of that time God withheld the rain from heaven, and afflicted the Adites with drought. All the cattle of Ad died, and the Adites fainted for lack of water. For three years no rain fell.

Hud said to the Adites, "Believe in God, and He will give you rain."

They replied, "Thou art mad." But they choose three men to send to Mecca with victims ; for the infidels believe in the sanctity of Mecca, though they believe not in the One true God.

But Eber said, "Your sacrifices will be unavailing, unless you first believe."

The three deputies started for Mecca with many camels, oxen, and sheep, as sacrifices. And when they reached Mecca they made friends with the inhabitants of that city, and were received with hospitality. They passed their days and nights in eating and drinking wine, and in their drunkenness they forgot their people, and the mission on which they had been sent. The inhabitants of Mecca ordered musicians to sing the afflictions of the Adites, to recall to the envoys the purpose of their visit. Then Lokman and Morthed, two of the deputies, declared to Qaïl, the third, that they believed in Allah ; and they added, "If our people had believed the words of the prophet Hud, they would not have suffered from drought,"

[1] Koran, Sura xi. verse 57.

and Lokman and Morthed were not drunk when they said these words.

Qaïl replied, "You do not partake in the affliction of our nation. I will go myself and will offer the victims."

He went and led the beasts to the top of a mountain to sacrifice them, and turning his face to heaven, he said, " O God of heaven, hearken unto my prayer, and send rain on my poor afflicted people."

Instantly there appeared three clouds is the blue sky: one was red, one was black, the third was white ; and a voice issued from the clouds, saying, " Choose which shall descend upon thy people."

Then Qaïl said within himself, " The white cloud, if it hung all day over my nation, would not burst in rain ; the red cloud, if it hung over them night and day, would not drop a shower ; but the black cloud is heavy with water." So he chose the black cloud.

And a voice cried, " It is gone to fall upon the people."

Qaïl returned full of joy, thinking he had obtained rain ; but that cloud was big with the judgments of God. Qaïl told what he had done to his companions, Lokman and Morthed, but they laughed at him.

Now the cloud, when it arrived over the land of Ad, was accompanied by a wind. And the Adites looked up rejoicing, and cried, " The rain, the rain is coming ! "

Then the cloud gaped, and a dry whirlwind rolled out from it, and swept up all the cattle that were in the land, and raised them in the air, spun them about, and dashed them lifeless on the ground.

But the Adites said, " Fear not ; first comes wind, then comes rain. And they rushed out of their houses into the fields. Hud thought they were coming forth to ask his assistance ; but they sought him not. Then the whirlwind caught them up and cast them down again. Now each of these men was like a palm-tree in statue, and they lay shattered and lifeless on the sand.

Hud was saved, along with those who had believed his word.

Now when the envoys at Mecca heard what had befallen their people, they went all three to the summit of the mountain, and Lokman and Morthed said to Qaïl, " Believe." But he answered, raising his face and hands to heaven : " O God of heaven, if thou hast destroyed my people, slay me also."

Then the whirlwind came, and rushed on him, and caught him up and cast him down, and he was dead.

But Lokman and Morthed offered their sacrifice, and a voice from heaven said, "What is your petition?"

Lokman answered: "O Lord, grant me a long life, that I may outlive seven vultures." Now a vulture is the longest-lived of all birds; it lives five hundred years.

And the voice replied, "However long thy life may be, death will close it."

Lokman said, "I know; that is true."

Then his prayer was granted. And Lokman took a young vulture and fed it for five hundred years, and it died; then he took a second, and at the expiration of five hundred years it died also; and so on till he had reached the age of three thousand five hundred years, and then he died also.

Morthed made his request, and it was, "O Lord, give me wheat bread," for hitherto in Ad he had eaten only barley bread. So Allah gave Morthed so much wheat, that he was able to make bread thereof all the rest of his life.

Hud lived fifty years with the faithful who had received his doctrine, and his life in all was one hundred and fifty years. The prophet Saleh appeared five hundred years after Hud; he was sent to the Thamudites.[1]

But there is another version of the story given by Weil.

Hud promised Schaddad, king of the Adites, a glorious city in the heavens, if he would turn to the true God. But the king said, "I need no other city than that I have built. My palace rests on a thousand pillars of rubies and emeralds; the streets and walls are of gold, and pearl, and carbuncle, and topaz; and each pillar in the house is a hundred ells long."

Then, at Hud's word, God let the city and palace of Schaddad fade away like a dream of the night, and storm and rain descended, and night fell, and the king was without home in the desert.[2]

Of Lokman we must relate something more. He was a great prophet; some say he was nephew of Job, whose sister was his mother; others relate that he was the son of Beor, the son of Nahor, the son of Terah.

One day, whilst he was reposing in the heat of the day, the angels entered his room and saluted him, but did not show

<hr>

[1] Tabari, i. c. xliv.; Abulfeda, Hist. Ante Islamica, pp. 19–21.
[2] Weil, pp. 47, 48.

themselves. Lokman heard their voices, but saw not their persons. Then the angels said to him,—

"We are messengers of God, thy Creator and ours ; He has sent us unto thee to announce to thee that thou shalt be a great monarch."

Lokman replied, "If God desires what you say, His will can accomplish all things, and doubtless He will give me what is necessary for executing my duty in that position in which He will place me. But if He would suffer me to choose a state of life, I should prefer that in which I now am,"—now Lokman was a slave,—"and above all would I ask Him to enable me never to offend Him ; without which all earthly grandeur would be to me a burden."

This reply of Lokman was so pleasing to Allah, that He gave him the gift of wisdom to such a degree of excellence, that he became capable of instructing all men ; and this he did by means of a great multitude of maxims, sentences, and parbles to the number of ten thousand, each of which is more valuable than the whole world.[1]

When Lokman did not know any thing with which others were acquainted, he held his tongue, and did not ask questions and thus divulge his ignorance.

As he lived to a great age, he was alive in the days King David. Now David made a coat of mail, and showed it to Lokman. The sage had seen nothing like it before, and did not know what purpose it was to serve, but he looked knowing and nodded his head. Presently David put the armor upon him, and marched, and said, "It is serviceable in war." Then Lokman understood its object ; so his mouth became unsealed and he talked about it.

Lokman used to say, " Silence is wisdom, but few practise it."[2]

Thalebi relates, in his Commentary on the Koran, that Lokman was a slave, and that having been sent along with other slaves into the country to gather fruit, his fellow-slaves ate them, and charged Lokman with having done so. Lokman, to justify himself, said to his master, "Let every one of us slaves be given warm water to drink, and you will soon see who has been the thief."

---

[1] Herbelot, Biblioth. Orientale, s. v. Lokman.
[2] Tabari, i. p. 432.

The expedient succeeded; the slaves who had eaten the fruit vomited it, and Lokman threw up only warm water.

The same story precisely is told of Æsop.

Lokman is always spoken of as black, with thick lips. He is regarded by the Arabs much as is Bidpay by the Indians, and Æsop by the Europeans, as the Father of Fable.

XXII.

THE PROPHET SALEH.

THE prophet Saleh was the son of Ad, son of Aram, son of Shem, and is not to be confused with Saleh, son of Arphaxad.

The Mussulmans say that he was sent to convert the Thamudites.

The Thamudites were in size and strength like their brethren the Adites, but they inhabited the rocks, which they dug out into spacious mansions. They had in the midst of their land an unfailing supply of sweet and limpid water. They were idolaters. Saleh came armed with the command of Allah to these men, and he preached to them that they should turn from the worship of stocks and stones to that of the living God who made them.

Now Saleh had been born among the Thamudites, but he had never been an idolater. When he was young, the natives of the land had laughed at him, and said, " He is young and inexperienced ; when he is old, and has grown wiser, he will adore our gods."

When Saleh grew old, he forbade the Thamudites to worship idols, and he spoke to them of the true and only God.

But they said, " What miracle can you work, to prove that your mission is from God ? " [1]

Then he said, " Oh, my people, a she-camel that shall come from God shall be to you for a sign. Let her go and eat on the earth, and do her no injury, that a terrible retribution fall not upon you." [2]

Now Saleh had asked them what miracle they desired, and they had answered, " Bring out of the rock a camel with red hair, and a colt of a camel also with red hair; let them eat grass, and we will believe."

[1] Koran, Sura xxvi. v. 153.   [2] Ibid, xi. v. 67.

Saleh said to them, "What you ask is easy," and he prayed.

Then the rock groaned and clave asunder, and there came out a she-camel with her foal, and their hair was red, and they began to eat grass.

Then the Thamudites exclaimed, "He is a magician!" and they would not believe in him.

The camel went to the perpetual fountain, and she drank it up, so that from that day forward from their spring they could get no water, and they suffered from thirst.

The Thamudites went to Saleh and said, "We need water!"

Saleh replied, "The fountain shall flow one day for you, and one day for the camel."

So it was agreed that the camel should drink alternate days with the people of the land, and that alternate days each should be without water whilst the other was drinking.

Then Saleh said, for he saw that the people hated the camel and her foal, "Beware that you slay not these animals for the day that they perish, great shall be your punishment.'

The she-camel lived thirty years among the Thamudites, but God revealed to Saleh that they were bent on slaying the camel, and he said, "The slayer will be a child with red hair and blue eyes."

Now the Thamudites ordered ten midwives to attend on the women in their confinement, and if a child were born with the signs indicated by the prophet, it was to be destroyed instantly.

Nine children had thus been killed, and the parents conceived a deadly animosity against Saleh the prophet, and formed a design to slay him.

One of the chiefs among the Thamudites had a son born to him with red hair and blue eyes, and the nurses would have destroyed it, but the nine men spake to the father of the child, and they banded together, and saved the infant.

Now when this child had attained the age of eleven, he became great and handsome; and each of the parents whose children had been put to death, when he saw him, said, "Such an one would have been my son, had not he been slain at the instigation of Saleh." And they combined to put the prophet to death. They said among themselves, "We will kill him outside the city, and returning, say we were elsewhere when he was murdered."

Having formed this project, they left the city and placed themselves under a rock, awaiting his exit from the gates

But God commanded the rock, and it fell and crushed them all.

Next day their corpses were recovered, but the Thamudites were very wroth, and said, " Saleh has slain our children, and now he slays our men ; " and they added, " We will be revenged on his camel."

But no one could be found to undertake the execution of this deed, save the red-haired child. He went to the fountain where the camel was drinking, and with one kick he knocked her over, and with another kick he despatched her.

But the foal, seeing the fate of her mother, ran away, and the boy with the red hair and blue eyes ran after her.

Saleh, seeing what had taken place, cried, " The judgment of God is about to fall."

The people were frightened, and asked, " What shall we do ? "

" The judgment of God will not fall as long as the colt remains among you."

Hearing this, the whole population went in pursuit of the young camel. Now it had fled to the mountain whence it had sprung, and the red-haired boy was close on its heels. And when the young camel heard the shouting of the inhabitants of the city, and saw the multitude in pursuit, it stood before the rock, turned round, uttered three piercing cries and vanished.

The Thamudites arrived and beat the rock, but they could not open it. Then said Saleh, "'The judgment of God will fall ; prepare to receive it. The first day your faces will become livid, the second day they will become black, and the third day red."

Things happened as Saleh had predicted. And when the signs befel them which Saleh had foretold, they knew that their end was near. The first day they became ash pale, the second day coal black, and the third day red as fire, and then there came a sound from heaven, and all fell dead on the earth, save Saleh and those who believed in him ; these heard the sound, but did not perish.

By the will of God, when the people were destroyed, one man was absent at Mecca ; the name of this man was Abou-Ghalib. When he knew what had befallen his nation, he took up his residence in Mecca ; but all the rest perished, as it is written in the Koran, " In the morning they were found dead in their houses, stretched upon the ground, as though they had never dwelt there."

From Saleh to Abraham there was no prophet. At the time of that patriarch there was no king over all the earth. The sovereignty had passed to Canaan, the son of Cush, the son of Ham, who was the son of Noah. [1]

The camel of the prophet Saleh was placed by Mohammed in the heavens, together with the ass of Balaam, and other favored animals.

Now wonderful as is this story, it is surpassed by that related by certain Arabic historians of the mission of Saleh. This we proceed to give.

Djundu Ibn Omar was king of the Thamudites, a people numbering seventy thousand fighting men. He had a palace cut out of the face of a rock, and his high priest, Kanuch Ibn Abid, had one likewise. The most magnificent building in the city was a temple which contained the idol worshipped by the people. This idol had the head of a man, the neck of a bull, the body of a lion, and the feet of a horse. It was fashioned out of pure gold, and was studded with jewels.

One day, as Kanuch, the high priest, was worshipping in the temple, he fell asleep, and heard a voice cry, " The truth will appear, and the madness will pass away." He started to his feet in alarm, and saw the idol prostrate on the floor, and its crown had fallen from its head.

Kanuch cried out for assistance, and fled to the king, who sent men to set up the image, and replace on its head the crown that had fallen from it.

But doubt took possession of the heart of Kanuch ; he no longer addressed the image in prayer, and his enthusiasm was at an end. The king observed this, and sent two vizirs with orders to imprison and execute him. But Allah struck the vizirs with blindness, and he sent two angels to transport Kanuch to a well-shaded grotto, well supplied with all that could content the heart of man.

As Kanuch was nowhere to be found, the king appointed his kinsman Davud to be high priest. But on the third day he came to the king to announce to him that the idol was again prostrate.

The monarch set it up once more, and Eblis, entering the

[1] Tabari, i. c. xlv.

image, spoke through its mouth, exhorting all men to beware of novel doctrines which were about to be introduced.

Next feast-day Davud was about to sacrifice two oxen to the idol, when one of them opened its mouth, and thus addressed him :—

"Will you sacrifice creatures endued with life by the living God to a mass of lifeless metal? O God, do thou destroy this sinful nation!" And the oxen broke their halters, and ran away.

Horsemen were deputed to pursue and capture them, but they escaped, for Allah screened them.

But God in his mercy resolved to give the Thamudites another chance of repenting of their idolatry.

Raghwah, Kanuch's wife, had shed incessant tears since the disappearance of her husband. Allah despatched a bird out of Paradise to guide her to the grotto of Kanuch.

This bird was a raven; its head was white as snow, its back was green as emerald. Its feet were purple; its beak of heaven's blue. Its eyes were gems; only its body was black, for this bird did not fall under the curse of Noah, as it was in Paradise.

It was midnight when the raven entered Raghwah's dark chamber, where she lay weeping on a carpet; but the glory of its eyes illumined the whole room, as though the sun had suddenly flashed into it. Raghwah rose from her place, and gazed in wonder on the lovely bird, which opened its beak and said, "Arise and follow me! God has seen thy tears, and will reunite thee to thy husband."

Raghwah followed the raven, which flew before her, and with the light of its eyes turned the night into day. The morning star had not risen, when they stood before Kanuch's grot. Then cried the raven, "Kanuch, open to thy wife!" and so vanished.

Nine months after that Raghwah had rejoined her husband, she bore him a son, who was the image of Seth, and had on his brow the prophetic light; and Kanuch, in the hope of drawing him to the knowledge of the true God and to a pious life, gave him the name of Saleh (The Blessed).

Not long after Saleh's birth, Kanuch died; and the raven of Paradise returned to the grotto to lead back Saleh to his own people.

Saleh grew in beauty and strength, to the admiration of his mother and all who saw him.

A war was being waged between the descendants of Ham and the Thamudites, and the latter had lost many battles and a large portion of their army, when Saleh suddenly appeared in the battle-field at the head of a few friends, and, by his personal heroism, turned the tide of victory, and routed the enemy.

This success drew upon him the gratitude and love of the people, but the envy of the king was kindled, and he sought the life of the young prophet. But as often as assassins were sent by the king to take his life, their arms shrivelled up, and were only restored by the intercession of Saleh. These circumstances tended to increase and confirm the number of his adherents, so that he was able to build a mosque, and occupy with worshippers of the true God one whole quarter of the city.

But one day the king surrounded the mosque with his troops, and threatened Saleh and his followers with death if they would not work a miracle to prove their worship to be the true one.

Saleh prayed, and instantly the leaves of the date-tree that stood before the mosque were transformed into serpents and scorpions, which fell over the king and his soldiers; whilst two doves, which dwelt on the terrace of the mosque, sang aloud, " Believe in Saleh, he is a prophet and messenger of God ! "

But Saleh was moved with compassion when he saw the anguish of those who had been bitten by the scorpions and vipers, and he prayed to God, and the noxious reptiles were transformed back again into date-leaves, and those who had been stung were made whole. Nevertheless the king hardened his heart, and continued to worship false gods.

When Saleh saw the impenitence of the Thamudites, he besought God to destroy them ; but an angel appeared to him in a cave, and sent him to sleep for twenty years.

When he awoke he betook himself towards the mosque he had built, never doubting that he had slept but a single night. The mosque was gone, his friends and adherents were dead or dispersed, a few remained, but they were old, and he hardly recognized them. Falling into despair, the angel Gabriel came to him and said,—

"Thou wert hasty in desiring the destruction of this people, therefore God hath withdrawn from thy life twenty years, which He has taken from thee in sleep. Now He sends thee precious relics wherewith to establish thy mission, to wit, Adam's shirt, Abel's sandals, Seth's overcoat, Enoch's seal ring, Noah's sword, and Hud's staff."

Next day, as the king Djundu with his brother Schihab, and the priests and the princes of the people formed a procession to an idol temple near the town, Saleh ran before the procession entered the temple, and stood in the door.

"Who art thou?" asked the king in astonishment: for he did not recognize Saleh, so greatly had God changed him in his sleep of twenty years.

He answered: "I am Saleh, the messenger of the only God, who preached to you twenty years ago, and showed to you many signs and wonders, but you would not believe. And now once more I appear unto you to give you a proof of my mission. Ask what miracle I shall perform and it shall be done."

Then the king said, "Bring me here out of the rock a camel one hundred ells long, of every color under the sun, whose eyes are like lightning, and whose feet are swifter than the wind."

Saleh consented. Then said Davud, "Let its fore feet be golden and its hinder feet silver, its head of emerald and its ears of ruby. Let it bear on its hump a tent of silver, woven with gold threads and adorned with pearls, resting on four pillars of diamonds!"

When Saleh agreed to this also, the king added, "And let it bring with it a foal like to its mother, just born, and running by her side; then will I believe in Allah, and in thee as His prophet."

"And wilt thou believe too?" asked Saleh of the high priest.

"Yes," answered Davud, "if she give milk without being milked, cold in summer and warm in winter."

"And one thing more," threw in the king's brother, Schihab, "the milk must heal the sick, enrich the poor, and the camel must of its own accord go into every house, and fill the pails with milk."

"Be it according to your will," said Saleh. But I warn you,—no one must injure the camel, deprive it of its food or drink, attempt to ride it, or use it for any other kind of labor."

When they consented, Saleh prayed to God, and the earth opened under his feet and a well of fragrant water gushed up, and poured over the rock, and the rock was rent, and the camel started forth in every particular such as the king and his high priest had desired. So they cried, " There is no God but God, and Saleh is his prophet."

Then the angel Gabriel came down from heaven, having in his hand a flaming sword, wherewith he touched the camel, and she bore instantly a foal like her parent.

Then the king fell on Saleh's neck, and kissed him and believed. But his brother Schihab and Davud attributed all that had been done to magic, and they labored to convince the people that the camel was the work of necromancy.

But as daily the camel gave her milk, and, whenever she drank, said her grace with formality, the number of true believers increased daily, and the high priest and all the chiefs of the infidels resolved on her destruction. Schihab, the king's brother, hoping to overturn the king and take his place, by adhering to the established religion and ignoring all novelties, was resolute in his resistance to the true religion. Therefore he promised his daughter Rajan in marriage to whosoever should kill the wondrous camel.

Now there was a young man of humble origin, named Kaddar, who had long loved the maiden, but had never ventured to show his passion ; he armed himself with a great sword and attacked the camel as it was drinking, in the rear, and wounded it in the hock.

Instantly all nature uttered a piercing cry. Then the youth, filled with compunction, ran to the top of a mountain, and cried, " God's curse on you, ye sinful people ! "

Saleh betook himself with the king, who would not be separated from him, into the town, and demanded the punishment of Kaddar and his accomplices. But Schihab, who in the ,mean time had seized on the throne, threatened them with death, and Saleh, obliged to fly to save his life, had only time to speak his threat, " Three days are given you for repentance ; after that ye shall be slain."

Next day every man's face was yellow as the leaves in autumn, and wherever the wounded camel limped a spring of blood bubbled out of the soil.

On the second day the faces of all were blood-red, and on the third they were coal-black.

Towards evening the camel spread a pair of scarlet wings and flew away, and then mountains of fire were rained from heaven on the city, by the hands of angels ; and the keepers of the fire beneath the earth opened vents, and blew fire from below in the form of flaming camels.

When the sun went down, all that remained of the Thamudites was a heap of ashes.

Saleh alone, and the king Djundu, were saved.[1]

XXIII.

THE TOWER OF BABEL.

FIRST we will take Jewish traditions, and then Mahommedan legends.   The Rabbis relate as follows :—

After the times of the great Deluge, men feared a recurrence of that great overthrow, and they assembled on and inhabited the plain of Shinar.   There, they no longer obeyed the gentle guidance of Shem, the son of Noah ; but they cast the kingdom of God far from them, and choose as their sovereign, Nimrod, son of Cush, son of Ham.[2]   Nimrod became very great in power.   Having been born when his father was old, he was dearly beloved, and every whim had been gratified.   Cush gave him the garment which God made for Adam when he was expelled from Paradise, and which Adam had given to Enoch, and Enoch to Methuselah, and Methuselah had left to Noah, and which Noah had taken with him into the ark.   Ham stole it from his father in the ark, concealed it, and gave it to his son Cush.   Nimrod, vested in this garment, was unconquerable and irresistible.[3]   All beasts and birds fell down before him, and his enemies were overcome almost without a struggle.

It was thus that he triumphed over the king of Babylon. His kingdom rapidly extended, and he became daily more powerful, till at last he was sole monarch over the whole world.[4]

Nimrod rejected God as his ruler ; he trusted in his own might, therefore it is said of him, " He was mighty in hunting, and in sin before the Lord ; for he was a hunter of the sons of men in their languages.   And he said to them, Leave the judgments of Shem, and adhere to the judgments of Nimrod."[5]

[1] Weil, pp. 48–61 ; Abulfeda, p. 21.
[2] Pirke of Rabbi Eliezer, c. xi.   [3] Ibid., c. xxiv.   [4] Ibid., c. xi.
[5] Targums, ed. Etheridge, i. p. 187.

But Nimrod was uneasy in his mind, and he feared lest some one should arise who would be empowered by God to overthrow him; therefore he said to his subjects, "Come, let us build a great city, and let us settle therein, that we may not be scattered over the face of the earth, and be destroyed once more by a flood. And in the midst of our city let us build a high tower, so lofty as to overtop any flood, and so strong as to resist any fire. Yea, let us do further, let us prop up the heaven on all sides from the top of the tower, that it may not again fall and inundate us. Then let us climb up into heaven, and break it up with axes, and drain its water away where it can do no injury. Thus shall we avenge the death of our ancestors. And at the summit of our tower we will place an image of our god with a sword in his hand, and he shall fight for us. Thus shall we obtain a great name, and reign over the universe."

Even if all were not inspired with the same presumption, yet all saw in the tower a means of refuge from a future deluge; and therefore they readily fell in with the proposal of the king. Six hundred thousand men were set to work under a thousand captains, and raised the tower to the height of seventy miles (*i. e.*, fifty-six English miles). A great flight of stairs on the east side was used by those carrying up material, and a flight on the west side served those who descended, having deposited their burdens. If a workman fell down and was killed, no one heeded; but if any of the bricks gave way, there was an outcry. Some shot arrows into the sky, and they came down tinged with blood, then they shouted and cried, "See, we have killed every one who is in heaven."[1] Curiously enough a similar story is told by the Chinese of one of their earlier monarchs, who thought himself so great that he might war against heaven. He shot an arrow into the sky, and a drop of blood fell. "So," said he, "I have killed God!"

At this time Abraham was forty-eight. He was filled with grief and shame at the impiety of his fellow-men, and he prayed to God, "*O Lord! confound their tongues, for I have spied unrighteousness and strife in the city!*"

Then the Lord called the seventy angels who surround His throne, that they should confuse the language of the builders, so that none should understand the other.

[1] Bechaji, Comm. in 1 Mos. xi.; Pirke of R. Eliezer, c. xi.; Talmud Sanhedrim, 109a; Targums, i. pp. 189–90, etc.

The angels came down, and cast confusion among the subjects of Nimrod, and seventy distinct languages sprang up, and
the men could not understand each other ; so they separated
from one another, and were spread over the surface of the earth.
The tower itself was destroyed in part.   It was in three portions : the upper story was destroyed by fire from heaven, the
basement was overthrown by an earthquake, only the middle
story was left intact,—how, we are not informed.[1]

We will now take the Mussulman tradition.   Nimrod, who,
according to the Arabs, was the son of Canaan, and brother of
Cush, sons of Ham, having cast Abraham, who refused to acknowledge him as supreme monarch of the world, into a burning, fiery furnace, from which he issued unhurt, said to his
courtiers, " I will go to heaven and see this God whom Abraham preaches, and who protects him."

His wise men having represented to him that heaven is
very high, Nimrod ordered the erection of a tower, by which
he might reach it.   For three years an immense multitude of
workmen toiled at the erection of this tower.   Every day Nimrod ascended it and looked up, but the sky seemed to him as
distant from the summit of his tower as it had from the level
ground.

One morning he found his tower cast down.   But Nimrod
was not to be defeated so easily.   He ordered a firmer founda-
tion to be laid, and a second tower was constructed ; but however high it was built, the sky remained inaccessible.   Then
Nimrod resolved on reaching heaven in another fashion.   He
had a large box made, and to the four corners he attached gigantic birds of the species Roc.   They bore Nimrod high into
the air, and then fluttered here and fluttered there, and finally
upset the box, and tumbled him on the top of a mountain,
which he cracked by his fall, without however materially injuring himself.

But Nimrod was not penitent, nor ready to submit to the
Most High, therefore God confounded the language of his
subjects, and thus rent from him a large portion of his kingdom.[2]

God sent a wind, says Abulfaraj, which overthrew the Tower
of Babel and buried Nimrod under its ruins.[3]

---

[1] Talmud, Sanhedrim ; see also the history of Nimrod in Yaschar, pp
1107–8.   [2] Herbelot, s. v. Nimroud.
[3] Hist. Dynast., p. 12.

Of Babel we find fewer traditions preserved amongst the ancient nations, than we did of the Deluge.

The Zendavesta makes no mention of such an event; and it is equally unknown to the Chinese books, though curiously enough, in Chinese hieroglyphics, the *tower* is the symbol of *separation*.[1]

The Chaldeans, however, says Abydessus, probably quoting Berosus, the priest of Bel, related, " That the first inhabitants of the earth, glorying in their own strength and size, and despising the gods, undertook to raise a tower whose top should reach the sky in the place where Babylon now stands; but when it approached the heavens, the winds assisted the gods, and overthrew the work of the contrivers; and its ruins are said to be still in Babylon; and the gods introduced a diversity of tongues among men, who till that time had all spoken the same language; and a war arose between Kronos and Titan. The place on which they built the tower is now called Babylon."[2]

Alexander Polyhistor relates the events as follows, and quotes the Sibyl. " The Sibyl says, when all men had one speech, they built a great tower in order to climb into heaven, but the gods blowing against it with the winds, threw it down, and confounded the language of the builders, therefore the city is called Babylon."[3] The writings of this Sibyl, commonly called the Chaldean Sibyl, formed part of the sacred scriptures of the Babylonians. Eupolemus, quoting apparently Syro-phœnician traditions, relates the matter somewhat differently. " The city Babylon," says he, " was built after the Deluge by those who were saved. But they were giants, and they built the famous tower then. But when this was overthrown by the will of the gods, the giants were scattered over the whole face of the earth."[4] The Armenian tradition recorded by Moses of Chorene, is to this effect: " From them (*i. e.*, from the first dwellers on the earth) sprang the race of the giants, with strong bodies and of huge size. Full of pride and envy, they formed the godless resolve to build a high tower. But whilst they were engaged on the undertaking, a fearful wind overthrew it, which the wrath of God had sent against it, and un-

---

[1] Mémoires conc. les Chinois, i. p. 213.
[2] Euseb., Præp. Ev., ix. 14 ; Cory, Ancient Fragments, pp. 34–50.
[3] George Syncellus, Bibl. Græc., v. p. 178.
[4] Euseb., Præp. Ev., ix. 17.

known words were at the same time blown about among men, wherefore arose strife and contention." [1]

The Hindu story of the confusion of tongues and the separation of nations is not connected with the erection of a tower, but with the pride of the Tree of Knowledge, or the world tree. This tree grew in the centre of the earth, and its head was in heaven. It said in its heart, I shall hold my head in heaven, and spread my branches over all the earth, and gather all men together under my shadow and protect them, and prevent them from separating. But Brahm, to punish the pride of the tree, cut off its branches and cast them down on the earth, where they sprang up as Wata trees, and made differences of belief and speech and customs to prevail in the earth, to disperse men over its surface. [2]

The Dutch traveller, Hamel van Gorcum, found a tradition of the Tower of Babel, in the seventeenth century, in the Korea, in the midst of a sect which had not adopted Buddhism, but which retained much of the old primitive Schamanism of the race. They said, "That formerly all men spake the same language, but, after building a great tower, wherewith they attempted to invade heaven, they fell into confusion of tongues." [3]

The Mexican story was, that after the Deluge the sole survivors Coxcox and Chichequetzl engendered many children who were born dumb, but one day received the gift of speech from a dove, which came and perched itself on a lofty tree: but the dove did not communicate to them the same language, so they separated in fifteen companies. And Gemelli Carrer. and Clavigero describe an ancient Mexican painting represent ing the dove with thirty-three tongues, answering to the languages and dialects he taught. [4]

At Cholula they related that Xelhuaz began to build a tower on Mount Tlalok to commemorate his having been saved along with his brothers from the Flood. And the tower he built in the form of a pyramid. The clay was baked into bricks in the province of Tlamanalco, at the foot of the Sierra Cocotl, and to bring them to Cholula a row of men was placed, that the bricks might be passed from hand to hand. The gods

[1] Mos. Chorene, i. 9.
[2] Müller, Glauben u. Wissen. d. Hindus ; Mainz, 1822, i. p. 303.
[3] Allgem. Hist. d. Reisen, vi. p. 602.
[4] Lüken, p. 287 ; Amerikanische Urreligionen, p. 517, etc.

saw this building, whose top reached the clouds, with anger
and dismay, and sent fire from heaven, and destroyed the
tower.[1]

XXIV.

ABRAHAM.[2]

I. HIS YOUTH AND EARLY STRUGGLES.

ABRAHAM or Abram, as he was first called, was the son of
Terah, general of Nimrod's army, and Amtelai, daughter of
Carnebo. He was born at Ur of the Chaldees, in the year
1948 after the Creation.

On the night on which Abraham was born, Terah's friends,
amongst whom were many councillors and soothsayers of Nimrod, were feasting in the house. On leaving, late at night, they
observed an unusual star in the east; it seemed to run from
one quarter of the heavens to another, and to devour four stars
which were there. All gazed in astonishment on this wondrous
sight. "Truly," said they, "this can signify nothing else but
that Terah's new-born son will become great and powerful, will
conquer the whole realm, and dethrone great princes, and seize
on their possessions."

Next morning they hastened to the king, to announce to him
what they had seen, and what was their interpretation of the
vision, and to advise the slaughter of the young child, and that
Terah should be compensated with a liberal sum of money.

Nimrod accordingly sent gold and silver to Terah, and asked
his son in exchange, but Terah refused. Then the king sent
and threatened to burn down and utterly destroy the whole
house of Terah, unless the child were surrendered. In the
mean time one of the female slaves had born a son; this Terah
gave to the royal officers, who, supposing it to be the son of the
householder, brought it before Nimrod and slew it.

Then, to secure Abraham, Terah concealed him and his
mother and nurse in a cave.

[1] Humboldt, Ansichten d. Cordilleren, i. p. 42.
[2] For the Rabbinic traditions relating to Abraham I am indebted to
the exhaustive monograph of Dr. B. Beer. "Leben Abraham's nach Auffassung der jüdischen Sage," Leipzig, 1859, to which I must refer my readers
for references to Jewish books, which are given with an exactitude which
leaves nothing to be desired.

But there is another version of the story, and it is as follows :—

Nimrod had long read in the stars that a child would be
born who would oppose his power and his religion, and would
finally overcome both.

Acting on the advice of his wise men, he built a house, sixty
ells high and eighty ells broad, into which all pregnant women
were brought to be delivered, and the nurses were instructed to
put to death all the boys that were born, but to make handsome
presents to the mothers who were brought to bed of daughters.

After seventy thousand male children had thus perished,
the angels of heaven turned to the All Mighty, and besought
Him with tears to stay this cruel murder of innocents.

"I slumber not, I sleep not," God answered. "Ye shall
see that this atrocity shall not pass unpunished."

Shortly after, Terah's wife was pregnant; she concealed
her situation as long as was possible, pretending that she was
ill; but when she could conceal it no more, the infant crept
behind her breasts, so that she appeared to every eye as if nothing were about to take place.

When the time came for her delivery, she went in fear out
of the city, and wandered in the desert till she lighted on a
cave, into which she entered.   Next morning she was delivered
of a son, Abraham, whose face shone, so that the grotto was
as light as though the sun were casting a golden beam into it.
She wrapped the child in a mantle, and left it there to the custody of God and His angels, and returned home.   God heard
the cry of the weeping infant, and He sent His angel Gabriel
to the cave, who let the child suck milk out of his fore-finger.
But according to another account he opened two holes in the
cave, from which dropped oil and flour to nourish Abraham.
Others, however, say that Terah visited the cave every day, and
nursed and fed the child.

According to the Arab tradition, which follows the Jewish
in most particulars, the mother, on visiting the cave, found the
infant sucking its two thumbs.   Now out of one of its thumbs
flowed milk, and out of the other, honey, and thus the babe
nourished itself: or, say others, from one finger flowed water
when he sucked it; from a second, milk; from a third, honey;
from a fourth, the juice of dates; and from the little finger,
butter.[1]

[1] Weil, p. 69.

When Abraham had been in the cave, according to some, three years, according to others ten, and according to others thirteen, he left the cavern and stood on the face of the desert. And when he saw the sun shining in all its glory, he was filled with wonder, and he thought, "Surely the sun is God the Creator!" and he knelt down and worshipped the sun. But when evening came, the sun went down in the west, and Abraham said, "No! the Author of creation cannot set." Now the moon arose in the east, and the stars looked out of the firmament. Then said Abraham, "This moon must indeed be God, and all the stars are His host!" And kneeling down he adored the moon.

But after some hours of darkness the moon set, and from the east appeared once more the bright face of the sun. Then said Abraham, "Verily these heavenly bodies are no gods, for they obey law: I will worship Him who imposed the law upon them."

The Arab story is this. When Abraham came out of the cave, he saw a number of flocks and herds, and he said to his mother, "Who is lord of these?" She answered, "Your father Azar (Terah)." "And who is the lord of Azar?" he further asked. She replied, "Nimrod." "And who is the lord of Nimrod?" "Oh, hush, my son," said she, striking him on the mouth; "you must not push your questions so far." But it was by following this train of thought that Abraham arrived at the knowledge of the one true God.

Another Rabbinical story is, that Abraham was only ten days in the cave after his birth, and then he was able to walk, and he left it. But his mother, who visited the grotto, finding him gone, was a prey to anguish and fear.

Wandering along the bank of the river, searching for her child, she met Abraham, but did not recognize him, as he had grown tall; and she asked him if he had seen a little baby anywhere.

"I am he whom you seek," answered Abraham.

"Is this possible!" exclaimed the mother. "Could you grow to such a height, and be able to walk and talk, in ten days?"

"Yes, mother," answered the youthful prodigy; "all this has taken place that you might know that there is but one living and true God who made heaven and earth, who dwells in heaven and fills the earth with His goodness."

"What!" asked Amtelai, "is there another god besides Nimrod?"

"By all means," replied the infant son; "there is a God in heaven, who is also the God who made Nimrod. Now go to Nimrod and announce this to him."

Abraham's mother related all this to her husband, who bore the message to the king. Nimrod, greatly alarmed, consulted his council what was to be done with the boy.[1]

The council replied that he had nothing to fear from an infant of ten days,—he, the king and god of the world! But Nimrod was not satisfied. Then Satan, putting on a black robe, mingled with the advisers of the monarch and said, "Let the king open his arsenal, arm all his troops, and march against this precocious infant. This advice fell in completely with Nimrod's own personal fears, and his army was marched against the baby. But when Abraham saw the host drawn up in battle array, he cried to heaven with many tears, and Gabriel came to his succor, enveloped the infant in clouds, and snatched him from the sight of those who came against him; and they, frightened at the cloud and darkness, fled precipitately to Babylon.

Abraham followed them on the shoulders of Gabriel, and reaching the gates of the city in an instant of time, he cried, "The eternal One is the true and only God, and none other is like Him! He is the God of heaven, God of gods and Lord of Nimrod! Be convinced of this, all ye men, women and children who dwell here, even I am Abraham, his servant." Then he sought his parents, and bade Terah go and fulfil his command to Nimrod.

Terah went accordingly, and announced to the king that his son, whom the army had been unable to capture, had, in a brief space of time, traversed a country across which was forty days' journey.

Nimrod quaked, and consulted his princes, who advised him to institute a festival of seven days, during which every subject and dweller on the face of the earth was to make a pilgrimage to his palace, and there to worship and adore him.

In the mean time Nimrod, being very curious to see Abraham,

---

[1] The Mussulman history of the patriarch relates that Azar brought Abraham before Nimrod and said, "This is thy God who made all things." "Then why did he not make himself less ugly?" asked Abraham,—for Nimrod had bad features.

ordered Terah to bring him into his royal presence. The child
entered the throne-room boldly, and going to the foot of the
steps which led to the throne, he exclaimed; " Woe to thee,
accursed Nimrod, blasphemer of God! Acknowledge, O
Nimrod, that the true God is without body, everlasting, never
·slumbering nor sleeping; acknowledge that He created the
world, that all men may believe in Him likewise!"

At the same moment all the idols in the palace fell, and
the king rolled from his throne in convulsions, and remained
in a fit for two hours.

When he came to himself again, he said to Abraham, "Was
that thy voice, or was it the voice of God?"

Abraham answered, "It was the voice of the meanest of
His creatures."

"Then your God must be great and mighty, and a King
of kings."

Nimrod now suffered Abraham to depart, and as his anger was abated, the child remained in his father's house, and
no attempts were made against his life.

Here must be inserted a legend of the childhood of Abraham, which I have ventured to render into verse.

THE GIFT OF THE KING.

Nimrod the Cushite sat upon a throne
Of gold, encrusted with a sapphire stone,
And round the monarch stood, in triple rank,
Three hundred ruddy pages, like a bank
    Of roses all a-blow,
Two gentle boys, with blue eyes clear as glass,
And locks as light as tufted cotton grass,
    And faces as the snow
That lies on Ararat, and flushes pink
On summer evenings, as the sun doth sink,
Were stationed by the royal golden chair
With fillets of carnation in their hair,
And clothed in silken vesture, candid, clean,
To flutter fans of burnished blue and green,
    Fashioned of peacock's plume.
A little lower, on a second stage
On either side, was placed a graceful page,
    To raise a fragrant fume—
With costly woods and gums on burning coals
That glowed on tripods, in bright silver bowls;
And at the basement of the marble stair,
Sweet singing choirs and harping minstrels were,
In amber kirtles purple gilt and sashed.

7*

The throbbing strings in silver ripples flashed,
    Where slaves the choral song
Accompanied with psaltery and lyre,
In red and saffron, like to men of fire,
    Whilst hoarsely boomed the gong:
Or silver cymbals clashed, or, waxing shrill,
Danced up the scale a flute's melodious thrilL

Now at the monarch's signal, pages twain,
With sunny hair as ripened autumn grain,
And robed in lustrous silver tissue, shot
With changing hues of blue forget-me-not,
    Start nimbly forth, and bend
Before the monarch, at his gilded stool,
And crystal goblets brimming, sweet and cool,
    Obsequiously extend ;
But Nimrod, slightly stirring, stately, calm,
Towards the right-hand beaker thrusts his arm,
And languid, raises it towards his lips ;
Yet ere he of the ruby liquor sips,
He notices upon the surface lie—
Fallen in and fluttering—a feeble fly,
    With draggled wings outspread.
Then shot from Nimrod's eyes an angry flare,
And passionately down the marble stair
    The costly draught he shed.
He spoke no word, but with a finger wave,
Made signal to a scarlet-vested slave ;
And as the lad before him, quaking, kneels,
Above him swift the gleaming falchion wheels,
Then flashes down, and, with one leap, his head
Bounds from his shoulders, and bespirts with red
    The alabaster floor.
And, mingled with the outpoured Persian wine,
Descends the steps a sliding purple line
    Of smoking, dribbled gore ;
And floats the little midge upon a flood
Of fragrant grape-juice, and of roseate blood.

Then Nimrod said : " I would you ugly stain
Were wiped away ; and thou, my chamberlain,
Obtain for me a stripling, to replace
This petty fool.   Let him have comely face,
    And be of slender mould :
Be lithely built, of noble birth ; a youth,
The choicest thou canst find.   His cost, in sooth !
    I heed not.   Stint no gold,
But buy a goodly slave : for I, a king,
Will have the best, the best of every thing—
Of gems, of slaves, of fabrics, meats, or wine ;
The best, the very best on earth be mine."

Then, prostrate flung before his master's throne,
The servant said, "Sire ! Terah hath a son
Whose equal in the whole round world is none,
    Beloved as himself.
But, Sire ! I fear the father will not deign
To yield his son as slave through love of gain,
    For great is he in wealth."
"Go !" said the monarch, " I must have the child:
Be sure the father can be reconciled,
If you expend of gold a goodly store,
And, if he haggles at your price, bid more ;
    I will it, chamberlain !
I care not what the cost.   I'll have the lad ! "
And then, he leaned him idly back, and **bade**
    The slaves to fan again.

Now on the morrow, to the royal court,
Terah Ben-Nahor from old Ur was brought—
Protesting loud he would not yield his son
As slave, at any price, to any one.
    " My flesh and blood be sold !
Fie on you !   Do you reckon that I prize
My first-begotten as mere merchandise,
    To barter him for gold !
A curse on him who would the old man's **stay,**
That bears him up, with money buy away !
Require me not to offer child of mine
To serve and brim a tyrant's cup with wine ;
To waste a life from morning to its grave,
Branded in mind and soul and body ' Slave !'
    How could I be repaid?
His artless fondlings, all his childish ways :
The reminiscences of olden days,
    That sudden flash and fade,
Of her who bore him—her, my boyhood's choice—
Resemblances in feature, figure, voice,
In gesture, manner, ay ! in very tone
Of pealing laugh, of that dear partner gone?
Thou, Nimrod, to an old man condescend
To hear his story ; your attention lend,
    And judge if acted well.
Last year to me thou gav'st a goodly steed,
From thine own stud, of purest Yemen **breed:**
    And thus it me befel.
A stranger offered me a price so fair
That I accepted it, and sold the mare."
" My gift disposed of !" with an angry start,
King Nimrod thundered : " Thou, old man, shalt **smart**
For this thy avarice. A royal gift,
Thou knowest well, must never owners shift,
    As thing of little worth.

> Then Terah raised his trembling hands, and said,
> "From thine own mouth, O King has judgment sped.
>   The Lord of Heaven and Earth,
> The King of Kings to me my offspring gave,
> And shall I sell His gift to be a slave?
> Nimrod! that child, which is His royal gift,—
> Thy mouth hath said it,—may not owners shift."

At this time idolatry was commonly practised by all. Nimrod and his servants Terah and his whole house worshipped images of wood and stone. Terah had not only twelve idols of the twelve months which he adored, but he manufactured images and sold them.

One day, when Terah was absent, and Abraham was left to manage the shop, he thought the time had come when he must make his protest against idolatry. This he did as follows. Every purchaser who came, was asked by Abraham his age; if he answered fifty or sixty years old, Abraham exclaimed, "Woe to a man of such an age who adores the work of one day!" and the purchaser withdrew in shame.

Another version of the incident is more full.

A strong, lusty fellow came one day to buy an idol, the strongest that there was. As he was going away with it, Abraham called after him, "How old are you?"

"Seventy years," he answered.

"Oh, you fool!" said Abraham, "to adore a god younger than yourself."

"What do you mean?" asked the purchaser.

"Why, you were born seventy years ago, and this god was made only yesterday."

Hearing this, the buyer threw the idol away.

Shortly after, an old woman brought a dish of meal to set before the idols. Abraham took it, and then with a stick smashed all the gods except the biggest, into whose hands he placed the stick.

Terah, who was returning home, heard the noise of blows, and quickened his pace. When he entered, his gods were in pieces.

He accused Abraham angrily; but Abraham said, "My father, a woman brought this dish of meal for the gods: they all wanted to have it, and the strongest knocked the heads off the rest, lest they should eat it all." And this, say the

Mussulmans, was the *first* lie that Abraham told, but it was not a lie, but a justifiable falsehood.

Terah said this could not be true, for the images were of wood and stone.

"Let thine ear hear what thy mouth hath spoken," said Abraham, and then he exhorted his father against idolatry.

Terah complained to Nimrod, who sent for Abraham, and he said to him, "Wilt thou not worship these idols? Well, then, adore fire."

"Why not water which quenches fire?" asked Abraham.

Nimrod.—"Very well; then worship water."

Abraham.—"Why not the clouds which swallow the water?"

Nimrod.—"So be it; adore the clouds."

Abraham.—"Rather let me adore wind which blows the clouds about."

Nimrod.—"So be it; pray to the wind."

Abraham.—"But man can stand up against the wind, and build it out of his house."

Then Nimrod in a fury exclaimed, "Fire is my god, and that shall consume you."

According to another version, a woman came to Abraham to buy a god, because thieves had stolen her former god; this gave the patriarch a text for his homily against idolatry. The woman was convinced.

"Believe in the true God," said he, "and you will recover the things the thieves stole from your house."

A few days after, the woman recovered all her lost goods, amongst them her image. Then she took a stone, and smashed its head, saying, "Oh, thou blockhead, not to be able to preserve my property and thyself from thieves!"

The report of what she had said and done reached the king, who ordered her to be executed. But Nimrod was uneasy, and he announced a grand ceremony to last for seven days, during which every one was to produce his gods and carry them about the streets, which were to be hung with gold and silks. His object was to dazzle Abraham's eyes by the splendor of idol worship. He sent for Terah and Abraham, but the latter refused to attend. The Mussulmans say that Abraham excused himself thus: "I see in the stars that I am going to be very sick to-day." This was the *second* lie Abraham told, but it was not a lie, it **was a** justifiable falsehood. Then the king sent his guard, who arrested him and cast him into a dungeon.

He lay in the dungeon ten days. The angel Gabriel brought him food, and a crystal fountain bubbled up through the soil of his cell.

Nimrod called his council together, and it was unanimously decided that Abraham should be burnt alive. The king therefore published a decree ordering every man to bring wood or other fuel for the heating of the kiln.[1] The wood was piled about the furnace to the height of five ells, for a circle of five ells diameter, and for three days and three nights the fire was kept up, and the flames licked the heavens, so that the oven was at a white heat. Then Nimrod ordered his jailer to produce Abraham. The prison-keeper humbly answered, that it was impossible that Abraham could be alive, for he had been given neither meat nor drink. But Nimrod answered, " Produce him alive or dead."

Then the jailer went to the prison door and cried, " Abraham, livest thou ? "

" I live," answered the prisoner, " and am hearty."

" How is that possible? " asked the jailer, astonished.

" Because the Almighty has wrought a miracle on my behalf. He is sole God, invisible, the Creator of the world, and the Lord of Nimrod."

The jailer believed.

The news was conveyed to Nimrod, who ordered the immediate execution of the jailer ; but as the executioner was about to smite off his head, he cried, " The Eternal One is alone the true God of the world, and the God of Nimrod who denies him." And lo ! the sword was blunted, and shivered into a thousand fragments.

Here we must add a few particulars from Mussulman sources.

" Who is your God? " asked Nimrod of Abraham, when brought before him.

" He who kills and makes alive again," said Abraham.

---

[1] The Mussulman story, which is precisely the same as the Jewish, adds that the camels refused to bear wood to form the pyre, but cast it on the ground ; therefore Abraham blessed the camels. But the mules had no compunction, therefore he cursed them that they should be sterile. The birds who flew over the fire were killed, the city was enveloped in its smoke, and the crackling of its flames could be heard a day's journey off.

"I can do that," exclaimed Nimrod, and he ordered two prisoners before him ; one he slew, the other he spared.

But Abraham said, "Behold the power of my God !" and he bade a dead man who had been four years in his grave, rise and bring him a white cock, a black raven, a green pigeon, and a gayly-colored peacock. The dead man rose and obeyed. Then Abraham cut up the birds, but preserved their heads ; and lo ! from the heads new bodies sprouted.

"Now," said Abraham, "do the same."

But Nimrod could not.

"If thou art a God," said Abraham again, "command the sun to rise to-morrow in the west and set in the east."

But this he could not do.[1]

Nimrod was highly incensed, and ordered that Abraham should be at once precipitated into the fire. When he was brought before the king, say the Rabbis, the soothsayers recognized him as the boy at whose birth they had warned the king that one was come into the world who would be the father of a great nation which would subdue that of Nimrod, and would possess the whole earth and heaven.

"This is the man against whom we cautioned you," they said ; "his father Terah must have deceived you, O king, and not have given you up the right child."

Terah, on being questioned, owned the truth.

"Who gave you this advice ?" asked the king ; "confess it, and your life shall be spared."

Out of fear Terah told a lie, and said that Haran, his other son, had suggested the deception.

"For having given this advice," said Nimrod, "Haran shall perish along with Abraham. Cast them both into the flames." Abraham and Haran were now to be stripped and their hands and feet bound by ropes, and then they were to be thrown into the fire. But the servants of Nimrod who approached the brothers were caught by the flames which, like the tongues of serpents, shot out, curled round them, drew them into the fire, and consumed them.

Then Satan appeared to Nimrod, and instructed him how to make a catapult which would throw stones to a distance, and by means of which Abraham and Haran could be projected into the midst of the fire.

[1] Weil, p. 73.

Haran was undecided in his mind whether to worship God or idols; sometimes he sided with Abraham, and sometimes with Terah. Now, the moment Haran was shot into the flames, his heart failed him, and he cried out that he would worship idols if his life were spared. But it was too late, he was burnt to ashes. But Abraham was unharmed. The cords which bound him were consumed, but for three days and nights he walked about in the flames, and felt no inconvenience.[1]

Then the king cried aloud. "Abraham, servant of the God of Heaven, come forth from the furnace to me."

And Abraham came forth. Then the king said to him, "How is it that thou art not consumed?" And Abraham answered, "The Lord God of Heaven and Earth, whom I serve, hath delivered me."

Instantly the flames were extinguished, and the wood burst forth into flower and fruit; and the pile was like a grove of flowering shrubs to look upon, and Angels descended and took Abraham and seated him in the midst.

The Arabic version of this part of the story is something different.

Nimrod could not see into the fire, so he ascended a high tower in his palace, and from the top looked down into the furnace, and saw that in the midst was a garden with flowers and a fountain of sparkling water, and Abraham seated on the grass beside the spring, conversing with an angel.[2]

Nimrod now loaded Abraham with presents, amongst which were two slaves named Oni and Eliezer; according to some, the latter was a son of the tyrant. Many followed Abraham home, and brought their children to him, and said, "Now we see that the God in whom thou trustest, is the only true God; teach our children the truth, that they may serve Him in righteousness." Thus three hundred persons accompanied Abraham home, most of whom were servants of the king, and of noble race.

Here follows in the Mussulman account the story of Nimrod's attempt to reach heaven in a box, to which were attached four vultures. His object was, says Tabari, to kill the God of Abraham. He went up along with his vizir. After a night

---

[1] Both the Rabbinic commentators and the Mussulman historians tell a long story about the discussion carried on between Gabriel and Abraham in the air, as he was being shot into the flames. It is hardly worth repeating.	[2] Tabari, i. p. 147.

and day in the air, the king said to his vizir, "Open the window of the box towards the earth and tell me what you see."
He did so, and replied, "I see the earth." After another day
and night, he again looked out and saw the earth still; on the
third day, at the king's command he looked out and saw nothing. Then said Nimrod, "Open the window towards heaven
and look out." He did so and saw nothing. Then Nimrod
shot three arrows into the sky, and they fell back with blood
on them. So Nimrod said, "I have killed the God of Abraham." But whence the blood came is unsettled. Some say
that the arrows hit a bird which flew higher than the vultures;
but others, with more probability, say they struck a fish, which
was being carried by the wind, that had caught it up with the
rain out of the sea.[1]

Abraham now married the daughter of his brother Haran,
named Sarai or Jisha, "the seeress," because she was endowed with the spirit of prophecy, say some, or, say others, because she was so beautiful that every one wanted to see her.
At the time of his marriage, Abraham was aged fifty; others,
however, suggest twenty-five.

Two years later, Nimrod was visited with a dream. He
saw himself and all his army in a valley, near the furnace into
which he had cast Abraham. A man resembling the latter
stepped out of the furnace and approached the king, holding a
naked sword. When Nimrod recoiled, the man cast an egg at
his head; the egg broke and became a mighty river, which
swept all his hosts away, saving only three men; and on looking at them, the king saw that they wore royal robes, and exactly resembled himself. Then the stream retreated into the
egg, and when all the water was gathered into it, from the egg
hopped out a chicken, which seated itself on Nimrod's head,
and pecked out one of his eyes.

Next morning the king sent for his soothsayers to explain
the dream, and this was their interpretation; "Hear, O king!
this dream presages to thee great misfortune, which Abraham
and his posterity shall bring upon thee. The time will come
when he will war with his forces against thee and thy forces,
and will overcome them and put them to the sword. Thou
alone wilt escape with three of thy confederates; but a messenger of Abraham will cause thy death. Therefore, O king!

---

[1] Weil, p. 78.

remember that thy council of wise men foretold this fifty-two years ago, in the stars at Abraham's birth. As long as Abraham lives thou art in jeopardy. Wherefore could he be suffered to live any longer?"

Nimrod believing what was said, sent a servant to assassinate Abraham. But Eliezer, the slave, whom Nimrod had given to the patriarch, had been with the councillors when this advice was given, and he fled and told Abraham before the emissary of the tyrant arrived ; and Abraham left his house and took refuge with Noah and Shem, and remained hidden with them for the space of one month.

Here Terah sought him in secret ; and Abraham addressed him a long discourse on the vanity of idol-worship and the evil of serving the godless tyrant Nimrod. And Noah and Shem supported him.

Then Terah, who grieved over the death of his son Haran, consented to all that Abraham had said, and he went forth with Abraham and his wife Sarah, and Lot his grandson, the son of Haran, and all his household, and they settled at Charan, where the land was fruitful and well watered. The dwellers in Charan associated themselves with Abraham, who instructed them in the knowledge and fear of the Lord.

2. THE CALL OF ABRAHAM, AND THE VISIT TO EGYPT.

For three years Abraham dwelt in Charan, till God called him to go further with his wife Sarah, and to take up his abode in Canaan ; but Terah and Lot remained at Charan. Abraham reached Canaan and pitched his tent among the inhabitants of that land ; and on the spot where God promised that He would give him all that pleasant country for his inheritance, he erected an altar to the Eternal One.

For fifteen years he had dwelt in Canaan, and Abraham was now aged 70, when, on the 15th day of the first month (Nisan), on the self-same day on which, in after years, the children of Israel went out of Egypt, the voice of God came to him saying, " I am the Lord that brought thee out of the furnace of Chaldæa ; to thee will I give this land to inherit it." And he said, " Lord God, whereby shall I know that I shall inherit it ? Shall my descendants be faithful and true, and serve Thee the living God, or will they rebel against God, against Thee, as did the men before the Flood, and as did the men of Shinar who builded the tower?"

Then God bade him take an heifer of three years old, or a she-goat of three years old, and a ram, and a turtle-dove, and a young pigeon. And he took all these and divided them in the midst, and laid each piece one against another; but the birds divided he not.[1] And God said to him, "When, in after days, thy descendants shall build me a temple, in it shall these five kinds of victims be offered to me.

"But," said Abraham, "should the temple be destroyed, what then shall they do?"

"Then," answered the Most Holy, "They shall offer to me in spirit, and I will pardon their sins." The beasts and birds also signified the races over which his seed was to reign; the beasts he divided, and they betokened the Gentile races, from which they were to purge away their idolatry; but *the birds divided he not;* for the birds signified the elect nation.

Then came ravens and vultures down upon the carcases, but Abraham drove them away (ver. 11); a symbol of the protection which God would accord to the people, for His promise sake, and the sake of their father Abraham, when the powers of evil, or mighty princes, menaced them.

And when the sun was going down, a deep sleep fell upon Abraham (ver. 12), and he saw the four realms,—the horror-awakening Babylonian, Medo-Persian, Syro-Grecian, and Roman empires. And God said to Abraham (ver. 13), "*Know of a surety that thy seed shall be a stranger in a land that is not theirs, and shall serve them; and they shall afflict them four hundred years.* But in the fourth generation thy seed shall come hither again, after I have plagued the nation that has held them in bondage with 250 plagues."

"Is this decree spoken to punish me for my crimes?" asked Abraham.

"No," answered the Almighty: "*Thou shalt go to thy fathers in peace; thou shalt be buried in a good old age* (ver. 15); and Terah, who now bewails his former idolatry, has a share in the eternal happiness; also Ishmael, thy son, who shall be born to thee, will, in thy lifetime, repent and return to good, and the profanity of thy grandson Esau shalt thou not see."

And when the sun was set, it was dark, and the various pe-

---

[1] Gen. xv.

riods of futurity passed before the eyes of the seer. He beheld *a smoking furnace* (ver. **17**) ; this was the flaming Gehinom, Hell, where sinners shall expiate their iniquities. Then he saw *a burning lamp :* that was the Law given on Sinai, and it *passed between those pieces ;* that is, he saw Israel go through the Red Sea.

Then said the voice of God to the patriarch, "I have showed thee the Temple-worship, Law, Bondage, and Hell. I must tell thee that in the times to come, through the sins of thy children, the Temple will be destroyed, and the Law will be dis-regarded.

Choose now, whether thou wilt have for their punishment, Bondage or Hell."

And Abraham after long hesitation answered, "I choose Hell ;" for he thought, "It is better to fall into the hands of God, than into the hands of men."

But the Lord answered and said, " Not so ; thou hast chosen wrongly, for from Bondage there will come deliverance, but from Gehinom, never."

After that, Abraham returned to the land of Charan, and dwelt there many years ; and he instructed the men, and Sarah the women, in the true religion. And when his father Terah was dead, God called him again, and bade him go forth to the land which God had promised him ; and he went obediently, and Lot his brother's son accompanied him.   And he reached the land of Canaan, and pitched first his wife's tent, and then his own, on the plain between Gerizim and Ebal ; and he erected three altars in thanks to God for His call, for His having brought him into the promised land, and for having cast down his enemies before him.   Then he went south, and pitched on the spot where stands Jerusalem.

And now a famine came upon the land ; this was the third famine since the world was formed, and it was sent to prove Abraham.   He murmured not, but went down with Sarah his wife, and his servants.

When he reached the River of Egypt (Wadi el Arisch), Abraham rested some days. As Abraham and Sarah walked together by the water-side, Abraham saw for the first time, reflected in the water, the beauty of Sarah ; for he was so modest that he had never lifted his eyes to her face, and knew not what she was like, till he saw her in the water. Then, when he saw how beautiful she was, he persuaded her to pass as his sister in Egypt, for he feared lest he should be slain for her sake; but as a further precaution he shut her up in a chest.

On the frontier, the Custom-house officers insisted on his paying the customs, due for the box, and required that it should be opened. Abraham offered to pay for the box as if it contained gold dust or gems, if only they would not enforce their right of search.

" Does it contain silk ? " asked the officers.

" I will pay the tenth, as of silk," he answered.

" Does it contain silver ? " they further asked.

" I will pay for it as silver."

" Nay, then it must contain gold."

" I will pay for it as gold."

" Maybe it contains the most rare and costly gems."

" I will pay for it as for gems."

In the altercation the chest was violently broken open, and lo ! in it was seated a beautiful woman, so beautiful that her countenance illumined all Egypt ; and the news reached the ears of Pharaoh. All this occurred in the night of the 15th of the month Nisan.

Abraham and Sarah were sorely troubled, and prayed to God to protect them. Then the angel of the Lord was sent to watch over Sarah, and the angel comforted her with these words, " Fear not ; God has heard thy petitions ! "

Pharaoh asked Sarah who that man was who accompanied her, and when she answered " My brother," Pharaoh bade him to be brought before him, and he gave him rich gifts.

And Pharaoh asked Abraham, " Who is this woman ? " He answered " She is my sister." This say the Mussulmans, is the *third* lie that Abraham told ; but it was not a lie, but a justifiable falsehood.

Pharaoh was filled with love for Sarah, and he offered her as his present for her hand, all his possessions of gold and silver and slaves, and the land of Goshen. And when he pressed his suit upon her with great vehemence, she cried to God and told him she was already married ; then he was smitten with paralysis, and great plagues afflicted all his servants. But Pharaoh sent for Abraham, and returned him Sarah, his wife, and dismissed him with costly presents, and he gave to Sarah also his daughter, Hagar, to be her servant.

" Truly, my daughter, it is better," said Pharaoh, " to be servant in a house which God has taken under His protection, than to command elsewhere."

After a three months' sojourn in Egypt, Abraham returned to Canaan.

According to Tabari, Hager loved Sarah greatly. On their way back to Canaan the provisions failed, and Abraham went out one day to get food, with a sack on his back; but the day was hot, so that he laid down and went to sleep. He did not awake till evening, and then he returned, but was ashamed to appear with the sack empty before his wife, so he filled it with sand. On reaching the tent he put the sack under his head and went to sleep again. Very early in the morning Sarah said to Hagar, " What has Abraham in his sack? open it and look." So Hager untied it, put in her hand and drew out flour. She and Sarah baked cakes of the flour, and woke Abraham and bade him eat. Then, full of wonder, he asked where they had obtained meal. They told him, and he understood that God had wrought a miracle. [1]

Now Abraham's flocks and herds, and those of Lot, pastured together. Abraham's cattle were muzzled that they should not feed in the lands of the neighbouring people; but Lot's cattle were not muzzled. And when Abraham's shepherds complained of this to those of Lot, the latter answered, " Your master is old, and has no children; soon he will die, and then all will belong to our master Lot."

But Abraham spake to Lot and said, " Thy ways and my ways do not agree: we must part; do thou go to the left, and I will go to the right." So they separated; and Lot departed from Abraham, and from the way of righteousness, and from the living God; but Abraham camped in Mamre.

3. THE WAR WITH THE KINGS.

After the failure of the Tower of Babel, and the people had been scattered over the whole earth, Chedorlaomer, one of Nimrod's chief captains, had left his service, and had established a kingdom of his own in Elam. He speedily brought into subjection all the Canaanitish peoples that dwelt in the fertile valley of Jordan,—Sodom, Gomorrah, Admah, Zebojim, and Zoar, and made them tributary to himself. These cities bore his yoke for twelve years, and then they rebelled. Five years after did Nimrod, who is also called Amraphel in

[1] Tabari, i. p. 156.

the sacred text,[1] march against Chedorlaomer, but Nimrod was defeated, along with his allies, Arioch, king of Ellasar, and Tidal, king of many confederate nations ; and obliged to enter into alliance with his former general, Chedorlaomer, and agree to assist him in bringing back the revolted cities—Sodom, Gomorrah, Admah, Zebojim, and Zoar—to their allegiance.

Consequently a huge army of confederates, under Chedorlaomer, Nimrod or Amraphel, Arioch, and Tidal, overran the plain and valley of Jordan, and slew all the giants that were there. The country before them was a garden, and behind them it was a desert.

They resolved also to defeat, and utterly to destroy Abraham, the servant of the Most High ; for Nimrod (Amraphel) remembered the perils to which his soothsayers had assured him he was exposed so long as Abraham lived.

The rulers of the five cities—Bera (Ruffian), king of Sodom ; Birsha (Evil-doer), king of Gomorrah ; Shirrab (Covetous one), king of Admah ; Shemeber (the Strong one), king of Zebojim ; and the king (a nameless one) of Bela (the engulfing city)— went forth in battle array, and met the host of Chedorlaomer in the great plain of Siddim, from whose canals and fountains the Salt Sea, or Dead Sea, was afterwards formed ; and there they were utterly routed, and fled in precipitate haste to the mountains and to the desert.

The king of Sodom alone escaped unharmed of all the five kings, by a miracle which God wrought, to exhibit His power to the dwellers in the plain, who had begun to doubt the truth of Abraham's deliverance out of the burning, fiery furnace.

The conquerors took the spoils of Sodom, and carried away Lot, who was like Abraham in face, thinking that they had taken Abraham captive ; and they placed him in chains.

Abraham was, in prophetic spirit, performing all the sacred rites, and preparing the unleavened cakes for the Paschal feast, for it was the Eve of the Passover, when the only giant who escaped the overthrow of the Rephaim by Chedorlaomer and his confederate kings,—Og, who was afterwards king of Basan, and who had been saved alive in the Flood of Noah,—came in haste to announce to the Patriarch the captivity of Lot.

Now Og had long cast his lustful eyes on Sarah, and he thought in his heart, " This Abraham is full of fire and zeal,

---

[1] Gen, xiv. 19. The book Jasher also says that Amraphel and Nimrod are the same.

like a sportsman ; that I know well. He will rush into battle to deliver his kinsman Lot, and will perish ; and then Sarah, his beautiful wife, will be mine."

But, according to another version, it was the angel Michael who brought the news to Abraham ; and to another, it was Oni, one of the slaves Nimrod had given him, and who had been sent to observe the progress of the war.

No sooner had Abraham heard the tidings than, filled with anxiety on Lot's behalf, and with sympathy for the Sodomites, his neighbors, he called all his neighbors together, and all those who had followed him, and in earnest words exhorted them to prepare to fight and rescue Lot. But they, knowing the disparity of numbers, would make no promise ; then he threatened them, but could not persuade them to join in what they regarded as an infatuated course certain to lead to destruction. Consequently Abraham was obliged to go against the enemy with only his own servants. But as they neared the plain, and saw the devastations wrought by the host of Chedor laomer, they also slipped away in the night, and Abraham was left alone with Eliezer, his trusty slave, and his three friends Aner, Eshcol, Mamre. And he followed after the foe, as they retired with their spoil, till he reached one of the fountains of Jordan, which is named Paneas, or Dan.

Here his three friends forsook him, along with their wives, who had accompanied them thus far.

It was the night of the 15th Nisan, the self-same night in which in after-years the first-born of Egypt would be slain ; and Abraham's heart fainted as he overtook the mighty host, and saw that they were countless as the sands of the sea-shore, and as grasshoppers for number.

But lo ! God fought for Abraham. The grass-blades changed into swords, and the stubble into spears, and battled all that night ; and in the morning, when he looked upon the host, they were all dead corpses. Thus he delivered Lot and all the captives, men, women, and children, and the spoil that had been carried away ; and none stayed them, for all their foes lay dead upon the ground.

The King of Sodom came forth to meet Abraham, full of pride of heart because he had been miraculously delivered, and attributing all the glory of the victory to Divine interposition on his own behalf. But all the people knew that Abraham was the favored of God, and their deliverer, and they built a throne of the trees that covered the plain, and which had been burnt in the war, and set Abraham as their prince and king thereon ; therefore is that place called to this day, " The king's dale." [1]

But Abraham was little pleased with this exhibition of honor, and he thought upon what he had learnt of old from that aged man, Shem, consecrated by God to be His priest, when he fled to him in his cave from the tyranny of Nimrod.

Shem reigned now in the city of Salem, which was in later years called Jerusalem, and from his righteous government he was named Melchizedek (king of righteousness).　And Abraham thought, " Will Shem ever forgive me for having drawn the sword against his grandsons, the sons of Elam ? "

But Shem was of no less noble and considerate temper than Abraham ; and he mused within himself, and said, " What sort of opinion can Abraham have formed of me, that such godless and violent hosts should have sprung from my loins, and have devastated the fair plain of Jordan, and carried away captive even his near kinsman ! "

Then Shem full of noble resolution to reconcile himself with Abraham, rose up and went forth, bearing bread and wine as tokens of friendship.

The words of God flowed from his mouth ; he instructed Abraham in all that appertained to the high priest's office, which was in future times to belong to his family ; and before he left, he blessed Abraham with these words, " *Blessed be Abraham of the most high God, possessor of heaven and earth ; and blessed be the most high God, which hath delivered thine enemies into thy hand.*" [2]

But in so saying, Melchizedek erred grievously, for he blessed Abraham before he blessed God, and the Creator should be blessed first, and the creature blessed afterwards ; therefore the high priesthood was taken from him, and given to Aaron in after-times.

Of all the spoil which Abraham had taken, he separated a tenth part, and he gave it to Melchizedek, as the offering due to the priest, and this was the first tithe paid in the history of the world.　All the booty of Sodom Abraham returned to the king thereof, and he took an oath, " *I will not take from a thread even to a shoe-latchet, and I will not take any thing that is thine,*

---

[1] Gen. xiv 17.　　　　　　　　　　　　　　　[2] Ibid., 19, 20.

lest thou should say, I have made Abraham rich, save only that which the young men have eaten, and the portion of the men which went with me, Aner, Eshcol, and Mamre; let them take their portion." [1]

On account of this unselfishness, the remembrance of which was to be continued through all generations, God gave the descendants of Abraham maxims to be written on their phylacteries and shoe-latchets; and the promise was made, " *Over Edom will I cast out my shoe;"* [2] that is, Edom, the most cruel oppressor of the chosen people, should fall under the condemnation of the Most High.

The end of Nimrod and his confederate kings is related with greater fulness by the Mussulman historians.

According to Tabari, God sent an army of flies against the host of Chedorlaomer and Nimrod, and these flies attacked the soldiers in their faces; and the flies were so numerous that the soldiers could not see one another; and the horses stung by them went mad, and leaped, and fell; so that, what with the horses and the flies, the army was entirely dispersed. Nimrod escaped to Babylon, but he was pursued by the meanest of the gnats of that host; it was blind of one eye and lame of one leg. When Nimrod sat down on his throne, the gnat settled upon his knee. Then the tyrant smote at it; and it rose, flew up one of his nostrils and entered his brain, which it began to devour.

Nimrod beat his face and his head, and when he did so the fly ceased gnawing at his brain, but he had no repose from his agonies save when struck upon the head. Consequently there was, after that, always some one stationed by him to strike his head. The king had a large blacksmith's hammer brought into his throne-room, and with that his princes and nobles smote him on the head; and the more violent the blow, the greater was the relief afforded. Nimrod reigned a thousand years before he felt the torment of the gnat; up to that moment he had suffered no pains. He lived for five hundred years with the fly eating at his brain; and all that while, night and day, there were relays of men to strike his head with the hammer.[3]

Precisely the same story is told by the Jewish Rabbis of Titus.[4]

---

[1] Gen. xiv. 23, 24.   [2] Ps. ix. 8.   [3] Tabari, i. c. xlviii.
[4] Gittin, fol, 56 b; Pirke of R. Eliezer, fol. 49.

There is, however, another version of the tradition ; which is, that the gnat fattening on the brain grew in size till it swelled to the dimensions of a pigeon, and then the skull of Nimrod burst, and the gnat flew away ; and this was fifteen days after it had entered by his nose.[1]

More shall be told of Melchizedek in a separate article.

4. THE BIRTH OF ISHMAEL.

Ten years passed, and yet Sarah was barren. Abraham, in sore distress, prayed to God, and reminded Him of His promises. Sarah then said to Abraham, "God has refused me children, therefore take Hagar to wife, the daughter of Pharaoh, who was given to be my servant ; I give her thee in all good-will, that my reproach may be taken away, and to her I give her freedom."

Abraham consented ; but Hagar, who had been virtuously brought up by Sarah, objected modestly, till Sarah pointed out to her how great an honor it would be to be the concubine of such a holy man.

But no sooner was Hagar installed as second wife, and felt in herself that she was about to become a mother, than her character changed ; she assumed the pre-eminence, and cast bitter words in the teeth of her mistress. "What," said she, "can Sarah be so holy and beloved of God, and He has never given her her heart's desire ? "

Sarah was stung to the quick by these words of her former slave. She turned to her husband and said, " I demand of thee my rights. For thee I forsook my father's house, and followed thee into a strange land ; for thee I passed myself off in Egypt as thy sister. And now what hast thou done ? Thou hast suffered my slave to assume the chief place in the house, and to take upon herself airs, and thou holdest thy peace. Depend upon it, if she bear thee a son there will be no peace in the house, for she is a daughter of Pharaoh, who is of the race of Nimrod, who cast thee into the furnace of fire."

" Hagar is in thy power," answered Abraham ; "but do her no harm. After thou gavest her her freedom, she may not again be brought into bondage."

But Sarah paid no attention to these words of gentleness,

[1] Weil, p. 80.

and treated Hagar with such cruelty, beat her, and cast an evil eye on her, so that she was delivered before her time of a dead child, and she fled for her life from the house.

The All-Righteous, for this offence, shortened Sarah's life, and made her die thirty-eight years before her husband.

Angels appeared to Hagar in the desert by the well of water whither she had fled, and bade her return to Abraham. So she went back, and was again pregnant, and bore a son, and called his name Ishmael.

5. THE DESTRUCTION OF SODOM AND GOMORRAH.

At noon on the 15th Nisan, the third day after the circumcision of Abraham, as recorded in the Book of Genesis, the heat of the sun was so great that Gehinom (Hell) was penetrated by it. And Abraham had not recovered the administration of the rite, which had been performed by the hands of Shem, king of Salem, priest of the Most High God.

Abraham was wont every day to go forth and invite any travellers he might see to feast with him. But this day, owing to the heat and to his being in pain, he sent Eliezer, his servant, forth, who looked and returned and said that there was no one to be seen.

But Abraham thought, " Can I trust the words of this slave, and neglect for one day the performance of my accustomed hospitality ? "

Then, notwithstanding the heat and his suffering, he went and sat in the shade of the door, and he beheld in the plain of Mamre the glory of the Lord that appeared. Abraham would have risen, but the voice of God called to him, saying, " Remain where thou art, and let thy pious, sitting posture teach future generations in their prayer and instruction to be seated ; and let judges, in delivering judgment, occupy the same position."

Then Abraham lifted his eyes, and beheld three men, who seemed to approach and then to withdraw. These were the angels Michael, Raphael, and Gabriel, sent to him with messages, whereof each bore one. They now stood before Abraham's tent, and they came to satisfy his desire to show hospitality : but when they observed the predicament in which he was, they attempted to withdraw, but Abraham supposed them to be travellers of the three neighboring races of Saracens,

Nabathæans, and Arabians; and as two of the angels were smaller of stature than the third, who stood in the middle—this was Michael—Abraham supposed him to be their chief; and he rose and bowed himself before him, and said to the Majesty of God which still shone, "If I have found favor in Thy sight, O Lord, may Thy majesty not depart from me whilst I receive hospitably these wanderers." And the Lord granted his request.

Then said Abraham to the men, "*Let a little water, I pray you, be fetched, and wash your feet, and rest yourselves under the tree; and I will fetch a morsel of bread, and comfort ye your hearts; after that ye shall pass on: for therefore are ye come to your servant.*"

Now the reason why he said "Let a little water be fetched and wash your feet," was, that he supposed the men were idolaters, and he would not have the dust from the feet of idolaters to pollute the floor of his tent.

And they said, "Do so."

Then Abraham hastened into the tent to Sarah, and said, "*Make ready quickly three measures of fine meal, knead it, and make cakes upon the hearth.*" And Abraham ran unto the herd, and fetched a calf which he had dressed, and set it before them; and he stood by them under the tree, and they did eat.

Abraham placed butter and milk on the table first, then calves' tongues, then the other dishes, and lastly Sarah's cakes; but some commentators doubt whether the men ate the cakes. It is asserted by some that the angels only appeared to eat, but by others we are assured that to reward Abraham's hospitality they really did eat, and this was the only occasion on which angels tasted the food of earth.

The angels, knowing that Sarah was within the tent, asked after her. And this betokens her great modesty, that she did not thrust herself forward to be seen of strange visitors. Abraham replied that she was within, engaged in women's household work. Then said Michael, the chief of the angels, "Truly shall such pious and seemly habits not pass unrewarded; but Sarah shall bloom again as fair as in her youth, and shall bear a son in her old age."

Sarah heard these words at the entrance of the tent; so did Ishmael, who stood near. Sarah stepped behind the angel, but the beauty of her countenance shone before her, and the angel turned to look at her, and then he saw she was laughing to herself, and saying, " I am good-looking, and smart dresses become me ; I could perfectly well produce a son, but then my husband is old."

Then the word of God came to Abraham, and said, " *Wherefore did Sarah laugh ?* Am I, the all-powerful God, too old to create miracles ? *At the appointed time Sarah shall have a son.*" To Sarah, who, out of fear, denied having laughed, the word came, " Fear not, *but thou didst laugh.*"

Then Michael withdrew, for his mission was accomplished ; and left the other two, Gabriel and Raphael, with Abraham. Then God revealed to Abraham, by Gabriel, that He was about to destroy the cities of the plain ; and by Raphael, that He would deliver Lot and his family in the overthrow.

These cities were very guilty before God. Eliezer, having been sent by Sarah to her brother Lot with a message, some years before, arrived in Sodom. An acquaintance invited him to a meal. But hospitality was a virtue abhorred in Sodom, and the news of the invitation having got wind, Eliezer's friend was driven out of the city. Now it was a custom in Sodom to make every stranger arriving within the walls rest in a certain bed ; and if the bed proved too long for him, his legs were pulled out to fit it ; and if it proved too short, his legs were pared down to its dimensions. Eliezer saw with horror what it was that they purposed to do with him, and he had recourse to a lie of necessity ; he declined to sleep in the bed, because he had taken an oath upon the death of his mother never to lie on a bed again ; and thus he escaped. Shortly after, having seen a Sodomite rob a poor stranger of his garment, Eliezer attempted to interfere, but the robber struck him over the head and made a gash, from which he lost much blood. Both being brought before the judge, this was the magistrate's decision :— That Eliezer was indebted to the Sodomite robber for having bled him. The servant of Abraham thereupon took up a large stone, flung it at the judge's head, which he cut open, and said, " Now, pay me for having bled thee ! " and then he fled out of the city.

From these incidents it may be seen how wicked the city was.

Now Abraham had interceded with God to spare the cities of the plain, for the intercession of His saints is mighty with God. And Abraham had obtained of God that if in Zoar, the smallest of the cities, five righteous could be found, and forty-five in all the rest of the country, God would spare them.

Then God ceased talking with Abraham. Next morning early, Abraham arose and took his staff, and went to the place where God had met him, to make further intercession for the cities of the plain, but the smoke of them rose as from a furnace, for brimstone and fire had been rained upon them out of heaven, and they had been consumed along with their inhabitants. Only Zoar was spared, as a place of refuge for Lot, and Lot was kept alive and his daughters ; for God remembered how he had been true to Abraham in Egypt, and had not betrayed the truth about Sarah when questioned by Pharaoh.

The Mussulman tradition is as follows :—

Lot, whom the Arabs called Loth, was sent by God as a prophet to convince the inhabitants of the cities of the plain of their ungodly deeds. But, though he preached for twenty years, he could not convince them. And whenever he visited Abraham he complained to him of the iniquity of the people. But Abraham urged him to patience.

At length the long-suffering of God was exhausted, and He sent the angels Michael, Gabriel, and Azrael, armed with the sword of destruction, against these cities.

They came to Abraham, who received them, and slaughtered a calf, and prepared meat and set it before them. But they would not eat. And he pressed them, and ate himself ; but they would not eat, being angels. Then Abraham's color went and he was afraid, for to refuse to eat with a man is a token that you seek his life.

Seeing him discouraged, the angels announced their mission. But Sarah, observing her husband's loss of color, laughed and said in her heart, "Why is he fearful, being surrounded with many servants and faithful friends ?"

Now the angels promised to Abraham a son in his old age, and that they would rescue Lot in the overthrow of Sodom. Then they rose up and went on their way, and entered into 'Sodom ; and they met a young maiden in the street, and asked her the way to Lot's house.

She answered, "He is my father, and I dwell with him ; but know you not, O strangers, that it is against the laws of this city to show hospitality ?"

But they answered her, "Fear not ; lead us to thy father."

So she led them, and ran before and told Lot, "Behold three men come seeking thee and asking shelter, and they are beautiful as the angels of God."

Then Lot went out to them, and told them the city was full of wickedness, and that hospitality was not permitted.

But they answered, "We must tarry this night in thy house." Then he admitted them, and he hid them. But Lot's wife was an infidel, a native of Sodom ; and finding that he lodged these strangers, she hastened to the chief men of the city and said, " My husband has violated your laws, and the customs of this people ; he has housed travellers, and will feed them and show them all courtesy."

Therefore the men of the city came tumultuously to the door of Lot's house, to bring forth the men that were come to him, and to cast them out of the city, having shamefully entreated them. They would not listen to the remonstrances of Lot, but went near to break in his door.

Then the three angels stepped forth and passed their hands over the faces of all who drew near, and they were struck blind, and fled from their presence.

Now, long before the day began to break, the angels rose up and called Lot, his wife and daughters, and bade them take their clothes and all that they had that was most precious, and escape out of the city. Therefore Lot and his family went forth.

And when they were escaped, the angel Gabriel went through the cities, and passed his wing over the soil on which they were built, and the cities were carried up into heaven ; and they came so near thereto that those on the confines of heaven could hear the crowing of the cocks in Sodom, and the barking of the dogs in Gomorrah. And then they were overthrown, so that their foundations were towards the sky and their roofs towards the earth. And God rained on them stones heated in the fire of hell ; and on each stone was written the name of him whom it was destined to slay. Now there were many natives of these accursed cities in other parts of the land, and where they were, there they were sought out by the red-hot stones, and were struck down. But some were within the sacred enclosure of the temple at Mecca, and the stones waited for them in the air ; and at the expiration of forty days they came forth, and as they came forth the stones whistled through the air, and smote them, and they were slain.

Now Lot's wife turned, as she went forth, to look back upon the city, and a stone fell on her, and she died.[1]

[1] Tabari, i. c. lii ; Abulfeda, p. 25.

It is related further of Lot that, after he had escaped, he committed in ignorance a very great sin; and Abraham sent him to expiate his crime to the sources of the Nile, to fetch thence three sorts of wood, which he named to him. Abraham thought, " He will be slain by ravenous beasts, and so will he atone for the sin that he has committed."

But Lot after a while returned, bringing with him the woods which Abraham had demanded—a cypress plant, a young cedar, and a young pine.

Abraham planted the three trees in the shape of a triangle, on a mountain, and charged Lot with watering them every day from Jordan. Now the mountain was twenty-four thousand paces from Jordan, and this penance was laid on Lot to expiate his sin.

At the end of three months the trees blossomed; Lot announced this to Abraham, who visited the spot, and saw to his surprise that the three trees had grown together to form one trunk, but with three distinct roots of different natures.

At the sight of this miracle he bowed his face to the ground and said, " This tree will abolish sin."

And by that he knew that God had pardoned Lot.

The tree grew and subsisted till the reign of Solomon, when it was cut down, and this was the tree which the Jews employed to form the Cross of Christ.[1]

This tradition is, of course, Christian; though Jewish in origin, it has been adapted to the Gospel story.

6. THE BIRTH OF ISAAC.

The country was wasted; travellers were few; those who passed by, and accepted Abraham's hospitality, spoke with scorn of the sin of Lot, his nephew; and the neighborhood became intolerable to the patriarch, who resolved to change his place of residence for a while.

He therefore went south, between Kadesh and Sur, and dwelt in Gerar.

Now Sarah had bloomed again as fair as in her youth, as the angel Michael had foretold; and Abraham persuaded her to pretend again to be his sister, though Sarah, remembering the ill-success of this deceit before, hesitated to comply.

---

[1] Apocrypha de Loto, apud Fabricium, t. i. pp. 428–431.

8*

Abimelech, king of Gerar, hearing of Sarah's beauty, sent for her to his palace. He asked Abraham, " Who is this woman?" and he answered, " She is my sister." Then Abimelech inquired of the camels and of the asses, and they answered the same, " She is his sister." But that same evening, as it grew towards dusk, as he sat on his throne, he fell asleep ; and in dream saw an angel of God approach him with a drawn sword in his hand to slay him. The king in his dream cried out to know why he was doomed to death ; and the angel answered, " Because thou hast received into thy house the wife of another man, the mistress of a house."

Abimelech excused himself, saying that Abraham had concealed the truth from him, and had said Sarah was his sister.

" The All-Holy knows that thou hast sinned in ignorance," said the angel ; " but is it seemly, when strangers enter thy land, to be questioning closely into their connections? Know that Abraham is a prophet, and foreseeing that thy people would entreat his wife ill, he resolved to call her his sister, and he knew, being a prophet, that thou couldst not harm her." [1]

That night—it was the Paschal eve—the angel with the drawn sword traversed all the streets of the city, and closed the wombs of those about to bear.

Next morning early, while it was yet dark, Abimelech sent for Abraham and Sarah, and gave Sarah back to her husband, and paid him a thousand ounces of silver, and to Sarah he gave a costly robe, which might conceal her from her eyes to her feet, that none might henceforth be bewitched by her beauty. " But," said Abimelech to Abraham, " because thou didst deceive me and blind my eyes with a lie, therefore thou shalt bear a son, whose eyes shall be dim so that he shall be deceived." And Abraham prayed to the Lord, and all the woman that were with child in Gerar were delivered of men-children, without the pangs of maternity, and those who were barren felt themselves with child. The angel hosts besought the Lord to look upon Sarah, and to remember His covenant. " O Lord of the whole world! Thou didst hear the cry of Abraham, and grant his petitions when he prayed for the barren women of Gerar ; and his own wife, from whom Thou didst promise him a son, is unfruitful and despised. Does it beseem a Lord, when he prepares a fleet, to free his subjects from pirates, but to leave the vessel of his best friend in bondage?"

[1] Solomon Jarschi, Comm. on Moses, xx. 5.

Now it was the first day of the seventh month, Tischri, the day on which, at the close of the world's history, the Lord will come to judge the quick and the dead, that the Lord God remembered Sarah, and the promise He had made, and looked upon her, and she conceived a son in her old age, one year and four months after her sojourn in Gerar; and nine months after, say some, but, say others, six months and two days after; at mid-day say some, others say in the evening of the fifteenth of Nisan; or, as others affirm, on the first of Nisan she was delivered of a son, without suffering any pains in the bringing forth. And the same time that Sarah's womb was blessed, God looked upon many other barren women and blessed them also; and on the day that the child was born they were delivered likewise; and the blind saw, the dumb spake, the deaf heard, and the lame walked, and the crazed recovered their senses. Also, the sun shone forty-eight times brighter than he shines at Midsummer, even with the splendor that he had on the day of his creation.

And when eight days were accomplished, Abraham circumcised his son, and called him Isaac.

But many thought it was an incredible thing that Abraham and Sarah should have a son in their old age, and they said, " This is a foundling, or it is the child of one of the slaves, which they pass off as their own." Now Abraham held a great feast on the day that Isaac was weaned, and he invited thereto all the princes and great men of the country. And there came Abimelech, king of Gerar, and Og, king of Basan, and all the princes of Canaan, sixty-two princes in all. Such an assembly was not seen before, yet all these princes fell in after-years by the hands of Joshua.[1]

Of this feast it is related that Og's companions said to him, " Do you believe that that old mule, Abraham, can be the father of this child ? "

Og replied with scorn, " I could crack this imp with the nail of my little finger."

Then came there a voice from heaven, saying, " Thou despisest this little child, but know thou that tens of thousands shall spring from his loins, and that before them thy pride shall be humbled."

Also, Abraham's ancestors, Shem and Eber, and his father,

---

[1] Josh. xii. 24.

Terah—though some say he was dead—and Nahor, Abraham's brother, attended the feast, and the Shekinah, the glory of the Lord, appeared to grace it.

But Satan also appeared in the form of a poor beggar-man, and he stood at the door and asked an alms. Now Abraham and Sarah were busy attending to their guests, so they perceived him not, but the servants thrust him away, and Satan received nothing ; therefore he presented himself before the Most High, and laid an accusation of inhospitality and churlishness against the Friend of God.

In the mean time Sarah had assembled, and was entertaining all the wives of the guests of Abraham. And it happened that the women found that they had no milk in their bosoms to give their infants, and the babes screamed that no one could hear the voice of another. The mothers were in despair, for the children were hungry, and they were all dry. Then Sarah uncovered her breasts, and there spirted from them jets of milk, and all the babes were nourished at her bosom, and yet there was more.

Now when they saw this, the women, who had doubted that the child was really the offspring of Sarah, doubted no more, and cried, " We are not worthy that our little ones should be nourished at thy bosom ! " And the story goes that all those who afterwards joined themselves to the people of Israel, and all those in every nation who in after-times became proselytes, were descended from those who sucked the breasts of Sarah. In allusion to this incident it is said in the Book of Psalms : " *Thou makest the barren woman to keep house, and to be the joyful mother of* (i. e., giving suck to) *children.*" [1]

The child Isaac was shown to every visitor, and all were astonished at his resemblance to Abraham. Both the babe and his father were so much alike that it was impossible to distinguish one from the other, and all doubt as to whose it was vanished before such evidence of likeness to the father, and before the fulness of Sarah's breasts. But as confusion was likely to arise through the striking similarity between father and son, Abraham besought God to give him wrinkles and white hair, that he might not be mistaken for the babe Isaac, or the babe Isaac be mistaken for him. [2]

---

[1] Psalm cxiii. 9.

[2] This climax of absurdity is found also in the Mussulman histories of the Patriarch.

7. THE EXPULSION OF HAGAR AND ISHMAEL.

Ishmael grew up, and became skilful with his bow; he was rough and undisciplined, and he occasionally lapsed into idolatry, but without his father knowing it. But Sarah was aware of his sin, and was grieved thereat.

Ishmael often boasted, "I am the eldest son, and I shall have a double portion of my father's inheritance." These words were reported to Sarah, and she hated Ishmael for them in her heart.

One day when Isaac was five years old, but others say fifteen, Ishmael said to him, "Come forth into the field and let us shoot." Isaac was well pleased. And when they were in the field, Ishmael turned his bow against his brother, but he did it in jest. Sarah saw him from the tent door, and she ran out, and caught away her son Isaac, and she went to Abraham and told him all the evil she knew of Ishmael; how he had gone after idols and had learnt the ways of the Canaanites that were in the land, how he had boasted of his majority, and how he had sought Isaac's life. And she said, "Give the maid-servant a writing of divorcement, and send her away. *Cast out this bond-woman and her son; for the son of this bond-woman shall not be heir with my son, even with Isaac.* Then she will no more vex Isaac. Do thou leave to Isaac all thy possessions. Never shall Ishmael inherit any thing from thee, for he is not my son."

Abraham was grieved at heart, for he loved Ishmael his son, but nothing that he said could alter Sarah's determination. She insisted on the expulsion of Hagar and her son, and she stirred up the wrath of Abraham against Ishmael, because he had fallen into idolatry.

Sarah, say the Mussulmans, was so fierce in her jealousy, that she would not be satisfied till she had washed her hands in the blood of Hagar. Then Abraham quickly pierced Hagar's ears, and drew a ring through them, so that Sarah could fulfil her oath, without endangering the life of Hagar.[1]

It was long before Abraham could be brought to consent to Sarah's desire, but God appeared to him in a dream and said, "Fear not to obey the voice of Sarah, for she is the wife of thy youth, and was chosen for thee from her mother's womb. But Hagar is not thy wife; she is but a bond-woman. Sarah

[1] Weil, p. 83.

also is a prophetess, and sees into things that shall be in the latter days, further than thou. Unto Isaac and those of his seed who believe in the Two Worlds are the promises made; and they alone shall be accounted as thy seed." [1]

Abraham now did what he was commanded. Next morning he gave Hagar a writing of dismissal, and took twelve loaves of bread and a pitcher of water, and laid them upon Hagar, for Sarah had cast an evil eye upon Ishmael, so that he was ill, and unable to carry any burden. And Abraham attached the pitcher by a cord to the hips of Hagar, that all might know she was a slave, and the pitcher hung down and trailed on the sand. Ishmael was sent away without garments; he went forth naked as he came into the world: thus it may be seen how implacable was the anger of Sarah, because he had boasted of his birthright, and the wrath of Abraham, because he had fallen into idolatry.

But when they went along their way, Abraham looked after them for long, standing in the door of his tent, for his bowels yearned after his son, and he saw the trail in the sand of the water pitcher which Hagar had dragged sadly along, and thereby Abraham knew the direction which they had taken.

Now God forsook not the outcast in her affliction, but filled the pitcher with water as fast as she and her son drank out of it, and the water was always sweet and cold. Thus they penetrated the wilderness, and there they lost their way, and Hagar forgot the God of Abraham, and in her distress turned to the false gods of her father Pharaoh, and besought their protection, for she said, " Where are the promises of the God of Abraham, that of Ishmael would He make a great nation ? "

Now Ishmael was sick of a burning fever, and the water in the pitcher failed when Hagar forsook the God of Abraham. So she cast him under a thorn bush, and went from him the space of two thousand ells, that she might not hear his cries. But Ishmael prayed to the Lord God of Heaven and Earth, and said, " O Lord God of my father Abraham ! thou canst send death in so many forms ; take my life speedily or give me a drop of water, that I suffer this agony no longer."

And the Lord in His compassion heard the prayer of the weeping child, and He sent His angel and showed Hagar that fountain which He had created on the sixth day at dusk, and

---

[1] It seems probable that S. Paul alludes to this traditional speech more than once, as for instance Gal. iii. 9.

of which the children of Israel were destined to drink when they came forth out of Egypt.

But the accusing angel murmured against this judgment of God, and said, "O Lord of the whole earth ! shall this one, of whom a nation of robbers shall arise, who will war upon thine elect people, and be a scourge upon the face of the earth, shall he be delivered now, and given to drink of a fountain destined for thine elect?"

The Lord answered, "Is the youth guilty, or is he not guilty?"

The angel answered, "He is not himself guilty, but his posterity will sin."

Then God said, "I punish men for what they have done, and not for what their children will do. Ishmael hath not merited a death of suffering, therefore shall he not die." And God opened the eyes of Hagar, and she saw the spring of water, and filled her pitcher, and took it to Ishmael to drink. She filled the pitcher before she gave her son a draught of water, for she had little faith, and thought that the fountain would be withdrawn before she could return to it again.

Then Ishmael was strengthened and could go, and he and his mother went further, and were fed by the shepherds; and they reached Paran, and there they found springs of water, and they settled there. Ishmael took a wife, a daughter of Moab, named Aischa, or Aifa, or Asiah ; but others say she was an Egyptian woman, and was named Meriba (the quarrelsome), and by her he had four sons and one daughter.

Ishmael lived a wandering life in tents with his wife and cattle ; and the Lord blessed his flocks, and he had great possessions. But his heart remained the same ; and he was a master of archery, and instructed his neighbors in making bows.

After three years, Abraham, whose heart longed after his son, said to Sarah, "I must see how my son Ishmael fares." And she answered, "Thou shalt go if thou wilt swear to me not to alight from off thy camel," for she hated Hagar, and feared to suffer her husband to meet her once more. So Abraham swore. Then he went to Paran, over the desert, seeking Ishmael's tent ; and he reached it at noon, but neither Hagar nor her son were at home. Only Ishmael's wife was within, and she was scolding and beating the children.

So Abraham halted on his camel before the tent door, and the sun was hot in the blue sky above, and the sand was white and glaring beneath. And he called to her, "Is thy husband within?"

She answered, without rising from her seat, "He is hunting." Or, say others, she said without looking at him or rising, "He is gathering dates."

Then Abraham said, "I am faint and hungry; bring me a little bread and a drop of water."

But the woman answered, "I have none for such as thee.'

So Abraham said to her, "Say to thy husband, even to Ishmael, these words: 'An old man hath come to see thee out of the land of the Philistines, and he says, The nail that fastens thy tent is bad; cast it away or thy tent will fall, and get thee a better nail.'" Then he departed, and went home.

Now when Ishmael returned, his wife told him all these words, and he knew that his father had been there, and he understood the tenor of his words, so he sent away his wife, and he took another, with his mother's advice, out of Egypt, and her name was Fatima.

And after three years, Abraham's bowels yearned once more after his son, and he said to Sarah, "I must see how Ishmael fares." And she answered, "Thou shalt go, if thou wilt swear to me not to alight from off thy camel." So Abraham swore.

Then he went to Paran, over the desert, seeking Ishmael's tent, and he reached it at noon; but neither Hagar nor her son was at home. Only Ishmael's wife, Fatima, was within, and she was singing to the children.

So Abraham halted on his camel before the tent door, and the sun was hot in the blue sky above, and the sand was white and glaring beneath. And when Fatima saw a stranger at the door, she rose from her seat, and veiled her face, and came out and greeted him.

Then said Abraham, "Is thy husband within?"

She answered, "My lord, he is pasturing the camels in the desert;" and she added, "Enter, my lord, into the cool of the tent and rest, and suffer me to bring thee a little meat."

But Abraham said, "I may not alight from off my camel, for my journey is hasty; but bring me, I pray thee, a morsel of bread and a drop of water, for I am hungry and faint."

Then she ran and brought him of the best of all that she had in the tent, and he ate and drank, and was glad.

So he said to her, "Say to thy husband, even to Ishmael, that an old man out of the land of the Philistines hath been here, and he says, The nail that fastens thy tent is very good ; let it not be stirred out of its place, and thy tent will stand."

And he returned. And when Ishmael came home, Fatima related to him all the words that the old man had spoken, and he understood the tenor of the words.

Ishmael was glad that his father had visited him, for he knew thereby that his love to him was not extinguished.[1]

Shortly after, he left his wife and children, and went across the desert to see his father in the land of the Philistines. And Abraham related to him all that had taken place with the first wife, and why he had exhorted him to put her away.

8. THE STRIFE BETWEEN THE SHEPHERDS.

Abraham lived twenty-six years in the land of the Philistines ; then he went to Hebron, and there his servants dug wells, and there they encamped.

When Abimelech's servants heard of these wells that they had dug, they came with their flocks, and desired to use them also, and the largest of the wells they claimed as their own. But Abraham's shepherds said, " Let the well belong to those to whom it gives water. The Lord shall decide between us ! "

To this the servants of Abimelech agreed. And when the flocks of Abraham came to drink, the well sprang up and overflowed ; but when the flocks of Abimelech drew near, the water sank and disappeared.

Now when Abimelech heard of the strife, he came with Phicol, his chief captain, to seek Abraham, and to be reconciled with him. " God is with all that thou doest," said Abimelech ; " He protected thee when Sodom was destroyed. He has given thee a son in thine old age. He rescued thy first born when perishing in the desert. Swear to me, as I have offered thee my whole land, my own palace not excepted, in which to dwell, that thou wilt show equal love and liberality to my descendants to the third generation."

Abraham swore to him, and they made a covenant together.[2]

And Abraham set apart seven lambs as a witness and token, that just as the well had sprung up when his flocks had come to water at it, so, in after days should it spring up to

---

[1] The same story is told by the Mohammedans : Weil, p. 90.
[2] Gen. xxi. 24–27.

water the descendants of Abraham ; as it is said, "*From thence they went to Beer, that is, the well whereof the Lord spake unto Moses, Gather the people together, and I will give them water Then Israel sang this song, Spring up, O well; sing ye unto it.*"

But such condescension and courtesy ill became Abraham in his dealings with a rude and savage people, and therefore there came to him a voice from heaven which said : " Because thou hast given these seven innocent lambs into the hands of a barbarous nation, therefore seven of thy descendants shall be slain by their hands (Samson, Hophni and Phinehas, Saul and his three sons) ; also seven dwellings that thy people shall raise to my Name shall they destroy (the Tabernacle, Gilgal Nob, Gibeon, Shiloh, and twice the Temple at Jerusalem), and seven months shall the ark of my covenant remain in the land of the Philistines."

9. THE GROVE IN BEER-SHEBA.

"*And Abraham planted a grove in Beer-sheba, and called there on the name of the Lord.*"[2] The reason was as follows :—

Once Abraham asked Shem the son of Noah, otherwise called Melchizedek, king of Salem, what service he and his father and brethren rendered to the Lord in the ark, which was so acceptable to God that He preserved them alive and brought them in safety to Ararat ; and Shem answered, " The service we rendered to God, all the time of our sojourn in the ark, was charity."

And when Abraham wondered and asked how that could possibly be, as there were none in the ark save themselves and the beasts, Shem answered,—

" Even so ; we showed charity and forethought and hospitality to the animals. We fed them regularly, and we slept not at night ; so busy were we with them in making them comfortable. Once, when we had delayed somewhat, the lion was hungry and bit Noah, my father."

Then said Abraham to himself, " In very truth, if it was reckoned to Noah and his sons as so great righteousness, that they fed and tended the dumb and senseless beasts, how much more pleasing must it be to the Most High, to be kind and generous to men who are made in His image, after His likeness ! "

[1] Numbers xxi. 16. 17.   [2] Gen. xxi. 33.

Filled with this thought, Abraham settled at Beer-sheba, where was an abundant spring of fresh water, and there he resolved to do service acceptable to the living God, and to honor His name, as Noah and his sons had done Him service and honored Him in the ark.

So Abraham planted a grove in Beer-sheba, one hundred ells long and one hundred ells broad, and he planted it with vines and figs, pomegranates and other fruit trees ; and he built a guest-house adjoining this garden, and he made in it four doors, one towards each quarter of the heavens ; and when a hungry man came by, Abraham gave him food ; if there came a man who was thirsty, he gave him drink ; if one who was naked, he clothed him ; if one who was sick, he took him in and nursed him ; and he gave to every man who passed by what he most needed for his journey.

He would receive neither thanks nor payment ; and when any one thanked him, he said hastily, " Give thanks, not to me the servant but to the Master of this house, *who openeth His hand, and filleth all things living with plenteousness."*

Then when the traveller asked, " Who, and where is this Master ? "

Abraham answered, " He is the God who rules over heaven and earth ; He is Lord of all ; He kills and makes alive ; He wounds and heals ; He forms the fruit in the mother's womb, and gives it life ; He makes the plants and trees to grow ; He brings man to destruction, and raises him from his grave again."

Thus Abraham instructed those whom he relieved. And if a traveller asked further, how he was to worship the great God, Abraham answered, " Say only these words, Praised be the Eternal One who reigns over heaven and earth ! Praised be the Lord of the whole world, who filleth all things living with plenteousness." And no traveller went on his way without thanking God.

Thus that guest-house was a great school, in which men were taught the true religion, and gratitude to the Almighty God.

10. THE OFFERING OF ISAAC.[1]

Abraham loved the son of his old age, and Isaac grew up

---

[1] The Mussulmans tell the story of Ishmael almost in every particular the same as that given below.

in the fear of God, and his good conduct heightened the love Abraham bore him ; but the Patriarch thought in his heart, "I prepare gifts to give of my abundance to every man that asks of me, and to every passer-by ; but to my Lord and God, the Giver of all good things, have I given nothing !"

There was a day when the sons of God (the angels) stood before the Eternal One, and amongst them was the accusing angel, Satan or Sammael. The Lord asked them, "Whence comest thou ?"

"From walking to and fro upon the face of the earth," he replied.

"And what hast thou beheld there of the doings of the sons of men ?"

The accuser answered, "I saw that the sons of earth no longer praise Thee, and adore Thee ; when they have obtained their petition, then they forget to give Thee thanks. I saw that Abraham, the son of Terah, as long as he was childless, built altars and proclaimed Thy name to all the world : now he has been given a son at the age of a hundred, and he forgets Thee. I went to his door as a beggar, on the day that Isaac was weaned, and I was turned away without an alms. I have seen him strike alliance with the king of the Philistines, a nation that knows Thee not, and to him has he given seven lambs. He has built a large house and he gives to strangers, but to Thee he gives no sacrifice of value. Ask of him any sacrifice that is costly, and he will refuse it."

"What shall I ask?" inquired the Almighty.

"Ask of him now his son, and he will refuse him to Thy face."

"I will do so, and thou shalt be confounded," answered the Holy One.

The self-same night God appeared to Abraham, and addressed him gently so as not to alarm him, and He said to him, "Abraham !"

The patriarch in deep humility answered, "Here am I, Lord what willest Thou of Thy servant?"

The Lord answered, "I have come to ask of thee something. I have saved thee in all dangers ; I delivered thee out of the furnace of Babylon ; I rescued thee from the army of Nimrod ; I brought thee into this land, and gave thee menservants and maid-servants and cattle and sheep and horses, and I have given thee a son in thine old age, and victory over all thine enemies, and new temptations await thee, for I must prove thee, and see if thou art grateful in thy heart, and that thy righteousness may be manifest unto all, and that thy obedience may be perfected. Take therefore thy son—"

Abraham answered trembling, "Which son? I have two."

The voice of God.—"That son which alone counteth with thee."

Abraham.—"Each is the only son of his mother."

The voice of God.—"The one you love."

Abraham.—"I love both."

The voice of God.—"The one you love best."

Abraham.—"I love both alike."

The voice of God.—"Then I demand Isaac."

Abraham.—"And what shall I do with him, O Lord?"

The voice of God.—"Go to the place that I shall tell thee, where, unexpectedly, hills shall arise in sight out of the valley bottom. Go to that place whence once My Light, My Teaching issued, which My eye watches over untiringly, and where the smoke of incense shall arise to Me, to the place where prayer is heard and sacrifice shall be offered, where at the end of time I shall judge the nations, and cast the ungodly into the pit of Gehinom ;—to the land of Moriah that I shall show thee, there shalt thou take thy son Isaac as a whole burnt offering."

Abraham.—"Shall I bring Thee such an offering as this, O Lord? Where is the priest to prepare the sacrifice?"

The voice of God.—"I have taken from Shem his priesthood, and thou art clothed therewith."

Abraham.—"But in that country there are many hills; which shall I ascend?"

The voice of God.—"A mountain on which shall rest my Glory ; there shall it be told thee further what thou must do."

Abraham prepared to fulfil the command of God, but he dreaded the separation between Sarah and her son. If he took Isaac away secretly, then he feared that, in the excess of her distress, she would do herself harm. At last he decided on this course; he went to Sarah's tent, and he said to her, " My dearest, prepare this day a little banquet, that in our old days we may rejoice our hearts."

Sarah answered, " Wherefore this day, my husband? Are you about to lose any thing this day?"

Abraham said, " Think, my wife, Sarah! how good God has

been to us ; therefore it behoves us to thank Him all the days of our life."

Sarah did as Abraham had commanded.

As they sat and ate, Abraham said, " Thou knowest well, dear wife, that I knew the one true God from the time that I was three years old. Isaac is older, and it behoves him to know more of the law of God. Therefore I design to take him with me to Shem and Eber, our ancestors, who live not far from here, that they may instruct him. Hast thou any thing to object to this, Sarah ?"

She answered, " No ; do that which is pleasing in thine eyes ; only let not Isaac be away too long, for thou knowest how precious the sight of him is to me."

Then Sarah put her arms round her son, and kissed him, and they parted with many tears ; and she exhorted Abraham to have great care of the youth, that the journey might not be too great for him."

Next morning, very early, Abraham rose, and he saddled the ass himself, though he had many slaves, for he was eager to be gone, and to go where the Lord called him. This was the ass, born of the she-ass created by God on the eve of the sixth day, upon which Moses afterwards rodewhen he went to Egypt :[1] it is the ass which spake to Balaam, and it is the ass of which the prophet Zechariah has spoken, that on it Messiah shall ride.[2]

This ass was of a hundred colors.[3]

Sarah clothed Isaac in the garment that Abimelech had given her, and placed a jewel-studded fillet about his head. She provided the travellers with food for their journey, and accompanied them with her maids, till Abraham bade them return. Then she clasped Isaac once more to her breast, and said with tears, " God be gracious to thee, my son ; how know I that I shall see thee again ? "

Abraham had two to accompany him, Eliezer and Ishmael ; he had cut fig and palm wood and made a fagot. On the way this discourse took place between Eliezer and Ishmael.

Ishmael said, " I perceive clearly that my father is about

---

[1] Exod. iv. 20.   [2] Zech. ix. 9.

[3] When King Sapor heard the R. Samuel explain that Messiah would come riding on an ass, the king said, " I will give him a horse ; it is not seemly that he should ride an ass." " What," answered the Rabbi, " hast thou a horse with a hundred colors?" (Talmud, Tract. Sanhedrim, fol 98, col. 1.)

to offer Isaac as a whole burnt offering; therefore I, his eldest son, will inherit his possessions."

But Eliezer said, "That is false: I am his trusty servant! Did not thy father drive thee away from home? He will leave all to me."

Whilst they thus spake, there came a voice from heaven, "O ye fools! neither of you knows the truth."

Abraham in the mean time walked forward. Then came Satan to him in the form of an old man bowed upon a staff, and said to him, "Whither goest thou?"

He answered, "I go to offer up my prayers."   .

"Wherefore this knife, and fuel, and fire?" asked Satan.

"I take them in case we have to spend much time on the mountain, that we may bake bread and slay beasts."

"Old man, thou deceivest me," said Satan. "Was I not by when a voice bade thee slay thy son, thine only son; ane now, what art thou about to do? Thinkest thou that thou shalt have another son, now that thou art a hundred years old? Art thou then about to cut down with thine own hands the main pillar of thy tent, the staff on which thou mayest lean in' thine old age? Knowest thou not the proverb, 'He who destroys his own goods, how shall he get more?' That was not the voice of God, it was the voice of the Tempter, and thou didst listen to it. Dost thou think that God, who promised to make of thee a great nation, and to bless all generations through Isaac, would thus persuade thee to make void His own promises?"

Abraham answered, "No, it was not the Tempter who spake, it was the voice of God; therefore I will not hearken to thy words, but walk on still in mine uprightness."

"But if God were to ask of thee some further sacrifice, wouldst thou grant it?"

"Of a truth would I," answered Abraham.

"Thy piety is folly," said Satan impatiently. "To-morrow God will punish thee for this murder thou art about to commit, since thou wilt shed the blood of thine own son."

But when Satan saw that Abraham was not to be moved from his purpose, then he took the form of a blooming youth, and joined himself to Isaac, and asked him the object of his journey.

Isaac replied that he was going to receive instruction in the law of the Most High.

"Art thou going to receive this instruction living or dead?" asked Satan, scornfully.

Isaac.—"Can a man receive instruction after he is dead?"

Satan.—"O thou son of a mother much to be pitied, knowest thou not that thy father is leading thee to death?"

Isaac.—"Nevertheless I shall follow him."

Satan.—"Then all the tears and prayers of thy mother, beseeching Heaven to grant her a son, end in this! All the pains and grief in child-bearing! All the afflictions she laid on Hagar and Ishmael! All the care she has taken of thy youth! All the love she has expended upon thee! All these things for nothing!"

Isaac.—"As my father wills."

Satan.—"Then the inheritance passes to Ishmael. How he will glory in being the first-born, and his mother Hagar will despise Sarah, and maybe will drive her out!"

Isaac.—"I obey the command of my father and the will of God, be they what they may."

But these words were not without some effect on Isaac. With piteous voice he urged his father to suspend or delay what he had undertaken. But Abraham exhorted his son not to listen or give credence to the words he had heard, for they were the temptations of Satan to draw him from the path of obedience and the fear of God.

They went a little further and came to a broad stream. Abraham, Isaac, and their followers sought to wade it; the water at first reached their knees, but when they were in the middle, it rose to their necks.

Abraham, who knew well the spot, and that there was neither brook nor river there by nature, recognized this as a deception of Satan, to divert them from the right way. He told Isaac that this was his opinion, and raising his eyes to heaven he prayed; "Thou, O Lord, didst declare to me Thy will, that I should take Isaac my son and offer him to Thee in pledge of my obedience. I did not hesitate, I did not refuse, and now the water overwhelms us and we sink; how then can I perform that which Thou badest me do?"

The Lord answered, "Fear not, through thee shall My Name be known."

Then the stream vanished away, and they stood upon dry land.

But now Satan made another attempt to turn Abraham from

his purpose. He drew him aside and said, "The object of thy journey has failed. I caught a whisper in heaven, and it was this—God will prepare a lamb for the sacrifice, and not thy son."

Abraham answered, "Even if thy words be true, it matters not; for this is the penalty of liars, that when they speak the truth they are not believed."

Abraham journeyed on the rest of that day, without seeing his appointed place. Next day he retraced his steps, but could find no signs of the place. The Almighty had so ordered it, that men might not say Abraham was hasty and acted precipitately, but might see that he had leisure and time for reflection on what he was about to do.

On the morning of the third day,[1] they reached the height of Zophim, and thence Abraham saw a beautiful mountain-land, and on the top of one of the mountains was a fiery pillar, which reached from earth to heaven,—it was the Glory of the Lord appearing in the cloud.

When Abraham asked Isaac if he beheld this sight, he answered that he did so: but when he asked his other companions, they replied that they saw nothing save the brown hills and purple valleys. Some say they answered that one hill was to them like every other hill.

From this, Abraham concluded that God was well pleased with Isaac as a victim. Then he said to Eliezer and Ishmael :

"Tarry ye here with the ass, for you are not worthy to behold the Shekinah nearer. But I and the youth will go on, *so many* only shall go."

Now, as he said these words, it suddenly came to his mind that God had promised him a great people descended from Isaac, *so many* as the stars for multitude, and with prophetic voice he said, "If the Lord will, *so many* as go on, *so many* shall return."

Then Abraham laid the wood of the sacrifice on his son Isaac, and took the fire and the knife in his hand ; and they went on both together, Abraham joyous, and Isaac without fear or thought.

---

[1] The day is uncertain. Some say it was the 3d Nisan ; others, it was the first of the seventh month, Tischri, New Year's day ; others, that it was the Day of Atonement. Some say Isaac's age was 37 ; others say 36 ; others 26 ; others 25 ; others 16 ; others 13 ; others, again, say 5 ; and others say only 2 years.

But after they had gone some way, Isaac turned to his father and said, "Father, whither are we going alone?"

Abraham.—"My son, we go to offer a sacrifice?"

Isaac.—"But art thou a priest to execute this undertaking?"

Abraham.—"Shem, the High Priest, will prepare the victim."

A great fear fell upon Isaac when he saw that they had no animal with them to offer, and he said, "Here are the fire and the wood, but where is a lamb for the whole offering?"

Abraham.—"The lamb which is to be offered is foreknown to the Almighty. He will provide the lamb; and if none other is here, then must thou be the offering, my son."

Isaac was silent, for the fear of death came over him. But presently he recovered himself and said, "If God chooses me, I place my soul in His hands."

Abraham.—"My son! Is there any blemish in thee within? For the offering must be without blemish of any sort."

Isaac.—"My father! There is none. I swear by God and by thy life, that in my heart there is not the least resistance to the Divine will. My limbs do not tremble, and there is no quaking at my heart. With gladness do I say, The Lord be praised, who has chosen me for a whole sacrifice."[1]

Abraham.—"O my son, with many a wish wast thou brought into this world. Since thou hast been in it, every care has been lavished on thee. I hoped to have had thee to follow me and make a great nation. But now I must, myself, offer thee. Wondrous was thy coming into this world, and wondrous will be thy going out of it![2] Not by sickness, not by war, but as a sacrifice. I had designed thee to be my comfort and stay in old age; now God himself must take thy place."[3]

Isaac.—"It were unworthy of thee were I to think to withstand the decree of God, and of thee. Had the decision been thine alone, I would have obeyed."

---

[1] In the Rabbinic tradition, the type of Christ comes out more distinctly than in Genesis, for here we see Isaac not merely offered by his father, but also giving himself as a free-will offering, immaculate without in his body, and within in his soul.

[2] Might not these words be spoken mystically of Christ?

[3] And these prophetic. Abraham means that God must take care of him in his old age. But they may also be taken by us thus, God must take thy place as the victim.

When they reached the top of Moriah, God said to Abraham,—

"This is the place where once Adam, when driven out of Paradise, built an altar to My name.   Here also Cain and Abel offered their sacrifice.   Then came the Flood, and when it was passed away, Noah offered victims to Me here.   When the people were scattered from the tower of Babel, then this altar was overthrown.   Now it is for thee, friend of God, to set it up again!"

Abraham built the altar, and Isaac brought him the stones. But, according to some authors, this was not so.   Abraham hid his son in a cave, lest Satan should take advantage of the opportunity, with a stone or clod of earth, to blemish him.

And when all was ready and the wood laid in order, then Isaac said to his father, "Bind me hand and foot, lest in the fear of death I start and thou wound me, and so I be blemished. Fold thy garments together, and gird thy loins, and bare thine arm, and strike me with the knife and then burn me to ashes, and lay up my ashes in a coffer, and let this coffer be preserved as a memorial of me in thy house, before my mother; and when thou passest by it, bid her remember me.   But remind her not of it near a well, or on the edge of a precipice, lest she cast herself down in her grief."[1]

And he continued, "When thou returnest home, how wilt thou console my mother?"

Abraham answered, "Well I know that he who comforted us before thou camest, will comfort us after thou art gone from us."[2]

Abraham now stood over his son, who was bound with his hands to his feet, upon the wood laid in order; and the eyes of Abraham rested on the eyes of his son.   But Isaac looked up into heaven, and saw the Angel hosts crowded about God's throne.   Abraham saw not this, and he lifted the knife; but he trembled and the knife fell from his hand, and he cried aloud, "O my son!   Would that another offering were found

---

[1] Here again—it may be fanciful—but I cannot help thinking we have the type continued of Christ's presence perpetuated in the Church, in the Tabernacle in which the Host is reserved, that all passing by may look thereupon and worship, and "Remember Me" in the adorable Sacrament. With a vast amount of utterly unfounded fable, the Rabbinic traditions may, and probably do, contain much truth.

[2] "If I go not away, the Comforter will not come unto you; but if I depart, I will send Him unto you."   (John xvi. 7.)

instead of thee ! But my help cometh only from the Lord who hath made heaven and earth ?"

Then he gathered up his resolution, and took the knife and held it once more to strike ; and Isaac's spirit left him, and he swooned away.

But the angels of God, who stood round about His throne, announced to the Most High all that took place, and they cried and wept, and even the fiery seraphim exclaimed, " Woe ! He slays his son."   And the tears of the angels fell upon the face of Isaac, and made him ever after sad of countenance.

Then God said, " Behold and see how great is the faith of My servant Abraham, how on earth a man can hallow My great name, and devote his best and dearest to My service ; see that, ye, who at the creation exclaimed, *What is man, that thou art mindful of him, aud the son of man that thou so regardest him ?* "

Then He ordered Michael to fly swiftly, and stay the hand of Abraham.

And the archangel, when he came near, cried aloud, " Abraham ! Abraham ! what doest thou ? "

Abraham looked in the direction of the voice, in doubt, and said, " *Here am I.*"

Then said the angel, " *Lay not thine hand upon the lad, neither do thou any thing unto him.*"

And Abraham said, " Who art thou ? "

Michael told him who he was.   Then said Abraham, " The Most High appeared to me in a vision, and bade me take my son as a whole offering to the place which He should say, and I may take no command from a servant of God, against that which God Himself hath laid upon me."

Then heaven opened, and he saw the glory of God, and God said to him, " *Touch not the lad to do him harm, for now I know that thou fearest God, seeing thou hast not withheld thy son, thine only son, from Me.*"

And Abraham said, " How is this, O Lord ! that Thou changest Thy purpose, and sayest one day, Do this, and the next, Do it not ? "

And the Lord answered, and said, " I said not unto thee, Slay the lad as a burnt offering, but I said, Take thy son to the place that I shall tell thee, as a whole burnt offering.   This hast thou done ; thou hast fulfilled My command, I exact no more of thee.   I change not my purpose, but I did suffer thee

to misunderstand the purport of My command, and to think
that I exacted more of thee ; and this I did to prove thee.
And now, *by Myself have I sworn ; for because thou hast done
this thing, and hast not withheld thy son, thine only son ; that
in blessing I will bless thee, and in multiplying I will multiply
thy seed as the stars of the heavens, and as the sand which is
upon the sea shore ; and thy seed shall possess the gate of his
enemies.*"

Then Isaac revived, and Abraham cut his cords, and he
stood up and said, " Praised be the eternal One, who quicken-
eth those that be dead."

And Abraham turned to the Shekinah and said, " Lord !
how shall I depart hence without having offered to Thee a sacrifice ?"   The Lord answered, " Lift thine eyes, and thou shalt
see a beast for sacrifice behind thee."

In the thicket of the wood was that ram which God created
at dusk on the sixth day, that it might serve this purpose.   An
angel had brought it out of Paradise, where it had lived since .
its creation, and had fed under the shadow of the Tree of Life,
and had drunk of the River that there flows.   And when the
ram was brought into this earth, all the earth was filled with
the fragrance from its fleece, on which hung the odors of the
flowers on which it had lain in Paradise.

But by Satan's fraud, the animal was frightened and strayed
away, and Abraham tracked it by its foot-prints.   Then Satan
decoyed the beast behind some bushes and entangled its horns
in the thicket ; and Abraham would have passed by, and not
seen it, but the ram caught him by his cloak.   So Abraham
slew it, and offered it in sacrifice, and sprinkled with its blood
the altar he had made.

Now the Last Trumpets that shall sound, the one to call
the just, the other the unjust, are made of the horns of this
wondrous ram.

11. THE DEATH OF SARAH.

Sarah,—who, as we have seen, accompanied Abraham and
Isaac part of the way to Moriah,—on her return to the tent,
found an old man awaiting her.   It was Satan.

He greeted her with profound respect, and asked after her
husband and son.

She answered that they had gone forth on a journey.

"Whither have they gone?" asked Satan.

" My lord has gone to visit the school of Shem and Eber, our grandsires, there to leave my son Isaac to be instructed in the law of God."

" Alas! alas!" exclaimed the Apostate Angel; "thou art greatly deceived."

Sarah was alarmed; and she asked wherefore he spake thus.

" Know then," said Satan, "that Abraham has gone forth with Isaac to sacrifice him, upon a mountain, to the Most High "

When she heard this, Sarah laid her head on the bosom of a slave and fainted. When she came to herself she hurried with her maidens to the school of Shem and Eber, and inquired after her husband and son, but they had neither seen nor heard any thing of them. So Sarah was convinced that what had been told her was true, and there was no spirit left in her.

Now when Satan knew that Abraham was bringing back his son, and that God had accepted the will for the deed, he was moved with envy and spite, and he could not rest to think of the joy that this would cause; so he went hastily to Sarah, and she was weeping in her tent, and sorely cast down and broken in spirit. Then he said suddenly to her, " Thy son liveth and is returning. God hath spared him ! "

And she rose up and uttered a cry, and fell, and was dead; for the joy had killed her."

Abraham and Isaac, in the mean time had returned from Moriah, and they sought Sarah at Beer-sheba, but she was not there; therefore they went to Hebron, and there they found her corpse. Isaac fell weeping upon the face of his mother, and he cried, " Mother, mother! why hast thou forsaken me? why hast thou gone away?"

Abraham wept aloud, and all the dwellers in Hebron wept and lamented over Sarah, and ceased from their labors, that they might mourn with Abraham and Isaac. Sarah's age was one hundred and seven-and-twenty years, and she was as fair to look upon when she died as in the bloom of her youth.

And as Abraham was bowed over the body of his wife, he heard the laugh of the Angel of Death, and his words, " Wherefore weepest thou? Thou bearest the blame of her death. Hadst thou not taken her son from her, she would have been alive now."

Abraham sought a place where to bury her ; and he went to the Hittites and asked them to suffer him to buy for his possession a parcel of land, where he might bury one dead body. But they said, " Nay, we will give thee land ;" but he would not. So they said, " Choose now a place where thou wouldst have thy sepulchre, and we will entreat the owner for thee."

Then Abraham said, " I desire the double cave of Ephron the son of Zohar. *If it be your mind that I should bury my dead out of my sight, hear me, and entreat for me to Ephron the son of Zohar, that he may give me the cave of Machpelah, which he hath ; for as much money as is worth he shall give it me, for a possession of a burying-place amongst you."*

And this was the reason why Abraham desired that cave. When he had gone after the calf, to slay it for the three angels that came to him before the destruction of Sodom, the calf had fled from him, and he had pursued it into this cave ; and on entering it, he found that it was roomy, and in the inner recesses he saw the bodies of Adam and Eve laid out with burning tapers around them, and the air was fragrant with incense.

The Hittites elected Emor their chief that he might deal with Abraham, for it did not become a chief and prince, like Abraham, to deal with an inferior ; and Emor said in the audience of the people of the land, *" My Lord, hear me ; the field give I thee, and the cave that is therein, I give it thee ; in the presence of the sons of my people give I it thee ; bury thy dead."*

But this he said with craft, for he sought to take an advantage of Abraham.[1]

Then Ephron said, " Put thine own price upon the land ; " but this Abraham would not do.

Then Ephron said to Abraham, *"My lord, Hearken unto me ; the land is worth four hundred shekels of silver ; what is that betwixt me and thee ? bury therefore thy dead."*

Now the land was not worth half that sum, but Emor said in his heart, " Abraham can afford to pay it, and he is in haste to bury his dead out of his sight."

Nevertheless, Abraham paid him in the sight of all his peo-

---

[1] This is one instance out of several in which the honorable and generous conduct of a Gentile is distorted by Rabbinical tradition ; the later Rabbis being unwilling to give any but their own nation credit for liberal and just dealing. It may have been observed in the account of Abimelech, how the frank exchange of promises between Abraham and the Philistine prince was regarded by them as sinful.

ple.   And the transfer of the land and cave was signed by Amigal, son of Abischna the Hittite; Elichoran, son of Essunass, the Hivite; Abdon, son of Ahirah, the Gomorrhite; and Akdil, son of Abdis, the Sidonian.

Machpelah (double cave) was so called, because, say some, it contained two chambers; or, say others, because Abraham paid double its value; or, say others, because it became doubly holy; but others again observe, with the highest probability, . because Adam's body had to be doubled up to get it into the cave.

Because the Hittites dealt honorably, and sought to procure a place for Abraham, where he might lay Sarah, their name is written ten times in the Holy Scriptures.

They took also an oath of Abraham, that he and his seed should never attack their city Jebus with violence; and they wrote his promise on brazen pillars, and set them up in the market-place of Jebus. Therefore, when the Israelites conquered Canaan, they left the Jebusites unmolested.[1] But when David sought to take the stronghold of Jebus,[2] its inhabitants said to him, "Thou canst not storm our city, because of the covenant of Abraham, which is engraven on these pillars of brass."

David removed these brazen pillars, for they were in time honored as idols; therefore the inhabitants of Jebus were *hated of David's soul;*[3] but he did not break the covenant of Abraham, for he obtained the city of Jebus, not by force of arms, but by purchase.[4]

Sarah was buried with the utmost honor; Shem (Melchizedek), his grandson Eber, Abimelech, Aner, Eschol and Mamre, together with all the great men of the land, followed the bier. Abraham caused a great mourning throughout the country to be made for seven days. After that, Abraham returned to Beer-Sheba, and Isaac went to be instructed in the law by Melchizedek. A year after, died Abimelech, king of Gerar, and Abraham attended his funeral. Soon after, also, died Nahor, Abraham's brother.

---

[1] Joshua i. 21.   [2] 2 Sam. v. 6; 1 Chron. xi. 4.   [3] 2 Sam. v. 8.
[4] 2 Sam. xxiv. 24; 1 Chron. xxi. 24. This is, however, in direct contravention of the account in the fifth chapter of the 2d Samuel.

12. THE MARRIAGE OF ISAAC.

After the death of Sarah, say some, Abraham had a daughter named Bakila, by Hagar, who returned to him now that her enemy was dead ; but, according to others, the great blessing of Abraham consisted in this, that he had no daughters. Ishmael abandoned his disorderly ways, and loved and respected his brother.

Isaac mourned his mother three years. When this time was elapsed, Abraham called to him his faithful servant Eliezer, and said to him, " I am old, and I know not the day of my death ; therefore must I no longer delay the marriage of my son Isaac. Lay thine hand upon my thigh, and swear to me by God Almighty to fulfil my commission. Do not take for my son a wife of the daughters of the Canaanites, but go to Haran, to the place whence I came, and bring thence a wife for my son Isaac." And he added the proverb, " When you have wheat of your own, do not sow your field with your neighbor's corn."

Eliezer asked, " But how, if a woman of that place will not accompany me hither ? "

But Abraham said, " Fear not ; go, and the Lord be with thee."

So the servant of Abraham went with ten camels, and he reached Haran in three hours, for the earth fled under the feet of his camels, and Michael, the angel, protected him on his way.

When he reached Haran, he besought the Lord to give him a sign, by which he might know the maiden who was to be the wife of Isaac. *" Let it come to pass, that the damsel to whom I shall say, Let down thy pitcher, I pray thee, that I may drink ; and she shall say, Drink, and I will give thy camels drink also ; let the same be she that Thou hast appointed for Thy servant Isaac."*

And there were many damsels by the fountain. And the servant said to them, " Let down the pitcher that I may drink." But they all said, " We may not tarry, for we must take the water home."

Then came Rebekah the daughter of Bethuel, son of Milcah, the wife of Nahor, Abraham's brother, out of the well, and she chid the maidens for their churlishness ; and lo ! the water in the well leaped to the margin, and she let down her pitcher and

9*

offered it to the man, and said, "*Drink; and I will give thy camels drink also.*" Then Eliezer leaped from his camel, and he brought forth his gifts, and he gave her a nose ring with a jewel of half a shekel weight, and bracelets of ten shekels weight. And he asked if he might lodge in her house one night.

She answered, "Not one night only, but many."

Now Rebekah's brother, Laban, so called from the paleness of his face, or, say some, from the cowardice of his breast, which made him pale,—coveted the man's gold, and resolved to kill him. Therefore he put poison in the bowl of meat which was offered him. But the bowl was changed by accident, and it fell to the portion of Bethuel, and he ate, and died that same night.

And Laban would have fallen upon Eliezer with his own hand, but that he saw him lead the two camels at once over the brook, and he knew thereby that he was stronger than he.

After the engagement had been drawn up, as it is written in the first book of Moses,[1] Eliezer urged for a speedy departure. Mother and brother consented, but on the following day they asked that, besides the seven days of mourning for Bethuel, they should tarry a year, or at least ten months, according to the usual custom. But Rebekah opposed them, and said that she would go at once.

It was noon when Eliezer and his retinue, together with Rebekah and her nurse Deborah, left Haran, and in three hours they were at Hebron.

At the self-same time Isaac was abroad in the fields, returning from the school of Seth, lamenting over his mother, and saying his evening prayer. Rebekah saw him with his hands outspread, and his angel walking behind him, and she said, "Who is that with a shining countenance, with another walking behind him?"

At the same moment she knew who it was, and with prophetic vision she saw that she would become the mother of Esau, and she trembled and fell from the camel.

Isaac took Rebekah to wife and led her into the tent of Sarah, and the door was once more open, and the perpetual lamp was again kindled, and it seemed to Isaac as if all the happiness that had gone with Sarah, had returned with Rebekah, so he was comforted for his mother.

[1] Gen. xxiv. 34–49.

Eliezer was rewarded for his faithful service, for Abraham gave him his freedom, and he was taken into Paradise without having tasted of death.

13. THE DEATH OF ABRAHAM.

Abraham, after the death of Sarah, had brought back Hagar, and she was called Keturah, which signifies "the Bondwoman," and this she was called because she had ever regarded herself as bound to Abraham, though he had cast her away. But others say that Keturah was not Hagar, but was a daughter of one of Abraham's slaves. She bare him six sons,[1] all strong, and men of clear understandings.

According to Mussulman traditions, she was the daughter of Jokdan, and was a Canaanitish woman.

Abraham said to the Most High, in gratitude of heart, "Thou didst promise me one son, Isaac, and thou hast given me many!"

All his substance he gave to Isaac; but some say he gave him a double portion only, and the rest he made over to his other sons. And to Isaac only he gave the right to be buried in the cave of Machpelah, and along with that, his blessing. But others say that he did not give his blessing to Isaac, lest it should cause jealousy to spring up between him and his brothers. He said, "I am a mortal man; to-day here and to-morrow in the grave; I have done all I can do for my children, and now I will depart when it pleases my heavenly Father."

He sent the sons of Keturah away, that they might not dwell near Isaac, lest his greatness should swallow them up; and he built them a city of iron, with walls of iron. But the walls were so high that the light of the sun could not penetrate the streets, therefore he set in them diamonds and pearls to illumine the iron city.

Epher, a grandson of Abraham and Keturah,[2] went with an army into Libya and conquered it, and founded there a kingdom, and the land he called after his own name, Africa.

Abraham was alive when Rebekah, after twenty years of barrenness, bare to Isaac his sons, Esau and Jacob; and he saw them grow up before him till their fifteenth year, and he died on the day that Esau sold his birthright.

---

[1] Gen. xxv. 2.   [2] Gen. xxv. 4.

The days of his life had been 175 years; he reached not the age of 180, to which Isaac attained, because God shortened his life by five years, lest he should know the evil deeds of Esau.

The Angel of Death did not smite him, but God kissed him, and he died by that kiss; and because the sword of the angel touched him not, but his soul parted to the kiss of God, his body saw no corruption

This is the Mussulman story of his death. The Angel of Death, when bidden to take the soul of the prophet, hesitated about doing so without his consent. So he took upon him the form of a very old man, and came to Abraham's door. The patriarch invited him in and gave him to eat, but he noted with surprise the great infirmity of the old man, how his limbs tottered, how dull was his sight, and how incapable he was of feeding himself, for his hands shook, and how little he could eat, for his teeth were gone. And he asked him how old he was. Then the angel answered, "I am 202." Now Abraham was then 200 years old. So he said, "What! in two years shall I be as feeble and helpless as this? O Lord, suffer me to depart; now send the Angel of Death to me, to remove my soul." Then the angel took him,[1] having first watched till he was on his knees in prayer.[2]

Isaac and Ishmael buried him in the double cave by the side of Sarah; and he was followed to his grave by all the inhabitants of Canaan, and Shem and Eber went before the bier. And all the people wailed and said, "Woe to the vessel when the pilot is gone! woe to the pilgrims when their guide is lost!"

A whole year was Abraham lamented by the inhabitants of the land; men, and women, and young children joined in bewailing him.

Never was there a man like Abraham in perfect righteousness, serving God, and walking in His way from the earliest youth to the day of his death.

Abraham was the first, say the Mussulmans, whose beard became white. He asked God when it became so, "What is this?" The Lord replied, "It is a token of gentleness, my son."

[1] Tabari, i. c. lvii.   [2] Weil, p. 98.

XXV.

MELCHIZEDEK.

WE have seen that, according to Jewish traditions, Melchizedek is Shem, the son of Noah, whom God consecrated to be a priest forever, and who set up a kingdom on Salem.[1]

It is also said that, before he died, Lamech ordered his son, Noah, to transport the body of Adam to the centre of the earth. Now the centre or navel of the earth is Salem, afterwards called Jerusalem.

Lamech also bade Noah confide to one of his children the custody of the body of Adam, obliging him to remain all his life in the service of God, and in the practice of celibacy, never to shed blood, and to offer to God only the sacrifice of bread and wine.

Noah chose, according to some, Shem ; according to others, Melchizedek, the son of Shem. He did not suffer him to wear other garments than the skins of beasts ; nor to shave his head nor cut his nails, nor to build a house.

A Christian tradition is that Adam was buried on Golgotha, and that when Christ died, His blood flowed down upon the head of Adam, and cleansed him of his sin.

Dom Calmet, in one of his dissertations, gives various curious opinions which have been entertained on the subject of Melchizedek : some affirmed that he was identical with the patriarch Enoch, who came from the Terrestrial Paradise to confer with Abraham ; and others, that the Magi who adored the infant Christ were Enoch, Melchizedek, and Elias.

And some have supposed that Melchizedek was created before Adam, and was of celestial race. Others again have supposed that he was our Lord Jesus Christ who appeared to Abraham.

S. Athanasius gives a curious tradition of Melchizedek.

A queen, named Salem, had a grandson named Melchi. He was an idolater. Where he reigned is unknown ; but it is supposed that it was where now stands the city Jerusalem. Melchi married a princess named Salem, like his grandmother.

---

[1] This the Targumim, or pharaphrases of the Sacred Text, distinctly say, "Melchizedek, who was Shem, son of Noah, king of Jerusalem." (Etheridge, i. p. 199.)

By her he had two sons, of whom the younger was called Melchizedek.

One day that Melchi was about to sacrifice to idols, he said to his son Melchizedek, " Bring me here seven calves to sacrifice to the gods."

Whilst going to execute his father's order, Melchizedek raised his eyes to heaven and said, " He who made heaven and earth, the sea and the stars, is the only God to whom sacrifice should be offered."

Then he returned to his father, who asked him, "Where are the calves?"

" My father," he replied, " hearken to me, and be not angry. Instead of offering thy victims to those gods which are no gods, offer them to Him who is above the heavens, and who rules all things."

King Melchi replied, " Go and do what I have commanded thee, as thou valuest thy life."

After that he turned to his wife Salem, and he told her that he purposed sacrificing one of his sons.   The queen wept bitterly, because she knew that the king designed the immolation of Melchizedek, and she said, " Alas ! I have suffered and labored in vain."

" Do not weep," said Melchi, somewhat touched.   "We will draw the lot : if it is mine, I will choose which of the sons is to die ; if it be thine, thou shalt keep the one dearest to thee."

Now the lot fell to the queen, so she chose Melchizedek, whom she loved : and the king adorned his eldest son for sacrifice.

There were in the temple troops of oxen and flocks of sheep and five hundred and three children, destined by their parents to be sacrificed.   The queen was at home weeping, and she said to Melchizedek, " Dost thou not weep for thy brother, whom we have brought up with so much care, and who is led to the slaughter?"

Melchizedek wept, and he said to his mother, " I will go and invoke the Lord, the only true God Most High."

He ascended Tabor, and kneeling down, he prayed, saying, " My God, Lord of all, Creator of heaven and earth, I adore Thee as the only true God ; hearken now unto my prayer.   May the earth open her mouth and swallow up all those who assist at the sacrifice of my brother ! "

God heard the cry of Melchizedek, and the earth parted asunder, and swallowed up the temple and all who were therein ; and the city of Salem also, and not a stone was left standing where it had been.

When Melchizedek came down from Tabor, and saw what God had done, he was filled with dismay, and retired into a forest, where he spent seven years, feeding on herbs and drinking the dew.

At the end of that time, a voice from heaven called Abraham, and said, "Take thine ass, lade it with rich garments, go to Tabor and cry thrice, O man of God !   Then a man of a savage appearance will come forth to thee out of the forest. And after thou hast cut his hair and pared his nails, clothe him with the garments thou hast taken with thee, and ask him to bless thee."

Abraham did as he was bidden.   He went to Tabor and called thrice, " O man of God ! " and there came out to him Melchizedek.   Then a voice was heard from heaven, which said, "As there remains no one on earth of the family of Melchizedek, it shall be said of him that he is without father and without mother, without beginning of days or end of life."

Therefore it is said of him, as of Enoch and Elias, that having been created a priest forever, he is not dead.

Afterwards he is said to have founded Jerusalem.[1]

Suidas the Grammarian gives the following account of this mysterious personage.

" Melchizedek, priest of God, king of Canaan, built a city on a mountain called Sion, and named it Salem ; which is the same as $E\ell\rho\eta\nu\delta\pi o\lambda\iota\varsigma$, the City of Peace.   In which, when he had reigned a hundred and thirteen years, he died, righteous and single.   For this reason he is said to have been without generation, because he was not of the seed of Abraham, but of the race of Canaan, and of abhorred seed.   Therefore he was without honorable generation.   Nor did it beseem him, the essence of all righteousness, to unite with the race of all unrighteousness.   Therefore he is said to have been without father or mother.   But that he was a Caananite, both as to country, of which he was lord ; and as to nation, of which he was king : and as to neighborhood, joining that of the iniquitous Sodomites,—that is evident enough.   Nevertheless Salem, of which he was king, is that celebrated Jerusalem, which, however, did not bear then the complete name of Hierusalem, but the ad-

---

[1] Fabricius, Codex Pseud. V. T. t. i. p. 311.   The Book of the Combat of Adam says Melchizedek was the son of Canaan.

jective ἱερο ῦ was added to Σαλήμ afterwards, and compounded into Hierusalem.   And because no genealogy is given to him, he is said to be without father and mother.   Therefore, when you hear him spoken of as God, by the sect of the Melchizedekites, remember the saying of the Apostle, that he was of another race, to wit, that of Canaan." [1]

Another apocryphal account of Melchizedek is in the "Chronicon Paschale :"—

"A certain ancient relates and affirms, concerning Melchizedek, this.   He was a man of the tribe of Ham, who, being found a holy seed in his tribe, pleased God; and God called him into the land beyond Jordan, even as He called Abraham out of the land of the Chaldeans.   And as this man was holy and just, he was made a priest of the Most High God, to offer bread and wine, and holy prayers to the Most High God.   He prayed for his tribe, saying, Lord, thou hast brought me from my own people, and hast had mercy on me; have mercy on them also.   But God answered him, and said, I will save them when I call my Son out of Egypt.   This promise God gave to Melchizedek.   The same ancient relates also that at this time it happened that Lot was carried away captive from Sodom by those who were of the tribe Gothologomos, whom Abraham pursued and destroyed, and he liberated all the captives; and Lot also, the son of his brother Aram, he delivered from their hands.   Therefore Abraham said within himself, Lord, if in my days Thou sendest Thy angel upon the earth, grant me to see that day!   The Lord said, It cannot be, but I will show thee a figure of that day; go down and cross the river Jordan and thou shalt behold it.

"Therefore Abraham crossed Jordan with his men, and Melchizedek came forth to meet him, called by the Holy Ghost, having in his hands the bread of Eucharists and the wine of thanksgiving.   Abraham did not see Melchizedek till he had passed over Jordan, which is the symbol of Baptism.

"Abraham then, seeing Melchizedek coming to meet him having the bread of Eucharists and the cup of thanksgiving, fell on his face upon the earth, and adored, since he saw the day of the Lord, and was glad.

"Melchizedek, king of Salem, priest of the Most High God, blessed Abraham and said, *Blessed be Abram of the Most High God, possessor of heaven and earth; and blessed be the*

[1] Suidas, Lexic. s. v. Μελχισεδεκ.

*Most High God, which hath delivered thine enemies into thy
hands.* And Abraham gave him tithes of all." [1]

Michael Glycas says: " Melchizedek, though he is said in
the Sacred Scriptures to have been without father and mother,
yet sprung from Sidos, son of Ægyptos, who built Sidon.
When he had built a city on Mount Sion, named Salem, he
reigned there thirteen years, and died a just man and a virgin." [2] And Cedrenus: " Melchizedek was the son of King
Sidos, son of Ægyptos, but he was said to be without father
and mother and of uncertain generation, because he was not
of Jewish extraction, and because his parents were bad and
not reckoned among the righteous." [3]

Joseph Ben-Gorion writes: " O Jerusalem! once the city
of the great King, by what name shall I designate thee? An-
ciently thou wast called Jebus, after thy founder; then thou
didst acquire the name of Zedek, and from thence did thy
king Jehoram take his title Melchi-zedek (or Melech-zedek,
Lord of Zedek), for he was a just king, and he reigned in thee
justly. And thou didst obtain the name of Justice, and in
thee justice dwelt, and the star that did illumine thee; thou
wast called Zedek, and in the same king's reign, to thee was
given the title Salem, as it is written in the Law: and Melchizedek was king of Salem, so called because thus the measure of the iniquity of the people was accomplished. But Abraham, our father, of pious memory, chose thee, to labor in thee
and to acquire in thee a possession, and in thee to lay a root
of good works, and because the majesty of God dwelt in thee,
when Abraham, our father, flourished." [4]

S. Epiphanius, however, says: " Although no names of the
parents of Melchizedek are given, yet some assert that his father was called Heraclas, and his mother Astaroth, or As-
teria." [5] The " Catena Arabica " on Genesis says: " Melchizedek was the son of Heraclis, the son of Peleg, the son of
Eber; and the name of his mother was Salathiel, the daughter
of Gomer, the son of Japheth, the son of Noah."

---

[1] Πασχάλιον, seu Chronicon Paschale a mundo condito ad Heraclii
imp. ann. vicesimum. Ed. C. du Fresne du Cange; Paris, 1688, p. 49.

[2] Michael Glycas, Βίβλος χρονική, ed. Labbe; Paris, 1660, p. 135.

[3] Georgius Cedrenus, Σς νοψιύ ίστοριῶν, ed. Goar; Paris, 1647. t.
i. p. 27.

[4] Josephus Ben-Gorion, lib. vi. c. 35, apud Fabricium, i. p. 326.

[5] S. Epiphanius Hæresi, lv. c. 2.

Melchizedek is said to have composed the cx. Psalm, *Dixit Dominus.*[1]

The tomb of Melchizedek is, or was, shown at Jerusalem, says Gemelli Carrere, the traveller in Palestine.

XXVI.

OF ISHMAEL AND THE WELL ZEMZEM.

THE Arabs call Hagar, Hagiar Anaï, the mother in chief, because of Ishmael her son. They do not suppose that she was the bond-servant of Sarah, but that she was the legitimate wife of the patriarch ; and she bore him Ishmael, who, as his eldest son, had the birthright, and obtained, as his double portion of Abraham's inheritance, the land of Arabia, whereas to Isaac was given the inferior land of Canaan.

They say that Hagar died at Mecca, and that she was buried in the exterior enclosure of the Kaaba, or square temple, built, say they, by Abraham.

Near the tomb is the well of Zemzem, which is the fountain which God revealed to her when she had been driven out of the house of Sarah, and had fled into Arabia.

As has been already mentioned, the Mussulmans say that it was Ishmael and not Isaac whom Abraham prepared to sacrifice. The story need not be related again, as all the particulars in the Jewish legends are absorbed into the Mussulman account.

One particular alone needs mention. Gabriel gave the ram to Abraham in the place where Mussulman pilgrims now cast stones ; namely, on the mountain of Mina. But the ram escaped out of the hands of Abraham, and the patriarch threw seven stones after it. Then Ishmael went forward, and the ram halted. Ishmael went up to the ram and brought it to Abraham, and he took it, and slew it. Some say that this was the same ram that Abel had offered in sacrifice, and which had been preserved in Paradise.[2]

Then God said to Abraham, "Go to Mecca along with Ishmael, and build me the temple there."

At Mecca had been the "Visited-house," to which Adam went in pilgrimage, and round which he walked in procession

---

[1] Talmud, Tract. Bava Bathra.   [2] Tabari, i. c. liii.

every year. When the Flood came, this house had been caught up into heaven.

When Abraham went in obedience to the command of God to visit Ishmael, and to call him to build the temple, he found him on a mountain engaged in making arrows. He said to him, "O my son, God has ordered me to build a house along with thee."

Ishmael replied, "I am ready to obey, O my father."

Then they prepared to build. But Abraham knew nothing of architecture.

God sent a cloud of the size of the Kaaba, to show them, by its shadow on the ground, what were to be the dimensions of the house, and to give them shade in which to build.

But some say that the Serpent arrived and instructed Abraham in the proportions of the house. After that, Abraham and Ishmael began to dig the trenches which were to receive the foundations; and they gave them the depth of a man's stature. Then they raised them to the level of the soil; after that, they cut stones out of the neighboring rocks for the walls of the edifice. Abraham built, and Ishmael handed the stones. Now, when the wall got above his reach, Abraham placed a stone on the ground, and stood upon that to build, and he left thereon the impression of his foot. The stone remains to this day, and is called Makam Ibrah'm.

And when the temple was built, God sent Gabriel to instruct Abraham in all the rights of pilgrimage, and how to visit Mina and Mount Arafat, and how to go processionally round the Kaapa, and to cast the stones, and to wear the pilgrim's dress, and to make sacrifice, and to shave the head, to visit the holy places, and all that concerns the pilgrimage.

That same year Abraham made the pilgrimage, and he confided the care of the temple to Ishmael, his son, and he said to him, "This land belongs to thee and to thy children till the Judgment Day."

Then Abraham, turning him about, went at God's command to the top of a high mountain, and cried, "O men, God has built you a house, and He calls you to visit it."

And all men and women, and the children yet unborn, answered from every quarter of the world, "We will visit it."

Then Abraham returned into Syria.[1]

---

[1] Tabari; Weil, Abulfeda, pp. 25–27, etc.

Now the well of Zemzem was formed when Hagar and Ishmael were in the desert. The angel Gabriel trod in the ground and the water bubbled up. At first it was sweet as honey, and as nourishing as milk. This well is one of the wonders of Mecca. We shall relate more of it presently.

And the stone that was white and shining, but now is black, that stone was an angel who wept over the sins of men till he has grown dark; that also is one of the wonders of Mecca.

Whilst Ishmael was engaged one day in building the Kaaba, there came to him Alexander the Two-horned, and asked him what he was doing.

Then Abraham answered, "We build a temple to the only God in whom we believe." And Alexander knew that he was a prophet of God; and he went on foot seven times round the temple.

About this Alexander authorities differ. Some say that he was a Greek, and that he was lord of the whole earth as Nimrod was before him, and as Soloman was after him.

Alexander was lord of light and darkness; when he went forth with his hosts, he had light before him, and behind him was darkness: thus he could overtake his enemies, but could not be overtaken by them. He had also two banners, one white and the other black, and when he unfurled the white one, it was instantly broad day; and when he unfurled the black one, it was instantly midnight. Thus he could have day in the darkest night, and night in the brighest day.

He was also unconquerable; for he could, at will, make his army invisible, and fall upon his enemies and destroy them, without their being able to see who were opposed to them. He went through the whole world in quest of the Fountain of Immortality, of which, as he read in his sacred books, a descendant of Shem was pre-ordained to drink, and become immortal.

But his vizir Al Hidhr[1] lighted on the fountain before him and drank, not knowing what were the virtues of this spring; and when Alexander came afterwards, the water had sunk away, for by God's command only one man was destined to drink thereof.

Alexander was called the Two-horned, according to some, because he went through the world from one end to the other;

---

[1] Or El Khoudr: he is identified in Arab legend with S. George and Elias.

according to others, because he wore two long locks of hair which stood up like horns; according to others, because he had two gold horns on his crown which symbolized the kingdoms of Grecia and Persia over which he reigned. But according to others, he once dreamed that he had got so near to the son, that he caught it by its two ends, and therefore he was given his name.

Learned men are also equally disagreed as to the time in which he lived, and as to the place of his birth and residence.

Most think that there were two Alexanders. One was descended from Shem, and went with El Khoudr to the end of the world after the Fountain of Immortality, and who was ordered by God to build an indestructible wall against the incursions of the children of Gog and Magog. The other Alexander was the son of Philip of Macedon, and was descended from Japheth, and was the pupil of Aristotle at Athens.[1]

And now let us return to the fountain or well of Zemzem, and relate what befel that.

Nabajoth, the eldest son of Ishmael, succeeded his father in the custody of the Kaaba, of the tombs of Adam and Eve, of the stone and the well. But having left only very young children to succeed him, Madad-ben-Amron, their maternal grandfather, took charge of their education, and at the same time became the protector of the Kaaba and of the well of Zemzem.

The children of Nabajoth, when they grew old, would not contest with their foster-father the possession of the Holy places, therefore it remained to him and his sons till the time when the Giorhamides took them by violence.

Then the posterity of Ishmael having attacked them, defeated them, and recovered the city and temple of Mecca. But the stone, and the two gazelles of gold which a king of Arabia had given to the Kaaba, had been lost, for they had been thrown into the well of Zemzem, which had been filled up.

The well remained choked and unregarded till the times of Abd-el-Motalleb, grandfather of Mohammed, who one day heard a voice bid him dig the well of Zemzem.

Abd-el-Motalleb asked the voice what Zemzem was.

Then the voice replied: " It is the well that sprang up to

---

[1] Weil. pp. 94–6.

nourish Ishmael in the desert, whereof he and his children drank."

Abd-el-Motalleb, not knowing whereabouts to dig, asked further, and the voice answered, "The well of Zemzem is near two idols of the Koraïschites named Assaf and Naïlah; dig on the spot where you shall see a magpie pecking in the ground and turning up a nest of ants."

Abd-el-Motalleb set about obeying the voice, in spite of the opposition of the Koraïschites, who objected to the overthrow of their idols. However, he dug, along with his ten sons, and he vowed that if God would show him the water, he would sacrifice one of his sons. And when he came to water, he found the gazelles of gold and the Black Stone.

Then he summoned his children before him and told them his vow. And he drew lots which of them should die, and the lot fell on Abd-Allah, the father of the prophet.

Then said Abd-el-Motalleb, "I am in a great strait; how shall I perform my vow?" For he loved Abd-Allah best of his ten sons. Now the mother of Abd-Allah belonged to the family of Benu-Zora, which is one of the chief in Mecca.

The Benu-Zora family assembled and said, "We will not suffer you to slay your son." But he said, "I must perform my vow." Then he consulted two Jewish astrologers, who said, "Go, and put on one side your child, and on the other your camel, and draw the lot; and if the lot fall on Abd-Allah, add a second camel to the first, and draw the lot again, and continue adding camels till the lot falls on them; then you will know how many camels will be accepted by God as an equivalent for your son."

He did so, and he put one camel, then two, then three, up to fifty. The lot fell on Abd-Allah up to the ninety-ninth camel; but when Abd-el-Motalleb had added the hundreth, then the lot fell on those animals, and he knew that they were accepted in place of his son, and he sacrificed them to the Lord; and this custom has continued among the Arabs, to redeem a man who is to be sacrificed by one hundred camels.[2]

Now when the Koraïschites saw what Abd-el-Motalleb had drawn from the well, they demanded a share of the treasure he had found. But he refused it, saying that all belonged to the temple that Abraham and Ishmael had built.

[2] Tabari, i. p. 181.

To decide this quarrel, they agreed to consult a dervish who dwelt on the confines of Syria, and passed for a prophet. It fell out that, on the way, Abd-el-Motalleb, exhausted with thirst, was obliged to ask water of the Koraïschites, but they fearing that they would not have enough for themselves, were obliged to refuse.

Then, from the ground pressed by the foot of the camel of Abd el-Motalleb, a fountain gushed forth, which quenched the thirst of himself and of those who had refused to give him water, and they, seeing the miracle, recognized him as a prophet sent from God, and they relinquished their pretensions to the well of Zemzem.

And when the well was cleared out, Abd-el-Motalleb gave to the temple of the Kaaba the two gazelles of gold, and all the silver, and the arms and precious things he found in the well. For long, Mecca was supplied with water from the well of Zemzem alone, till the concourse of pilgrims became so great, that the Khalifs were obliged to construct an aqueduct to bring abundance of water into the city.

Mohammed, to honor the town of Mecca, where he was born, gave great praise to the water of the well. It is believed among the Arabs that a draught of that water gives health, and that to drink much thereof washes away sin. It is related of a certain Mussulman teacher, who knew a great many traditions, that, having been interrogated on his memory, he replied, "Since I have drunk long draughts of the water of Zemzem, I have forgotten nothing that I learnt."

To conclude what we have to say of Ishmael.

He had a daughter named Basemath, whom he married to Esau, and many sons; two, Nabajoth and Kedar, were his sons who dwelt in Mecca. He was a hundred and thirty years old when he died, and he was buried at Mecca, after having appointed Isaac his executor.

XXVII.

ESAU AND JACOB.

THERE are few Oriental traditions, whether Rabbinic or Mussulman, concerning Isaac's life after he was married and his father died. Those touching his birth, early life, and marriage, have been given in the article on Abraham.

We proceed therefore, to his history as connected with Esau and Jacob.

Isaac, says Tabari, lived a hundred years after Ishmael. God granted him the gift of prophecy, and sent him to the inhabitants of Syria, in the country of Canaan, for he could not change his place of abode on account of his blindness; for Abimelech had wished him to be dim of sight, because Abraham had deceived him by saying, " Sarah is my sister ;" and, say the Rabbis, Isaac's eyes were made dim by the tears of the angels falling into them as he was stretched upon the altar by his father ; or because he had then looked upon the Throne of God, and had been dazzled thereby.

But others say he went blind through grief and tears at his son Esau having taken four Canaanitish women to wife.

Isaac had two sons, twins, by Rebekah his wife—Esau and Jacob.

The Cabbalists say that the soul of Esau, whom the Arabs call Aïs, passed into the body of Jesus Christ by metempsychosis, and that Jesus and Esau are one ; and this they attempt to prove by showing that the Hebrew letters composing the name of Jesus are the same as those of which Esau is compounded.[1]

The following curious story is told of the brothers by the Rabbi Eliezer :—" It is said that when Jacob and Esau were in their mother's womb, Jacob said to Esau, ' My brother, there are two worlds before us, this world and the world to come. In this world, men eat, and drink, and traffic, and marry, and bring up sons and daughters; but all this does not take place in the world to come. If you like, take this world, and I will take the other.' And Esau denied that there was a resurrection of the dead, and said, ' *Behold I am at the point to die; and what profit shall this birthright do to me ?* ' And he gave over to Jacob in that hour his right to the other world." [2] Therefore Esau and his descendants have no part or lot in Paradise, and none are admitted there.[3]

It is also said that the religious predilections of the children were developed before they were born. On the words of Gen-

---

[1] Maschmia Jeschua, fol. 19, col. 4.
[2] Nezach Israel, fol. 25, col. 3.
[3] Eisenmenger, ii. pp. 260, 304.

esis, "*The children struggled together within her,*"[1] a Rabbinic commentator says that when Rebekah passed before a synagogue, then Jacob made great efforts to escape into the world, that he might attend the synagogue, and this is the meaning of the words of the prophet Jeremiah, when God says of Jacob, *Before thou camest forth out of the womb I sanctified thee:*"[2] But whenever she went before an idol temple, Esau became excited, and desired to come forth.[3]

When Esau was born, he had on his heel the likeness of a serpent, and his name indicates that he was closely connected with Satan (Sammael ; for, says the Rabbi Isaiah, if you write the name Sammael in Hebrew characters, you will find it to be identical with that of Esau ; for the four letters of Esau turned one way make Sammael, and turned another way make Edom.[4] Esau had also a serpent in his inside coiled in his bowels.[5]

Esau was called Edom, or Red, because, say some, he sucked his mother's blood before he was born ; or, say others, because he was to shed blood ; or again, because he was born under the ruddy planet Mars ; or again, because he liked to eat his meat underdone and red ;[6] but the Targumim say that Esau had red hair over his body like a garment ; therefore he was called Esau.[7]

The lads grew ; and Esau was a man of idleness to catch birds and beasts, a man going forth into the field to kill, as Nimrod had killed, and Anak, his son. But Jacob was a man peaceful in his works, a minister of the school of Eber, seeking instruction before the Lord. And Isaac loved Esau, for words of deceit were in his mouth ; but Rebekah loved Jacob.[8]

On the day that Abraham died, Jacob dressed pottage of lentiles, and was going to comfort his father. And Esau came from the wilderness, exhausted ; for in that day he had committed five transgressions—he had worshipped with strange worship, he had shed innocent blood, he had pursued a betrothed damsel, he had denied the life of the world to come, and he had despised his birthright.[9]

---

[1] Gen. xxv. 22.   [2] Jer. i. 5.   [3] Bereschith Rabba, fol. 56., col. 2.
[4] Eisenmenger, i. p. 646.   [5] Ibid.   [6] Ibid., pp. 650–1.
[7] Targums, ed. Etheridge, i. p. 240.   [8] Ibid., p. 241.
[9] Ibid., also R. Bechai's Comment. on the Five Books of Moses, fol. 35, col. 1.

And Esau said to Jacob, "Let me now taste that red pottage, for I am faint." Therefore he called his name Edom.

And Jacob said, "Sell to me to-day what thou wouldst hereafter appropriate—thy birthright."

And Esau said, "Behold, I am going to die, and in another world I shall have no life; and what then to me is the birthright, or the portion in the world of which thou speakest?

And Jacob said, "Swear to me to-day that so it shall be."

And he swore to him, and sold his birthright to Jacob. And Jacob gave to Esau bread, and pottage of lentiles. And he ate and drank, and arose and went. And Esau scorned the birthright, and the portion of the world that cometh, and denied the resurrection of the dead.[1]

But according to certain Rabbinic authorities Esau sold his birthright not only for the mess of lentiles, but also for a sword that Jacob had—to wit, the sword of Methuselah, wherewith he had slain a thousand devils.[2]

Esau had the garment which God had made for Adam,[3] on which were embroidered the forms of all the wild beasts and birds that were on the face of the earth, in their proper colors. This garment had been stolen by Ham from Noah in the ark, and had been given by him to Cush, who gave it to Nimrod. Esau killed Nimrod, and took from him his painted dress, and thenceforth all the success in hunting which had attended Nimrod devolved upon Esau.[4]

The story of the blessing of Jacob and Esau has not become surrounded with many fables. The following are the most remarkable. Esau on that occasion went forth in such haste to catch the venison, that he forgot to take with him Nimrod's garment, and therefore was not successful in hunting, as on former occasions, and Jacob took advantage of this forgetfulness to assume the embroidered coat.[5]

And when the meat was ready, and Isaac began to eat thereof, he was thirsty, and there was no wine for him in the house. So an angel was sent to him out of Paradise, and

---

[1] Targum of Palestine and Jerusalem; Etheridge, i. 241, 242. The book Yaschar says the deed of transfer was written by Jacob on a leaf, and that he and Esau sealed it, p. 1151.

[2] Eisenmenger, i. p. 651.   [3] Gen. iii. 21.

[4] Yaschar, p. 1150, where is the story of the assassination of Nimrod by Esau.

[5] Ibid.

brought him the juice of the grape that grows there on the vine that was created before the foundations of the earth were laid.[1]

Isaac was so angry at having been deceived by Jacob, that he was about to doom him to Gehinnom, after he said, *" Where is he that hath taken vension, and brought it me, and I have eaten of all before thou camest, and have blessed him ? "* But he paused to prepare his curse.

Then God suddenly opened hell to him beneath his feet, and he looked into it, and saw the abyss of fire and darkness, and his horror rendered him speechless ; but when he recovered his voice, he resolved that no child of his should descend there ; therefore he added, *" Yea, and he shall be blessed."* [2]

The Mussulmans relate the history of Esau and Jacob much as it stands in the Book of Genesis. They add that the benediction of Esau was fulfilled in his having a son named Roum, from whom sprang the Greek and Roman empires.

This is also a Rabbinical tradition, for the Talmudists say that Esau had a son named Eliphaz, who had a son, Zepho, from whom Vespasian and his son Titus were descended, and thus they attribute the destruction of Jerusalem to the struggle of Esau to break the yoke of Jacob from off his neck.

Esau is said by the Rabbis to have had four wives, in imitation of Satan, or Sammael, as has been already related.

Abulfaraj says that Esau made war with Jacob, and was killed by him with an arrow.

Jacob feared Esau, for Esau said in his heart, " I will not do as Cain did, who slew his brother Abel in the lifetime of his father, after which his father begat Seth ; but I will wait till the days of mourning for my father are accomplished, and then I will kill Jacob, and so I shall be the sole heir." [3]

Therefore Jacob went out only at night ; during the day he hid himself away. Thus several years passed, and his life became intolerable to him. So his mother said, " Thy uncle Laban, the son of Bethuel, has great possessions, and is very old. Go, and ask him to give thee his daughter ; and if he consents, then tarry with him till thy brother's anger turn away." Jacob listened to the advice of his mother, and he fled away without letting Esau know.

Five miracles were wrought for the patriarch Jacob, at the

<hr>

[1] Eisenmenger, ii. p. 879. [2] Ibid., p. 262.
[3] Targums, i. p. 250.

time when he went forth from Beer-sheba. First, the hours of the day were shortened, and the sun went down before its time, because the Word desired to speak with him; secondly, the four stones, which Jacob had set for his pillow, he found in the morning had coagulated into one stone; thirdly, the stone which, when all the flocks were assembled, the shepherds rolled from the mouth of the well, he rolled away with one of his arms; fourthly, the well overflowed, and the water continued to flow all the days he was in Haran. The fifth sign—the country was shortened before him, so that in one day he went forth and came to Haran.[1]

And he prayed in the place where he rested, and took four stones of that place, and set them for a pillow, and went asleep. Of these stones this is the history. They were twelve in num-ber, and Adam had set them up as an altar. On them Abel had offered his sacrifice. The Deluge had thrown them down, but Noah reared them once more. They had been again over-thrown, but Abraham set them in their places, and of them built the altar on which to sacrifice Isaac. These twelve stones Jacob now found, and he placed them under his head as a pil-low. But a great wonder was wrought, and in the morning the twelve stones had melted together into one stone.[2]

Finally, this stone, so ancient and with such a history, was carried to Scotland, by whom I do not know, where it was placed at Scone, and was used for the consecration of the Scot-tish kings. Edward I. of England brought it to London, and it was set beneath the chair of the Confessor, as the following lines, inscribed on a tablet, announced :—

> " Si quid habent veri, vel chronica cana, fidesve,
>   Clauditur hac cathedra nobilis, ecce, lapis.
> Ad caput eximius Jacob quondam patriarcha
>   Quem posuit cernens numina mira poli.
> Quem tulit ex Scottis, spolians quasi victor honoris,
>   Edwardus primus, Mars velut omnipotens.
> Scottorum domitor, noster validissimus Hector,
>   Anglorum decus, et gloria militiæ."[3]

The stone may now be seen in Westminster Abbey.

When Jacob—to return to our narrative—slept with his

---

[1] Targums, i. p. 252.   [2] Pirke R. Eliezer, c. 35.
[3] William Sanderson, Vita Mariæ, reg. Scot., et Jacobi, reg. Anglorum ; also Beckmann, Notitiar. dignit. Dissert. 3, c. i. § 7.

head on the pillow of stones, he dreamed, and beheld a ladder fixed in the earth, and the summit of it reached to the height of heaven. And, behold! the angels who had accompanied him from the house of his father, ascended to make known to the angels on high, saying, "Come, see Jacob the pious, whose likeness is in the throne of glory, and whom you have been desirous to see!" These were the two angels who had been sent to Sodom to destroy it, and who had been forbidden to rise up to the throne of God again, because, say some, they had revealed the secrets of the Lord of the whole earth, or because, say others, they had threatened in their own name to destroy the cities of the plain.

Then the rest of the angels of God came down, at the call of these twain to look upon Jacob.

And the Glory of the Lord stood above him, and He said to him, "I am the Lord God of Abraham, thy father, and the God of Isaac. The land on which thou art lying I will give to thee and thy sons. And thy sons shall be many as the dust of the earth, and shall become strong in the west and in the east, and in the north and in the south; and all the kindreds of the earth shall be blessed through thy righteousness and the righteousness of thy sons."

When Jacob arrived at Haran, he saw a well in a field, and three flocks lying near it—because from that well they watered the flocks—and a great stone was laid upon the mouth of the well.

And Jacob said to the shepherds, "My brethren, whence are ye?"

They said, "From Haran are we."

And he said, "Know you Laban, son of Nahor?" They answered, "We know him."

And he said, "Hath he peace?"

They said, "Peace; and behold, Rachel, his daughter, cometh with the sheep."

And he said, "Behold, the time of the day is great; it is not time to gather home the cattle; water the sheep."

But they said, "We cannot, until all the shepherds be gathered, and then we can altogether roll away the stone."

While they were speaking with him, Rachel came with her father's sheep; for she was a shepherdess at that time, because there had been a plague among the sheep of Laban, and but few of them were left; and he had dismissed his shepherds, and had put the remaining flock before Rachel, his daughter.

Then Jacob went nigh, and rolled the stone which all the shepherds together could scarce lift, with one of his hands, and the well uprose, and the waters flowed, and he watered the sheep of Laban, his mother's brother ; and it uprose for twenty years.

And Jacob kissed Rachel, and lifted up his voice and wept.

And Jacob told Rachel that he was come to be with her father to take one of his daughters.   Then Rachel answered him : " Thou canst not dwell with him, for he is a man of cunning."

But Jacob said, " I am more cunning than he."

And when she knew that he was the son of Rebekah, she ran and made it known to her father.   And when Laban heard the account of the strength of Jacob, his sister's son, and how he had taken the birthright and the order of blessing from the hand of his brother, and how the Lord had revealed Himself to him in the way, and how the stone had been removed, and how the well had upflowed and risen to the brink,—he ran and kissed him, and led him into his house.

Laban had two daughters ; the name of the elder was Leah and the name of the younger, Rachel.   And the eyes of Leah were moist and running, from weeping and praying before the Lord, that He would not destine her for Esau the wicked.

Jacob served Laban seven years, and was given Leah to wife ; and he served seven years more; and he was given Rachel to wife ; and he served six years for cattle that Laban gave him ; and then, seeing that Laban's face was set against him, he fled away secretly from Laban's house, and Rachel stole the image that Laban worshipped.   And this image was the head of a man, a first-born, that Laban had slain, and he had salted it with salt and balsams, and had written incantations on a plate of gold for it, and this head spake to him and told him oracles, and Laban bowed himself down before it.[1]

Jacob drew near to the land of Esau, and he feared that his enmity was not abated ; therefore he sent a message before him to his brother, and he tarried all night at Mahanaim.   And he sent a present before him to Esau to abate his anger.

The Book of Jasher gives some curious details on the meeting of the brothers.

[1] The whole of the above is from the Targumim

Jacob, trusting to the support of the Most High, besought Him to stand by him, and deliver him from the wrath of his brother. And God sent four angels to protect him ; these angels went before him. The first who met Esau presented himself at the head of a thousand horsemen, armed at all points, who fell upon the troop that accompanied Esau, and dispersed it. As this body of men swept along, they shouted, "We are the servants of Jacob ; who can resist us?"

A second body followed, under the second angel ; then a third phalanx, under the third angel.

Esau, trembling, exclaimed, "I am the brother of Jacob. It is twenty years since I saw him, and you maltreat me as I am on my way to meet him!"

One of the angels answered, "If Jacob, the servant of God, had not been thy brother, we would have destroyed thee and all thy men."

The forth body passing, under the command of the fourth angel, completed the humiliation of Esau.

However, Jacob, who knew not what assistance had been rendered him by Heaven, prepared for Esau, to appease him, rich presents. He sent him four hundred and forty sheep, thirty asses, thirty camels, fifty oxen, in ten troops, each conducted by a faithful servant charged to deliver his troop as a gift from Jacob to his brother Esau.

This consoled and pleased Esau, who, as soon as he saw Jacob again, was, by the grace of God, placed in a better mind, and the brethren met, and parted with fraternal love.[1]

Now let us take another version of the story of this meeting.

It came to pass that Jacob spent one night alone beyond Jabbok, and an angel contended with him, having taken on him the body and likeness of a man. This angel was Michael, and the subject of their contention was this :—The angel said to Jacob, " Hast thou not promised to give the tenth of all that is thine to the Lord?" And Jacob said, "I have promised."

Then the angel said, " Behold thou hast ten sons and one daughter ; nevertheless thou hast not tithed them."

Immediately Jacob set apart the four first-born of the four mothers, and there remained eight. And he began to number from Simeon, and Levi came up for the tenth.

---

[1] Jalkut Cadasch, fol. 81, col. 1 ; Yaschar, p. 1161 et seq.

Then Michael answered and said, " Lord of the world, this is Thy lot." So Levi became the consecrated one to the Lord.

On account of this ready compliance with his oath, Michael was unable to hurt him, but he remained striving with Jacob, till the first ray of sunlight rose above the eastern hills.

And he said, " Let me go, for the column of the morning ascendeth, and the hour cometh when the angels on high offer praise to the Lord of the world : and I am one of the angels of praise ; but from the day that the world was created, my time to praise hath not come till now."

And he said, " I will not let thee go, until thou bless me."

Now Michael had received commandment not to leave Jacob till the patriarch suffered him ; and as it began to dawn, the hosts of heaven, who desired to begin their morning hymn, came down to Michael and bade him rise up to the throne of God and lead the chant ; but he said, " I cannot, unless Jacob suffer me to depart." [1]

Thus did God prove Jacob, as He had proved Abraham, whether he would give to Him his son, when He asked him of the patriarch.

But, according to certain Rabbinic authorities, it was not Michael who wrestled with Jacob, but it was Sammael the Evil One, or Satan. For Sammael is the angel of Edom, as Michael is the angel of Israel ; and Sammael went before Esau, hoping to destroy Jacob in the night. Sammael, says the Jalkut Rubeni, met Jacob, who had the stature of the first man, and strove with him ; but he could not do him an injury, for Abraham stood on his right hand, and Isaac on his left. And when Sammael would part from him, Jacob would not suffer it, till the Evil One had given him the blessing which Jacob had purchased from Esau. And from that day Sammael took from Jacob his great strength, and made him to halt upon his thigh. [2]

But when Michael appeared before God—we must now suppose the man who strove with Jacob to have been the angel—God said to him in anger, " Thou hast injured My priest ! "

Michael answered, " I am Thy priest."

" Yea," said the Most High, " thou art My priest in heaven, but Jacob is My priest on earth. Why hast thou lamed him ? "

<hr>

[1] Eisenmenger, i. p. 486.   [2] Jalkut Rubeni, fol. 61. col. 3.

Then Michael answered, " I wrestled with him, and let him overcome me, to Thy honor, O Lord ; that, seeing he had overcome an angel of God, he might have courage to go boldly to meet Esau."

But this was no excuse for having lamed him. Therefore Michael said to Raphael, " Oh, angel of healing ! come to my aid." So Raphael descended to earth, and touched the hollow of Jacob's thigh, and it was restored as before.

But God said to Michael, " For this that thou hast done, thou shalt be the guardian of Israel as long as the world lasteth." [1]

Jacob called the name of the place Peniel ; for he said, " I have seen the angel of the Lord face to face, and my soul is saved." And the sun rose upon him before its time, as, when he went out from Beer-sheba, it had set before its time.[2]

And Jacob lifted up his eyes and looked, and behold, Esau came, and with him four hundred men of war. And he divided the children unto Leah, and to Rachel, and to the two concubines, and placed the concubines and their sons foremost ; for he said, " If Esau come to destroy the children, and ill-treat the women, he will do it with them, and meanwhile we can prepare to fight ; and Leah and her children after, and Rachel and Joseph after them."[3] And he himself went over before them, praying and asking mercy before the Lord ; and he bowed upon the earth seven times, until he met with his brother ; but it was not to Esau that he bowed, though Esau supposed he did, but to the Lord God Most High.[4]

And Esau ran to meet him, and embraced him, and fell upon his neck and bit him, but by the mercy of God the neck of Jacob became marble, and Esau broke his teeth upon it ; therefore it is said in the Book of Genesis that he *fell on his neck, and kissed him; and they wept.*[5] But the Targumim apparently do not acknowledge that the neck of Jacob became marble, for the Targum of Palestine explains their weeping thus : " Esau wept on account of the pain of his teeth, which

---

[1] Jalkut Cadasch, fol. 91, col. 4.   [2] Targum of Palestine, i. p. 272.

[3] Jacob prepared three things against Esau—War, Gifts, and Prayer—as a token to all men that they must overcome evil by Resistance, by Alms, and by Supplication. (R. Bechai, Comm. on the Five Books of Moses, fol. 42, col. 4.)

[4] Jalkut Rubeni, fol. 62, col. 2.

[5] Bereschith rabba, fol. 71, col. 1 (70th Parascha).

10*

were shaken ; but Jacob wept because of the pain of his neck ;" and the Targum of Jerusalem, " Esau wept for the crushing of his teeth, and Jacob wept for the tenderness of his neck."

"The Lord God prospered Jacob," and he had one hundred and two times ten thousand and seven thousand (*i.e.*, a thousand times a thousand, seven thousand and two hundred) sheep, and six hundred thousand dogs ; but some Rabbis say the sheep were quite innumerable, but when Jacob counted his sheep-dogs he found that he had twelve hundred thousand of them ; others, however, reduce the number one-half. They say, one dog went with each flock, but those who say that there were twelve hundred thousand dogs, count two to each flock.[1]

Jacob, says the Rabbi Samuel, could recite the whole of the Psalter.[2] Of course this must have been in the spirit of prophecy, as the Psalms were not written, with the exception of Psalm civ., which had been composed by Adam.

Adam, after his fall, had been given by God six commandments, but Noah was given a seventh—to this effect, that he was not to eat a limb or portion of any living animal. Abraham was given an eighth, the commandment of circumcision ; and Jacob was communicated a ninth, through the mouth of an adder, that he was not to eat the serpent.[3]

If we may trust the Book of Jasher, the affair of Shechem, the son of Hamor, was as follows :—The men of the city were not all circumcised, only some of them, so as to blind the eyes of the sons of Jacob, and throw them off their guard ; and Shechem and Hamor had privately concerted to fall upon Jacob and his sons and butcher them ; but Simeon and Levi were warned of their intention by a servant of Dinah, and took the initiative.[4] But this is a clumsy attempt to throw the blame off the shoulders of the ancestors of the Jewish nation upon those of their Gentile enemies.

Jacob, say the Rabbis, would have had no daughters at all in his family, but only sons, had he not called himself El-elohe-Israel (Israel is God).[5] Therefore God was angry with him, for making himself equal with God, and in punishment he afflicted him with a giddy daughter.[6]

Esau, say the Mussulmans, had no prophets in his family

---

[1] Bereschith rabba, fol. 67, col. 1.   [2] Jalkut Cadasch, fol. 90, col. 3.
[3] Eisenmenger, i. p. 325.   [4] Tabari, i. p. 206.
[5] Gen. xxxiii. 20.   [6] Jalkut Cadasch, fol. 91, col. 3.

except Job.   All the prophets rose from the family of Jacob; and when Esau saw that the gift of prophecy was not in his family, he went out of the land, for he would not live near his brother.[1]

The father of the Israelites, from the land of Canaan which he inhabited, could smell the clothes of Joseph when he was in Egypt, being a prophet; and thus he knew that his son was alive.   He was asked how it was that he divined nothing when his beloved son was cast into the pit by his brothers, and sold to the Ishmaelites.   He replied that the prophetic power is sudden, like a lightning flash, piercing sometimes to the height of heaven; it is not permanent in its intensity, but leaves at times those favored with it in such darkness that they do not know what is at their feet.[2]

The Arabs say that Jacob, much afflicted with sciatica, was healed by abstaining from the meat he most loved, and that was the flesh of the camel.   At Jerusalem, say the Arabs, is preserved the stone on which Jacob laid his head when he slept on his way to Haran.

The custom of saying " God bless you! " when a person sneezes, dates from Jacob.   The Rabbis say that, before the time that Jacob lived, men sneezed once, and that was the end of them—the shock slew them ; but the patriarch, by his intercession, obtained a relaxation of this law, subject to the condition that, in all nations, a sneeze should be consecrated by a sacred aspiration.

XXVIII

JOSEPH.

JOSEPH'S story is too attractive not to have interested intensely the Oriental nations in any way connected with him, and therefore to have become a prey to legend and myth.

Joseph, say the Mussulmans, was from his childhood the best loved son of his father Jacob ; but the old man not only loved him, but yearned after the sight of him, for he was deprived of the custody of Joseph from an early age.   Joseph had been sent to his aunt, the sister of Isaac, and she loved

---

[1] Yaschar, pp. 1167, 1168.
[2] D' Herbelot, Bibliothèque Orientale, s. v. Ais, i. p. 142.

the child so dearly, that she could not endure the thought of parting with him. Therefore she took the family girdle, which she as the eldest retained as an heirloom, the girdle which Abraham had worn when he prepared to sacrifice his son, and she strapped it round Joseph's waist.

Then she drew him before the judge, and accused him of theft, and claimed that he should be made over to her as a slave to expiate his theft. And it was done so. Thus the child Joseph grew up in her house, and it was not till after her death that he returned to his father Jacob.

One morning Joseph related to his father a dream that he had dreamt; he said that he and his brothers had planted twigs in the earth, but all the twigs of his brothers had withered, whereas his own twig had brought forth leaves, and flourished.

Jacob was so immersed in thought over the dream, that he allowed a poor man who came begging to go away unrelieved, because unnoticed.[1] And this act of forgetfulness brought upon him some trouble, as we shall see.

One morning Joseph related to him another dream; he saw the sun, the moon, and the stars bow down before him. Jacob could no longer doubt the significance of these dreams, which showed him how great Joseph would be, but he cautioned him on no account to let his brothers know about them, lest they should envy him.

He was so beautiful that he was called the Moon of Canaan, and he had on one of his shoulders a luminous point like a star, a token that the spirit of prophecy rested upon him. The brothers of Joseph, however, heard of the dreams, and they were greatly enraged, and they said, "Joseph and Benjamin are more loved of their father than we ten; let us kill Joseph, or drive him out of the country, and when we have done this, we will repent at our leisure, and God will forgive us."[2]

One day the brothers went to feed their father's flock in Shechem. Then Israel said to Joseph, "Do not thy brethren feed in Shechem? I am afraid lest the Hivite come upon them and smite them, and repay on me what Simeon and Levi

---

[1] This was Sammael, and he complained to God that Jacob had neglected the duty of hospitality, therefore he was suffered to afflict him for a season.

[2] Tabari, i. p. 210.

did to Shechem and Hamor, because of Dinah their sister. I will send thee to them to caution them to go elsewhere."

And he said, "I am ready." So Joseph arose, and went to Shechem ; and Gabriel, in the likeness of a man, found him wandering in the field. And he said to him, "Thy brethren have journeyed hence. I heard of them, when I was in the presence of God, behind the veil, and that, from this day, the bondage of Egypt begins."[1]

When Joseph came in sight, the brothers conspired to slay him, but Judah said, "Slay not Joseph, for to slay is a crime ; but cast him into a well on the way that the caravans pass, that he may be found by a caravan, and be drawn out." Joseph was then aged seventeen.

His brethren fell on him and stripped him, and were about to cast him into the well which was by the wayside to Jerusalem, when he said, "O my brothers, wherewith shall I cover my nakedness in this pit?"

They replied, "Bid the sun, the moon, and the stars, which adored thee, bring thee clothes to cover thy nakedness."

Having thus mocked him, they let him down into the well. There was much water in it ; and a stone had fallen into it : on this Joseph stood, and was above the surface of the water.[2] Not so, say the Rabbis, it was dry, but it was full of scorpions and adders.[3]

Judah, according to the Mussulman account, had not consented to this, he being absent ; and when he had learned what had been done, he took food and let it down into the well, and told Joseph to be of good cheer, his brothers' anger would turn away, and then he would bring him back to them. But the Jews say that Reuben was absent, as he was fasting on a mountain, because he had incurred his father's anger, and was in disgrace, and he hoped, by restoring Joseph to Israel, to recover his father's favor.

The sons of Jacob then slew a lamb and dipped the garment of Joseph in the blood, and brought it to their father, and said, "We left Joseph in charge of our clothes, and a wolf has fallen upon him, and has devoured him."

But Jacob looked at the garment and said, "I see that it

---

[1] Targums, i. p. 287.   [2] Tabari, i. p. 211.
[3] Targums, i. p. 288. The account of the sale in Yaschar is very long, and full of details too numerous for insertion here (pp. 1185-8).

is bloody, but I see no rents; the wolf was merciful to my son Joseph, for he ate him and left his garment whole!"[1]

Then Jacob went to commune with God, and the spirit of prophecy came upon him, and he said, "No wolf, no enemy has slain him, but a bad woman is against him."[2]

Now Joseph was three days and three nights in the pit, but it was not dark, for the angel Gabriel hung in it a precious stone to give him light.[3]

The brethren of Joseph, seeing that their father mistrusted them, said to him, "We will go and catch the wolf that slew Joseph."

He said, "Go and do so."

So they went and chased and caught a monstrous wolf, and they brought him to their father and said, "This is the beast whereof we spoke to thee, that it had slain Joseph."

But God opened the mouth of the wolf, and he said, "Son of Isaac, believe not the words of thy envious sons. I am a wolf out of a foreign land; I one morning lost my young one when I woke up, and I have been straying in all directions to find it; is it likely that I, mourning over the loss of a wild cub, should attack and kill a young prophet?"

Jacob released the wolf out of the hands of his sons, and he dismissed his sons, for he abhorred the sight of their faces; only Benjamin, the brother of Joseph, and the youngest child of Rachel, did he retain near him.[4]

On the third morning, a party of Arabs passed near the well, and were thirsty. Now the chief of these Arabs was Melek-ben-Dohar; the second, who accompanied Melek, was an Indian, a freed man of Melek, and his name was Buschra.

Melek reached the well carrying a bucket and a rope, and let down the bucket into the well. Then Joseph put his hand on it, and, however much Melek and Buschra pulled, they could not raise the bucket. Then Melek looked down into the pit, and exclaimed: "O Buschra, the bucket was heavy because a young man has hold of it."

Now the face of Joseph illumined the well like a lamp: Buschra and Melek tried to raise Joseph, but they could not.

Then Melek asked, "What is thy name, and whence art thou?"

---

[1] Tabari, i. p 212.   [2] Targums, i. 289.   [3] Weil, p. 102.
[4] Yaschar, tr. Drachs, p. 1192.

Joseph answered, "I am a young man of Canaan; my brothers have cast me into this cistern, but I am not guilty."

Melek said to his companions, "If we tell the rest of the caravan that we have drawn this youth out of the well, they will demand a share in the price he will fetch. Now I can sell this youth for a large sum in Egypt. I will therefore tell my comrades that I have bought him from some people who were at the well. Do thou say the same thing, and we will share the money between us."

Next day, being the fourth day, the brethren, finding that their father's face was turned against them, went to the cistern to draw forth Joseph, and when they found him not, they went to the caravan, and they saw Joseph among the Arabs.

Then they asked, "Whose is this lad?"

Melek-ben-Dohar replied, "He his mine."

They answered, "He belongs to us; he ran away from us."

Melek replied, "Well, I will give you money for him."[1]

So he bought him for twenty pieces of silver; thus each of the brothers obtained two drachmæ, and therewith they bought shoes.[2] To this the prophet Amos refers in two places (ii. 6; viii. 6), and in the Testament of the Twelve Patriarchs, which is received as canonical by the Armenian Church, Zebulun relates the same circumstance, that the brethren supplied themselves with sandals from the money which they got by the sale of Joseph.

Joseph went along with the Ishmaelites till they passed his mother's tomb; then his grief overcame him, and he burst forth into bitter tears and cried, "O mother, mother! I am an outcast and a slave, I the child of the wife Jacob loved. When thou wast dying, thou didst show me to my father, and bade him look on me, and be comforted for my loss. O mother, mother! hast thou no thought of thy son? Awake and see the miserable condition of thy child; shake off thy sleep; be my defence against my brethren, and comfort my father. Awake and stand up to judge my quarrel, awake and plead my cause with God! awake and look upon the desolation of the soul of my father who cherished thee, and who for fourteen years served a hard bondage for his beloved Rachel! Console him, I pray thee, and by the voice that he loves, soothe the grief of his last days."

---

[1] Tabari, i. pp. 213, 214.   [2] Targums, i. 288.

It was moonlight, and the caravan was resting.

A low voice issued from the tomb, "My son! my son Joseph! my child! I have heard the voice of thy crying. I know all thou hast suffered, my son, and my grief is as deep as the sea. But put thy trust in God, who is the help of thy countenance and thy God! Rise, my child, and have patience. If thou knewest the future, thou wouldst be comforted.[1]

One of the chiefs of the caravan, wearied with the cries of Joseph, came to drive him from the tomb, but suddenly a dark and threatening cloud appeared in the sky over his head, and he desisted in fear.

In the Testament of the Twelve patriarchs, Benjamin says that a man struck Joseph as he lagged on the way, whereupon a lion fell upon the man and slew him.

The sun was about to set, when the caravan entered Heliopolis, the chief city of Egypt, which was then under the government of Rajjan, an Amalekite. Joseph's face shone brighter than the mid-day sun; and as this new light from the east shone in the city, and cast the shadows towards the declining sun, all the women and damsels ran out upon the terraces or to the windows to see.

Next day he was placed for sale before the palace of the king. All the wealthy ladies of Heliopolis sent their husbands or relations to bid for the beautiful youth, but he was purchased by Potiphar, the king's treasurer,[2] who was childless, and designed making Joseph his adopted son and heir.

Zuleika,[3] Potiphar's wife, received him with great friendliness, gave him new clothes and a garden-house in which to live, as he would not sit down to eat with the Egyptians. He was occupied in tending the fruit and the flowers in Potiphar's garden; and from her window Zuleika watched him.

Thus Joseph served as gardener to Potiphar for six years.

A graceful Arab legend of this period of Joseph's life deserves not to be omitted.

One day an Ismaelite passed the gate of Potiphar's garden, leading a camel. As the beast approached Joseph, who was

---

[1] Yaschar, pp. 1188–9; Parrascha Wajescheb. This touching incident is common to Rabbinic and Mussulman traditions. It has been gracefully versified by Dr. Le Heris, "Sagen aus der Orient;" Mannheim, 1852.

[2] His name in Arabic is Aziz.

[3] Zuleika is the name in Yaschar; it is that also given her by the Arabs.

standing at the door, it bowed, refused to follow its master, and turning to Joseph, fell before him, and shed tears over his feet.

Joseph recognized the camel as having once belonged to his father, and he remembered having often given it bread. He questioned the Ishmaelite, who acknowledged he had purchased the beast from Israel.

Now Joseph loved Zuleika as much as she loved him, but he did not venture to hope that he was precious to his mistress.

One day when a great feast of the gods was observed, all the household had gone to the temple, save Zuleika, who pretended to be ill, and Joseph, who worshipped the One true God. Zuleika prepared a table with wine and fruit and sweet cakes, and invited Joseph to eat with her.

He was rejoiced, and his heart beat with passion ; and when he took the goblet of wine she offered him, he looked into her eyes, and saw that she loved him. Then, says the Rabbi Ishmael in the Midrash, the form of his father Jacob appeared in the window or doorway, and thus addressed him : " Joseph ! hereafter the names of thy brothers engraven on gems shall adorn the breastplate of the High Priest, and shall thine be absent from among them ? " Then Joseph dug his ten fingers into the ground, and so conquered himself.[1]

The Mussulmans say also that Joseph was brought to his senses by seeing the vision of his father in the door biting his finger reproachfully at him.[2]

When Potiphar returned home, Zuleika brought false accusations against Joseph, but a babe who was in its cradle, in the room,—the child was a relation of Zuleika,—lifted up its voice in protest, and said, " Potiphar, if you want to know the truth, examine the torn portion of the garment. If it is from the front of the dress, then know that Zuleika was struggling to thrust Joseph from approaching her ; if from the back, know that she was pursuing him."

Potiphar obeyed the voice of the sucking child, and found that his wife had spoken falsely, and that Joseph was innocent.[3]

Now one of the neighbors had seen all that took place, for

---

[1] Tract. Sota., fol. 36, col. 2. The original account of this final detail is too absurd and monstrous to be narrated more particularly.

[2] Tabari, i. p. 217.

[3] Yaschar, p. 1197. Nearly all these incidents in the life of Joseph are common to Jewish and Mussulman traditions.

she was sick, and had not attended the feast, so the whole affair was soon a matter of gossip throughout the town. Then Zuleika invited all the ladies who had blamed her to a great feast in her house ; and towards the close of the banquet, when the fruit and wine were brought in, an orange and a knife were placed before each lady ; and at the same moment Joseph was brought into the room. The ladies, in their astonishment, cut their fingers in mistake for the oranges, for their eyes were fixed upon him, and they were amazed at his beauty ; and the table was deluged with blood.

"This," said Zuleika, "is the youth on whose account you blame me. It is true that I loved him, but his virtue has opposed me ; and now love is turned to hate, and I shall cast him into prison." [1]

She was as good as her word, and thus it fell out that Joseph was placed in the king's prison. But God would not suffer the innocent to be punished. He illumined his cell with a celestial light, made a fountain spring up in the midst of it, and a fruit-bearing tree to grow before the door. [2]

Joseph was five years in prison, and then the King of the Greeks, who was warring against Egypt, sent an ambassador to Rajjan desiring peace. But his true purpose was to throw him off his guard, that he might with treachery destroy him. The ambassador sought the advice of an old Greek woman who had long lived in Egypt. She said, "I know of only one way of accomplishing what you desire, and that is to bribe the butler or the baker of the king to poison him ; but it would be better to put the drug in the wine than in the bread."

The ambassador then bribed the chief baker with much gold, and he promised to put poison in Pharaoh's meat. After that he told the old woman that one of the two she had named to him had been persuaded to destroy the king.

Then the ambassador returned, and when he was gone, the woman disclosed all to Pharaoh, and she said, "Either the butler or the baker has taken a bribe to poison thee, O king." Thereupon the king cast both into prison, till it should be made manifest which was guilty. Now the name of the baker was Mohlib, and that of the butler was Kamra.

---

[1] Tabari, p. 220 ; Weil, p. 112 ; both taken from the Rabbinic story in Yaschar, p. 1195.

[2] Weil, p. 113.

After they had been in prison some time, they had dreams ; and they told their dreams to Joseph.

The chief butler said, " I saw in my dream, and, behold, a vine was before me. And in the vine were three branches : and as it sprouted it brought forth buds, and immediately they ripened into clusters, and became grapes. And I saw till they gave the cup of Pharaoh into my hand, and I took the grapes and squeezed them into Pharaoh's cup, and I gave the cup into Pharaoh's hand."

And Joseph said to him, " This is the interpretation of the dream. The three branches are the three Fathers of the world, Abraham, Isaac, and Jacob, whose children*are to be enslaved in Egypt in clay and brickwork, and in all labors of the face of the field ; but afterward shall they be delivered by the hand of three shepherds. As for the cup thou didst give into Pharaoh's hand, it is the vial of the wrath of God, which Pharoah is to drink at the last. But thou, the chief butler, shalt receive a good reward : the three branches to thee are three days un til thy liberation."

Joseph, leaving his higher trust in God, now turned and reposed it in man, for he added, " Be thou mindful of me when it shall be well with thee, and obtain my release from this prison-house."

And the chief baker, seeing that Joseph had interpreted well, began to speak with an impatient tongue, and said to Joseph, " I also saw in my dream, and, behold, three baskets of hot loaves were upon my head ; and in the upper basket of all, delicious meat for Pharaoh, made by the confectioner ; and the birds ate them from the basket upon my head."

Joseph answered, " This is its interpretation. The three baskets are the three enslavements with which the house of Israel are to be enslaved. But thou, the chief baker, shalt receive an evil award. At the end of three days, Pharoah shall take away thy head from thy body, and will hang thee upon a gibbet, and the birds shall eat thy flesh from off thee."

And it fell out as Joseph had foretold. But because Joseph had withdrawn from putting his trust in God, and had laid it on man, therefore he was forgotten by the butler and left in prison for two years more.[1]

Joseph had now been seven years in prison, and this is why

____

[1] Targums, i. pp. 296—9 ; Midrash, fol. 45 ; Yaschar, p. 1200.

he had been so long there.   Potiphar's wife persuaded her friends to bring against Joseph the same accusation that she had laid against him, and their husbands complained to Pharaoh; so he was kept in prison that he might not cause strife and evil in the city.[1]

When the seven years were elapsed, one day the butler came to the prison and bade Joseph follow him, as the King had been troubled with a dream, and desired to have it explained. But Joseph refused to leave till his innocence was proclaimed. He named to the butler the ladies who had attended the banquet of Zuleika, and before whom she had confessed that she loved him, and besought that they might be called as witnesses before the king.   Pharoah agreed; the ladies, when interrogated, related all that had been said, and Zuleika herself confessed the truth.

Then Pharaoh sent and fetched Joseph out of prison, and gave him his liberty.

"I dreamed," said the king, when Joseph stood before his throne, "that seven lean cows ate seven fat cows, and that seven empty husks ate seven full ears of corn.   What is the interpretation of this dream?"

"God will give thee seven fruitful years, and then seven years of famine," answered Joseph.   "Therefore must thou gather together all the superfluity in the first seven years to sustain the starving people in the seven years of dearth."[2]

The king was so well pleased with this interpretation, that he made Joseph his chief treasurer in Potiphar's room.   Joseph went through all the land, and purchased corn, which, on account of the good harvests, was at a very low price.

One day as he rode out of the town to view his magazines, he observed a beggar-woman whose whole appearance was most woe-begone, but bespoke her having seen better days. Joseph approached her with compassion, and held out to her a handful of gold.   She hesitated about taking it, and said, sobbing, "Great prophet of God! I am not worthy to receive this at thy hand, though it was my love for thee which was the first step on the ladder on which thou mountedst to thy present exaltation."   And Joseph saw that the poor beggar-woman was Zuleika, wife of Potiphar.

<hr>

[1] Midrash, fol. 45.
[2] Weil, p. 116; Tabari, i. c. 44; Gen. xli.; Yaschar, pp. 1202–8.

He asked about her husband, and learned that shortly after he had been deposed from office, he had died of distress of mind and body. "Thou hast thought evil of me," she said, "but I have great excuses, thou wast so beautiful; and moreover I was young, and only a wife in name, for I am as I left my mother's womb, a maiden, with the seal of God upon me."

Then Joseph was filled with joy. He extended his hands to her, and he brought her to the king's palace, and she was treated there with care as a sister, till she recovered her bloom and joy, and then Joseph took her to be his wife.[1] And by her he had two sons before the seven years of dearth began, during which the Egyptians gave first their gold, and their apparel and all their movable goods; then their land, then their slaves, and last of all themselves, their wives and children, as bondsmen, that they might have food.

But not only did Egypt suffer, the adjoining lands were also afflicted with scarcity. There was no corn in Canaan, and Jacob sent his ten sons into Egypt to buy corn, retaining Benjamin at home. He cautioned his sons not to create mistrust by their numbers, nor cause the evil eye to light on them, and advised them to enter the city of Pharaoh by different gates, for it had ten.

But Joseph expected that his brothers would be coming to Egypt, and therefore he bade the gatekeepers every day bring him the names of those who had entered the city. One day one porter gave him the name of Reuben, son of Jacob; and so on to the tenth, Asher, son of Jacob. Joseph at once gave orders for every storehouse to be closed with the exception of one, and gave the keepers of the open magazine the names of his brothers, and said to them, "When these people arrive take them prisoners, and bring them before me."

And when they appeared before him, he charged them with being spies: "For," said he, "if ye were true men, ye would have come in together; but ye entered by different gates, and that shows that ye are set upon evil."[2]

When, to excuse themselves, they told their family history,

---

[1] This conclusion of the loves of Zuleika and Joseph completes the romance, and makes it a most popular subject for poets in the East. Both Jewish and Mussulman traditions give Zuleika a very different character from that which Holy Scripture leads one to attribute to her.

[2] Midrash, Jalkut, fol. 46.

he bade them go and bring Benjamin down to him, and, to secure their return, he kept Simeon in prison as hostage.

When Joseph wanted to imprison Simeon, his brothers desired to assist him by force, but Simeon refused their assistance. Joseph ordered seventy fighting men of Pharaoh's body-guard to cast him down and handcuff him. But when they approached, Simeon gave a scream, and the seventy fell back on the ground, and their teeth went down their throats. "Hah!" said Joseph to his son Manasseh, who stood near him, "throw a chain about his neck."

Manasseh dealt Simeon a blow, and chained him. "Then," said Simeon, "this blow comes from one of the family."[1]

Jacob, reluctant to part with Benjamin, was however obliged to do so, being pressed with famine. Joseph received the brethren, measured out to them the wheat, and, by his orders, his steward secretly put the silver cup of Joseph into the sack of Benjamin. Then at the gate of the city they were charged with theft, and were brought back to the palace of Joseph.

"What is the penalty due to him who has stolen my cup?" asked Joseph.

"Let him be thy slave," answered the brethren, feeling confident in their innocence. But when the sacks were opened, and his cup was found in that of Benjamin, they said to their youngest brother, "Woe to thee! what hast thou done? Wast thou resolved to follow the example of thy lost brother, who stole his grandfather Laban's idol, and his aunt's girdle?"

But as they had sworn to their father to restore Benjamin to him, they besought Joseph to take one of them in the place of Benjamin. But Joseph persisted that he would keep Benjamin.

Then said Reuben to his brothers, "Go back to our father, and tell him all that has occurred; I, the eldest of you, who undertook on the security of my life to bring Benjamin home, must remain here till he himself calls me back, for he will see that we have stood hostages for a thief."[2]

Now Reuben had a fierce temper, and when he became furious, all the down or hair on his skin bristled and penetrated his clothes like needles; he pulled off his head-gear, and uttered a scream so terrible that all who heard it died of terror. This frenzy of Reuben's could only be abated by one of the

---

[1] Midrash, Jalkut. fol. 46.   [2] Weil, p. 122.

family of Jacob placing his hand upon him. Reuben went up
to Joseph, and said, "O great one of Egypt, I am in a rage;
and if I scream out, all who hear me will die of fright. Restore to me my brother, or I shall scream, and then thou and
all the inhabitants of Egypt will perish."

Joseph knowing that Reuben spoke the truth, and seeing
his hair bristling through his clothes like needle-points, and
knowing also that if any one of the house of Jacob were to lay
his hand on the body of Reuben, his force would pass away,—
he said to Ephraim, his son, "Go softly, so that Reuben may
not observe thee, and lay thine hand upon his shoulder that
his anger may abate." Ephraim did as he was bidden, and instantly the hairs of Reuben sank, and his fury passed away,
and he felt that the power to scream was gone from him.

Then Joseph said calmly, "I shall retain Benjamin, do
what you will."

Reuben made an effort to scream, but it was unavailing.
Then astonishment got hold of him, and he said to Joseph,
"I think that there must be one of the family of Jacob in
this house."[1]

Then Joseph ordered Benjamin to be chained. And when
Judah saw this he roared like a lion, and his voice was so
piercing, that Chuschim, the son of Dan, who was in Canaan,
heard him, and began to roar also.

And Judah drew his sword, and roared, and pursued the
Egyptian soldiers sent to bind Benjamin, and the fear of him
fell on them all, and they fell, and he smote them up to the
gates of the king's palace; and he roared again, and all the
walls of Memphis rocked, and the earth shook, and Pharaoh
was shaken off his throne and fell on his face, and the roar of
Judah was heard four hundred miles off.

Joseph feared to be killed by Judah. When Judah was
angry, blood spirted from his right eye. Judah wore five sets
of clothes upon him, one above another; and when he was
angry, his heart swelled so as to tear them all. Joseph, fearing
him, roared at him, and his voice shivered a pillar of the palace
into fine dust, so that Judah thought, "This is a great hero!
he can master me."[2]

[1] Tabari, i. p. 247; taken from the Rabbinic Yaschar (Sepher Hajaschar), p. 1226.

[2] Midrash, Jalkut. fol. 47; Yaschar, p. 1225; Berescheth Rabba,
fol. 84, col. 4.

Then said Judah to Joseph, " Let our brother go, or we will devastate this land."

Then Joseph answered, " Go home, and tell your father that a wild beast has devoured him."

Then Judah beckoned to his brother Naphtali, who was very swift of foot, and said to him, " Run speedily and count all the streets in Egypt, and come swiftly back and tell me."

But Simeon said, " There is no need ; I will break a stone out of the mountains and throw it down on the land of Egypt, and will utterly destroy it." [1]

Then Joseph saw that it was not well to press them further ; so he took a bowl, and filled it, and looked into it as though he were divining by it, and said suddenly, " Ye are liars ! Ye told me that your brother Joseph was dead, and behold he is alive, and I see him in this bowl ! Ye sold him."

Then he bade Zuleika bring the deed of sale, and he handed it to Judah.   Thereupon the brothers knew him, and fell down before him, and besought him to pardon them.

Then he told them how God had exalted him, and he comforted their hearts, and after that he asked news of his father.

They replied, " He is blind with grief at having to part with Benjamin."

Therefore Joseph said, " Take my shirt and go to my father, and pass my shirt before his face, and he will recover his sight. Then take all that you have, and come down into Egypt." [2]

When the caravan left Memphis, the sons of Jacob carried with them abundance of corn and the shirt of Joseph ; and the wind was in their backs, and blew the scent of the shirt from the gate of Memphis into Canaan.   And Jacob snuffed the wind, and said, " O women ! O children ! I can smell Joseph."

They all thought, " He is deranged," but they said, " It is forty years since Joseph died, and thou canst think of nothing else ; thou art always insisting that he is alive."

When the caravan was near the dwelling of Jacob, Judah brought the shirt of Joseph in, and said, " On the day upon which I bore the bloody coat of Joseph, I said a wolf had devoured him.   Now I bring thee good news."   And he cast

---

[1] Yaschar, p. 1226.

[2] This was the shirt given Abraham by Gabriel, to preserve him from the fire into which Nimrod cast him ; it was fragrant with the odors of Paradise.

the shirt upon the face of his father, and Jacob recovered his sight.[1]

The story in the Sepher Hadjaschar, or Book of Jasher, is more poetical. As the sons were approaching the home of their father, Sarah, the adopted daughter of Asher, came to meet them. She was very beautiful and graceful and modest, and could play sweetly on the harp. They gave her the kiss of peace, and told her the tidings. Then she went singing home, accompanying her words upon the harp, " Joseph is not dead, God has been his protector, and he lives, and is gov- ernor in Egypt; rejoice and be glad of heart!" Then Jacob was filled with hope and consolation, and he said, " Because thou hast revived my spirit, my daughter, death shall never seize on thee."[2]

After that, Jacob went down into Egypt, that he might see his son Joseph before he died. And when they met, they fell on one another's neck and wept, and kissed; and Jacob said to his son, " Tell me, I pray thee, what evil thy brothers did to thee." But Joseph answered, " Nay, my father, I will tell thee only how great good the Lord did to me."

We have heard how that Joseph married Zuleika, the wife Potiphar, but this is not a universal tradition. It is said in Genesis that he had to wife Asenath, daughter of Potipherah, priest of On. Many suppose that this Asenath was the daughter of Potiphar, the old master of Joseph, and that her mother was Dinah, the daughter of Jacob, and the following story is related of Asenath :—

She was a maid of wondrous beauty, of which she was very proud, and she greatly despised all men, though she had never seen any, saving her father. She dwelt in a tower next to her father's house, ten stories high, which contained every thing that the eye could desire, and also idols in gold and silver, which she daily worshipped. Asenath was as tall as Sarah, as comely as Rebekah, and as beautiful as Rachel.

Now Joseph, being on his way through Egypt, sent down to the priest Potipherah, to command him to bring his daughter before him. Thereupon Potipherah was glad, and told his daughter that Joseph, the Strength of God, was coming, and that she should become his wife. At this Asenath was very indignant, and spoke angry words of Joseph, declaring that she

---

[1] Koran, Sura xii. ; Tabari, i. pp. 250, 251.   [2] Yaschar, p. 1227.

would be wife to no man, saving to a king's son.   Now, while she thus spake, Joseph came, seated in the chariot of Pharaoh, which was all of gold, drawn by four horses white as snow, with gilt reins.   And Joseph was dressed in a radiant tunic, with gold embroidery, and a robe of crimson woven with gold hung from his shoulders, and a fillet of gold was about his temples, and in his hand was an olive branch full of fruit.

Then Potipherah came with his wife, and did him homage. Joseph entered the hall, and the doors were shut, and Asenath beheld him, and she was troubled at what she had said of him, and thought, " This is the sun come from heaven ; I knew not before that Joseph was divine.   What father hath begotten so much beauty, or what mother borne so much light ? "

Then Joseph said, " Who was that woman that was here, but hath gone ? " for Asenath had hastened to her chamber.

And Potipherah said, " My lord, my daughter is a maiden, and very modest ; she hath, till this day, seen no man save my-self.   If it please thee, she shall come and salute thee."

Then Joseph said, " If thy daughter be a maiden, I will treat her as a sister."

They brought her into his presence, and Potipherah said to her, " Salute thy brother, who hateth women as thou hatest men."

And Asenath said, " Hail, blessed of God, who giveth life to all ! "

Then Potipherah bade his daughter kiss Joseph, but when she approached him, he thrust forth his hand and said, " It becomes not the man worshipping the living God to kiss an outlandish woman whose lips kiss dumb idols."

Asenath hearing these words, fell into great grief and wept. Joseph had compassion on her, and laid his hand on her head and blessed her, and Asenath was glad because of his bene-diction.   But she went to her couch in the tower, and was ill with fear and pain, and she turned with penitence from her idols, and renounced them, and cast them out of her window.

Joseph ate and drank, and went his way, promising to re-turn in eight days.   Then Asenath put on a black robe, and closed her door and prayed, and cast her food to the dogs, and laid her head on the pavement, and wept seven days.

Then an angel visited her, and gave her honey gathered from the roses of paradise ; and the honey was so sweet, that when she had tasted it she could not doubt whence it had

come, and she felt herself enlightened by the true God ; and
the angel signed the honey with the cross, and the trace of his
finger was blood.   Along with faith and hope, charity enlightened her heart, and she besought of the angel to give of this
honey to the seven maidens who attended on her ; and when
they obtained this favor, they all became like their mistress,
servants of the Most High.   Then the angel bade her lay
aside her tears and black garment, and rejoice, for her prayer
was heard.

At that moment one of the servants of Potipherah entered,
saying, " Behold, Joseph, the Strength of God, approaches ; go
ye out to meet him ? "

Now when Joseph had alighted down from his chariot, he
came into the hall ; and when he knew that Asenath had cast
away her idols, he rejoiced greatly, and he sought her in mar
riage of Potipherah, and the Priest of On made a great supper,
and gave his daughter to Joseph, and he called Joseph the
lord of lords, and Asenath he called the daughter of the Most
High.[1]

XXIX.

THE TESTAMENTS OF THE TWELVE PATRI-ARCHS.

THE " Testaments of the Twelve Patriarchs " is one of the
seventy-two apocryphal books of the Old Testament which
were at one time in circulation, and, according to Epiphanius,
it formed one of the twenty-two canonical books sent by the
Jews to Ptolemy, king of Egypt.[2]

It was a work of Jewish origin, which has been tampered
with and interpolated by Christian copyists.   S. Augustine
numbers it with the Apocrypha ; he says, " There are the apocryphal books of the Old Testament : the works falsely attributed to Enoch, the Patriarchs, the Discourse of Joseph, the
Assumption of Moses, the pseudographia of Abraham, Eldad
and Medad, Elias the prophet, the prophet Zephaniah, Zechariah, Baruch, Habakkuk, Ezekiel, and Daniel."

---

[1] Vita Aseneth, filiæ Potipharis ; a Greek apocryphal book, in Fabri
cius, iii. p, 85.

[2] Lib. de Mensuris et Ponderibus, § 10.

Curiously enough, the Testament of the Patriarchs contains a large number of alleged quotations from the book of Enoch, which are not, however, to be found in that book as we now have it.

This Testament was read by the Jews at the time of Christ's coming, and S. Paul seems to have been acquainted with it, for he quotes it, "*Awake, thou that sleepest, and arise from the dead;*"[1] and again he quotes the Testament of Levi, "*The wrath is come upon them to the uttermost.*"[2]   S. Jerome remarks on this, "The Apostle Paul quoted from the hidden prophets and from those books which are called Apocrypha," and he adds, "That he did so in several other places is very evident."[3] And Origen says, "It is evident that many examples were quoted and inserted in the New Testament by the Apostles and the Evangelists from those Scriptures which we do not read as canonical, but these passages are found in the apocryphal books, and it is evident that these passages were extracted from them;" and he gives the reason why that was lawful to the Apostles which is not lawful to us.

He says, "It may have been, that the Apostles and Evangelists, filled with the Holy Ghost, may have known what was to be taken from these writings and what was to be rejected; but for us to presume to do such a thing would be full of danger, not having the Spirit in the same measure to guide us."[4]

'Robert Grostête, Bishop of Lincoln, translated the Testament of the twelve Patriarchs into Latin, in 1242, according to Matthew Paris.   "Also in this time, Robert, Bishop of Lincoln, a man most skilled in Latin and Greek, translated accurately the Testaments of the Twelve Patriarchs from the Greek into Latin; which for many years had been unknown and concealed, through the jealousy of the Jews, because of the prophecies concerning our Saviour therein contained.   But the Greeks, the most indefatigable investigators of all writings, being the first who learnt about this, translated it from Hebrew into Greek, and kept it to themselves until our own time.   For in the time of S. Jerome, or of any other holy interpreter, it could not in any way whatever come to the knowledge of the Christians, on account of the scheming malice of the Jews. Therefore the above-named Bishop, assisted by Master Nich-

---

[1] Ephes. v. 14.   [2] Thess. ii. 16.   [3] Commen. in Eph. loc. cit.
[4] Prolog. infin. Duarum Hom. in Cant. Canticorum.

olas, a Greek, and clerk to the Abbey of S. Albans, translated clearly, evidently, and word for word, into Latin, that glorious treatise, to the strengthening of the Christian faith, and to the greater confusion of the Jews." [1]

The Testaments were published by Grabe, at Oxford, in 1698, and were republished by Fabricius in his " Codex Pseud-epigraphus Vet. Testamenti," at Hamburg, in 1722. [2]

XXX.

J O B.

JOB was the great grandson of Esau.   He was the son of Amos the son of Zara, the son of Esau, and he had to wife Rahma, daughter of Ephraim, son of Joseph.   Ephraim left two sons, who were prophets after him ; but amongst the children of Esau there was no prophet, saving Job.

Job was more patient than any other prophet ; therefore it is said of him in the Koran, " Certainly we have found this excellent servant patient." [3]

The Rabbis say that Job, Jethro, and Balaam were King Pharaoh's three councillors, and they were also his chief magi-cians.   They, by their enchantments, drew a line round the land of Egypt, so that no slave could escape out of it ; for when he came to the line, he was held back and could not overleap it.   But when the Israelites broke away and disre-garded the enchanted line, Job, Jethro, and Balaam gave up their witchcrafts, and turned to the service of the living God. [4]

Job lived in Bashan, which lies between Damascus and Ramla, and there he reigned as a prince.   Job had five hun-dred yoke of oxen, and to every yoke there was a she-ass to carry the instruments of husbandry.   He had also a thousand flocks of sheep, and a thousand sheep in each flock.   He had ten children, seven sons and three daughters ; all were grown up. [5]

In the " Testament of Job," [6] we read that this great man,

[1] Matt. Paris, Chronicle. ed. Bohn. vol. i. pp. 437, 438.
[2] T. i., pp. 496–759.
[3] Koran. Sura xxxviii. v. 43-4.   Job in Arabic is Aïub.
[4] Eisenmenger, ii. p. 439.   [5] Tabari, i. p. 256.
[6] Maï (Angelus), Test. Job : Romæ, 1839.

illumined by the Divine light, comprehended that the idols which his people adored were no gods, and that there was but one only true God, the Creator and Preserver of all things. There was near his house an idol which attracted great worship. He prayed the Lord to show him whether this idol were a demon or not ; and he promised, in that case, to destroy it and purify the place ; and this he was able to do, being a sovereign.

God sent him an angel, who illumined him, and strengthened him in his resolution.   So he destroyed the idol, and abolished its worship.   But this act drew upon him the wrath of Satan.   The angel had foreseen the disasters which would befall Job if he resolved to strive against the Evil One, and he had warned Job what to expect ; but Job answered that, being convinced of the truth, he was ready to suffer for it.

Satan presented himself at the door of Job's house. He had taken upon him the form of a pilgrim, and he said to the portress, " I desire to see the faithful servant of the Most High."

Now Job, who had received the gift of prophecy, knew that this was the Evil One, and he refused to see him, saying to the gate-keeper when she brought the message, " Tell him that I am occupied, and that I cannot receive him."

Satan retired, but he returned soon after, disguised as a beggar, and he said to the portress, " Go and ask Job to give me a morsel of bread."

" Tell him," replied Job, " that I will not give him of the bread I eat, because I will not have any thing in common with him.   But offer him this burnt crust, that he may not say I sent him empty away."

The servant, not venturing to give the burnt crust, because she was not aware who the beggar was, offered him some good bread.   But Satan, who knew what Job had commanded, thrust it away, saying, " Begone, bad servant, and bring me the bread you were told to give me."

The portress replied : " You say well, I am a bad servant, for I have not done that which I was commanded to do.   Here is the crust my master ordered me to give you.   He will not have any thing in common with you ; no ! not even the bread he eats ; but he sends you this, that it may not be said of him that he dismissed thee empty from his door without an alms."

Satan took the charred crust, and bade the servant tell Job

that he would soon render to him such measure as he had dealt to him.[1]

Then Satan ascended to God, and desired permission to afflict and prove Job. And when leave was given him, he descended to earth, and breathed such a hot blast, that all the cattle, and sheep, and servants of Job were burnt up. Then Satan took the form of a slave, and ran and told the prophet. Job answered, "*The Lord gave, and the Lord hath taken away; blessed be the name of the Lord!*"

Then Satan went and shook the earth under the house where the sons and daughters of Job were assembled, and the house fell and destroyed them all.

Satan immediately hastened in the disguise of a servant to Job, and told him what had taken place. He said, "O Job! God has shaken down the house about your children, and they are dead. Had you seen their bleeding faces and broken limbs, and their brains bespattering the stones, and had heard their piercing cries, you would have been heart-broken."

Job wept, and lifted his eyes to God; and he knew who addressed him, and he said, "Satan! it is thou who comest to tempt me and to cast doubt into my heart, and mistrust in the wisdom and goodness of God; get thee hence."

Satan then blew a hot breath up the nose of Job, and poisoned all his blood. His body became scarlet next day, and the day after was covered with ulcers from head to foot; there was no whole place in him, except the head, the tongue, the eyes, and the heart; for over these portions God had not given Satan power.

All Job's friends deserted him and fled; Rahma,[2] his wife, alone remained, and she spent on him the rest of his possessions, but he was not cured of his disease. And this was why all his possessions went—Satan stole them away; and thus in a short time he was reduced to penury, and Rahma went frcm house to house begging alms for his support.

Satan saw that he could not triumph so long as the wife remained with her husband; she was a comfort and joy to him, and he cared not for possessions, or children, or health, so long as his wife was at his side; therefore, he sought occasion to separate them. One day, as Rahma was carrying food

[1] Maï (Angelus), Test. Job; Romæ, 1839.
[2] In the "Testament of Job" she is called Sitis.

to Job, Satan presented himself before her in the form of an old man, and asked her, "O Rahma! art thou not the daughter of Ephraim, the son of Joseph?" She replied, "I am."

Then said the Evil Angel, "In what condition do I see thee?" She answered, "My husband Job has fallen into poverty, and I serve him."

He said, "Do not serve him, for when thou touchest him, the poison of his disease passes into thy veins."

She replied, "He is my husband, and I must attend on him as long as I live, in health or sickness."

Then Satan retired, despairing of seducing her from her duty. Rahma told Job all that had been said to her.

The prophet said, "O woman! he whom you have seen is Satan, and he desired to separate us. Do not speak to him again when he addresses you."

Some time after, the Evil One presented himself before the faithful wife under the form of a beautiful youth; and said to her, "What woman art thou, who art so radiant in beauty?" She answered, I am the wife of a poor man, named Job."

He said, "O woman! what hast thou, with thy wondrous beauty, to do with a poor sick husband? Go, be divorced from thy husband, and marry me. I have great possessions, and I will treat thee as a queen."

She answered, "I am the wife of a prophet; I desire nothing higher."

Then Satan withdrew, despairing of seducing her from her duty. Rahma told Job all that had been said to her.

Job said, "O woman! did I not tell thee to speak with him no more; why hast thou disobeyed my voice? That was Satan, and he sought to separate us. Do not speak to him again when he addresses thee."

Some time after, the Evil One presented himself before the faithful wife, under the form of an angel; and said to her, "O woman, daughter of a prophet! I am an angel sent from God with a message to thee."

She said, "What message?"

He said, "Behold the Most High is wroth with Job, for he renders no thanks for all the good things He gave to him; therefore hath the Lord rejected him from being a prophet, and he shall fall from worse to worse, till he is cast into the flames of hell; we, the angels of God, curse him, and do thou, daughter of a prophet, avoid him, lest thou come into the same condemnation."

When Rahma heard these words, she wept, and said, " After so many afflictions, shall the name of Job be taken from the number of the prophets ?   And after so many sufferings shall he perish everlastingly ? "

Then she went to Job and told him all that had been said to her.

Job was greatly angered when she told him the tenor of the words, and he cried out, " Have I not warned thee these two times not to speak with him, who is the author of my affliction ?   Wait till I am well, and I will give thee a hundred strokes with a rod." [1]

But the story is told differently by others.   It is said that the third time Satan appeared as a baker, and Rahma wanted bread, but had nought to pay.   Then said the pretended baker, " Thou hast locks of very beautiful hair ; cut off thy hair and give it me, and thou shalt take the largest of my loaves."

Then she cut off three locks and gave them to him.

And when Job saw that she had done this, he was filled with fury, and he swore that when he was well he would beat her for having cut off her hair. [2]

Thus Satan triumphed in making Job to sin by swearing. and threatening to ill-treat a true and good woman.

Next the Evil One went as an angel, and announced to all the people of the land that he came from God to declare to them that Job was no more reckoned among the prophets ; and that they were not to trust his words and believe his doctrine, but were to return to the worship of those gods he had blasphemed and cast out.

Soon after, Job heard his three friends, Bildad, Eliphaz, and Zophar, converse together, and repeat what had been told them by Satan ; and the thought that he was supposed to be rejected by God from among His prophets, was so distressing to him, that he cried out, " Truly, O God ! evil has befallen me ; but Thou art the most merciful of those who show mercy." [3] That is, the words of men are cruel, but Thou, O God, wilt deliver me out of all my evils.

Job was sick for seven years, and all that while his wife ministered to him.

But the mediæval commentators draw a very different pic-

---

[1] Tabari, i. c. lxvi ; Abulfeda, pp. 27–29.   [2] Testament of Job.
[3] Koran, Sura xxi. v. 83.

ture of this wife, relying on the words of Scripture which make her tempt Job to "*curse God and die.*" They say that her tongue was one of the plagues of Job. That he bore patiently the loss of his cattle, of his children, and of his health, was indeed wonderful; but that he also endured the nagging of his wife with equanimity,—that was the most wonderful of all.

Then God looked on Job and had compassion upon him, and he said to him, "Strike the earth with thy foot."[1] Job stamped, and from the dung-heap on which he had been seated a clear stream of water issued, the sweetest that there is, and the water continued to flow. Then God said to Job, "Wash in this water."

Rahma, the wife of Job, poured the water upon his head and over his body, and he washed himself. All the sores that were on his flesh disappeared, and he was healed; there was not a scar left, and he appeared more beautiful than before he was afflicted.

Then God said to Job, "Drink of the water."

Then all the worms that were in the inside of Job died, and he was quite whole. Now this took place in Bashan, and the fountain remains to this day, and is called Qarya-Aïyub, and the city near which it is, Aïrs-Aïyub. "I have seen the city of the fountain," says the Persian translator of Tabari: "every person who goes there, affected by internal or external maladies, and washes and drinks of that water, is healed of his disease."[2]

Then God said to Job, "Fulfil thy vow, and take in thine hand a bundle of rods."[3] But the rods God told him to take were light sticks; and he took a hundred of these, and bound them together and smote Rahma with them, and he did not hurt her. By this action of Job, the Mussulman doctors support their advice to those who have taken rash oaths to clear themselves by a subterfuge. Thus, if a man has sworn he will not enter his house again, he is recommended to allow himself to be bound hand and foot and be carried into his home. Or, if he has sworn to recite the whole Koran, it will be sufficient for him to say the word "Koran," and listen to the imaum reading before the assembly.

Then God restored to Job double all that he had lost; and

---

[1] Koran, Sura xxxviii. v. 41. [2] Tabari, i. p. 263.
[3] Koran, Sura xxxviii. v. 43.

Job lived, after he was recovered of his disease, twenty years, and he died at the age of ninety-three.

The worms which had devoured the body of the prophet, God turned into silk-worms; and the flies which had bitten him and tormented his sores, converted He into honey-bees; and before this there were neither silk-worms nor honey-bees on the earth. Also the rain and the snow which fell within his possessions, were grains of gold and pearl.

Isidore of Seville places the fountain which cured Job in Idumæa. He says, it is clear during three months of the year, troubled during the next three, then for three months it is green, and for the last three, it is red.

In the "Testament of Job," we read some details concerning his death, written by his brother Nahor.

After three days of sickness, Job, lying on his bed, saw the angels come to receive his soul. After having divided his substance between his seven sons (for, after his troubles, he became the father of seven sons and three daughters), he gave his daughters three mantles of inestimable price, which he had received from heaven. To the eldest, Hemera (Jemima), he gave his harp; to the second, Cassia (Keziah), he handed his censer; to the third, Keren-happuch, he remitted his tamborine: and as he sang his last hymn to the Most High on his death-bed, Hemera and Keren-happuch accompanied him with harp and timbrel, and Cassia cast up fumes of sweet incense. Thus they greeted the messengers of heaven who came for the soul of Job.

XXXI.

JETHRO.

As has already been related, Jethro formed one of the council of Pharaoh till he found that his incantations had no effect on the Israelites. He escaped from Egypt before Job; for he had found in the palace of the king the staff of Joseph which had been cut from the Tree of Life, and therewith he hied him into the land of Midian, along with his daughter Zipporah.

According to Mussulman tradition, Jethro, whom the Arabs call Schohair or Schohaib, was a great prophet; and he was sent by God to the Midianites to call them to repentance and the rejection of polytheism. Jethro was old and nearly blind. He preached to the people and exhorted them with many words and for a long season, but all his words were in vain ; the Midianites would not be converted, and at length they openly accused him of being a false prophet, and denied that God had sent him.

Therefore God gave over this nation to destruction. He sent a fiery breath upon the land, and the people could not bear the great heat, and retired into the fields, where there was shadow ; for God sent a cloud to hide the face of the sun, and it cast a blot of shade upon the fields. But there were old men and women and little children, and the sick who could not leave the city and take refuge in the shade.

Slowly the cloud came down from heaven, like the lid of a saucepan, and covered all the Midianites that were in the field, and the cloud was of fire, and they fried "as fish fry in an oven." Then the angel Gabriel gave a great shout, and all that were in the city, saving Jethro and his family, died of fright when they heard his cry.

Then Jethro lived in the land of Midian till Moses came to him out of Egypt.[1]

XXXII.

MOSES.[2]

I. ISRAEL IN EGYPT.

AFTER the death of Jacob, his descendants were drawn into servitude by soft and hypocritical speeches. Fifty-four years had passed since the death of Joseph.

Joseph had had the good fortune to acquire the favor of Mechron, the son and successor of that Pharoah who had

---

[1] Tabari, i. c. lxvii ; Abulfeda p. 31.

[2] The early portion of the life of Moses has been elaborated from Rabbinic sources by Dr. B. Beer. Unfortunately he died before the work was completed, and it has been published as a fragment by his friend, G. Wolf. It extends only as far as his marriage with Zipporoh. (Leben Moses nach Auffassung der Jüdischen Sage, von Dr. B. Beer ; ein Fragment. Leipzig, 1863.) It is for the most part, compiled from the Sepher Hajasher, or Book of Jasher.

raised him from the dungeon to be second in the kingdom. Almost all the inhabitants of Egypt had loved Joseph ; only a few voices were raised in murmurs at a foreigner exercising such extensive powers.

The successors of the patriarchs mingled among the people of the land and learned their ways ; and many of them abandoned the rite of circumcision, and spoke the language of Mizraem.

Then God withdrew His protection for a while ; and the former love of the Egyptians towards the Hebrews was turned into implacable hatred.   By degrees the privileges of the children of Israel were encroached upon, and they were oppressed with heavy taxes, from which hitherto they had been held exempt.

Afterwards the king exacted from them their labor without pay ; he built a great castle and required the Hebrews to erect it for him at their own cost.

Twenty-two years after the death of Joseph, Levi died, who had outlived all his other brothers.

Fields, vineyards, and houses, which Joseph had given to his brethren, were now reclaimed by the natives of Egypt, and the children of Israel were enslaved.

The Egyptians, effeminate, and hating work, fond of pleasure and display, had envied the prosperity of the Hebrews, who had thriven in Goshen, and whose wives bore sometimes six and sometimes twelve infants at a birth.

They also feared lest this people, increasing upon them, should become more numerous than they, and should seize upon the power, and enslave the native population.

Nine years after the death of Joseph, King Mechron died, and was succeeded by his son Melol.

But before pursuing the history of the oppression of the Hebrews, we must relate some events that had occurred before this time.

When the body of Jacob, according to the last will, had been taken to the cave of Machpelah, Esau and his sons and a large body of followers hastened to oppose the burial of Jacob. After the death of Isaac, Esau and Jacob had come to an agreement, by which all the movable property of the father was made over to Esau, and all that was immovable, especially the burial cave, was apportioned to Jacob.   But now Esau desired to set aside this agreement, and, as first-born, to claim the tomb as his, trusting that the sons of Jacob could not prove the agreement.

But no sooner had he raised this objection, than Naphtali, who was swift of foot, ran into Egypt, and returned in a few hours with the writing of agreement.

Esau, seeing himself baffled, had recourse to arms ; and a fight took place, in which Esau was killed, and his followers were put to flight or taken as captives to Egypt, where they became the slaves of the Israelites.   Amongst those captives was Zepho, son of Eliphaz, son of Esau.

Even in Joseph's lifetime, the Edomites made incursions into Egypt to recover their captive relatives, but their attempts led to no other result than the tightening of the chains which bound the captives.   Later, however, Zepho succeeded in effecting his escape, and he took refuge with Angias, king of Dinhaba (Ethiopia), who made him chief captain of his host.

Zepho persuaded the king to make war upon Egypt.   Among the servants of Angias was a youth of fifteen, named Balaam, son of Beor, very skilful in the arts of witchcraft.   The king bade the youthful necromancer divine who would succeed in the proposed war.   Balaam formed chariots and horses and fighting men of wax, plunged them in water, which he stirred with palm twigs ; and it was seen by all who stood by, that the men and horses representing the Egyptians and Hebrews floated, whereas those representing the Ethiopians sank.

Angias, deterred by this augury, refused to have any thing to do with a war against Egypt. Then Zepho left him, and betook himself to the land of the Hittites, and he succeeded in combining that nation, the Edomites, and the Ishmaelites together in making an invasion of Egypt.

To repel them, the Hebrews were summoned from the land of Goshen, but the Egyptians would not receive their allies into the camp, fearing lest they should unite with their kindred nations, and deliver them up to destruction.

Zepho now asked Balaam, who had followed him, to divine the end of the battle, but the attempt failed ; and the future remained closed to him.   But Zepho, full of confidence, led the combined army against the Egyptians, repulsed them at every point, and drove them back upon the camp of the Hebrews. Then the Israelites charged the advancing forces flushed with victory, who, little expecting such a determined onslaught, were thrown into confusion, and routed with great loss.   The Hebrews pursued them to the confines of Ethiopia, cutting them down all along the way, and then they desisted and returned: and on numbering their band—they were but a handful—they found that they had not lost one man. They now looked out for their allies, the Egyptians, and found that they had deserted and fled; therefore, full of wrath, they returned to Goshen in triumph, and slew the deserters, with many words of contempt and ridicule.[1]

Thus the Hebrews were puffed up with pride, regarding themselves as invincible; and the Egyptians were filled with dread, lest this small people should resolve on seizing upon the supremacy, and should subjugate them.

Therefore the reigning Pharaoh and his council assembled to consult what should be done; and this was decided:—" The cities Pithom and Rameses (Tanis and Heliopolis) are not strong enough to withstand a foe, therefore they must be strengthened." And a royal decree went forth over all the land of Egypt and Goshen, commanding all the inhabitants, both Egyptians and Hebrews, to build. Pharaoh himself set the example by taking trowel and basket in hand, and putting a brick mould on his neck. Whoever saw this hastened to do likewise, and all who were reluctant were stimulated by the overseers with these words, " See how the king works. Will you not imitate his activity?"

Thus the Israelites went to the work, and laid the mould upon their necks, little suspecting the guile that was in the hearts of the king and his councillors.

At the close of the first day, the Hebrews had made a large number of bricks; and this number was now imposed upon them as the amount of their daily task.

Thus passed a month, and by degrees the Egyptian workmen were withdrawn, yet the Hebrews were paid the regular wage.

When a year and four months had elapsed, not an Egyptian was to be seen making bricks and building; and the wage was stopped for the future, but the Hebrews were kept to their work.

The harshest and most cruel men were appointed to be their overseers, and if one of the Israelites asked for his wage, or fainted under his burden, he was beaten or put in the stocks.

---

[1] Yaschar, pp. 1241–53. The history of Zepho is quite a romance, too long for insertion here.

2*

When Pithom and Rameses were walled, the Israelites were employed to strengthen with forts all the other cities of Egypt, then to build storehouses and pyramids, to dig canals for the Nile, and to rear dykes against the overflow. They were also employed to dig and plough the fields, to garden and prune the fruit-trees, and to exercise trades. They were engaged from early dawn till late at night, and because the way from their homes was often far, they were forced to sleep in the open air, upon the bare ground.[1]

As the life of the Israelites became embittered to them, they called the king Meror, "the embitterer," instead of Melol, "the grinder," though that was appropriate enough, one would have supposed.[2]

But matters grew worse; the Edomites and Hittites again threatened Egypt, and Pharaoh ordered a closer guard to be kept, and heavier tasks to be laid upon the Hebrews.

Notwithstanding all attempts to crush the spirit of this unfortunate people and to diminish their numbers, they were sustained by hope in God, for a voice was heard from heaven, "This people shall increase abundantly, and multiply."

Whilst the men of Israel slept exhausted after their unspeakable oppression of mind and body, the faithful women labored to relieve and strengthen them. They hastened to the springs to bring pure water to their husbands to drink, and, by the mercy of the All Merciful, it fell out that their pitchers were found, each time, to contain half water and half fish.

These gentle and diligent women dressed the fish, and prepared other good meats for their husbands, and they sought them at their work with the food, and with their cheerful words of encouragement. This loving attention of the women soothed the hearts of the men, and gave them fresh energy.

When 125 years had elapsed since Jacob came into Egypt, the fifty-fourth year after Joseph's death, the elders and councillors of Egypt presented themselves before Pharaoh, and complained to him that the people increased and multiplied and became very great in the land, so that they covered it like the bushes in the wood; and two of the king's councillors, of whom one was Job of Uz, said to Pharaoh, "It was well that heavy tasks were laid upon the Hebrews, but that doth not suffice; it is needful that they should be diminished in number as well

---

[1] Yaschar, pp. 1248, 1249; 1253, 1254.   [2] Ibid., p. 1255.

as enslaved. Therefore give orders to the nurses to kill every male child that is born to the Hebrews, but to save the women children alive."

This council pleased the king well; and what Job had advised was put in operation.

Pharaoh summoned the two Hebrew midwives before him; they were mother and daughter; some say their names were Jochebed and Miriam, but others Jochebed and Elizabeth. Now, Miriam was only five years old, nevertheless she was of the greatest assistance to her mother in nursing women. Both showed the utmost kindness to the new-born children, washed and brushed them up, said pretty things to them, and strengthened the mothers with cordials and tonic draughts. To their care the Israelites were indebted for the graceful and vigorous forms of their children; and the two women were such favorites with the people, that they called the one Shiphrah (the soother or beautifier) and the other Puah (the helper).

When they appeared before the king, and heard what he designed, Miriam's young face flushed scarlet, and she said, in anger, "Woe to the man! God will punish him for his evil deed."

The executioner would have hurried her out, and killed her for her audacity, but the mother implored pardon, saying, "O king! forgive her speech; she is only a little foolish child."

Pharaoh consented, and assuming a gentler tone, explained that the female children were to be saved alive, and that the male children were to be quietly put to death, without the knowledge of the mothers. And he threatened them, if they did not obey his wishes, that he would cast them into a furnace of fire. Then he dismissed them. But the two midwives would not fulfil his desire.

And when Pharaoh found that the men-children were saved alive, he shut up the two midwives, that the Hebrew women might be without their succor. But this availed not. And God rewarded the midwives; for of the elder Moses was born.

Five years passed, and Pharaoh dreamed that, as he sat upon his throne, an old man stood before him holding a balance. And the old man put the princes, and nobles, and elders of Egypt, and all its inhabitants into one scale, and he put into the other a sucking child, and the babe outweighed all that was in the first scale.[1]

<hr>

[1] Midrash, fol. 51 ; Yaschar, p. 1157.

When Pharaoh awoke, he rehearsed his dream in the ears of his wise men and magicians and soothsayers, and asked them the interpretation thereof.

Then answered Balaam, who, with his sons Jannes and Jambres, was at the court, and said, "O king, live forever! The dream thou didst see has this signification. A child shall be born among the Hebrews who shall bring them with a strong hand out of Egypt, and before whom all thy nations shall be as naught. A great danger threatens thee and all Egypt."

Then said Pharaoh in dismay, "What shall we do? All that we have devised against this people has failed."

"Let the king suffer me to give my advice," said Jethro, one of his councillors. And when Pharaoh consented, he said, "May the king's days be multiplied! This is my advice; the people that thou oppressest is a great people, and God is their shield. All who resist them are brought to destruction; all who favor them prosper. Therefore, O king, do thou withdraw thy hand, which is heavy upon them; lighten their tasks, and extend to them thy favor."

But this advice pleased not Pharaoh nor his councillors; and his anger was kindled against Jethro, and he drove him from his court and from the country. Then Jethro went with his wife and daughter, and dwelt in the land of Midian.

Then said the king, "Job of Uz, give thy opinion."

But Job opened not his lips.

Then rose Balaam, son of Beor, and he said, "O my king, all thy attempts to hurt Israel have failed, and the people increase upon you. Think not to try fire against them, for that was tried against Abraham their father, and he was saved unhurt from the midst of the flames. Try not sword against them, for the knife was raised against Isaac their father, and he was delivered by the angel of God. Nor will hard labor injure them as thou hast proved. Yet there remains water, that hath not yet been enlisted against them; prove them with water. Therefore my advice is—cast all their new-born sons into the river." [1]

The king hesitated not; he appointed Egyptian women to be nurses to the Hebrews, and instructed them to drown all the male children that were born; and he threatened with death

---

[1] Midrash Jalkut, fol. 52; Yaschar, pp. 1257–9.

those who withstood his decree. And that he might know what women were expecting to be delivered, he sent little Egyptian children to the baths, to observe the Hebrew women, and report on their appearance.

But God looked upon the mothers, and they were delivered in sleep under the shadow of fruit-trees, and angels attended on them, washed and dressed the babes, and smeared their little hands with butter and honey, that they might lick them, and, delighting in the flavor, abstain from crying, and thus escape discovery. Then the mothers on waking exclaimed :— "O most Merciful One, into Thy hands we commit our children !" But the emissaries of Pharaoh followed the traces of the women, and would have slain the infants, had not the earth gaped, and received the little babes into a hollow place within, where they were fed by angel hands with butter and honey.

The Egyptians brought up oxen and ploughed over the spot, in hopes of destroying thereby the vanished infants ; but, when their backs were turned, the children sprouted from the soil, like little flowers, and walked home unperceived. Some say that 10,000 children were cast into the Nile. They were not deserted by the Most High. The river rejected them upon its banks, and the rocks melted into butter and honey around them and thus fed them,[1] and oil distilled to anoint them.

This persecution had continued for three years and four months, when, on the seventh day of the twelfth month, Adar, the astrologers and seers stood before the king and said, " This day a child is born who will free the people of Israel ! This, and one thing more, have we learnt from the stars, *Water* will be the cause of his death ;[2] but whether he be an Egyptian or an Hebrew child, that we know not."

"Very well," said Pharaoh ; " then in future all male children, Egyptians as well as Hebrews, shall be cast indiscriminately into the river."

And so was it done.[3]

2. THE BIRTH AND CHILDHOOD OF MOSES.

Kohath, son of Levi, had a son named Amram, whose life

---

[1] The curious passages, Isaiah vii. 15, 22, may allude to this tradition.

[2] Moses' life was shortened because he brought water out of the rock contrary to God's command (Numb. xxvii. 14), striking the rock instead of speaking to it.

[3] Beer. pp. 112–6.

was so saintly, that death could not have touched him, had not the decree gone forth, that every child of Adam was to die.

He married Jochebed, the daughter of Levi, his aunt, and by her he had a daughter Miriam; and after four years she bore him a son, and he called his name Aaron.

Now when it was noised abroad that Pharaoh would slay all the sons of the Hebrews that were born to them, Amram thrust away his wife, and many others did the same, not that they hated their wives, but that they would spare them the grief of seeing their children put to death.[1] After three years, the spirit of prophecy came on Miriam, as she sat in the house, and she cried, " My parents shall have another son, who shall deliver Israel out of the hands of the Egyptians ! " Then she said to her father, " What hast thou done ? Thou hast sent thy wife away, out of thine house, because thou couldest not trust the Lord God, that He would protect the child that might be born to thee."

Amram, reproved by these words, sought his banished wife ; the angel Gabriel guided him on his way, and a voice from heaven encouraged him to proceed. And when he found Jochebed, he led her to her home again.[2]

One hundred and thirty years old was Jochebed, but she was as fresh and beauteous as on the day she left her father's house.[3] She was with child, and Amram feared lest it should be a boy and be slain by Pharaoh.

Then appeared the Eternal One to him in a dream, and bade him be of good cheer, for He would protect the child, and make him great, so that all nations should hold him in honor.

When Amram awoke, he told his dream to Jochebed, and they were filled with fear and great amazement.

After six months she bore a son, without pain. The child entered this world in the third hour of the morning, of the seventh day of the month Adar, in the year 2368 after the Creation, and the 130th year of the sojourn of the Israelites in Egypt. And when he was born, the house was filled with light, as of the brightest sunshine.

---

[1] Some authorities say that Jochebed, when thrust away, married Eliph-azan, the son of Parnach (Numb. xxxiv. 25), and bare him two sons, Eldad and Medad (Numb. xi. 15) ; but others, with more probability, assert that she married Eliphazan after the death of Amram. (Yaschar, p. 1259.)

[2] Yaschar, p. 1260.   [3] Targum of Palestine, i. p. 446.

The tender mother's anxiety for her son was increased when she noted his beauty,—he was like an angel of God,—and his great height and noble appearance. The parents called him Tobias (God is good) to express their thankfulness, but others say he was called Jokutiel (Hope in God). Amram kissed his daughter, Miriam, on the brow, and said, "Now I know that thy prophecy is come true."[1]

Jochebed hid the child three months in her chamber where she slept. But Pharaoh, filled with anxiety, lest a child should have escaped him, sent Egyptian women with their nurslings to the houses of the Hebrews. Now it is the custom of children, when one cries, another cries also. Therefore the Egyptian women pricked their babes, when they went into a house, and if the child were concealed therein, it cried when it heard the Egyptian baby scream. Then it was brought out and despatched.

Jochebed knew that these women were coming to her house, and that, if the child were discovered, her husband and herself would be slain by the executioner of Pharaoh.

Moreover they feared the astrologers and soothsayers, that they would read in the heavens that a male child was concealed there. "Better can we deceive them," said Amram, "if we cast the child into the water."

Jochebed took the paper flags and wove a basket, and pitched it with pitch without, and clay within, that the smell of the pitch might not offend her dear little one; and then she placed the basket amongst the rushes, where the Red Sea at that time joined the River Nile.

Then weeping and wailing, she went away, and seeing Miriam come to meet her, she smote her on the head, and said, "Now, daughter, where is thy prophesying?"

Miriam followed the little ark, as it floated on the wash of the river, and swam in and out among the reeds; for Miriam was wondering whether the prophecy would come true, or whether it would fail. This was on the twenty-first of the month Nisan, on the day, chosen from the beginning, on which in after times Moses should teach his people the Song of Praise for their delivery at the Red Sea.[2]

Then the angels surrounded the throne of God and cried, "O Lord of the whole earth, shall this mortal child fore-or-

---

[1] Rabboth, fol. 118 a.   [2] Exod. xv. 1.

dained to chant, at the head of Thy chosen people, the great song of delivery from water, perish this day by water?"

Tne Almighty answered, "Ye know well that I behold all things. They that seek their salvation in their own craftiness and evil ways shall find destruction, but they who trust in Me shall never be confounded. The history of that child shall be a witness to My almighty power."

Melol, king of Egypt, had then only one daughter, whom he greatly loved; Bithia (Thermutis or Therbutis)[1] was her name. She had been married for some time to Chenephras, prince of a territory near Memphis, but was childless. This troubled her greatly, for she desired a son who might succeed her father upon the throne of Egypt.

At this time God had sent upon Egypt an intolerable heat, and the people were affected with grievous boils.[2] To cure themselves, they bathed in the Nile. Bithia also suffered, and bathed, not in the river, but in baths in the palace; but on this day she went forth by the Nile bank, though otherwise she never left her father's palace. On reaching the bathing-place she observed the ark lodged among the bulrushes, and sent one of her maids to swim out and bring it to her; but the other servants said, "O princess, this is one of the Hebrew children, who are cast out according to the command of thy royal father. It beseems thee not to oppose his commands and frustrate his will."

Scarcely had the maidens uttered these words than they vanished from the surface of the earth. The angel Gabriel had sunk them all, with the exception of the one who swam for the ark, into the bosom of the earth.

But the eagerness of the princess was so great, that she could not wait till the damsel brought her the basket, and she stretched forth her arm towards it, and her arm was lengthened sixty ells, so that she was able to take hold of the ark and draw it to land, and lift the child out of the water.

No sooner had she touched the babe, than she was healed of the boils which afflicted her, and the splendor of the face of the child was like that of the sun.[3] She looked at it with wonder, and admired its beauty. But her father's stern law made her fear, and she thought to return the child to the wa-

---

[1] The Arabic name for her is Asia; Yaschar, p. 1261.
[2] Targum of Palestine, i. p. 446; Yaschar, p. 1261.
[3] Midrash, fol. 51.

ter, when he began to cry, for the angel Gabriel had boxed his ears to make him weep, and thus excite the compassion of the princess. Then Miriam, hid away among the rushes, and little Aaron, aged three, hearing him cry, wept also.

The heart of the princess was stirred; and compassion, like that of a mother for her babe, filled her heart. She felt for the infant yearning love as though it were her own. "Truly," said Bithia, "the Hebrews are to be pitied, for it is no easy matter to part with a child, and to deliver it over to death."

Then, fearing that there would be no safety for the babe, if it were brought into the palace, she called to an Egyptian woman who was walking by the water, and bade her suckle the child. But the infant would not take the breast from this woman, nor from any other Egyptian woman that she summoned; and this the Almighty wrought that the child might be restored to its own mother again.

Then Miriam, the sister, mingled with those who came up, and said to Bithia, with sobs, "Noble lady! vain are all thine attempts to give the child the breast from one of a different race. If thou wouldst have a Hebrew woman, then let me fetch one, and the child will suck at once."[1]

This advice pleased Bithia, and she bade Miriam seek her out a Hebrew mother.

With winged steps Miriam hastened home, and brought her mother, Jochebed, to the princess. Then the babe readily took nourishment from her, and ceased crying.

Astonished at this wonder, the king's daughter said, but unawares, the truth, for she spake to Jochebed, "Here is thy child; take and nurse the child for me, and the wage shall be two pieces of silver a day."

Jochebed did what she was bidden, but better reward than all the silver in Pharaoh's house was the joy of having her son restored to his mother's breast.

The self-same day the soothsayers and star-gazers said to Pharaoh, "The child of whom we spake to thee, that he should free Israel, hath met his fate in the water."

Therefore the cruel decree ordering the destruction of all male infants was withdrawn, and the miraculous deliverance of Moses became by this means the salvation of the whole generation. In allusion to this, Moses said afterwards to the people when he would restrain them (Numbers xi.): "Verily ye

---

[1] Midrash, fol. 51; Yaschar, p. 1262.

number six hundred thousand men, and ye would all have perished in the river Nile, but I was delivered from the water, and therefore ye are all alive as at this day."

After two years Jochebed weaned him, and brought him to the king's daughter. Bithia, charmed with the beauty and intelligence of the child, took him into the palace, and named him Moses (he who is drawn out of the water). Lo! a voice from heaven fell, "Daughter of Pharaoh! because thou hast had compassion on this little child and hast called him thy son, therefore do I call thee My daughter (Bithia). The foundling that thou cherishest shall be called by the name thou gavest him—Moses; and by none other name shall he be known, wheresoever the fame of him spreads under the whole heaven."

Now, in order that Moses might really pass for the child of Bithia, the princess had feigned herself to be pregnant, and then to be confined; and now Pharaoh regarded him as his true grandchild.

On account of his exceeding beauty, every one that saw him was filled with admiration, and said, "Truly, this is a king's son." And when he was taken abroad, the people forsook their work, and deserted their shops, that they might see him. One day, when Moses was three years old, Bithia led him by the hand into the presence of Pharaoh, and the queen sat by the king, and all the princes of the realm stood about him. Then Bithia presented the child to the king, and said, "Oh, sire! this child of noble mien is not really my son; he was given to me in wondrous fashion by the divine river Nile; therefore have I brought him up as my own son, and destined him to succeed thee on thy throne, since no child of my body has been granted to me."

With these words Bithia laid the boy in the king's arms, and he pressed him to his heart, and kissed him. Then, to gratify his daughter, he took from his head the crown royal, and placed it upon the temples of Moses. But the child eagerly caught at the crown, and threw it on the ground and then alighting from Pharaoh's knee, he in childish fashion danced round it, and finally trampled it under his feet.[1]

The king and his nobles were dismayed. They thought that this action augured evil to the king through the child that was before them. Then Balaam, the son of Beor, lifted up his

---

[1] Midrash, fol. 52; Yaschar, p. 1263.

voice and said, " My lord and king! dost thou not remember
the interpretation of thy dream, as thy servant interpreted it
to thee? This child is of Hebrew extraction, and is wiser and
more cunning than befits his age. When he is old he will take
thy crown from off thy head, and will tread the power of Egypt
under his feet. Thus have his ancestors ever done. Abraham
defied Nimrod, and rent from him Canaan, a portion of his
kingdom. Isaac prevailed over the king of the Philistines.
Jacob took from his brother his birthright and blessing, and
smote the Hivites and their king Hamor. Joseph, the slave,
became chief in his realm, and gave the best of this land to
his father and his brethren. And now this child will take from
thee the kingdom, and will enslave or destroy thy people.
There is no expedient for thee but to slay him, that Egypt become not his prey.'

But Pharaoh said, " We will take other counsel, Balaam,
before we decide what shall be done with this child."

Then some advised that he should be burnt with fire, and
others that he should be slain with the sword. But the angel
Gabriel, in the form of an old man, mingled with the councillors, and said, " Let not innocent blood be shed. The child
is too young to know what he is doing. Prove whether he has
any understanding and design, before you sentence him. O
king! let a bowl of live coals and a bowl of precious stones be
brought to the little one. If he takes the stones, then he has
understanding, and discerns between good and evil; but if he
thrusts his hands towards the burning coals, then he is innocent of purpose and devoid of reason." [1]

This advice pleased the king, and he gave orders that it
should be as the angel had recommended.

Now when the basins were brought in and offered to Moses,
he thrust out his hand towards the jewels. But Gabriel, who
had made himself invisible, caught his hand and directed it towards the red-hot coals; and Moses burnt his fingers, and he
put them into his mouth, and burnt his lips and tongue; and
therefore it is that Moses said, in after days, " I am slow of lips
and slow of tongue." [2]

Pharaoh and his council were now convinced of the sim-

---

[1] According to another version, it was Jethro who advised that the child
should be proved with the basins of rubies and coals (Rabboth, fol. 118 b;
Yaschar, pp. 1263, 1264).

[2] Exod. iv. 10.

plicity of Moses, and no harm was done him. Then Bithia removed him, and brought him up in her own part of the palace. '

God was with him, and he increased in stature and beauty, and Pharaoh's heart was softened towards him. He went arrayed in purple through the streets, as the son of Bithia, and a chaplet of diamonds surrounded his brows, and he consorted only with princes. When he was five years old, he was in size and knowledge as advanced as a boy of twelve.

Masters were brought for him from all quarters, and he was instructed in all .the wisdom and learning of the Egyptians ; and the people looked upon him with hope as their future sovereign.'

3. THE YOUTH AND MARRIAGE OF MOSES.

Moses, as he grew older, distinguished himself from all other young men of Egypt by the conquest which he acquired over himself and his youthful passions and impetuous will. Although the life of a court offered him every kind of gratification, yet he did not allow himself to be attracted by its pleasures, or to regard as permanent what he knew to be fleeting. Thus it fell out, that all his friends and acquaintances wondered at him, and doubted whether he were not a god appeared on earth. And, in truth, Moses did not live and act as did others. What he thought, that he said, and what he promised, that he fulfilled.

Moses had reached the summit of earthly greatness ; acknowledged as grandson to Pharaoh, and heir to the crown. But he trusted not in the future which was thus offered to him, for he knew from Jochebed, whom he frequently visited, what was his true people, and who were his real parents. And the bond which attached him to his own house and people was in his heart, and could not be broken.

Moses went daily to Goshen to see his relations ; and he observed how the Hebrews were oppressed, and groaned under their burdens. And he asked wherefore the yoke was pressed so heavily on the neck of these slaves. He was told of the advice of Balaam against the people, and of the way in which

---

[1] Beer, pp. 26–42. Abulfaraj says that Jannes and Jambres were the tutors of Moses in his youth (Hist. Dynast., p. 17).

Pharaoh had sought the destruction of himself in his infancy. This information filled Moses with indignation, and alienated his affections from Pharoah, and filled him with animosity towards Balaam.[1] But, as he was not in a position to rescue his brethren, or to punish Balaam, he cried, " Alas! I had rather die than continue to behold the affliction of my brethren." Then he took the necklace from off him, which indicated his princely position, and sought to ease the burden of the Israelites. He took the excessive loads from the women and old men, and laid them on the young and strong ; and thus he seemed to be fulfilling Pharaoh's intentions in getting the work of building sooner executed, whereas, by making each labor according to his strength, their sufferings were lightened. And he said to the Hebrews, " Be of good cheer, relief is not so far off as you suppose—calm follows storm, blue sky succeeds black clouds, sunshine comes after rain. The whole world is full of change, and all is for an object."

Nevertheless Moses himself desponded ; he looked with hatred upon Balaam, and lost all pleasure in the society of the Egyptians. Balaam seeing that the young man was against him, and dreading his power, escaped with his sons Jannes and Jambres to the court of Ethiopia.

The young Moses, however, grew in favor with the king, who laid upon him the great office of introducing illustrious foreigners to the royal presence.

But Moses kept ever before his eyes the aim of his life, to relieve his people from their intolerable burdens. One day he presented himself before the king and said, " Sire! I have a petition to make of thee."

Pharaoh answered, " Say on, my son."

Then said Moses, " O king! every laborer is given one day in seven for rest, otherwise his work becomes languid and unprofitable. But the children of Israel are given no day of rest, but they work from the first day of the week to the last day, without cessation ; therefore is their work inferior, and it is not executed with that heartiness which might be found, were they given one day in which to recruit their strength."

Pharaoh said, " Which day shall be given to them ? "

Moses said, " Suffer them to rest on the seventh day."

The king consented, and the people were given the Sab-

---

[1] Yaschar, p. 1265.

bath, on which they ceased from their labors; therefore they rejoiced greatly, and for a thousand years the last day of the week was called " The gift of Moses." [1]

As the command to destroy all the male children had been withdrawn the day that Moses was cast into the Nile, the people had multiplied greatly, and again the fears of the Egyptians were aroused. Therefore the king published a new decree, with the object of impeding the increase of the bondsmen.

He required the Egyptian task-masters to impose a tale of bricks on every man, and if at evening the tale of bricks was not made up, then, in place of the deficient bricks, even though only one brick was short, they were to take the children of those who had not made up their tale, and to build them into the wall in place of bricks.[2] Thus upon one misery another was piled.

In order that this decree might be executed with greater certainty, ten laborers were placed under one Hebrew overseer, and one Egyptian task-master controlled the ten overseers. The duty of the Hebrew overseers was to wake the ten men they were set over, every morning before dawn, and bring them to their work. If the Egyptian task-masters observed that one of the laborers was not at his post, he went to the overseer, and bade him produce the man immediately.

Now one of these overseers had a wife of the tribe of Dan, whose name was Salome, daughter of Dibri. She was beautiful and faultless in her body. The Egyptian task-master had observed her frequently, and he loved her. Then, one day, he went early to the house of her husband, and bade him arise, and go and call the ten laborers. So the overseer rose, nothing doubting, and went forth, and then the Egyptian entered and concealed himself in the house. But the overseer returning, found him, and drew him forth, and asked him with what intent he had hidden himself there; and Moses drew nigh. Now Moses was known to the Hebrews as merciful, and ready to judge righteously their causes; so the man ran to Moses, and told him that he had found the Egyptian task-master concealed in his house.

And Moses knew for what intent the man had done thus, and his anger was kindled, and he raised a spade to smite the man on the head and kill him.

[1] Yaschar, p. 1265.   [2] Ibid, p. 1263.

But whilst the spade was yet in his hand, before it fell, Moses said within himself, "I am about to take a man's life ; how know I that he will not repent ? How know I that if I suffer him to live, he may beget children who will do righteously and serve the Lord ? Is it well that I should slay this man ?"

Then Moses' eyes were opened, and he saw the throne of God, and the angels that surrounded it, and God said to him, " It is well that thou shouldst slay this Egyptian, and therefore have I called thee hither. Know that he would never repent, nor would his children do other than work evil, wert thou to give him his life."

So Moses called on the name of the Most High and smote ; but before the spade touched the man, as the sound of the name of God reached his ears, he fell and died.[1]

Then Moses looked on the Hebrews who had crowded round, and he said to them, " God has declared that ye shall be as the sand of the sea-shore. Now the sand falls and it is noiseless, and the foot of man presses it, and it sounds not. Therefore understand that ye are to be silent as is the sand of the sea-shore, and tell not of what I have this day done."

Now when the man of the Hebrews returned home, he drove out his wife Salome, because he had found the Egyptian concealed in his house, and he gave her a writing of divorcement and sent her away. Then the Hebrews talked among themselves at their work, and some said he had done well, and others that he had done ill. There were at their task two young men, brothers, Dathan and Abiram, the sons of Eliab, of the tribe of Reuben, and they strove together on this subject, and Dathan in anger lifted his hand, and would have smitten Abiram. Then Moses came up and stayed him, and cried, " What wickedness art thou doing, striking thy comrade ? It beseems you not to lay hands on each other."

Boldly did Dathan answer : " Who made thee, beardless youth, a lord and ruler over us ? We know well that thou art not the son of the king's daughter, but of Jochebed. *Will thou slay me as thou didst the Egyptian yesterday ?*"

" Alas ! " said Moses, " now I see that the evil words, and evil acts, and evil thoughts of this people will fight against

---

[1] Parascha of R. Solomon Jaschi, on Exod. ii. 12 ; also Targums of Palestine and Jerusalem, i. p. 447 ; Yaschar, pp. 1265, 1266.

them, and frustrate the loving-kindness of the Lord towards them."

Then Dathan and Abiram went before Pharaoh, and told him that Moses had slain an Egyptian task-master; and Pharaoh's anger was kindled against Moses, and he cried, " Enough of evil hath been prophesied against thee, and I have not heeded it, and now thou liftest thy hand against my servants ! "

For he had, for long, been slowly turning against Moses, when he saw that he walked not in the ways of the Egyptians, and that he loved the king's enemies, and hated the king's friends. Then he consulted his soothsayers and his councillors, and they gave him advice that he should put Moses to death with the sword. Therefore the young man, Moses, was brought forth, and he ascended the scaffold, and the executioner stood over him with his sword, the like of which was not in the whole world. And when the king gave the word, the headsman smote. But the Lord turned the neck of Moses into marble, and the sword bit not into it.

Instantly, before the second blow was dealt, the angel Michael took from the executioner his sword and his outward semblance, and gave to the headsman the semblance of Moses, and he smote at the executioner, and took his head from off his shoulders. But Moses fled away, and none observed him. And he went to the king of Ethopia.[1]

Now the king of Ethiopia, Kikannos (Candacus) by name, was warring against his enemies ; and when he left his capital city, Mero, at the head of a mighty army, he left Balaam and his two sons regents during his absence.

Whilst the king was engaged in war, Balaam and his sons conspired against the king, and they bewitched the people with their enchantments, and led them from their allegiance, and persuaded them to submit to Balaam as their king. And Balaam strengthened the city on all sides. Sheba, or Mero, was almost impregnable, as it was surrounded by the Nile and the Astopus. On two sides Balaam built walls, and on the third side, between the Nile and the city, he dug countless canals, into which he let the water run. And on the fourth side he assembled innumerable serpents. Thus he made the city wholly impregnable.

When King Kikannos returned from the war, he saw that

[1] Pirke, R. Eliezer, c. 40 ; Rabboth, fol. 119 a ; Yaschar, p. 1266.

his capital was fortified, and he wondered ; but when he was refused admission, he knew that there was treason.

One day he endeavored to surmount the walls, but was repulsed with great slaughter ; and the next day he threw thirty pontoons across the river, but when his soldiers reached the other side, they were engulfed in the canals, of which the water was impelled with foaming fury by great mill-wheels. On the third day he assaulted the town on the fourth side, but his men were bitten by the serpents and died. Then King Kikannos saw that the only hope of reducing the city was by famine ; so he invested it, that no provisions might be brought into it.

Whilst he sat down before the capital, Moses took refuge in his camp, and was treated by him with great honor and distinction.

As the siege protracted itself through nine years, Kikannos fell ill and died.

Then the chief captains of his army assembled, and determined to elect a king, who might carry on the siege with energy, and reduce the city with speed, for they were weary of the long investment. So they elected Moses to be their king, and they threw off their garments and folded them and made thereof a throne, and set Moses thereon, and blew their trumpets, and cried " God save King Moses ! " [1]

And they gave him the widow of Kikannos to wife, and costly gifts of gold and silver and precious stones were brought to him, but all these he laid aside in the treasury. This took place 157 years after Jacob and his sons came down into Egypt, when Moses was aged twenty-seven years.

On the seventh day after his coronation came the captains and officers before him, and besought of him counsel, how the city might be taken. Then said Moses, " Nine years have ye invested it, and it is not yet in your power. Follow my advice, and in nine days it shall be yours."

They said, " Speak, and we will obey."

Then Moses gave this advice, " Make it known in the camp that all the soldiers go into the woods, and bring me storks' nests as many as they can find."

So they obeyed, and young storks innumerable were brought to him. Then he said, " Keep them fasting till I give you word, and he who gives to a stork food, though it were but a

___
[1] This illustrates the passage 2 Kings ix. 13.

crumb of bread, or a grain of corn, he shall be slain, and all that he hath shall become the king's property, and his house shall be made a dung-heap."

So the storks were kept fasting.   And on the third day the king said, " Let the birds go."

Then the storks flew into the air, and they spied the serpents on the fourth side of the city, and they fell upon them, and the serpents fled, and they were killed and eaten by the storks or ever they reached their holes, and not a serpent remained. Then said Moses, " March into the city and take it."

And the army entered the city, and not one man fell of the king's army, but they slew all that opposed them.

Thus Moses had brought the Ethiopian army into possession of the capital.   The grateful people placed the crown upon his head, and the queen of Kikannos gave him her hand with readiness.   But Balaam and his sons escaped, riding upon a cloud.

Moses reigned in wisdom and righteousness for forty years, and the land prospered under his government, and all loved and honored him.   Nevertheless, some thought that the son of their late king ought to ascend the throne of his ancestors ; —he was an infant when Moses was crowned, but now that he was a man, a party of the nobles desired to proclaim his right.

They prevailed upon the queen to speak ; and when all the princes and great men of the kingdom were assembled, she declared the matter before all.   " Men of Ethiopia," said she, " it is known to you that for forty years my husband has reigned in Sheba.   Well do you know that he has ruled in equity, and administered righteous judgment.   But know also, that his God is not our God, and that his faith is not our faith.   My son, Mena-Cham (Minakros) is of fitting age to succeed his father ; therefore it is my opinion that Moses should surrender to him the throne."

An assembly of the people was called, and as this advice of the queen pleased them, they besought Moses to resign the crown to the rightful heir.   He consented, without hesitation, and, laden with gifts and good wishes, he left the country and went into Midian.[1]

Moses was sixty-seven years old when he entered Midian. Reuel or Jethro,[2] who had been a councillor of Pharaoh, had,

<hr>

[1] Midrash, fol. 52 ; Yaschar, pp. 1265–1274.
[2] These were two of his seven names,

as has been already related, taken up his residence in Midian, where the people had raised him to be High Priest and Prince over the whole tribe. But Jethro after a while withdrew from the priesthood, for he believed in the one True God, and abhorred the idols which the Midianites worshipped. And when the people found that Jethro despised their gods, and that he preached against their idolatry, they placed him under the ban, that none might give him meat or drink, or serve him.

This troubled Jethro greatly, for all his shepherds forsook him, as he was under the ban. Therefore it was, that his seven daughters were constrained to lead and water the flocks.[1]

Moses arrived near a well and sat down to rest. Then he saw the seven daughters of Jethro approach.

The maidens had gone early to the well, for they feared lest the shepherds, taking advantage of their being placed under ban, should molest them, and refuse to give their sheep water. They let down their pitchers in turn, and with much trouble filled the trough. Then the shepherds came up and drove them away, and led their sheep to the trough the maidens had filled, and in rude jest they would have thrown the damsels into the water, but Moses stood up and delivered them, and rebuked the shepherds, and they were ashamed.

Then Moses let down his pitcher, and the water leaped up and overflowed, and he filled the trough and gave the flocks of the seven maidens to drink, and then he watered also the flocks of the shepherds, lest there should be evil blood between them.

Now when the maidens came home, they related to their father all that had taken place ; and he said, " Where is the man that hath shown kindness to you?—bring him to me."

So Zipporah ran—she ran like a bird—and came to the well, and bade Moses enter under their roof and eat of their table.

When Moses come to Raguel (Jethro), the old man asked him whence he came, and Moses told him all the truth.

Then thought Jethro, " I am fallen under the displeasure of Midian, and this man has been driven out of Egypt and out

---

[1] It may be noticed in this as in several other instances, such as those of Rebekah and Rachel, the Rabbis have invented stories to explain the circumstance of the damsels watering the flock, which they supposed derogated from their dignity. This indicates the late date of these traditions, when the old pastoral simplicity was lost.

12*

of Ethiopia ; he must be a dangerous man ; he will embroil me with the men of this land, and, if the king of Ethiopia or Pharaoh of Egypt hears that I have harbored him it will go ill with me."

Therefore Raguel took Moses and bound him in chains, and threw him into a dungeon, where he was given only scanty food ; and soon Jethro, whose thoughts were turned to reconciliation with the Midianites, forgot him, and sent him no food. But Zipporah loved him, and was grateful to him for the kindness he had showed her, in saving her from the hands of the shepherds who would have dipped her in the water-trough, and every day she took him food and drink, and in return was instructed by the prisoner in the law of the Most High.[1]

Thus passed seven, or, as others say, ten years ;[2] and all the while the gentle and loving Zipporah ministered to his necessities.

The Midianites were reconciled again with Jethro, and restored him to his former position ; and his scruples about the worship of idols abated, when he found that opposition to the established religion interfered with his temporal interests.

Then, when all was again prosperous, many great men and princes came to ask the hand of Zipporah his daughter, who was beautiful as the morning star, and as the dove in the hole of the rock, and as the narcissus by the water's side. But Zipporah loved Moses alone ; and Jethro, unwilling to offend those who solicited her by refusing them, as he could give his daughter to one only, took his staff, whereon was written the name of God, the staff which was cut from the Tree of Life, and which had belonged to Joseph, but which he had taken with him from the palace of Pharaoh, and he planted it in his garden, and said, " He who can pluck up this staff, he shall take my daughter Zipporah."

Then the strong chiefs of Edom and of Midian came and tried, but they could not move the staff.

One day Zipporah went before her father, and reminded him of the man whom he had cast into a dungeon so many years before. Jethro was amazed, and he said, " I had forgotten him these seven years ; he must be dead ; he has had no food."

But Zipporah said meekly, " With God all things are possible."

<hr>

[1] Pirke R. Eliezer, c. 40 ; Yaschar, p. 1274.
[2] The Targum of Palestine, "ten years ;" i. p. 448.

So Jethro went to the prison door and opened it, and Moses was alive. Then he brought him forth, and cut his hair, and pared his nails, and gave him a change of raiment, and set him in his garden, and placed meat before him.

Now Moses, being once more in the fresh air, and under the blue sky, and with the light of heaven shining upon him, prayed and gave thanks to God ; and seeing the staff, whereupon was written the name of the Most High, he went to it and took it away, and it followed his hand.

When Jethro returned into the garden, lo ! Moses had the staff of the Tree of Life in his hand ; then Jethro cried out, " This is a man called of God to be a prince and a great man among the Hebrews, and to be famous throughout the world." And he gave him Zipporah, his daughter, to be his wife.[1]

One day, as Moses was tending his flock in a barren place, he saw that one of the lambs had left the flock and was escaping. The good shepherd pursued it, but the lamb ran so much the faster, fled through valley and over hill, till it reached a mountain stream ; then it halted and drank.

Moses now came up to it, and looked at it with troubled countenance, and said,—

" My dear little friend ! Then it was thirst which made thee run so far and seem to fly from me ; and I knew it not ! Poor little creature, how tired thou must be ! How canst thou return so far to the flock ? "

And when the lamb heard this, it suffered Moses to take it up and lay it upon his shoulders ; and, carrying the lamb, he returned to the flock.

Now whilst Moses walked, burdened with the lamb, there fell a voice from heaven, " Thou, who hast shown so great love, so great patience towards the sheep of man's fold, thou art worthy to be called to pasture the sheep of the fold of God."[2]

4. MOSES BEFORE PHARAOH.

One day that Moses was keeping sheep, his father-in-law, Jethro, came to him and demanded back the staff that he had

---

[1] Beer, pp. 42–02 ; Pirke R. Eliezer. The Targum of Palestine says the rod was in the chamber of Jethro, not in the garden ; i. p. 448. Yaschar, pp. 1277, 1278.

[2] Rabbot., fol. 120 a. It is possible that our Blessed Lord's parable of the Good Shepherd may contain an allusion to this popular and beautiful tradition.

given him.   Then Moses cast the staff from him among a number of other rods, but the staff ever returned to his hand as often
as he cast it away.   Then Jethro laid hold of the rod, but he
could not move it.   Therefore he was obliged to let Moses
retain it.   But he was estranged from him.

Now Pharaoh was dead.   And when the news reached
Moses in Midian, he gat him up, and set his wife Zipporah and
his son Gershom on an ass, and took the way of Egypt.

And as they were in the way, they halted in a certain place ;
and it was cloudy, and cold, and rainy.   Then they encamped,
and Zipporah tried to make a fire, but could not, for the wood
was damp.

Moses said, " I see a fire burning at the foot of the mountain.   I will go to it, for there must be travellers there ; and I
will fetch a brand away and will kindle a fire, and be warm."

Then he took his rod in his hand and went.   But when he
came near the spot, he saw that the fire was not on the ground,
but at the summit of a tree ; and the tree was a thorn.   A
thorn-tree was the first tree that grew, when God created the
herb of the field and the trees of the forest.   Moses was filled
with fear, and he would have turned and fled, but a voice [1]
called to him out of the fire, " *Moses, Moses !*"   And he said,
" *Here am I.*"   And the voice said again, " *Put off thy shoes
from off thy feet, for the place whereon thou standest is holy
ground.*"   This was the reason why he was bidden put off his
shoes ; they were made of asses' hide, and Moses had trodden
on the dung of his ass as he followed Zipporah and Gershom.

Then God gave Moses his commission to go into Egypt,
and release his captive people.   But Moses feared, and said,
" I am of slow lips and tongue ! " for he had burnt them, with
his finger, when he took the live coal before Pharoah, as already related.   But God said to him, " I have given thee Aaron
thy brother to speak for thee.   And now, what is this that thou
hast in thy hand ? "

Moses answered, " This is my rod."

" And to what purpose dost thou turn it ? "

" I lean on it when I am walking, and when I come where
there is no grass, I strike the trees therewith, and bring down
the leaves to feed my sheep withal."   And when he had narrated all the uses to which he put the staff, God said to him,

---

[1] Gen. iii. 4.   It was the angel Zagnugael who appeared and spoke to
him from the bush.   (Targum of Palestine, i. p. 449 ; Abulfeda, p. 31.)

"With this staff shalt thou prevail against Pharaoh. Cast it upon the ground." And when he cast it down, it was transformed into a serpent or dragon, and Moses turned his back to run from it; but God said, "Fear not; take it up by the neck;" and he caught it and it became a rod in his hands. Then said the Most Holy, "Put thy hand into thy bosom." And he did so, and drew it forth, and it was white, and shining like the moon in the dark of night.

Then Moses desired to go back to Zipporah his wife, but the angel Gabriel retained him, saying, "Thou hast higher duties to perform than to attend on thy wife. Lo! I have already reconducted her to her father's house. Go on upon thy way to Pharaoh, as the Lord hath commanded thee."

The night on which Moses entered Egyptian territory, an angel appeared to Aaron in a dream, with a crystal glass full of good wine in his hand, and said, as he extended it to him :—

"Aaron, drink of this wine which the Lord sends thee as a pledge of good news. Thy brother Moses has returned to Egypt, and God has chosen him to be His prophet, and thee to be his spokesman. Arise, and go forth to meet him ! "

Aaron therefore arose from his bed and went out of the city to the banks of the Nile, but there was no boat there by which he could cross. Suddenly he perceived in the distance a light which approached ; and as it drew nearer he saw it was a horseman. It was Gabriel mounted on a steed of fire, which shone like the brighest diamond, and whose neighing was hymns of praise, for the steed was one of the cherubim.

Aaron at first supposed that he was pursued by one of Pharaoh's horsemen, and he would have cast himself into the Nile ; but Gabriel stayed him, declared who he was, mounted him on the fiery cherub, and they crossed the Nile on his back.

There stood Moses, who, when he saw Aaron, exclaimed, "Truth is come, Falsehood is passed." Now this was the sign that God had given to Moses, "*Behold he cometh to meet thee.*" [1] And they rejoiced over each other.

But another account is this: Moses entered Memphis with his sheep, during the night. Now Amram was dead, but his wife Jochebed was alive. When Moses reached the door, Jochebed was awake. He knocked at the door; then she opened, but knew him not, and asked, "Who art thou ?"

---

[1] Exod. iv. 14.

He answered, " I am a man from a far country ; I pray thee
.odge me, and give me to eat this night."

She took him in, and brought him some meat, and said to
Aaron, " Sit down and eat with the guest, to do him honor."
Aaron, in eating conversed with Moses and recognized him.

Then the mother and sister knew him also. And when the
meal was over, Moses acquitted himself of his mission to
Aaron, and Aaron answered, " I will obey the will of God."[1]

Moses spent the night, and the whole of the following day,
in relating to his mother the things that had befallen him.

And on the second night, Moses and Aaron went forth to
Pharoah's palace. Now the palace had four hundred doors,
a hundred on each side, and each door was guarded by sixty
thousand fighting men. The angel Gabriel came to them and
led them into the palace, but not by the doors.

When they appeared before Pharoah they said: " God hath
sent us unto thee, to bid thee let the Hebrews go, that they
may hold a feast in the wilderness."

But Pharoah said, " *Who is the Lord, that I should obey His
voice to let Israel go? I know not the Lord, neither will I let
Israel go.*"[2]

Tabari tells a different story. Moses and Aaron sought
admittance during two years. Now Pharoah gave himself out
to be a god.

But Moses and Aaron, when they spake at the door with
the porters, said, " He is no god." One day the jester of
Pharoah heard his master read the history of his own life,
and when he came to the passage which asserted he was a
god, the jester exclaimed, " Now this is strange ! For two
years there have been two strangers at thy gate denying thy
divinity."

When Pharoah heard this, he was in a fury, and he sent
and had Moses and Aaron brought before him.

But to return to the Rabbinic tale. Moses and Aaron were
driven out from the presence of Pharoah ; and he said, " Who
admitted these men ? " And some of the porters he slew, and
some he scourged.

Then two lionesses were placed before the palace to protect
it, and the beasts suffered no man to enter unless Pharoah
gave the word.

---

[1] Tabari, i. c. lxxiii. p. 24.   [2] Midrash, fol. 54.

And the Lord spake to Moses and Aaron, saying, " When Pharoah talketh with you, saying, Give us a miracle, thou shalt say to Aaron, Take thy rod and cast it down, and it shall become a basilisk serpent ; for all the inhabitants of the earth shall hear the voice of the shriek of Egypt when I destroy it, as all creatures heard the shriek of the serpent when I stripped it, and took from it its legs and made it lick the dust after the Fall." [1]

On the morrow, Moses and Aaron came again to the king's palace, and the lionesses would have devoured them. Then Moses raised his staff, and their chains brake, and they followed him, barking like dogs, into the house. [2]

When Moses and Aaron stood before the king, Aaron cast down the rod before Pharaoh, and before his servants, and it became a serpent, which opened its jaws, and it laid one jaw beneath the throne, and its upper jaw was over the canopy above it ; then the servants fled from before it, and Pharaoh hid himself beneath his throne, and the fear it caused him gave him bowel-complaint for a week. Now before this Pharaoh was only moved once a week, and this was the occasion of his being lifted up with pride, and giving himself out to be a god. [3]

Pharaoh cried out from under the throne, "O Moses, take hold of the serpent, and I will do what you desire." [4]

Moses took hold of the serpent, and it became a rod in his hands. Then Pharaoh crawled out from under his throne, and sat down upon it. And Moses put his hand into his bosom, and when he drew it forth, it shone like the moon.

The king sent for his magicians, and the chief of these were Jannes and Jambres. He told them what Moses had done.

They said, "We can turn a thousand rods into serpents."

Then the king named a day when Moses and Aaron on one side should strive with Jannes and Jambres [5] and all the magicians on the other ; and he gave them a month to prepare for the contest.

---

[1] Targum of Palestine, i. p. 460.   [2] Yaschar, p. 1280.
[3] Tabari, p. 326.
[4] Some say that Pharaoh entreated Moses to spare him for the sake of Asia (Bithia), and that at the mention of his name Moses was softened (Weil, p. 159).
[5] In Arabic, Risam and Rijam ; and Shabun and Gabun, in Persian.

On the day appointed—it was Pharaoh's birthday—all the inhabitants of Memphis were assembled in a great plain outside the city, where lists were staked out, and the royal tent was spread for the king to view the contest.

Moses and Aaron stood on one side and the magicians on the other.

The latter said, "Shall we cast our rods, or will you?"

Moses answered, "Do you cast your rods first."

Then the magicians threw down a hundred ass-loads of rods, tied the rods together with cords, and by their enchantment caused them to appear to the spectators like serpents, leaping and darting from one side of the arena to the other.

And all the people were filled with fear, and the magicians said, "We have this day triumphed over Moses."

Then the prophet of God cast his rod before Pharaoh, and it became a mighty serpent. It rolled its tail round the throne of the king, and it shot forth its head, and swallowed all the rods of the enchanters, so that there remained not one.

After that all had disappeared, Moses took the serpent, and it became a rod in his hand again, but all the rods of the magicians had vanished.

And when the magicians saw the miracle that Moses had wrought, they were converted, and worshipped the true God. But Pharaoh cut off their hands and feet, and crucified them; and they died. Pharaoh's own daughter Maschita believed; and the king in his rage did not spare her, but cast her into a fire, and she was burnt. Bithia was also denounced to him, and she was condemned to the flames, but the angel Gabriel delivered her. The Mussulmans say that he consoled her by telling her that she would become the wife of Mohammed in Paradise, after which he gave her to drink, and when she had tasted, she died without pain.

Then Moses and Aaron met Pharaoh in the morning as he went by the side of the river, and Moses said to the king, "*The Lord of the Hebrews hath sent me unto thee, saying, Let My people go, that they may serve Me in the wilderness.*"

But Pharaoh would not hearken to him. Then Aaron stretched out his rod over the river, and it became blood.

All the water that was in the vessels also became blood, even the spittle that was in the mouth of the Egyptians. The Rabbi Levi said that by this means the Israelites realized large fortunes; for if an Israelite and an Egyptian went together to

the Nile to fetch water, the vessel of the Egyptian was found
to contain blood, but that of the Israelite pure water ; but if
an Israelite brought water to the house of an Egyptian and sold
it, it remained water.[1]

But Pharaoh's heart was hard ; and seven days passed,
after that the Lord had smitten the river.

Then went Moses and Aaron to him. But the four hundred doors of the palace were guarded by bears, lions, and other
savage beasts, so that none might pass, till they were satisfied
with flesh. But Moses and Aaron came up, collected them
together, drew a circle round them with the sacred staff, and
the wild beasts licked the feet of the prophets and followed
them into the presence of Pharaoh.[2]

Moses and Aaron repeated this message to Pharaoh, but
he would not hearken to them, but drove them from his
presence. Aaron smote the river ; but Moses on no occasion
smote the Nile, for he respected the river which had saved his
life as a babe.[3] Then the Lord brought frogs upon the land,
and filled all the houses ; they were in the beds, on the tables,
in the cups. And the king sent for Moses and said : " *Intreat
the Lord, that He may take the frogs from me and from my people.*" So the Lord sent a great rain, and it washed the frogs
into the Red Sea.

The next plague was lice.[4]

The fourth plague was wild beasts.

The fifth was murrain.

The sixth was boils and blains upon man and beast.[5]

The seventh was hail and tempest. Now Job regarded the
word of Moses, and he brought his cattle within doors, and
they were saved ; but Balaam regarded it not, and all his cattle
were destroyed.[6]

The eighth was locusts ; these the Egyptians fried, and
laid by in store to serve them for food ; but when the west wind
came to blow the locusts away, it blew away also those that had
been pickled and laid by for future consumption.[7]

The ninth plague was darkness.

---

[1] Midrash, fol. 56. The Targums say that the enchanters turned the water of Goshen into blood, so that there was no water to the Israelites as to
the Egyptians ; i, p. 462.

[2] Midrash, fol. 55.   [3] Targum of Palestine, i. p. 463.

[4] Venomous insects (Kalma), gnats (Kinnim). See Wisdom xvi. 1, 3.

[5] Targums, i. 464.   [6] Targums, i. p. 467.   [7] Ibid., i. p. 471.

The tenth was the death of the first-born.

The Book of Jasher says that, the Egyptians having closed their doors and windows against the plagues of flies, and lo-custs, and lice, God sent the sea-monster Silinoth, a huge polypus with arms ten cubits long, and the beast climbed upon the roofs and broke them up, and let down its slimy arms, and unlatched all the doors and windows, and threw them open for the flies and locusts and lice to enter.[1]

But the Mohammedans gave a different order to the signs :—(1) the rod changed into a serpent ; (2) the whitened hand ; (3) the famine ; (4) a deluge, the Nile rose over the land so that every man stood in water up to his neck ; (5) locusts ; (6) anommals—these are two-legged animals smaller than locusts ; (7) blood ; (8) frogs ; (9) every green thing through-out the land, all fruit, all grain, eggs, and every thing in the houses were turned to stone.[2]

After the plague of the darkness, Pharaoh resolved on a general massacre of all the children of the Hebrews. The Mussulmans put the temporary petrifaction of all in the land in the place of the darkness. The Book of Exodus says that during the darkness "*they saw not one another, neither rose any from his place;*" but the Arabs say that they were turned to stone. Here might be seen a petrified man with a balance in his hand sitting in the bazaar ; there, another stone man count-ing out money ; and the porters at the palace were congealed to marble with their swords in their hands.[3] But others say that this was a separate plague, and that the darkness followed it.

And now Gabriel took on him the form of a servant of the king, and he went before him and asked him what was his desire.

" That vile liar Moses deserves death," said Pharaoh.

" How shall I slay him ? " asked Gabriel.

" Let him be cast into the water."

" Give me a written order," said the angel. Pharaoh did so.

Then Gabriel went to Moses and told him that the time was come when he was to leave Egypt with all the people, for the measure of the iniquity of Pharoah was filled up, and the Lord would destroy him with a signal overthrow.

[1] Yaschar, p. 1283.   [2] Tabari, i. p. 338.   [3] Weil, p. 165.

5. THE PASSAGE OF THE RED SEA.

The Israelites had made their preparations to depart out of Egypt a month before the call came to escape.

And when all was ready, Moses called together the elders of the people and said to them, " When Joseph died, he ordered his descendants to take up his bones, or ever they went out of the land, and to bear them to the cave of Machpelah, where lie the bones of his father Jacob. Where are the bones of Joseph ? "

The elders answered him, " We do not know."

Now there was an old Egyptian woman, named Miriam, and she believed in the Lord. She said to Moses, " I will show thee where is the tomb of Joseph, if thou wilt swear unto me that thou wilt take me with thee from Egypt, and that thou wilt ask the Most High to admit me into Paradise."

Moses said, " I will do these things that thou askest."

Then the woman said, " The tomb of Joseph is in the middle of the river Nile, which flows through Memphis, at such a spot."

Moses prayed to God, and the water fell till the bed of the river was left dry ; and then he and the women went into it, and came on the tomb of Joseph ; it was a sarcophagus of marble without joints.[1]

Moses made preparations for departure, and said to the children of Israel, " God will destroy the Egyptians, and will give you their precious things."

Then every one among the Hebrews who had an Egyptian neighbor said to him, if he was rich : " I am going to a feast in the country, I pray thee lend me jewels of gold and silver to adorn my wife and children."

The Egyptians lent their precious things, and the Israelites by this means found themselves possessed of borrowed jewels in great abundance. Then Moses said, " We will leave Egypt this night when the Egyptians are asleep. Let every housekeeper softly desert his house, and bring with him his precious things, and meet outside the town. And let every one slay a lamb, and sprinkle with the blood the lintel and door-posts of the house, that the neighbors may know, when they see the blood, that the house is empty."

When the middle of the night was passed, the Israelites

---

[1] Talmud, Sota, fol. 13.

were assembled outside Memphis, at the place which Moses had appointed. Then the host was numbered, and it contained six hundred thousand horsemen, not including those who were on foot, the women, the children, and the aged. All who were under twenty were accounted infants, and all who were over sixty were accounted aged.

After that, Moses placed Aaron in command of the first battalion, and he said to him, "March in the direction of the sea, for Gabriel has promised to meet me on its shores." At that time one branch of the Nile (the Pelusiac branch) flowed into the Red Sea, which extended over where is now sandy desert to Migdol.

Moses made the host follow Aaron, troop by troop, and tribe by tribe ; and he brought up the rear with a strong guard of picked men.

It was dawning towards the first day of the week when Israel escaped out of Egypt.

And when day broke, behold, they were gone away. Then the Egyptians came and told Pharaoh. He sent to search all the houses of the Israelites, but they were all empty, only their lamps were left burning. Pharaoh said, "We will pursue them." The Egyptians said, "They have borrowed our jewels ; we must follow after them, and recover what is our own."

Now Moses had used craft touching these ornaments, in order that the Egyptians might be constrained to follow. For if the Israelites had gone without these, the Egyptians would have rejoiced at their departure. But because they had borrowed of the Egyptians, therefore the Egyptians went after them to recover their ornaments, and by this means rushed into destruction.

And Israel marched all day through the wilderness protected by seven clouds of glory on their four sides : one above them, that neither hail nor rain might fall upon them, nor that they should be burned by the heat of the sun ; one beneath them, that they might not be hurt by thorns, serpents, or scorpions ; and one went before them, to make the valleys even, and the mountains low, and to prepare them a place of habitation.[1]

Also, when the morning dawned, there was not a house in all Egypt in which there was not a first-born dead. And this

---

[1] Targum of Palestine, i. p. 1478.

delayed the people from pursuing after the Israelites ; for they were engaged in bewailing their dead, and in digging graves for them. Thus they were not at leisure to follow after their former slaves, till they had escaped clean away.

Also that night was every metal image in Egypt molten, and every idol of stone was broken, and every idol of clay was shattered, and every idol of wood was dissolved to dust.[1]

The same day Pharaoh sent into all the cities of Egypt and collected an army. When even was come the whole army was assembled about the king, and Pharaoh said to Dathan and Abiram, who had remained behind,[2] "The Israelites are few in number, *they are entangled in the land, the wilderness hath shut them in.*" For all the way was full of marshes and canals of water and desert tracts. "They have acted wrongly by us, for they have carried away the ornaments and jewels of our people ; and Moses, by magic, has slain all our first-born, so that there is not a house in which there is not one dead."

On the morrow—it was the second day of the week—the army was reviewed, and Pharaoh numbered the host, and he had six hundred chosen chariots, and two million foot soldiers, and five million horsemen, and, in addition, there were one million seven hundred thousand horses, and on these horses were black men.

When the sun rose on the third day, Pharaoh marched out of Memphis, and he pursued for half a day with forced marches. At noon, Pharaoh had come up with Moses, and the fore-front of Pharaoh's army thrust the rear-guard of the army of Moses. Then the children of Israel cried unto the Lord, and they said to Moses, " *Because there were no graves in Egypt, hast thou taken us away to die in the wilderness ? Wherefore hast thou dealt thus with us, to carry us forth out of Egypt ?* "

They were divided into four opinions. One set said, "Let us fling ourselves into the sea." Another set said, "Let us return and surrender ourselves." The third set said, "Let us array battle against the Egyptians." The fourth recommended," Let us shout against them, and frighten them away with our clamor."[3]

And Moses said unto the people, " *Fear ye not, stand still, and see the salvation of the Lord. The Lord shall fight for you, and ye shall hold your peace.*"[4]

---

[1] Targums, i. p. 475. [2] Ibid., i. p. 485.
[3] Targum of Jerusalem, i. 488 ; Yaschar, p. 1287.
[4] Exod. xiv. 13, 14.

Then Moses raised his rod over the sea, and it divided, and let twelve channels of dry land appear traversing it, one for each of the twelve tribes. "When Moses had smitten," says the Koran, "the sea divided into twelve heaps, and left twelve ways through it, and each heap was as a great mountain."[1]

The Israelites hesitated to enter ; for they said, "O Moses ! the bottom of this sea is black mud, and when we place our feet on it we shall sink in and be swallowed up."

But Moses prayed to God, and he sent a wind and the rays of the sun, and the wind and the sun dried the mud, and it became as sand.

Then Gabriel and Michael appeared to Moses and said, "Pass on, and lead the people through. As for us, we have orders to tarry for Pharaoh." So Moses galloped forward into the sea, crying, "In the name of the merciful and glorious God !" and all the people went in after him. But as they marched by twelve ways, and there were walls of water between, they could not see each other, and they were in fear ; therefore Moses prayed to the Lord, and the Lord made the water-heaps rise and arch over them like bowers, and shelter them from the fire of the sun ; and He made the watery walls so clear they were as sheets of glass, and through them the columns of the advancing army were visible to each other.

Moses traversed the sea in two hours, and he came forth with all the people on the other side.

Then Pharoah and his host came to the water's side, but he feared to enter in. Now Pharaoh was mounted on an entire horse of great beauty. He reined in his steed and would not go forward, for he thought that this was part of the enchantment of Moses.

But now Gabriel appeared mounted on a mare, and this was the cherub Ramka.[2] And when the horse of Pharaoh saw the mare of Gabriel, he plunged forward and followed the mare into the sea. Then, when the Egyptian army saw their king enter fearlessly into one of the channels, they also precipitated themselves into the ways through the deep.

They advanced till they reached the middle of the Red Sea, and then Gabriel reined in and turned and unfurled before Pharaoh the order he had given for the destruction of Moses

---

[1] Koran, Sura xxvi. v. 63.
[2] Weil, p. 168 ; see also Midrash, fol. 176.

in the water, and it was signed by Pharoah and sealed with his own signet.

"See!" exclaimed the angel, "What thou wouldest do to Moses, that shall be done to thee ; for thou art but a man, thou who fightest against God."

Then the twelve heaps of water overwhelmed the host. But Pharaoh's horse was so fleet of foot that he outfled the return-ing waters, and he brought the king to the shore. He would have been saved, had not Gabriel smitten him on the face, and he fell back into the sea and perished with the rest. Then said Miriam, as he sank, "*Sing ye to the Lord, for he hath triumphed gloriously ; the horse and his rider hath He thrown into the sea.*" [1]

Another curious incident is related by Tabari. When the water reached Pharaoh, and he knew that he must perish, he cried out, "I believe in the God of Israel!" Gabriel, fearing lest Pharaoh should repeat these words, and that God in His mercy should accept his profession of faith, and pardon him, passed his wing over the bottom of the sea, raised the earth, and threw it into the mouth of Pharaoh so as to prevent him from swallowing again, and said, "Now thou believest, but before thou wast rebellious ; nevertheless, thou art numbered with the wicked." [2]

It was the ninth hour of the day when the children of Is-rael stood on dry land on the further side of the sea.

On the morrow, the children of Israel assembled around Moses, and said to him, "We do not believe that Pharaoh is drowned, for he had peculiar power. He never suffered from headache, nor from fever, nor from any sickness, and was in-ternally moved but once a week."

Then Moses clave the sea asunder with his rod, and they saw Pharaoh and all his host dead at the bottom of the sea. The bodies of the Egyptians were covered with armor and much gold and silver, and on the corpse of Pharaoh were chains and bracelets of gold. The children of Israel would have spoiled the dead, but Moses forbade them, for he said, "It is lawful to spoil the living, but it is robbery to strip the dead." Nevertheless many of the Hebrews went in and took from the Egyptians all that was valuable. Then God was wroth, because they had disobeyed Moses, and the sea was troubled, and for ten days it raged with fury, and even to this

---

[1] Exod. xv. 21. [2] Tabari, p. 350.

day the water is not at rest where the Israelites committed this sin. And the name of that place at this day is Bab el Taquath." [1]

6. THE GIVING OF THE LAW.

As long as Moses was with them, the Israelites did not venture to make idols, but when God summoned Moses into the Mount to talk with Him face to face, then they spake to Aaron that he should make a molten god to go before them.

Aaron bade them break off their earrings and bracelets and give them to him, for he thought that they would be reluctant to part with their jewels. Nevertheless the people brought their ornaments to him in great abundance, and one named Micah cast them into a copper vessel ; and when the gold was melted, he threw in a handful of the sand which had been under the hoof of Gabriel's horse, and there came forth a calf, which ran about like a living beast, and bellowed ; for Sammael (Satan) had entered into it. "Here is your god that shall go before you," cried Micah ; and all the people fell down and worshipped the golden calf. [2]

And when Moses came down from the Mount and drew near to the camp, and saw the calf, and the instruments of music in the hands of the wicked, who were dancing and bowing before it, and Satan among them dancing and leaping before the people, the wrath of Moses was suddenly kindled, and he cast the tables of the Commandments, which he had received from God on the Mount, out of his hand and brake them at the foot of the mountain ; but the holy writing that was on them flew, and was carried away into the heavens ; and he cried and said, " Woe upon the people who have heard from the mouth of the Holy One, ' Thou shalt not make to thyself any image, a figure, or any likeness ; ' and yet at the end of forty days make a useless molten calf ! "

And he took the calf which they had made, and burned it with fire, and crushed it to powder, and cast it upon the face of the water of the stream, and made the sons of Israel drink ;

---

[1] Tabari, i. p. 355.

[2] Both the Rabbis and the Mussulmans lay the blame, not on Aaron, but on another. The Rabbis say it was Micah who made the calf; the Mussulmans call him Samiri. (Weil, p. 170.)

and whoever had given thereto any trinket of gold, the sign of it came forth upon his nostrils.[1]

Of all the children of Israel only twelve thousand were found who had not worshipped the calf.[2]

The Mussulmans say that the Tables borne by Moses were from ten to twelve cubits in length, and were made, say some, of cedar wood, but others say of ruby, others of carbuncle; but the general opinion is that they were of sapphire or emerald;[3] and the letters were graven within them, not on the surface, so that the words could be read on either side. When the golden calf had been pounded to dust, Moses made the Israelites drink water in which was the dust, and those who had kissed the idol were marked with gilt lips. Thus the Levites were able to distinguish them; and they slew of them twenty and three thousand.[4]

It is a common tradition among the Jews that the red hair which is by no means infrequently met with in the Hebrew race is derived from this period; all those who had sinned and drank of the water lost their black hair and it became red, and they transmitted the color to their posterity.

Another version of the story is as follows. Samiri (Micah), who had fashioned the golden calf, was of the tribe of Levi. When Moses came down from the Mount, he would have beaten Aaron, but his brother said, " It is not I, it is Samiri who made the calf." Then Moses would have slain Samiri, but God forbade him, and ordered him instead to place him under ban.

From that time till now, the man wanders, like a wild beast, from one end of the earth to the other; every man avoids him, and cleanses the earth on which his feet have rested; and when he comes near any man, he cries out, " Touch me not! "

But before Moses drave Samiri out of the camp, he ground the calf to powder, and made Samiri pollute it; then he mixed it with the water, and gave it to the Israelites to drink. After Samiri had departed, Moses interceded with God for the people. But God answered, " I cannot pardon them, for their sin is yet in them, and it will only be purged out by the draught they have drunk."

When Moses returned to the camp, he heard a piteous cry.

---

[1] Targum of Palestine i. p. 552.   [2] Tabari, i. p. 362.
[3] Targum of Palestine, ii. p. 685.   [4] Pirke R. Eliezer. c. 45.

13

Many Israelites with yellow faces and livid bodies cast themselves before him, and cried, " Help! Moses, help ! the golden calf consumes our intestines ; we will repent and die, if the Lord will pardon us."

Some, really contrite, were healed. Then a black cloud came down on the camp, and all those who were in it fought with one another and slew one another ; but upon the innocent the swords had no power. Seven thousand idolaters had been slain, when Moses, hearing the cry of the women and children, came and prayed ; and the cloud vanished, and the sword rested.[1]

According to some, the complaint caused by swallowing the dust of the calf was jaundice, a complaint which has never ceased from among men since that day. Thus the calf brought two novelties into the world, red hair and jaundice.

And Moses went up again into the Mount, and took with him seventy of the elders. And he besought the Lord, " Suffer me, O Lord, to see Thee ! "[2] But the Lord answered him, " Thinkest thou that thou canst behold Me and live ? " And He said, " Look at this mountain ; I will display Myself to this mountain."

Then the mountain saw God, and it dissolved into fine dust. So Moses knew that it was not for him to see God, and he repented that he had asked this thing.[3] After that he went with the seventy elders to Sinai, and a cloud, white and glistening, came down and rested on the head of Moses, and then descended and wholly enveloped him, so that the seventy saw him not ; and when he was in the cloud, he received again the Tables of the Commandments, and he came forth out of the cloud. But they murmured that they had not also received the revelation. Then the cloud enveloped them also, and they heard all the words that had been spoken to Moses ; and after that they said, " Now we believe, because we have heard with our own ears."

Then the wrath of God blazed forth, and a thundering was heard so great and terrible that they fainted and died. But Moses feared, and he prayed to God, and God restored the seventy men to life again, and they came down the Mount with him.[4]

And it was at this time that the face of Moses shone with the splendor which had come upon him from the brightness

[1] Weil, pp. 172, 173.   [2] Koran, Sura vii. v. 139.
[3] Tabari, i. p. 364.   [4] Ibid., i. c. lxxv.

of the glory of the Lord's Shekinah in the time of His speaking
with him. And Aaron and all the sons of Israel saw Moses,
and, behold, the glory of his face was dazzling, so that they
were afraid to come near to him. And Moses called to them,
and Aaron, and all the princes of the congregation; and he
taught them all that the Lord had spoken to him on Mount
Sinai. And when Moses spoke with them, he had a veil upon
his face; and when he went up to speak with the Lord, he removed the veil from his countenance until he came forth.[1]

This was the reason why the face of Moses shone. He saw
the light which God had created, whereby Adam was enabled to
see from one end of the earth to the other. God showed this
light now to Moses, and thereby he was able to see to Dan.[2]

When Moses went up into the Mount, a cloud received
him, and bore him into heaven. On his way, he met the door-
keeper Kemuel, chief of twelve thousands of angels of destruction; they were angels of fire; and he would have prevented
Moses from advancing: then Moses pronounced the Name in
twelve letters, revealed to him by God from the Burning Bush,
and the angel and his host recoiled before that word twelve
thousand leagues. But some say that Moses smote the angel,
and wounded him.

A little further, Moses met another angel; this was Hadar-
niel, who had a terrible voice, and every word he uttered split
into twelve thousand lightnings; he reigned six hundred thousand leagues higher than Kemuel. Moses, in fear, wept at his
voice, and would have fallen out of the cloud, had not God
restrained him. Then the prophet pronounced the Name of
seventy-two letters, and the angel fled.

Next he came to the fiery angel Sandalfon, and he would
have fallen out of the cloud, but God held him up. Then he
reached the river of flame, called Rigjon, which flows from the
beasts which are beneath the Throne, and is filled with their
sweat; across this God led him.[3]

It is asserted by the Rabbis that Moses learnt the whole
law in the forty days that he was in the Mount, but as he descended from the immediate presence of God, he entered the
region where stood the angels guarding the Mount, and when
he saw the Angel of Fear, the Angel of Sweat, the Angel of
Trembling, and the Angel of Cold Shuddering, he was so fill-

[1] Targum of Palestine, i. p. 561. [2] Jalkut Rubeni, fol. 117, col. 1.
[3] Jalkut Rubeni, fol. 107, cols. 2. 3.

ed with consternation, that he forgot all that he had learnt. Then God sent the Angel Jephipha, who brought back all to his remembrance ; and, armed with the law, Moses passed the ranks of all the angels, and each gave him some secret or mystery ; one the art of mixing simples, one that of reading in the stars, another that of compounding antidotes, a fourth the secret of name, or the Kabalistic mystery.[1]

It is said by the Mussulmans, that when the law was declared to the children of Israel by Moses, they refused to receive it ; then Mount Sinai rose into the air, and moved above them, and they fled from it ; but it followed them, and hung over their heads ready to crush them. And Moses said, " Accept the law, or the mountain will fall on you and destroy you."

Then they fell on their faces and placed the right side of the brow and right cheek against the ground and looked up with the left eye at the mountain that hung above them, and said, "We will accept the law." This is the manner in which the Jews to this day perform their worship, says Tabari ; they place the brow and right cheek and eye upon the ground, and turn the left cheek and eye to heaven, and in this position they pray.[2]

7. THE MANNA. (Exod. xvi.)

All the time that Israel wandered in the wilderness they were given manna, or angels' food. This food is ground by the angels in heaven, as Moses saw when he was there. For when Moses was in heaven, he knew not when it was night and when it was day, till he listened to the song of the angels ; and when they sang " Holy God," then he knew it was morning below on earth ; and when they sang " Blessed be thou," he knew it was evening below. Also he observed the angels grinding the manna and casting it down ; and then he knew it was night, and they were strewing it for the Israelites to gather in the morning.[3] It is in the third firmament, called Schechakim (clouds), that the mills are in which manna is ground.[4] Along with the manna fell pearls and diamonds, and on the mountain it was heaped so high that it could be seen from afar.[5]

---

[1] Jalkut Rubeni, fol. 107, col. 3.
[2] Tabari, i. p. 371 ; also Midrash, fol. 30.
[3] Parascha R. Bechai, fol. 116.
[4] Talmud, Tract. Hajada, fol. 12, col. 2.
[5] Talmud, Tract. Joma, fol. 75, col. 1.

And the manna, this bread from heaven, contained in it-self all sweetness; and whatsoever any man desired to eat, the manna tasted to him as if it were that food.[1] Thus, if any one said, "I wish I had a fat bird," the manna tasted like a fat bird. But usually it had the taste of cakes made of oil, honey, and fine flour, according to the words of the Lord, "*My meat also which I gave thee, fine flour, and oil, and honey where-with I fed thee*" (Ezek. xvi. 10).[2] The Targum of Palestine thus describes the fall of the manna :—In the morning there was a fall of holy dew, prepared as a table,[3] round about the camp ; and the clouds ascended and caused manna to descend upon the dew ; and there was upon the face of the desert a minute substance in lines, minute as the hoar frost upon the ground. And the sons of Israel beheld, and wondered, and said to one another, " Man hu ? " (What is it ?) for they knew not what it was. And Moses said to them, " It is the bread which hath been laid up for you from the beginning in the heavens on high, and now the Lord will give it you to eat. This is the word which the Lord hath dictated : You are to gather of it ; every man according to the number of the per-sons of his tabernacle."

And the children of Israel did so, and gathered manna more or less. And Moses said to them, " Let no man reserve of it till the morning."

But some of them, Dathan and Abiram, men of wickedness, did reserve of it till the morning ; but it produced worms, and putrefied. And they gathered from the time of the dawn until the fourth hour of the day ; when the sun had waxed hot upon it, it liquefied and made streams of water, which flowed away into the great sea ; and wild animals that were clean, and cat-tle, came to drink of it ; and the sons of Israel hunted, and ate them.[4]

Some of the Gentiles, the Edomites and Midianites, came up, and, seeing the chosen people eating, they also gathered of the manna and tasted, but it was to them as wormwood.[5]

---

[1] This is sanctioned by Scripture : " *Thou feddest Thine own people with angels' food, and didst send them from heaven bread prepared without their labor, able to content every man's delight, and agreeing to every taste.*" (Wisdom, xvi. 20.)

[2] Talmud, Tract. Joma, fol. 75, col. 1 ; Schemoth Rabba, fol. 115, col 4.

[3] To this tradition perhaps David refers, Ps. xxiii, 5, lxxviii. 19.

[4] Targum of Palestine, i. pp. 499, 500

[5] Jalkut Shimoni, fol. 73, col. 4.

8. THE SMITTEN ROCK. (Exod. xvii. 1–7.)

And all the congregation of the sons of Israel journeyed from the desert of Sin and encamped in Rephidim, a place where their hands were idle in the commandments of the law, and the fountains were dry, and there was no water for the people to drink.

And the wicked of the people contended with Moses, and said " Give us water that we may drink." And Moses said to them, " Why contend ye with me ? Why tempt ye the Lord ? "

But the people were athirst for water, and the people murmured against Moses and said, " Why hast thou made us come up out of Egypt to kill us, and our children, and our cattle, with thirst ? "

And Moses prayed before the Lord, saying, " What shall I do for this people ? Yet a little while, and they will stone me."

And the Lord said to Moses, " Pass over before the people, and take the rod, with which thou didst smite the river, in thine hand, and go from the face of their murmuring. Behold, I will stand before thee there, on the spot where thou sawest the impression of the foot on Horeb ; and thou shalt smite the rock with thy rod, and therefrom shall come forth waters for drinking, and the people shall drink."

And Moses did so before the Elders of Israel. And he called the name of that place Temptation and Strife ; because the people strove with him there, and tempted God.[1]

Tabari gives these particulars concerning the smitten rock. In the desert there was no water. Moses prayed to God, and He commanded him to strike a rock with his staff.

Some say that this was an ordinary stone in the desert, others that it was a stone from Sinai which Moses carried about with him that he might stand on it whenever he prayed. Moses struck the rock, and twelve streams spouted from it.

Then Moses said, " You have manna and quails in abundance, gather only sufficient for the day, and you shall have fresh on the morrow." But they would not obey his word ; therefore the Lord withdrew the birds, and the people were famished. Then Moses besought the Lord, and the quails were restored to them. And this is how the quails fell in the camp.[2] A wind smote them as they flew over the camp, and broke their wings.

---

[1] Targum of Palestine, i. pp. 501, 502.   [2] Tabari, i. p. 393.

Then the people murmured again, and said to Moses, "The heat is intolerable, we cannot endure it."

So he prayed, and God sent a cloud to overshadow Israel; and it gave them cool shade all the day.[1]

After that they complained, "We want clothes." Then God wrought a marvel, and their clothes waxed not old and ragged, nor did their shoes wear out, nor did dirt and dust settle on their garments.[2]

It is also commonly related that the rock followed the Israelites, like the pillar of fire and the manna, all the time they went through the wilderness; to this tradition S. Paul alludes when he says, "*They drank of that spiritual rock that followed them, and that rock was Christ.*"[3]

9. MOSES VISITS EL KHOUDR.

One day, say the Mussulmans, Moses boasted before Joshua of his wisdom. Then said God to him, "Go to the place where the sea of the Greeks joins the Persian Gulf, and there you will find one who surpasses you in wisdom."

Moses therefore announced to the Hebrews, who continued their murmurs, that, in punishment for their stiffneckedness and rebellion, they were condemned by God to wander for forty years in the desert.

Then having asked God how he should recognize the wise man of whom God had spoken to him, he was bidden take a fish in a basket; "and," said God, "the fish will lead thee to my faithful servant."

Moses went on his way with Joshua, having the fish in a basket. In the evening he arrived on the shore of the sea and fell asleep.

When he awoke in the morning, Joshua forgot to take the fish, and Moses not regarding it, they had advanced far on their journey before they remembered that they had neglected the basket and fish. Then they returned and sought where they had slept, but they found the basket empty. As they were greatly troubled at this loss, they saw the fish before them, standing upright like a man, in the sea; and it led them,

---

[1] Koran, Sura ii. v. 54.
[2] Tabari, i. p. 394; but also Deut. viii. 4, Nehemiah ix. 21.
[3] 1 Cor. x. 4.

and they followed along the coast; and they did not stay till their guide suddenly vanished.

Supposing that they had reached their destination, they explored the neighborhood, and found a cave, at the entrance to which were inscribed these words, " In the Name of the all-powerful and all-merciful God." Joshua and Moses, entering this cavern, found a man seated there, fresh and blooming, but with white hair and a long white beard which descended to his feet. This was the prophet El Khoudr.

Some say he was the same as Elias, some that he was Jeremiah, some that he was Lot, and some that he was Jonah. The greatest uncertainty reigns as to who El Khoudr really is. All that is known of him is that he went with Alexander the Two-horned, to the West, and drank of the fountain of immortality, and thenceforth he lives an undying life, ever fresh, but also marked with the signs of a beautiful old age.

El Khoudr derives his name from the circumstance of his having sat on a bare stone, and when he rose from it the stone was green and covered with grass.[1]

In later times he was put to death for the true faith with various horrible tortures, by an idolatrous king, but he revived after each execution.

The explanation of the mystery of El Khoudr is this. He is the old Sun-god Thammuz of the Sabæans, and when he was dethroned by Mohammed, he sank in popular tradition to the level of a prophet, and all the old myths of the Sun-god were related of the prophet.

His wandering to the West is the sun setting there; his drinking there of the well of immortality is the sun plunging into the sea. His clothing the dry rock with grass is significant of the power of the sun over vegetation. His torments are figures of the sun setting, in storm, in flames of crimson, or swallowed by the black thunder-cloud: but from all his perils he rises again in glory in the eastern sky.[2]

Moses said to El Khoudr, " Take me for thy disciple, permit me to accompany thee, and to admire the wisdom God hath given thee."

---

[1] Tabari, i. p. 373.

See my " Curious Myths of the Middle Ages," article on S. George. I have no doubt whatever that El Khoudr, identified by the Jews with Elias, is the original of the Wandering Jew. I did not know this when I wrote on the " Wandering Jew " in my " Curious Myths," but I believe this to be the key to the whole story.

"Thou canst not understand it," answered the venerable man. "Moreover, thy stay with me is short."

"I will be patient and submissive," said Moses; "for God's sake, reject me not."

"Thou mayest follow me," said the sage. "But ask me no questions, and wait till I give thee, at my pleasure, the sense of that which thou comprehendest not."

Moses accepted the condition, and El Khoudr led him to the sea, where was a ship at anchor. The prophet took a hatchet, and cut two timbers out of her side, so that she foundered.

"What art thou doing?" asked Moses; "the people on board the ship will be drowned."

"Did I not say to thee that thou wouldst not remain patient for long?" said the sage.

Pardon me," said Moses; "I forgot what I had promised."

El Khoudr continued his course. Soon they met a beautiful child who was playing with shells on the sea-shore. The prophet took a knife which hung at his girdle, and cut the throat of the child.

"Wherefore hast thou killed the innocent?" asked Moses, in horror.

"Did I not say to thee," repeated El Khoudr, "that thy journey with me would be short?"

"Pardon me once more," said Moses; "if I raise my voice again, drive me from thee."

After having continued their journey for some way, they arrived at a large town, hungry and tired. But no one would take them in, or give them food, except for money.

El Khoudr, seeing that the wall of a large house, from which he had been driven away, menaced ruin, set it up firmly, and then retired. Moses was astonished, and said, "Thou hast done the work of several masons for many days. Ask for a wage which will pay for our lodging."

Then answered the old man, "We must separate. But before we part, I will explain what I have done. The ship which I injured belongs to a poor family. If it had sailed, it would have fallen into the hands of pirates. The injury I did can be easily repaired, and the delay will save the vessel for those worthy people who own her. The child I killed had a bad disposition, and it would have corrupted its parents. In its place God will give them pious children. The house which I

13*

repaired belongs to orphans, whose father was a man of substance. It has been let to unworthy people. Under the wall is hidden a treasure. Had the tenants mended the wall, they would have found and kept the treasure. Now the wall will stand till its legitimate owners come into the house, when they will find the treasure. Thou seest I have not acted blindly and foolishly."

Moses asked pardon of the prophet, and he returned to his people in the wilderness.[1]

The same story, with some variation in the incidents, is related in the Talmud.

God, seeing Moses uneasy, called him to the summit of a mountain, and deigned to explain to him how He governed the world. He bade the prophet look upon the earth. He saw a fountain flowing at the foot of the mountain. A soldier went to it to drink. A young man came next to the fountain, and finding a purse of gold, which the soldier had left there by accident, he kept it and went his way.

The soldier, having lost his purse, returned to search for it, and demanded it of an old man whom he found seated by the spring. The old man protested that he had not found it, and called God to witness the truth of his assertion. But the soldier disbelieving him, drew his sword upon him and killed him.

Moses was filled with horror. But God said to him : " Be not surprised at this event ; this old man had murdered the father of the soldier ; the soldier would have wasted the money in riotous living ; in the hands of the youth it will serve to nourish his aged parents, who are dying of poverty.[2]

10. THE MISSION OF THE SPIES. (Numb. xiii. xiv.)

And the Lord spake with Moses, saying, " Send thou keen-sighted men men who may explore the land of Canaan, which I will give to the children of Israel ; one man for each tribe of their fathers shalt thou send from the presence of all their leaders."

And Moses sent them from the wilderness of Paran ; all of them acute men, who had been appointed heads over the sons of Israel. And Moses said to them, " Go up on this side by

[1] Weil, pp. 176–81 ; Tabari, i. c. lxxvi. ; Koran, Sura xviii.
[2] Voltaire has taken this legend as the basis of his story of " Zadig."

the south, and ascend the mountain, and survey the country, what it is, and the people who dwell in it ; whether they be strong or weak, few or many ; what the land is in which they dwell, whether good or bad ; what the cities they inhabit, whether they live in towns that are open or walled ; and the reputation of the land, whether its productions are rich or poor, and the trees of it be fruitful or not ; and do valiantly, and bring back some of the fruit of the land."

And the day on which they went was the nineteenth of the month Sivan, about the days of the first grapes. They came to the stream of the grapes in Eshkol, and cut from thence a branch, with one cluster of grapes, and carried it on a rod between two men ; and also of the pomegranates, and of the figs ; and the wine dropped from them like a stream.[1]

And when they returned, they related, "We have seen the land which we are to conquer with the sword, and it is good and fruitful. The strongest camel is scarcely able to carry one bunch of grapes ; one ear of corn yields enough to feed a whole family ; and one pomegranate shell could contain five armed men. But the inhabitants of the land and their cities are in keeping with the productions of the soil. We saw men, the smallest of whom was six hundred cubits high. They were astonished at us on account of our diminutive stature, and laughed at us. Their houses are also in proportion, walled up to heaven, so that an eagle could hardly soar above them."[2]

When the spies had given this report, the Israelites murmured, and said, "We are not able to go up to the people, for they are stronger than we."

And the spies said, " The country is a land that killeth its inhabitants with diseases ; and all the people who are in it are giants, masters of evil ways. And we appeared as locusts before them."

And all the congregation lifted up their voices and wept ; and it was confirmed that that day, the ninth of the month Ab, should be one of weeping for ever to that people ; and it has ever after been one of a succession of calamities in the history of the Jews.

" Would that we had died in the land of Egypt," said the people ; "would that we had died in the wilderness. Why has the Lord brought us into this land, to fall by the sword

---

[1] Targums, ii. pp. 380, 381.   [2] Weil, p. 175.

of the Canaanites, and our wives and little ones to become a prey?"[1]

Then the Lord was wroth with the spies, and the earth opened her mouth and swallowed them up, saving only Joshua and Caleb, who had not given an evil report of the land.[2]

The account of the Targum of Palestine is different. The Targum says that the men who had brought an evil report of the land died on the seventh day of the month Elul, with worms coming from their navels, and with worms devouring their tongues.[3]

The Rabbis relate that though for the wickedness of men the fruitfulness of the Holy Land diminished, yet in places it remained as great as of old. "The Raf Chiji, son of Ada, was the teacher of the children of the Resch Lakisch; and once he was absent three days, and the children were without instruction. When he returned, the Resch Lakisch asked him why he had been so long absent. He answered, 'My father sent me to his vine, which is bound to a tree, and I gathered from it, the first day, three hundred bunches of grapes, which gave as much juice as would fill two hundred and eighty and eight egg-shells (three gerabhs). Next day I cut three hundred bunches, of which two gave one gerabh. The third day I cut three hundred bunches, which yielded one gerabh of juice; and I left more than half the bunches uncut.' Then said the Resch Lakisch to him, 'If thou hadst been more diligent in the education of my children, the vine would have yielded yet more.'

"Rami, son of Ezechiel, once went to the inhabitants of Berak, and saw goats feeding under the fig-trees, and the milk flowed from their udders, and the honey dropped from the figs, and the two mingled in one stream. Then he said, 'This is the land promised to our forefathers, flowing with milk and honey.'

"The Rabbi Jacob, son of Dosethai, said that from Lud to Ono is three miles, and in the morning twilight I started on my way, and I was over ankles in honey out of the figs.

"The Resch Lakisch said that he had himself seen a stream of milk and honey in the neighborhood of Zippori, sixteen miles long and the same breadth.

"The Rabbi Chelbo and Rabbi Avera and Rabbi Jose, son of Hannina, once came to a place where they were offered a

[1] Targums, ii. p. 382.   [2] Weil, p. 176.   [3] Targums, ii. p. 386.

honeycomb as large as the frying-pan of the village Heiro; they ate a portion, they gave their asses a portion, and they distributed a portion to any one who would take it.

"Rabbi Joshua, son of Levi, once came to Gabla, and saw grape-bunches in a vineyard, as big as calves, hanging between the vines, and he said, 'The calves are in the vineyard.' But the inhabitants told him they were grapes. Then said he, 'O land, land! withdraw thy fruits. Do not offer to these heathen those fruits which have been taken from us on account of our sins.'

"A year after, Rabbi Chija passed that way, and he saw the bunches like goats. So he said, 'The goats are in the vineyard.' But the inhabitants said, 'They are grape-bunches; depart from us and do not unto us as did your fellow last year.'"[1]

11. OF KORAH AND HIS COMPANY.   (Numb. xvi.)

And the Lord said to Moses, "Speak to the sons of Israel, and bid them make fringes not of threads, nor of yarn, nor of fibre, but after a peculiar fashion shall they make them. They shall cut off the heads of the filaments, and suspend by five ligatures, four in the midst of three, upon the four corners of their garments, and they shall put upon the edge of their gar ments a border of blue (or embroidery of hyacinth)."[2]

But Korah, son of Ezhar, son of Kohath, son of Levi, with Dathan and Abiram, the sons of Eliab, and On, the son of Peleth, sons of Reuben, refused to wear the blue border.

Moses had said, "The fringes are to be of white, with one line of blue;" but Korah said, "I will make mine altogether of blue;" and the two hundred and fifty men of the sons of Israel, who had been leaders of the congregation at the time when the journeys and encampments were appointed, supported Korah.[3]

Korah was a goldsmith, and Moses greatly honored him, for he was his cousin, and the handsomest man of all Israel. When Moses returned from the mount, he bade Korah destroy the calf; but the fire would not consume it. Then Moses prayed and God showed him the philosopher's stone, which is

[1] Tract. Kethuvoth, fol. 111, col. 2.
[2] Targums, ii. p. 391.   [3] Targum of Palestine, ii. p. 390.

a plant that grows in great abundance by the shores of the Red Sea, but none knew of its virtues before. Now, this plant turns metals into gold, and also if a twig of it be cast into gold, it dissolves it away. Moses instructed Korah in the virtues of this herb. Then Korah dissolved the calf by means of it, but he also used it to convert base metals into gold, and thus he became very rich.

Korah had great quantities of this herb, and he made vast stores of gold. He accumulated treasures. What he desired he bought, and he surrounded himself with servants clad in cloth of gold. He built brick houses with brass doors, and filled them to the roof with gold, and he made his servants walk before him with the keys of his treasure-houses hung round their necks. He had twenty men carrying these keys ; and still he increased in wealth, so he placed the keys on camels ; and when he still built more treasuries and turned more sub-stance into gold, he increased the number of keys to such an extent that he had sixty camel loads of them. Moses knew whence Korah derived his wealth, but the rest of the congrega-tion of Israel knew not.

After that, Korah did that which was wrong, and he broke the commandment of Moses, and would have no blue border on his servants' tunics, but habited them in scarlet, and mount-ed them on red horses. Neither did he confine himself to the meats which Moses permitted as clean.

Then God ordered Moses to ask Korah to give one piece of money for every thousand that he possessed. But Korah refused. This state of affairs continued ten years. When his destiny was accomplished, he was lifted up with pride, and he resolved to humble Moses before all the people.

Now, there was among the children of Israel a woman of bad character. Korah gave her large bribes, and said to her, "I will assemble all the congregation, and bring Moses before them, and do thou bring a false accusation against him."

The woman consented.

Then Korah did as he had said ; and when all the assem-bly of Israel was gathered together, he spake against Moses all that the lying witness had invented. Then he brought forth the woman. But when she saw all the elders of the congrega-tion before her, she feared, and she said, "Korah hath suborned me with gold to speak false witness against Moses, to cause him to be put to death."

And when Korah was thus convicted, Moses cried, " Get yourselves up and separate from him." Then all the people fled away from him on either side. And the earth opened her lips and closed them on Korah's feet to the ankles.

But Korah laughed, and said, " What magic is this ? "

Moses cried, " Earth, seize him ! "

Then the earth seized him to his knees.

Korah said, " O Moses ! ask the earth to release me, and I will do all thou desirest of me."

But Moses was very wroth, and he would not hearken, but cried, " Earth seize him ! "

Then the earth seized him to the waist.

Korah pleaded for his life. He said, " I will do all thou desirest of me, only release me ! "

But Moses cried again, " Earth, seize him ! "

And the earth gulped him down as far as his breast, and his hands were under the earth.

Once more he cried, " Moses ! spare me and release me, because of our relationship ! "

Moses was filled with bitterness, and he bade the earth swallow him ; and he went down quick into the pit, and was seen no more.

Then, when Moses was returning thanks to God, the Lord turned His face away from him and said, " Thy servant asked of thee forgiveness so many times, and thou didst not forgive him."

Moses answered, " O Lord, I desired that he should ask pardon of Thee and not of me."

The Lord said, " If he had cried but once to Me, I would have forgiven him." [1]

The earth swallowed Korah and seventy men, and they are retained in the earth along with all his treasures till the Resurrection Day.

Every Thursday, Korah, Dathan and Abiram go before the Messiah, and they ask, " When wilt Thou come and release us from our prison ? When will the end of these wonders be ?"

But the Messiah answers them, " Go and ask the Patriarchs ; " but this they are ashamed to do. [2]

---

[1] Tabari, i. c. lxxvii. ; Weil, pp. 182, 183 ; Abulfeda, p. 33.

[2] Eisenmenger, ii. p. 305. Possibly the passage Zech. ix. 11, 12, may contain an allusion to this tradition.

They sit in the third mansion of Sheol, not in any lowest one; nor are they there tormented, because Korah promised to hear and obey Moses, as he was being engulfed.[1]

The Arabic name for Korah is Karoun, and under this name he has returned to Rabbinic legends, and the identity of Korah and Karoun has not been observed.

The Rabbis relate of Karoun that he is an evil angel, and that Moses dug a deep pit for him in the land of Gad, and cast him into it. But whenever the Israelites sinned, Karoun crept out of his subterranean dwelling and plagued them.[2]

This is a curious instance of allegorizing upon a false interpretation of a name. The Karoun of the Mussulmans is clearly identical with Korah, but Karoun in Hebrew means Anger, and Karoun was supposed to be the Angel of the Anger of the Lord, and the story of his emerging from his pit to punish the sinful Israelites is simply a figurative mode of saying that the anger of the Lord came upon them.

12. THE WARS OF THE ISRAELITES.

The children of Israel had many foes to contend with. Amongst these were the Amorites. They hid in caves to form an ambuscade against the people of God, intending, when the Israelites had penetrated into a defile between two mountains, to sally forth upon them and to overthrow them. But they did not know that the ark went before Israel, smoothing the rough places and levelling the mountains.[3] Now, when the ark drew near the place where the ambush was, the mountains fell in upon the Amorites, and the Israelites passed on, and knew not that they had been delivered from a great danger. But there were two lepers named Eth and Hav, who followed the camp and they saw the blood bubbling out from under the mountain; and thus the fate of the Amorites was made known.[4]

The Israelites found a redoubtable enemy in Og, king of Bashan, who was one of the giants who had been saved from the old world by clambering on the roof of the ark; but his weight had so depressed the vessel, that Noah was obliged to

[1] Eisenmenger, ii. p. 305.   [2] Pirke R. Eliezer, c. 45.
[3] Perhaps the passage Isai. xl. 4 may be an allusion to this tradition.
[4] Talmud, Tract. Beracoth, fol. 54, col. 2; Targum of Palestine, ii., pp. 411–13.

turn out the hippopotamus and rhinoceros to preserve the ark from foundering.

Og determined to destroy Moses. Moses was ten cubits in height, and when Og came against him, he took a hatchet of ten cubits' length, and he made a jump into the air, and hit Og on the ankle. Og tore up a mountain, and put it on his head to throw it upon Moses; but the ants ate out the inside of the mountain, and it sank over Og's head to his neck, and he could not draw his head out, for his teeth grew into tusks and thrust through the mountain, and he was blinded and caught as in a trap. Thus Moses was able to slay him.[1]

Some further details on Og, furnished by the Rabbis, will assist the reader in estimating the powers of Moses.

At one meal, Og ate a thousand oxen and as many wild roes, and his drink was a thousand firkins; one drop of the sweat from his brow weighed thirty-six pounds.[2] Of his size the following authentic details are given. The Rabbi Johanan said, "I was once a grave-digger, and I ran after a deer, and went in at one end of a shin-bone of a dead man, and I ran for three miles and could not catch the deer or reach the end of the bone. When I went back, I inquired, and was told that this was the shin-bone of Og, king of Bashan."[3] The sole of his foot was forty miles long. Once, when he was quarrelling with Abraham, one of his teeth fell out, and Abraham made a bed out of the tooth, and slept in it; but some say he made a chair out of it.[4]

When the Israelites came to Edrei and fought against it, in the night Og came and sat down on the wall, and his feet reached the ground. Next morning Moses looked out and said, "I do not understand how the men of Edrei can have built a second wall so high during the night."

Then it was revealed to him that what he had taken for a wall was Og.[5] Og had built sixty cities, and the smallest was sixty miles high. These cities were in Argob.[6]

The Moabites also resisted Israel, and they were encouraged by Balaam the son of Beor.

---

[1] Talmud, Tract. Beracoth, fol. 54, col. 2; Targums, ii. p. 416; Yraschar, p. 1296.
[2] Talmud, Tract. Sopherim, fol. 42, col. 2.
[3] Ibid., Tract. Nida, fol. 24, col. 2.
[4] Jalkut Cadasch, fol. 16, col. 2.   [5] Eisenmenger, i. p. 389.
[6] Talmud, Tract. Sopherim, fol. 14. col. 4.

Balak, king of Moab, sent to Balaam to curse Israel. Then Balaam rose in the morning and made ready his ass, and went with the princes of Moab. The Mussulman account is that Balaam, having been told by God not to go, resolved to obey, but the princes of Moab bribed his wife, and she gave him no peace till he consented to go to Balak with his messengers.[1] But the anger of the Lord was kindled, because he would go to curse them, and the angel of the Lord stood in the way to be an adversary to him. But he sat upon his ass, and his two sons, Jannes and Jambres, were with him.

And the ass discerned the angel of the Lord standing in the way with a drawn sword in his hand, and the ass turned aside out of the road to go into the field ; and Balaam smote the ass. And the angel of the Lord stood in a narrow path that was in the midst between the vineyards, in the place where Jacob and Laban raised the mound, the pillars on this side and the observatory on that side,[2] that neither should pass the limit to do evil to the other. And as the ass discerned the angel of the Lord, and thrust herself against the hedge, and bruised Balaam's foot by the hedge, he smote her again. Ten things were created after the world had been founded at the coming in of the Sabbath between sunset and sunrise,—the manna, the well, the rod of Moses, the diamond, the rainbow, the cloud of glory, the mouth of the earth, the writing on the tables of the covenant, the demons, and the speaking ass.

Then the Lord opened the mouth of the ass, and she said to Balaam, " What have I done to thee, that thou hast smitten me twice ? "

And Balaam said to the ass, " Because thou hast been false to me ; if there were now a sword in my hand, I would kill thee."

And the ass said to Balaam, " Woe to thee, wanting in understanding ! Behold thou hast not power with all thy skill to curse me, an unclean beast, which am to die in this world and not to enter the world to come ; how much less canst thou curse the children of Abraham, Isaac and Jacob, on whose account the world was created."[3]

Balaam finding that he could not curse the people, and that they were under the protection of the Most High, saw that the only way to ruin them was by leading them into sin. Therefore he advised Balak, and the king appointed the daughter

<hr>

[1] Tabari, i. p. 398.   [2] Gen. xxxi. 51   [3] Targums ii. pp. 419–21.

of the Midianites for the tavern-booths at Beth Jeshimoth, by the snow mountain, where they sold sweetmeats cheaper than their price. And Israel trafficked with them for their sweet cakes; and when the maidens brought out the image of Peor from their bundles, the Israelites did not notice it to take it away, and becoming accustomed to it they went on to sacrifice to it.[1]

And Moses saw one of the sons of Israel come by, holding a Midianitess by the hand, and Moses rebuked him. Then said the man, "What is it that is wrong in this? Didst not thou thyself take to wife a Midianitess, the daughter of Jethro?"

When Moses heard this, he trembled and swooned away. But Phinehas cried, "Where are the lions of the tribe of Judah?" and he took a lance in his hand, and slew the man and the woman.

Twelve miracles were wrought for Phinehas, but they need not be repeated here.[2]

Then all the Israelites went forth against the Midianites and defeated them; and when they numbered the slain, Balaam and his sons were discovered among the dead.

13. THE DEATH OF AARON. (Numb. xx. 22–29.)

Moses was full of grief when the word of the Lord came to him that Aaron, his brother, was to die. That night he had no rest, and when it began to dawn towards morning, he rose and went to the tent of Aaron.

Aaron was much surprised to see his brother come in so early, and he said, "Wherefore art thou come?"

Moses answered, "All night long have I been troubled, and have had no sleep, for certain things in the Law came upon me, and they seemed to me to be heavy and unendurable; I have come to thee that thou shouldst relieve my mind." So they opened the book together and read from the first word; and at every sentence they said, "That is holy, and great, and righteous."

Soon they came to the history of Adam; and Moses stayed from reading when he arrived at the Fall, and he cried bitterly, "O Adam, thou hast brought death into the world!"

---

[1] Targums, ii. pp. 432–3. [2] Ibid., pp. 434–5.

Aaron said, " Why art thou so troubled thereat, my brother? Is not death the way to Eden?"

" It is however very painful. Think also that both thou and I must some day die. How many years thinkest thou we shall live?"

Aaron.—" Perhaps twenty."

Moses.—" Oh no! not so many."

Aaron.—" Then fifteen."

Moses.—" No, my brother, not so many."

Aaron.—" Then ten years."

Moses.—" No, not so many."

Aaron.—" Then surely it must be five."

Moses.—" I say again, not so many."

Then said Aaron, hesitating, " Is it then one?"

And Moses said, " Not so much."

Full of anxiety and alarm, Aaron kept silence. Then said Moses gently, " O my beloved! would it not be good to say of thee as it was said of Abraham, that he was gathered to his fathers in peace?" Aaron was silent.

Then said Moses, " If God were to say that thou shouldst die in a hundred years, what wouldst thou say?"

Aaron said, " The Lord is righteous in all His ways, and holy in all his works."

Moses.—" And if God were to say to thee that thou shouldst die this year, what wouldst thou answer?"

Aaron.—" The Lord is righteous in all His ways, and holy in all his works."

Moses.—" And if He were to call thee to-day, what wouldst thou say?"

Aaron.—" The Lord is righteous in all His ways, and holy in all His works."

" Then," said Moses, " arise and follow me."

At that same hour went forth Moses, Aaron, and Eleazer, his son ; they ascended into Mount Hor, and the people looked on, nothing doubting, for they knew not what was to take place.

Then said the Most High to His angels, " Behold the new Isaac ; he follows his younger brother, who leads him to death."

When they had reached the summit of the mountain, there opened before them a cavern. They went in and found a death-bed prepared by the hands of the angels. Aaron laid himself down upon it and made ready for death.

Then Moses cried out in grief, " Woe is me ! " we were two, when we comforted our sister in her death ; in this, thy last hour, I am with thee to solace thee ; when I die, who will comfort me ? "

Then a voice was heard from heaven, " Fear not ; God himself will be with thee."

On one side stood Moses, on the other Eleazer, and they kissed the dying man on the brow, and took from off him his sacerdotal vestments to clothe Eleazer his son with them. They took off one portion of the sacred apparel, and they laid that on Eleazer ; and then they removed another portion, and laid that on Eleazer ; and as they stripped Aaron, a silvery veil of clouds sank over him like a pall and covered him.

Aaron seemed to be asleep.

Then Moses said, " My brother, what dost thou feel ? "

" I feel nothing but the cloud that envelopes me," answered he.

After a little pause, Moses said again, " My brother, what dost thou feel ? "

He answered feebly, " The cloud surrounds me and bereaves me of all joy."

And the soul of Aaron was parted from his body. And as it went up Moses cried once more, "Alas, my brother ! what dost thou feel?"

And the soul replied, " I feel such joy, that I would it had come to me sooner."

Then cried Moses, "Oh thou blessed, peaceful death! Oh, may such a death be my lot ! "

Moses and Eleazer came down alone from the mountain, and the people wailed because Aaron was no more. But the coffin of Aaron rose, borne by angels, in the sight of the whole congregation, and was carried into heaven, whilst the angels sang : " The priest's lips have kept knowledge, have spoken truth ! " [1]

The Mussulman story is not quite the same.

One version is that both Moses and Aaron ascended Hor, knowing that one of them was to die, but uncertain which, and they found a cave, and a sarcophagus therein with the inscription on it, " I am for him whom I fit."

Moses tried to lie down in it, but his feet hung out ; Aaron next entered it, lay down, and it fitted him exactly.

[1] Jalkut, fol. 240 ; Rabboth, fol. 275, col. 1 ; Midrash, fol. 285.

Then Gabriel led Moses and the sons of Aaron out of the cave, and when they were again admitted Aaron was dead.[1]

Another version is this: God announced to Moses that he would call Aaron to Himself. Then Moses took his brother from the camp, and they went into the desert, till they came to a tree. When Aaron saw the shadow, he said, "O my brother, whose tree is this?"

Moses said, "God alone knows."

Then spake Aaron, "I am weary, and the shadow is cool; suffer me to repose a little while under the tree."

Moses said, "Lie down my brother; and may thy rest be sweet."

Aaron lay down, and Moses sat by him till he died.

Then suddenly the tree, the shadow, and Aaron vanished; and Moses returned alone to the Israelites. They were angry with him, that he had not brought back Aaron, and they took up stones against him. But Moses cried to the Lord, and the Lord showed them Aaron on a bed, and he was dead; and the people looked, and wondered, and wept: then said a voice from heaven, "God hath taken him." The people bewailed him many days.[2]

14. THE DEATH OF MOSES.

When the time came for Moses to die, the Lord called Gabriel to Him, and said, "Go and bring the soul of My servant Moses to Paradise."

The angel Gabriel answered in astonishment, "Lord, Lord, how can I venture to give death to that man, the like of whom all generations of men have not seen?"

Then the Most High called to Him Michael, and said, "Go and bring the soul of My servant Moses to Paradise."

The angel Michael answered in fear, "Lord, Lord, I was his instructor in heavenly lore! How can I bear death to my pupil?"

Then the Most High called to Him Sammael, and said, "Go and bring the soul of My servant Moses to Paradise."

The angel Sammael flushed red with joy. He clothed himself in anger, and grasped his sword, and rushed down upon the holy one. But he found him writing the incommunicable name of God, and he saw his face shine with divine light.

---

[1] Weil, p. 185.   [2] Tabari, i. c. lxxix.; Abulfeda, p. 35.

Then he stood irresolute, and his sword sank with the point to earth.

"What seekest thou ?" asked Moses.

"I am sent to give thee death," answered the trembling angel. "All mortals must submit to that."

"But not I," said Moses, "at least from thee; I, consecrated from my mother's womb, the discloser of divine mysteries, the mouthpiece of God, I will not surrender my soul into thy hand."

Then Sammael flew away.

But a voice fell from heaven, "Moses, Moses, thine hour is come ! "

"My Lor l," answered Moses, "give not my soul into the hands of the Angel of Death."

Then the Bath-kol, the heavenly voice, fell again, "Be comforted. I myself will take thy soul, and I myself will bury thee." [1]

Then Moses went home, and knocked at the door. His wife Zipporah opened ; and when she saw him pale and trembling, she inquired the reason.

Moses answered, "Give God the praise. My hour of death is come."

"What ! must a man who has spoken with God die like ordinary mortals ? "

"He must. Even the angels Gabriel, Michael, and Israfiel must die ; God alone is eternal, and dies not."

Zipporah wept and swooned away.

When she recovered her senses, Moses asked, "Where are my children ? "

"They are put to bed, and are asleep."

"Wake them up ; I must bid them farewell."

Zipporah went to the children's bed and cried, "Arise, poor orphans ! arise and bid your father farewell ; for this is his last day in this world, and the first in the world beyond."

The children awoke in terror, and cried, "Alas ! who will pity us when we are fatherless? who will stand protector on our threshold ? "

Moses was so moved that he wept. Then God said to him, "What mean these tears ? Fearest thou death, or dost thou part reluctantly with this world ? "

Rabboth, fol. 302 b ; Devarim Rabba, fol. 246, col. 2.

" I fear not death, nor do I part reluctantly with this world ; but I lament these children, who have lost their grandfather Jethro and their uncle Aaron, and who now must lose their father."

" In whom then did thy mother confide, when she cast thee in the bulrush ark into the water ? "

" In Thee, O Lord."

" Who gave thee power before Pharaoh ? who strengthened thee with thy staff to divide the sea ? "

" Thou, O Lord."

" Who led thee through the wilderness, and gave thee bread from heaven, and opened to thee the rock of flint ? "

" Thou, O Lord."

" Then canst thou not trust thy orphans to Me, who am a father to the fatherless ?   But go, take thy staff, and extend it once more over the sea, and thou shalt have a sign to strength-en thy wavering faith."

Moses obeyed.   He took the rod of God in his hand, and he went down to the sea-beach, and he lifted the rod over the water.   Then the sea divided, and he saw in the midst a black rock.   And he went forward into the sea till he reached the rock, and then a voice said to him, " Smite with thy staff ! " And he smote, and the rock clave asunder, and he saw at its foundations a little cavity, and in the cavity was a worm with a green leaf in its mouth.   The worm lifted up its voice and cried thrice,·" Praise be God, who doth not forget me, though I, a little worm, lie in loneliness here !   Praised be God, who hath nourished and cherished even me ! "

When the worm was silent, God said to Moses : " Thou seest that I do not fail to consider and provide for a little worm in a rock of which men know not, far in the depths of the sea ; and shall I forget thy children, who know Me ? "

Moses returned with shame to his home, comforted his wife and children, and went alone to the mountain where he was to die.[1]

And when he had gone up the mountain, he met three men who were digging a grave ; and he asked them, " For whom do you dig this grave ? "

They answered, " For a man whom God will call to be with Him in Paradise."

[1] Weil, pp. 188, 189.

Moses asked permission to lend a hand to dig the grave of such a holy man. When it was completed, Moses asked, " Have you taken the measure of the deceased ? "

" No ; we have quite forgotten to do so. But he was of thy size ; lie down in it, and God will reward thee, when we see if it be likely to suit."

Moses did so.[1]

The three men were the three angels Michael, Gabriel, and Sagsagel The angel Michael, had begun the grave, the angel Gabriel had spread the white napkin for the head, the angel Sagsagel that for the feet.

Then the angel Michael stood on one side of Moses, the angel Gabriel on the other side, the angel Sagsagel at the feet, and the Majesty of God appeared above his head.

And the Lord said to Moses, " Close thine eyelids." He obeyed.

Then the Lord said, " Press thy hand upon thy heart." And he did so.

Then God said, " Place thy feet in order." He did so.

Then the Lord addressed the spirit of Moses, and said, " Holy soul, my daughter ! For a hundred and twenty years hast thou inhabited this undefiled body of dust. But now thine hour is come ; come forth and mount to Paradise ! "

But the soul answered, trembling and with pain, " In this pure and undefiled body have I spent so many years, that I have learned to love it, and I have not the courage to desert it."

" My daughter, come forth ! I will place thee in the highest heaven beneath the Cherubim and Seraphim who bear up My eternal throne."

Yet the soul doubted and quaked.

Then God bent over the face of Moses, and kissed him. And the soul leaped up in joy, and went with the kiss of God to Paradise.

Then a sad cloud draped the heavens, and the wind wailed, " Who lives now on earth to fight against sin and error ? "

And a voice answered, " Such a prophet never arose before."

And the Earth lamented, " I have lost the holy one ! "

And Israel lamented, " We have lost the Shepherd ! "

[1] Weil, p. 190

14

And the angels sang, "He is come in peace to the arms of God!"[1]

But the Mussulmans narrate the last scene differently.

They say that the Angel of Death stood over Moses, as he lay in the grave, and said, "Prophet of God, I must take thy soul."

"How wilt thou take it?"

"From thy mouth."

"Thou canst not, for my mouth hath spoken with God."

"Then from thine eyes."

"Thou canst not, for my eyes have seen the uncreated Light of God."

"Then from thy ears."

"Thou canst not, for my ears have heard the Voice of "God."

"Then from thy hands."

"Thou canst not, for my hands have held the diamond tables, on which was engraven the Tora."

Then God bade the Angel of Death obtain from Rhidwan, the porter of Paradise, an apple from the garden, and give it to Moses to smell.

Moses took the apple out of the hand of the Angel of Death, and smelt at it; and as he smelt thereat, the angel drew his soul forth at his nostrils.

None know where is the grave of Moses, save Gabriel, Michael, Israfiel, and Azrael, for they buried him and defend his grave to the Judgment Day.[2]

> By Nebo's lonely mountain,
>   On this side Jordan's wave,
> In a vale in the land of Moab
>   There lies a lonely grave.
> And no man knows that sepulchre,
>   And no man saw it e'er,
> For the angels of God upturned the sod,
>   And laid the dead man there.
>
> That was the grandest funeral
>   That ever passed on earth;
> But no man heard the trampling,
>   Or saw the train go forth—
> Noiselessly as the daylight
>   Comes back when night is done,
> And the crimson streak on Ocean's cheek
>   Grows into the great sun;

---

[1] Rabboth, fol. 302 b.   [2] Well, pp. 190, 191.

> Noiselessly as the spring-time
>   Her crown of verdure weaves,
> And all the trees on all the hills
>   Open their thousand leaves ;
> So without sound of music,
>   Or voice of them that wept,
> Silently down from the mountain's crown
>   The great procession swept.
>   *   *   *   *
>
> And had he not high honor—
>   The hill-side for a pall,
> To lie in state, while angels wait
>   With stars for tapers tall ;
> And the dark rock-pines, like tossing plumes.
>   Over his bier to wave,
> And God's own hand in that lonely land
>   To lay him in the grave? [1]

Once when the Persian Empire was at the summit of its power, an attempt was made to discover the body of Moses. A countless host of Persian soldiers was sent to search Mount Nebo. When they had reached the top of the mountain, they saw the sepulchre of Moses distinctly at the bottom. They hastened to reach the valley, and then they clearly distinguished the tomb of Moses at the summit. Thus, whenever they were at the top, they saw it at the foot ; and when they were at the foot, it appeared at the top ; so they were forced to abandon the prosecution of their search. [2]

The incident of the contention of Michael with Satan for the body of Moses mentioned by S. Jude is contained in the apocryphal " Assumption of Moses," now lost, but which has been quoted by Origen and other Fathers.

XXXIII.

JOSHUA.

Hitherto Israel had required a lawgiver, and they had been given one in Moses ; now they needed a general, and they were provided with one in Joshua.

After the death of Moses and his brother Aaron, the children of Israel remained seven years in the wilderness, till the forty

---

[1] Lyra Anglicana, London, 1864, " The burial of Moses."
[2] Talmud, Tract. Sota, fol. 14 a.

years were acomplished.   Then God conferred on Joshua the function of prophet, and ordered him to lead the chosen people out of the desert and to attack the three cities of the giants.

Joshua was of the tribe of Joseph.   He was the son of Nun, who was the son of Ephraim, who was the son of Joseph ; and his mother was Miriam, the sister of Moses and Aaron.[1]

Before Joshua led the people of the Lord to the conquest of the Holy Land, Joshua sent three deputations into Canaan ; of these the first proclaimed, " Let any one who will escape death, leave the country."

Then came the second deputation, and declared, " Let such people as will make an alliance with us, do so, and we will receive them."

Then came the third deputation, and cried, " Let those who persist in desiring war prepare for it."

The result of these deputations was that one nation deserted the country and settled in Africa, and that another nation made terms with Israel.   But thirty-one princes made ready for war.[2]

Joshua marched with his army against Jericho, took the city, and slew all the men therein ; they were giants, and it took a hundred men to cut off the head of each giant.

After the capture of Jericho, Joshua went against Ai, which is beside Beth-aven, on the east side of Bethel.   And as the people went up, the men of Ai came forth, and routed them, and they fled.[3]

Then Joshua rent his clothes, and fell on his face to the earth before the ark of the Lord, until eventide, he and the elders of Israel, and put dust on their heads.

And the Lord said to Joshua, " Get thee up.   I am wroth with the people, for there is amongst them a sin which is not put away, and till that accursed thing is cast out, victory shall not attend their arms."

Now Joshua had ordered all the plunder of Jericho to be burnt with fire ; but although it was heaped up, the fire would not consume it.   Then he knew that the pile could not be complete, for the flames danced up, but would consume nothing, as though they waited for the entirety of their prey.

So Joshua made inquisition ; and it was found that Achan

---

[1] Tabari, i. p. 396.   [2] Talmud of Jerusalem ; Tract. Terumoth.
[3] Josh. vii. 1–5.

(Adjezan in Arabic) had concealed a portion of the booty, which he desired to appropriate to his own use.

Then the booty taken by Achan was added to the heap, and instantly the flames roared up, and devoured the whole of the spoil.[1]

And when Ai was taken, Joshua said: " Enter into this town ; for God has taken it from the giants, and has given it to you to be your inheritance. But when you pass through the gates, prostrate yourselves, with your heads in the dust, and adore God, saying, Hittaton, hittaton, which is by interpretation, Pardon our sins."

Some of those who entered Ai obeyed the voice of Joshua, and God gave them a possession in that city, and their posterity retain it to this day.

But there were some ungodly men who disobeyed the voice of Joshua, and when they passed through the gates, they did not prostrate themselves, but they raised their heads to heaven, and instead of saying " *hittaton*," as commanded, they said " *hintaton*," asking for corn.

Then the wrath of God was kindled against these men, and fire fell from heaven, and consumed all that had said *hintaton* in place of *hittaton*.[2]

Near Ai there were mountains, in which reigned two kings, Kuma and Djion (Sihon). These Amorites were wealthy. When Joshua attacked these kings, they asked to make a league with the people of Israel ; and they were accepted, on condition that they believed in the religion of Moses.

Another of these mountain kingdoms was governed by a king called Barak (Adoni-bezek). He also sought by submission to escape ruin, and Joshua accepted him on the same terms as Kuma and Djion.

To the west were five cities, whose inhabitants were also Amorites. The kings of these cities made war on Joshua. Joshua routed them, and these five kings took refuge in a cave. Joshua ordered the cave to be closed with a stone, whilst he pursued the routed army. Then God sent hail from heaven, and each hailstone struck down and killed a man.[3]

On that day Joshua cried to the Lord, for the sun hasted to go down, and it was a Friday, and he feared that he should not have utterly discomfited the host before the Sabbath came in.

[1] Tabari, i. p. 402.
[2] Koran, Sura ii. v. 55, 56.   [3] Tabari, p. 404.

Then the Lord lengthened the day one hour, so as to enable him to complete his victory.[1]

After the battle, it was announced to him that Barak and the other kings who had made submission to him had taken advantage of the rising of the kings of the five cities to renounce their allegiance, and to return to the worship of false gods. Therefore Joshua prayed, " O Lord! because they have become unfaithful, take from them their riches, and make them poor, that they may become bondsmen ; and that their king may fall into misery ! "

Joshua was sick and unable to march against them. He was aged a hundred and twenty-eight years. He was a hundred years old when Moses died, and he governed Israel twenty-eight years.[2]

For the benefit of coin-collectors, the following information is inserted. " On the coins struck by Abraham are figured, on the obverse, an old man and an ass ; on the reverse, a boy and a girl. On the coins of Joshua are, on one side a bull, on the other a unicorn. On those of David, on one side a staff and wallet, on the other a tower. On those of Mordecai, on the obverse, sackcloth and ashes; and on the reverse a crown.'"[3]

After Joshua, Caleb, the son of Jephunneh, and Othniel, the son of Kenaz,[4] Caleb's brother, governed Israel. They collected the people, and marched against Barak (·Adoni-bezek)[5] and his people who had apostatized, and attacked them, and slew great numbers of them.

They took the king and cut off his thumbs. This Barak had, during his reign, treated seventy kings in like fashion, so that they were unable to pick up any thing off the ground. And when Barak was feasting, these kings were brought before him. Then he cast bread among them, but they were unable to pick it up, having no thumbs, and they were obliged to stoop to the ground, and take it in their mouths like dogs ; and this caused huge merriment to the king.[6]

---

[1] Tabari, p. 401.　　　[2] Ibid., p. 404.　　　[3] Berescheth Rabba.
[4] The Mussulmans say Khasqîl or Ezechiel.　　[5] Judges i. 4.
[6] Tabari, i. p. 404.

XXXIV.

THE JUDGES.

IF Joshua, the first of the Judges, has, to a great extent, escaped the hands of legend manufacturers, the same may be said of his successors, Phinehas, Othniel, Ehud, Deborah and Barak, Gibeon, Abimelech, Tola, Jair, Jephthah, Ibzan, Elon, and Abdon. Even Samson has not been surrounded by such a multitude of traditions as might have been expected.

The Mussulmans have little to say of him, and the Jewish legends are not numerous.

The Rabbi Samuel, son of Nahaman, said that Samson once took two mountains, one in each hand, and knocked them together, as a man will strike together two pebbles. The Rabbi Jehuda said that when the Spirit of the Lord rested on him he strode in one stride from Zorah to Eshtaol. The Rabbi Nahaman added that his hair stood up, and one hair tinkled against another, so that the sound could be heard, like that of bells, from Zorah to Eshtaol.[1]

Abulfaraj says that Phinehas, the son of Eleazer, the son of Aaron, after the death of Joshua, was commanded by an angel to put the manna, the rods, the tables of the covenant, and the five books of Moses in a brazen urn, seal it with lead, and conceal it in a cave, as the Israelites were too wicked to be entrusted with such a treasure.[2]

XXXV.

SAMUEL.

GJALOUT (Goliath) was king of the Philistines. He was of the race of the ancient giants, the Adites and the Themudites, who were from fifty to a hundred cubits in height.

The children of Israel were grievously oppressed by him, and they besought God to send them a prophet who would reinstruct them in the law of Moses, and in the true religion. For thirty years they besought God, but no prophet was given to them. In the meanwhile, the Philistines oppressed them

---

[1] Eisenmenger, i. p. 395.   [2] Hist. Dynast. p. 24.

more and more, and whenever the Israelites rose against them
they defeated the Israelites with great slaughter.

There died a man of the tribe of Levi, Rayyan (Elkanah),
son of Elkama, who was descended from Aaron the brother of
Moses.   The elders of Israel hearing that he had died, leaving
his wife pregnant, went to her and surrounded her with the
greatest care and comforts.

There was amongst them a wise man named Hil (Eli) who
was high-priest ; to him they confided the care of the widow.   In time she bore a son, who was named Ischmawil
(Samuel).

Eli brought up the child Samuel in the temple, to the age
of seven years, and he taught him the Pentateuch and the
religion of Moses.

Samuel regarded Eli as his father, because he had been
brought up by him, and he loved and reverenced him greatly.

One night when he was asleep, Gabriel came into the room
and made a noise, so that Samuel awoke.

He saw no one, so he called to Eli, " Master ! didst thou
summon me ? "

Eli replied, " No, my son, I did not summon thee."

Next night the same occurred ; so also the third night.

Then Eli thought that God wished to give to Samuel the
gift of prophecy ; therefore he said, " My son, if thou art
called again in the night, reply, Here am I ; what wouldest
Thou ?   I am in Thy hands."

Samuel did so.   Then Gabriel appeared to him and cum-
municated to him the message of God.

Samuel told Eli that the Lord had given him the gift of
prophecy, by the mouth of His messenger Gabriel.

Then Eli was rejoiced, and he announced the glad tidings
to all Israel.

Eli had two sons whom he had instructed in the art of offering sacrifice according to the law of Moses, but he had
taught them nothing else.   Eli himself moreover neglected to
sacrifice, and he allowed his sons to live after their lusts, unre-
strained by his paternal and priestly rebuke.

Therefore God spake to Samuel that He would punish Eli
and his sons ; but Samuel feared to show it to the high priest.

Then said Eli to him, " Has God given thee a message to
me ? "

And Samuel answered, " God has said, Why hast thou neglected to offer sacrifice, so that thy sons add thereto or detract therefrom ?   And why hast thou not constrained them ?   Because of this sin, I shall deliver thee into the hands of an enemy, who shall slay thy sons, and take the ark, and cause thee to perish also." [1]

Then Gjalout came, and made war against the children of Israel, and there was a great battle, and Hophni and Phinehas, the sons of Eli, were slain, and the ark was taken ; and Eli fell backward from off his seat when he heard the news, and his neck brake, and he died.

In the ark, that now fell into the hands of the Philistines, were preserved the tables of the Law, which God had given to Moses, and a basin in which the angels washed and purified the hearts of the prophets, and the mitre and breastplate and potifical robes of Aaron.

The Israelites had been accustomed, in times of peril, to produce the ark, and it had delivered them from evil by virtue of the sacred relics it contained.   As for the Shekinah which rested upon it, and from which the ark took its name of Tabut-Shekinah, the Mussulman authors assure us it had the form of a leopard, which, whenever the ark was carried against the enemies of God's people, rose on its legs, and uttered so potent a roar, that the foes of Israel fell to the ground.   These authors, however, derive this fable from Rabbinic writers.[2]

The king of the Philistines, having obtained possession of the ark, placed it in a draught-house, purposing thereby to express his hatred of the Jews, and his contempt for that which they regarded as most sacred.

But a terrible disease broke out among the Philistines, and the ark was sent from Gaza to another city.   There the plague appeared immediately, and the Philistines were at length obliged to return the ark to the Israelites.

In the mean time, the Israelites, in consternation at the loss of their ark, gathered about Samuel, and besought him to consecrate a king for them, who might go forth to battle before them, and recover for them the ark.

Then Samuel said : " If I consecrate a king for you, will you not desert him, and refuse to obey him ? "

But they all protested, " We will follow him wherever he leads, and we will obey all his commands." [3]

[1] Tabari, i. c. lxxxvii.   [2] D'Herbelot, Bibl. Orient., s. v. Aschmouil.
[3] Koran, Sura ii. v. 247, 248.

Then Schareh, who was surnamed Thalout (Saul), on account of the greatness of his stature, was chosen by Samuel to be their king.   He was poor, and by trade a water-carrier, and his ancestors had all been water-carriers.

Now the father of Saul had lost an ass, which had escaped into the desert.   Saul went after it.

Then Samuel came to meet him, and said to him : " Thou shalt reign as king over the people of Israel."

Saul replied : " O prophet of God ! thou knowest that my tribe is the least among the tribes, and that I am the poorest among the members of my tribe.

Samuel said : " Nevertheless, God has ordered that so it should be."

Then he poured on his head the sacred oil which had been brought to Samuel out of heaven by Gabriel.

But some say that this oil belonged to Joseph the son of Jacob, and it was preserved by the prophets.   When this oil was poured on Saul's head and face, it made his skin brilliant and pure.

Now the prophets all came out of the tribe of Levi, and the tribe of Benjamin was despised greatly by the Israelites. And when they heard that their king was from that tribe, and was a water-carrier, they were angry, and exclaimed, " Why should he reign over us ?   We are as worthy to reign as he ! " [1]

Samuel answered, " God gives power to whom He wills."

The Israelites said, " Show us a sign."

Samuel brought the sacred oil forth, and it boiled in the presence of Saul.[2]

But that did not suffice them.   They then asked another sign ; and Samuel said, " The ark shall return."

And they lifted their eyes, and lo! the ark was coming to them attached to the tails of two cows, and angels guided the cows.[3]

Then the children of Israel doubted no longer, but accepted Saul as their king.

Then said Samuel to the people : " The God of your fathers has sent me unto you, to promise you victory over the Philistines, and deliverance from your bondage, if you will turn and leave your evil ways."

[1] Koran. Sura ii. v. 248.   [2] D'Herbelot, Bibl. Orientale, t. i. p. 263.
[3] Tabari, i. p. 417.

"What shall we do?" asked one of the elders, "that we may obtain the favor of God?"

Samuel answered, "Ye must pray to God alone, and offer no sacrifices to idols, nor eat the flesh of swine, or blood; neither must you eat any thing which is not slaughtered in the name of the Most High. Ye must assist one another, honor your parents, entreat your wives with kindness, and support the widows, orphans, and poor. Ye shall believe in the prophets who have gone before me, especially in Abraham, for whom God turned a fiery pile into a pleasure garden; in Ishmael, whose neck God made as a flint stone, and for whom He opened a fountain in the stony desert; and in Moses, who with his staff opened twelve clay paths through the sea. Also ye shall believe in the prophets who shall follow after me, especially in Isa Ibn Mariam (Jesus, Son of Mary), the Spirit of God, and in Mohammed Ibn Abd-Allah."

"And who is this Isa?" asked one of the elders of Israel.

"Isa," pursued Samuel, "is the prophet foretold in the Tora as the Word of God. His mother Mariam (Mary) shall conceive him by the will of God, and by a breath of the angel Gabriel. In his mother's womb will he praise the almighty power of God, and testify to the immaculate purity of his mother; afterwards will he heal the sick and crippled, will quicken the dead, and will create living birds out of clay.[1] His godless cotemporaries will deal cruelly with him, and will crucify him; but God will deceive their eyes and will let another die in his room, and he will be carried up into heaven like the prophet Idris (Enoch)."

"And Mohammed," asked the same Israelite, "who is he? His name sounds strange in our ears, never have we heard that name before."

"Mohammed," answered Samuel, "does not belong to the race of Israel; he will descend from the seed of Ishmael, and he will be the last and greatest of the prophets, before whom Moses and Christ will bend at the Resurrection Day. His name, which signifies the Much Praised, is prophetic of the laud and honor he will receive from all creatures on earth, and all the angels in heaven. The miracles he will work are numberless, so that a man's life is not long enough to relate them

---

[1] This incident, from the apocryphal gospels of the childhood of Christ, shall be related in the Legendary Lives of New Testament Characters.

all. I shall be able to tell you only the events of a single night.

"One fearful night of tempest, in which neither cock will crow nor dog bark, Mohammed shall be aroused from sleep by Gabriel, who shall appear to him in the shape he has when he appears before God, with seven hundred wings streaming with light; between each a space such as a fleet-footed horse could scarce traverse in five hundred years. Gabriel will lead the prophet forth into the open air, where the wondrous horse Borak will be ready. That is the horse on which Abraham mounted when he made his pilgrimages from Syria to Mecca. This horse has two wings as an eagle, and feet like a dromedary, and a body like a costly gem, shining like the sun, and a head like the fairest maiden. On this wondrous beast, whose brow bears the inscription, 'There is no God save God, and Mohammed is his prophet,' he will mount and ride, first to Medina, then to Sinai, thence to Bethlehem, and finally to Jerusalem, to view the holy places, and at them to offer up his prayers. From Jerusalem he will ascend on a golden ladder, with rungs of rubies, emeralds, and jacinths, into the seventh heaven, where he will be instructed in all the mysteries of the creation, and the governance of the world. He will see the blessed in all their joy, in Paradise, and the sinners, in all their pain, in Hell. There will he see many pasturing wild cattle in unfruitful fields. These are they who in the time of life used the gifts of God without giving to those in need. Others will he see running about, and carrying in one hand fresh, and in the other putrid, meat, and as often as they attempt to taste the former, a fiery rod will smite them on the hand, till they devour the latter. This is the punishment of those who have violated marriage, and have preferred forbidden pleasures. Others have a swollen body, swelling daily more and more; these are the fraudulent and avaricious. Others have their tongues and lips fastened together with iron clamps; these are the slanderers and backbiters. Between Paradise and Hell sits Adam, laughing with joy when the gate of Heaven opens to receive one of his sons, and he hears the songs and shouts of the blessed; weeping with self-reproach when the gate of Hell uncloses to take in one of his descendants, and he hears the sobbing of the damned. On this night will Mohammed also see, besides Gabriel, the other angels, who have each seventy thousand heads, and in each head seventy thousand faces, and in each face seventy thousand mouths, and in each mouth seventy thousand tongues, wherewith they cease not day or night to praise God in seventy thousand diverse languages. He will also see the angel of atonement, who is half fire, half ice ; also the angel who watches the treasure of fire with gloomy countenance and flashing eyes ; also the angel of death, with a great writing-table in his hand, whereon are inscribed many names, and from which at every instant he wipes off several hundreds ; finally, the angel who guards the waters, and weighs in great scales the water allotted to each spring and well, and brook and river ; and the angel who bears up the throne of God on his shoulders, and has a horn in his mouth, wherewith he will blow the blast that is to wake the dead. Moreover, the prophet will be conducted through many seas of light near to the throne itself, which is so great that the whole world will be beside it as a link in a coat of mail dropped in the desert. What will be further revealed to him," answered Samuel, " is unknown to me ; this only I know, that, after having contemplated the Majesty of God a bowshot off, he will descend the ladder precipitately, and, mounting Borak, will return to Mecca. Now the whole of this journey, his sojourn in Medina, Bethlehem, Jerusalem, and the seventh heaven, will occupy so little time, that a water-pitcher which he upset as he left the house in Mecca will not have run all its waters out by his return."

The assembled Israelites listened to Samuel, and when he was silent they cried with one voice, " We believe in God and in all the past prophets, and in all those who are yet for to come. Pray for us that we may escape the tyrany of Gjalout (Goliath)."

Thus Saul was chosen king of Israel, and Samuel was prophet to the people of God.[1]

XXXVI.

S A U L.

I. WAR WITH THE PHILISTINES.—GOLIATH SLAIN.

SAMUEL ordered Thalout (Saul) to make war upon Gjalout (Goliath), and to assemble the fighting men of the tribes of

[1] Weil. pp. 193–8.

Israel. Saul summoned all the men and they numbered eighty thousand. Samuel gave Saul a suit of mail, and said to him, " He who can wear this coat with ease will decide the war, and Goliath will perish by his hand."

Saul started with his army ; his way led through a desert, a day's journey across ; and it was very hot weather. On the other side of the desert was a broad river, between Jordan and Palestine, and the children of Israel had to pass this river to reach the army of Goliath. Saul thought that now he would prove his soldiers, for Samuel had bidden him take into battle only as many men as he could rely upon.

The men were faint with heat and thirst as they reached the river of Palestine, and Saul said, " He who drinks of this water shall not come with me, but he who drinks not thereof shall follow after me." [1] For he would not have them slake their thirst till they reached Jordan. [2]

But, according to another version of the story, the men were fainting in the wilderness, and murmured against Saul. Then Samuel prayed, and God brought a water-spring out of the dry, stony ground, and made standing water in the desert, fresh as snow, sweet as honey, and white as milk. [3]

Samuel spake to the soldiers, and said, " Ye have sinned against your king and against God, by murmuring. Therefore refuse to drink of this water except in the hollow of your hand, and so expiate your fault." [4]

Samuel's words were disregarded. Only three hundred and thirteen men were found who had sufficient control over themselves not to drink except slightly out of the hollow of their hand ; but these felt their thirst quenched, whereas those who had laid down and lapped were still parched with thirst.

Saul and his army came before that of Goliath ; then said the majority of those who had lain down and lapped, " We have no strength to-day to stand against the Philistines." So Saul dismissed them to their homes, to the number of seventy-six thousand men ; he had still with him four thousand men. Next day, when they saw the array of the Philistines, and the gigantic stature of their king, and their harness flashing in the sun, the hearts of more of the warriors failed, and they would

---

[1] Koran, Sura ii. v. 250.   [2] Tabari, i. p. 418.
[3] Perhaps the Passage in Psalm cvii. 35 may refer to this miracle, unrecorded in Holy Scripture.
[4] Weil, pp. 200, 201.

not follow Saul into battle, but said, "We have no strength to-day to stand against the Philistines!"

So Saul dismissed three thousand six hundred men, and there remained to him only three hundred and thirteen, the same number as those who on the day of Bedr remained with the prophet Mohammed.

Then said Saul, "God is favorable to us!" and he advanced, and set his army in array against Goliath. And he prayed, saying, "Grant us, O Lord, perseverance."[1]

However, God sent an order by Samuel saying, "Go not into battle this day, for the man who is to slay Goliath is not here ; he is Daud (David), son of Jesse, son of Obed, son of Boaz ; he is a little man, with grey eyes, and little hair, timid of heart, and slender of body. By this shalt thou know him : when thou placest the horn upon his head, the oil will overflow and boil."

Then Samuel went to Jesse, and said to him, "Amongst thy sons there is one who will slay Goliath."

Jesse said, "I have eleven sons, men stalwart and comely.'

Samuel placed the horn on their heads, but the oil was not to be seen.

Then God gave him a vision, and he said to him, "Look not at the beauty and strength of these men, but on the purity of their hearts and their fear of God."

Samuel said to Jesse, "God says thou art a liar, and He says thou hast another son besides these."

Jesse answered, "It is true ; but he is diminutive in stature, and I am ashamed to bring him into the company of men ; I make him tend sheep ; he is somewhere with the flock to-day."

Samuel went to the place, and it was a valley into which a torrent fell. He saw David drawing the sheep out of the torrent by twos. Samuel said, "Certainly this is the man I seek." He placed the horn on his head, and the oil overflowed.

Now Goliath, seeing the small number of the children of Israel, despised them, and scorned to fight them. He sent a messenger to Saul, saying. "Thou hast come out to fight against me with this handful, and I disdain to attack thee with my large army. If thou wilt, come forth that we may fight each other, or send any one out of the army, whom thou wilt, to fight with me."

---

[1] Koran, Sura ii. v. 251.

None in Saul's army would venture against the giant, and Saul was himself afraid.   He produced the shirt of mail Samuel had given him, and he tried it upon each of his soldiers in turn; but it was too short for one, too long for another, too tight for a third, and too loose for a fourth.

Now the father of David had come with his eleven sons into the host; but he had left David, because he was young and small of stature, to keep the sheep: and he had bidden him, from time to time, bring him supplies of food.   David came with the provisions.   He was dressed in a woollen shirt, and he bore in his hand the staff, and a pouch attached to his waist.

As he passed over a pebbly strip of soil, a stone cried to him, "Pick me up, and take me with thee."   He stooped and picked up the stone, and placed it in his pouch.   And when he had taken a few paces, another stone cried to him, "Pick me up, and take me with thee."   He did so.   And a third stone cried in like manner, and was in like manner taken by David.   The first stone was that wherewith Abraham had driven away Satan, when he sought to dissuade the patriarch from offering up his son; and the second stone was that on which the foot of Gabriel rested when he opened the fountain in the desert for Hagar and Ishmael; and the third stone was that wherewith Jacob strove against the angel whom his brother Esau had sent against him.[1]   But, according to another account, the first was the stone which Moses cast against the enemies of God, the second was that cast by Aaron, the third was destined to cause the death of Goliath.[2]   When David came into the army, Saul had finished trying on the suit of mail upon the soldiers, and he said, "It fits none of them." Then he spied David, and he said, "Young man, let me place this shirt of mail on thee."   Then he cast it over him, and it fitted him exactly.

Saul said, "Wilt thou fight Goliath?"

David answered, "I will do so."

Saul said, "With what horse and arms wilt thou go?"

David answered, "I will have no horse and no arms, save these stones of the brook."

David was feeble in body, he had grey eyes, was short, yellow-complexioned, thin-faced, and had red hair.[3]

Saul had little hope that David would overcome the giant,

---

[1] Weil, p. 203.   [2] Tabari, i. p. 421.   [3] Ibid.

but he thought his example might shame and stimulate others, therefore he let him go.

Now when Goliath came forth and defied the army of Israel, David went to meet him, wearing only his linen shirt, and belt, and pouch, and he had his shepherd's staff in his hand.

Then cried Goliath, " Who art thou, that comest out to meet me ? "

Then David replied, " I am come out to fight with thee."

Goliath said, " Go back, petty fool, and play with children of thine own age. I despise thee ; thou art unarmed."

" And I despise thee, dog of a Philistine ! " cried the stripling ; " thou deservest to be dealt with as men deal with dogs, —pelting them with stones till they turn tail."

Then Goliath was in a rage, and he lifted his spear against David ; but David hasted and loosed his belt, and laid in it one of the stones, and slung it ; and the wind caught the helmet of Goliath, and lifted it in the air above his head, and the stone struck him on the brow, and sank in, and crushed all his skull, and strewed his brains all over the horse he rode ; then the giant fell out of his saddle, and died.

Then again David placed the second stone in his sling, and he cast it, and it smote the right wing of the army of the Philistines ; then he cast the third stone, and it smote the left wing, and the host of the Philistines fled before him.[1]

2 SAUL'S JEALOUSY OF DAVID.

Saul had promised his daughter to the man who should slay Goliath. When the Philistines had been routed, Saul told Samuel all that had taken place ; and the prophet exhorted the king to fulfil his promise, and to give to David his daughter in marriage.

To this Saul agreed, and he gave David his ring, and made him manager of all his affairs, and he exalted him to be his son-in-law.

Several years passed, and Saul became envious of David, whose praise was in everybody's mouth.

He sent David into the wars, in hopes of his there meeting his death ; but it was all in vain. Then he spoke to his daughter Michal, that she should introduce him into her husband's

---

[1] Tabari, i. p. 422 ; Weil, pp. 202–4 ; D'Herbelot, i. p. 362.

chamber at night, that he might slay David with his own hand.

Michal told David her father's resolution, with many tears ; but David bade her be comforted. " For," said he, " the God of my fathers, who preserved Abraham and Moses from the hands of the executioner, will deliver me from thy father. But do as he bade thee, open the door at night, and fear not for me."

Then David went into his smithy and wrought a suit of chain mail. He was the inventor of chain-armor. And he had received from God the power of moulding iron, like wax, in his fingers, without fire and without hammer.

Now he fashioned for himself a whole suit of chain mail ; it was so thin that it was like gossamer, and it fitted to his body like his skin, and it was impenetrable to the thrust of every weapon.

David put upon him his armor, and lay down in his bed. He slept, but was awakened at midnight by the knife of Saul stabbing at him as he lay. He sprang up, struck the weapon from the hands of his father-in-law, and thrust him forth out of the house.[1]

After this, Saul came to Michal and said, " He was not asleep, or I certainly would have slain him. Admit me again into his chamber at night."

Michal went to David and told him all with many tears.

Then said David, " I must escape from my house, for my life is not in security here. But do thou fill a leather bottle with wine, and lay it in my bed."

Michal did so ; she took a large skin of wine and placed it in the bed, and drew the cover over it. But David fled away to Hebron.

And in the night came Saul, and he felt the clothes, and he thought it was David in the bed, so he stabbed at him with his knife, and the wine ran out in the bed. Then Saul smelt it, and he said, " How much wine the fellow drank for his supper ! "[2]

But when he found that David had escaped him once more, he was wroth, and he gathered men together, and pursued after

[1] Weil, pp. 205–8.
[2] Tabari, i. p. 423. The same story is told of the escape of S. Felix of Nola, in the Decian persecution.

him ; in his anger, moreover, he sought to kill Michal, but she
fled away and concealed herself.

Saul pursued David in the mountains, but David knew all
the caves and lurking-places, and Saul was unable to catch
him. One night, David crept into the camp and thrust four
arrows, inscribed with his name, into the ground, round the
head of Saul. When Saul awoke, he saw these arrows, and
he said, " David has been here ; he might have slain me had
he willed it."

During the day, Saul came upon his enemy in a narrow
valley ; he was mounted, and he pursued David, who was on
foot. David fled as fast as he could run, and managed to
reach a cave a few moments before Saul could reach it.
Then God sent a spider, which spun a web over the mouth of
the cave ; and Saul saw it and passed on, saying, " Certainly
David cannot have entered in there, or the web would be
torn." [1]

One night, Saul and his soldiers lodged in a cavern. And
David was there, but they knew it not. In the night David
carried off the sword and banner and seal-ring of the king,
and he went forth out of the cave, for it had two openings. In
the morning, when Saul prepared to continue his search, he saw
him on a mountain opposite the mouth of the cave, and David
had girded the royal sword to his side, and brandished the flag,
and held forth his finger that all might note that he had on it
the king's signet. [2]

Then Saul said, " His heart is better than mine ; " and he
was reconciled with David, and he bade him return with him
and live at peace. And he did so.

3. THE DEATH OF SAUL.

Now when Saul had gone forth against David, the wise men
of Israel had gathered themselves together, and had remon-
strated with him. But Saul was wroth at this interference, and
he slew them all, and there escaped none of them save one
wise woman, whom his vizir spared. This vizir was a good
man, and he took the woman into his own house, and she lived
with his family.

Some time after that, Saul had a dream, and in his dream
he was reproached for having slain the wise men. And when

---

[1] Tabari, p. 429.   [2] Weil, p. 207.

he awoke he was full of remorse, and he went to his vizir and said, " It repents me that I have put to death all the wise men of my realm ; is there none remaining of whom I might ask counsel how I could expiate my crime ? "

Then the vizir answered, " There remains but one, and that is a woman."

Saul said, " Bring her hither before me."

Now, when the wise woman was come before Saul, the king was troubled in mind, and he said, " Show me how I can make atonement for the great sin that I have committed."

The woman answered, " Lead me to the tomb of a prophet ; I will pray, and may be God will suffer him to speak."

They went to the tomb of Samuel, and the woman prayed.

Then Samuel spake out of his sepulchre, and said, " Let his expiation be this : He shall go down, he and his sons, to the city of Giants, and they shall fall there."

Saul had twelve sons. He called them to him and said to them all the words of Samuel. They then answered, " We are ready, let us go down.

So they went to the city of Giants, and fought against it, and fell there, all in one day.[1]

XXXVII.

DAVID.

DAVID says of himself, " *Behold, I was shapen in wickedness ; and in sin did my mother conceive me.*"[2] The Rabbis explain this passage by narrating the circumstances of the conception of David, which I shall give in Latin. The mother of David they say was named Nitzeneth. " Dixerunt Rabbini nostri beatæ memoriæ, quod Isai (Jesse) habebat ancillam, eamque sollicitabat ad turpia ; quæ, cum esset pudica et fidelis uxori Isai, eidem retulit ; quæ seipsam aptavit (loco ancillæ) et congressa est cum Isai, ex quo concubitu egressus est David. Et quia Isai intentio fuerat in ancillam, quamquam res aliter evenerat, idcirco dixit David,—super eum sit pax : Ecce in iniquitate formatus sum, et peccato calefecit me mater mea."[3]

On this account, Jesse, having discovered the deception, lightly esteemed his son David, and sent him to keep sheep,

---

[1] Tabari, i. p. 424.   [2] Ps. li. 5.   [3] Midrash, fol. 204, col. 1.

and made him as a servant to his brethren. And to this David refers when he says, "*The stone which the builders rejected is become the head of the corner;*"[1] for, from being the despised brother, put to menial work, he was exalted before his brethren to be king over Israel.

When David was born he would have died immediately, had not Adam, when he saw his posterity marshalled before him, taken compassion on David, and given him seventy years.[2]

However, David was without a soul for the first fourteen years of his life, and was so regarded by God, as he was uncircumcised;[3] but other Rabbinic writers say that he was born circumcised.

The Jewish authors relate, as do the Mussulman historians, that David had red hair. In Jalkut (1 Sam. xvi. 12) it is said, " Samuel sent, and made David come before him, and he had red hair;"[4] and again in Bereschith Rabba, "When Samuel saw that David had red hair, he feared and said, He will shed blood as did Esau. But the ever-blessed God said, This man will shed it with unimpassioned eyes—this did not Esau. Esau slew out of his own caprice, but this man will execute those sentenced to death by the Sanhedrim."

David was very small, but when Samuel poured the oil upon his head and anointed him, he grew rapidly, and was soon as tall as was Saul. And this the commentators conclude from the fact of Saul having put his armor upon David, and it fitted him. Now Saul was a head and shoulders taller than any man in Israel; therefore David must have started to equal height since his anointing.[5]

David was gifted with the evil eye, and was able to give the leprosy by turning a malignant glance upon any man. " When it is written, ' *The Philistine cursed David by his gods,*'[6] David looked at him with the evil eye. For whoever was looked upon by him with the evil eye became leprous, as Joab knew to his cost, for after David had cast the evil glance on him, it is said, ' *Let there not fail from the house of Joab one that hath an issue, or that is a leper.*'[7]

" The same befell the Philistine when he cursed David. David then threw on him the malignant glance, and fixed it

---

[1] Ps. cxviii. 22.　　　　[2] See the story in the Legends of Adam.
[3] Zohar, in Bartolocci, i. fol. 85, col. 2.
[4] Jalkut, fol. 32, col. 2 (Parasch. 2, numb. 134).
[5] Ibid. (Parasch. 2, numb. 127).　　[6] 1 Sam. xvii. 43.　　[7] 2 Sam. iii. 29.

on his brow, that he might at once become leprous ; and at the same moment the stone and the leprosy struck him." [1]

But David was himself afflicted for six months with this loathsome malady, and it is in reference to this that he says, " *Thou shalt purge me with hyssop, and I shall be clean ; Thou shalt wash me, and I shall be whiter than snow.*" During this period, he was cast out and separated from the elders of the people, and the Divinity withdrew from him. [2] And this ex-plains the discrepancy apparent in the account of the number of years he reigned. It is said that he reigned over Israel forty years, [3] but he reigned seven years in Hebron and thirty and three in Jerusalem. In the Second Book of Samuel, how-ever, it is said, he reigned in Hebron seven years and six months ; [4] though the statement that he reigned only forty years in all, that is, thirty-three in Jerusalem, is repeated. Conse-quently these six months do not count, the reason being that David was at that time afflicted with the disorder, and cut off from society, and reputed as one dead. [5]

The Rabbis suppose that David sinned in cutting off the skirt of Saul's robe ; [6] and they say that he expiated this fault in his old age, by finding no warmth in his clothes, wherewith he wrapped himself. [7] For it is said, " *King David was old and stricken in years ; and they covered him with clothes, but he got no heat.*" [8]

To David is attributed by the Rabbi Solomon the power of calling down the rain, the hail, and the tempest, in vengeance upon his enemies. "Our Rabbis," says he, "say that these things were formerly stored in heaven, but David came and made them to descend on the earth : for they are means of vengeance, and it is not fitting that they should be garnered in the Treasury of God." [9] But the rain and hail fell at the Deluge, in Egypt, and on the Amorites ; therefore the signifi-cation to be attributed to this opinion of the Rabbis probably is, that David was the first to be able to call them down by his prayer.

David had a lute which he hung up above his head in the bed, and the openings of the lute were turned towards the

<hr>

[1] Zohar, in Bartolocci, i. fol. 99, col. 1.
[2] Talmud. Tract. Sanhedrim, fol. 107.   [3] 1 Kings ii. 11.
[4] 2 Sam. v. 5.   [5] Bartolocci, i. f. 100.   [6] 1 Sam. xxiv. 4.
[7] Bartolocci, i. f. 122. col. 1.   [8] 1 Kings i. 1.
[9] Bartolocci, i. f. 122. col. 2.

north, and when the cool night air whispered in the room towards dawn, it stirred the strings of the lute, which gave forth such sweet and resonant notes, that David was aroused from his sleep early, before daybreak, that he might occupy himself in the study of the Law.   And it is to this that he refers when he cries in his Psalm, "*Awake lute and harp: I myself will awake right early.*" [1]

When Absalom was slain, David saw Scheol (Hell) opened, and his son tormented, for his rebellion, in the lowest depths. The sight was so distressing to the king, that he wrapped his mantle about his face and cried, "*O my son Absalom! my son, my son Absalom! would God I had died for thee, O Absalom, my son, my son!*"   Here it is to be noted that David called Absalom either by name or by his relationship seven times. Now in Hell there are seven mansions, and as each cry escaped the father's heart, Absalom was released from one of these divisions of the Pit ; and he thus effected his escape from Gehenna through the love of his father, which drew him up out of misery. [2]

David was very desirous to build a temple to the Lord, but God would not suffer him to do so, as he was a man of blood. This is the reason why he so desired to erect a temple. When he was young, and pastured his father's sheep, he came one day upon a rhinoceros (unicorn) asleep, and he did not know that it was a rhinoceros, but thought it was a mountain, so he drove his flock up its back, and fed them on the grass which grew thereon.   But presently the rhinoceros awoke, and stood up, and then David's head touched the sky.   He was filled with terror, and he vowed that if God would save his life and bring him safely to the ground again, he would build to the Lord a temple of the dimensions of the horn of the beast, an hundred cubits. The Talmudists are not agreed as to whether this was the height, or the breadth, of the horn ; however, the vow was heard, and the Lord sent a lion against the rhinoceros ; and when the unicorn saw the lion, he lay down, and David descended his back, along with his sheep, as fast as possible ; but when he saw the lion, his spirit failed him again.   However he took the lion by the beard, and smote, and slew him. This adventure the Psalmist recalls when he says, "*Save me from the lion's mouth; Thou hast heard me also from among*

[1] Ps. lvii. 9 ; Bartolocci, i. fol. 125, col. 2.
[2] Talmud, Tract. Sota, fol. 10 b.

the horns of the unicorn;" [1] and to his vow he alludes in Psalm cxxxii., *"Lord, remember David, and all his trouble; how he sware unto the Lord, and vowed a vow unto the Almighty God of Jacob."* [2]

One day David was hunting in the wilderness. Then came Satan, in the form of a stag, and David shot an arrow at him, but could not kill him. This astonished him, for on one occasion, in strife with the Philistines, he had transfixed eight hundred men with one arrow.[3] Then he chased the deer, and it ran before him into the Philistine land. Now when Ishbibenob, who was of the sons of the giant, knew this, he said, " David has slain my brother Goliath ; now he is in my power ! " and he came upon him and chained him, and cast him down, and laid a wine-press upon him, that he might crush him, and squeeze all the blood out of him. But God softened the earth beneath him, so that it yielded to his body, and he was uninjured; as he says in the Psalms, *" Thou shalt make room enough under me for to go."* [4] And as David lay under the press, he saw a dove fly by, and he said, *" O that I had wings as a dove, that I might flee away, and be at rest ;"* [5] and he alludes to his being among the pots, and noting the wings of the dove as silver, in another Psalm.[6]

Now Abishai, the son of Zeruiah, heard the plaining of the dove, which had seen the trouble of the king, and came into Jerusalem in grief thereat. Then Abishai went to the chamber of David to search for him, but he was not there. Then he knew that the king must be in danger, and the only means of reaching him with speed was to mount the royal mule, which was fleet as the wind ; but this Abishai did not venture to do without advice, for he remembered the words of the Mischna, " Thou shalt not ride the king's horse, nor mount his throne, nor grasp his sceptre." But as the danger was pressing, Abishai went to the school, and consulted the doctors of the Law, who said, " In an emergency all things are lawful." Then he mounted the mule of King David, and rode into the desert, and the earth flew under him, and he reached the house of Ishbibenob. Now the mother of Ishbi-benob—her name was Orpha—sat without the door spinning. And when she saw Abishai galloping up, she brake her thread and flung the spindle at him, with intent to strike him dead. But the spindle fell

---

[1] Ps. xxii. 21.   [2] Midrash Tillim, fol. 21, col. 2.
[3] Eisenmenger, i. p. 409.   [4] Ps. xviii. 36.   [5] Ps. lv. 6.   [6] Ps. lxviii. 13

short of him.   So Orpha cried to him, "Give me my spindle,
boy."   Abishai stooped and picked it up, and cast it at her
with all his force, and it struck her on the brow, and broke her
skull, and she fell back and died.

Then, when Ishbi-benob saw what was done, he said,
"These two men will be too much for me!" so he drew David from under the wine-press, and flung him high into the air,
and set his lance in the ground, that David might fall upon it,
and be transfixed.   But Abishai cried the Sacred Name, and
David was arrested in his fall, and hung between heaven and
earth, and gradually was let down, not on the spear, but at a
distance.   Then Abishai and David slew Ishbi-benob.[1]

When David's life was run out, the Angel of Death came
to fetch his soul.   But David spent all his time in reading
the Law.   The angel stood before him, and watched that his
lips should cease moving, for he might not interrupt him in
this sacred work.   But David made no pause.   Then the angel went into the garden which was behind the house, and
shook violently one of the trees.   David heard the noise, and
turned his head, and saw that the branches of one of his trees
were violently agitated, but no leaf stirred on the other trees;
so he closed the book of the Law, and went into his garden,
and set a ladder against the tree and ascended into it, that he
might see what was agitating the leaves.   Then the angel withdrew the ladder, but David knew it not; so he fell and broke
his neck, and died.   It was the Sabbath day.   Then Solomon
doubted what he should do, for the body of his father was exposed to the sun, and to the dogs; and he did not venture to
remove it, lest he should profane the Sabbath; so he sent to
the Rabbis, and said, "My father is dead, and exposed to the
sun, and to be devoured by dogs; what shall I do?"

They answered, "Cast the body of a beast before the dogs,
and place bread or a boy upon thy father, and bury him."[2]

David had such a beautiful voice, that, when he sang the
praises of God, the birds came from all quarters and surrounded him, listening to his strains.   The mountains even and the
hills were moved at his notes.[3]   He could sing with a voice as
loud as the most deafening peal of thunder, or warble as
sweetly as the tuneful nightingale.

[1] Talmud, Tract. Sanhedrim, fol. 95, col. 1.
[2] Tract. Sabbath, fol. 30, col. 2.
[3] Tabari, i. p. 426; Weil, p. 208.

15

He divided his time, say the Mussulmans, into three parts. One day he occupied himself in the affairs of his kingdom, the second day he devoted to the service of God, and the third day he gave up to the society of his wives.

As he was going home from prayer, one day, he heard two of his servants discussing him and comparing him with Abraham.

"Was not Abraham saved from a fiery furnace?" asked one.

"Did not David slay the giant Goliath?" asked the other.

"But what has David done that will compare with the obedience of Abraham, who was ready to offer his only son to God?" asked the first.

When David reached home, he fell down before God and prayed: "Lord! Thou who didst give to Abraham a trial of his obedience in the pyre, grant that an opportunity may be afforded me of proving before all the people how great also is mine."[1]

But others relate this differently. They say that David besought the Lord to endue him with the spirit of prophecy. Then God answered, "When I give great gifts, he who receives them must suffer great trials. I proved Abraham by the fire, and by the sacrifice of one son, and separation from others; Jacob by his children; Joseph by the well and the prison; Moses by Pharaoh; Job by the worms. I afflicted all these, but thee have I not afflicted." But David said, "O Lord, prove me and try me also, that I may obtain the same degree of celebrity as they."[2]

One day, as David sang psalms before God and the congregation, a beautiful bird appeared at the window, and it attracted his whole attention, so that he could scarcely sing. David concluded his recitation of the psalms earlier than usual, and went in pursuit of the bird, which led him from bush to bush, and from tree to tree, till it suddenly disappeared near a secluded lake. Now this bird was Eblis, and he came to tempt David into evil.

When the bird vanished, David saw in the water a beautiful woman, bathing, and when she stood up, her hair covered her whole person.

David hid behind the bushes, that he might not startle her, till she was dressed; then he stood forth, and asked her her name.

---

[1] Weil, p. 207.   [2] Tabari p. 428.

"My name," said she, "is Bathsheba,[1] daughter of Joshua, and wife of Uriah, son of Hanan, who is with the army."[2]

Then David departed, but his heart was inflamed with love, and he sent a message to Joab, the captain of his host, to set Uriah before the ark in every battle. Now those who went before the ark must conquer or fall. Three times Uriah came out of battle victorious, but the fourth time he was killed.

Then David took Uriah's wife to his own house and made her his own wife. And she consented upon the condition that should she bear him a son, that son was to succeed him in the kingdom. Now David had, before he married her, ninety-nine wives. The day after his marriage, Michael and Gabriel appeared before him in human form, as he was in his court, and Gabriel said to him ; " This fellow here possesses ninety and nine sheep, but I have only one, and that I love, and cherish in my bosom. This man claims my little ewe lamb, and will take it from me, and, if I will not give it him, he says that he will slay me ; and take my lamb from me by force."

Then David's anger was kindled against Michael, and he said, " Thou who hast so many sheep, wherefore lustest thou after the poor man's ewe lamb ? Thou hast an evil heart and an insatiable spirit."

Then Michael exclaimed, " Thou hast given judgment against thyself: what thou rebukest in this man, thou hast allowed thyself to do !"[3]

And David knew that God had sent His angels to rebuke him, and he fell upon his face to the ground. But, some say, he drew his sword and rushed upon Michael : then Gabriel held him back, and said, " Thou didst ask to be tried ; now thou hast fallen under the temptation."[4]

Then the angels vanished, and David fell to the ground, tore off his purple robe, cast aside his golden crown, and wept, for forty days and forty nights. And his tears flowed in such

---

[1] The Arabs call her Saga.

[2] The story in the Talmud is almost the same, with this difference : Bathsheba was washing herself behind a beehive, then the beautiful bird perched on the hive, and David shot an arrow at it and broke the hive, and exposed Bathsheba to view. In the Rabbinic tale, David had asked for the gift of prophecy, and God told him he must be tried. This he agreed to, and the temptation to adultery was that sent him. (Talmud, Tract, Sanhedrim, fol. 107, col. 2 ; Jalkut, fol. 22, col. 2).

[3] Koran, Sura xxxviii. [4] Weil, pp. 212, 213.

abundance, that every now and then he plunged a cup into them and drank it off.

At the expiration of forty days Gabriel came to him, and said, "The Lord salutes thee!" But David felt this was an additional reproach, and he wept still more. It is said that during the ensuing forty days and nights David shed more tears than Adam and all his descendants had, and will, shed from the day of the Fall to the day of the Resurrection.

Then God sent Gabriel to him again, and Gabriel said, "The Lord salutes thee!" But David lifted his tearful face and said, "O Gabriel, what will Uriah say to me on the day of the general Resurrection?"

Gabriel answered, "The Lord will give him so great an inheritance in Paradise, that he will not have the heart to re-proach thee."

Then David knew that he was pardoned, and he rejoiced greatly. But he never forgot his sins. He wrote them on the palm of his hand, that he might have them always before him; therefore he says, "My shame is ever before mine eyes."

Nevertheless David's heart was lifted up with pride, when he considered that he was a king, a prophet, and a great general. And one day he said to Nathan, "I think I am perfect, I have every thing."

"Not so," answered Nathan, "thou exercisest no handi-craft."

Then David was ashamed, and he asked God to teach him a craft; and God made him skilful in fabricating coats of mail of rings twined together; his trade therefore was that of an armorer, and his disgrace was wiped away.

After his judgment between the two angels, David had no confidence in giving sentence in cases pleaded before him; therefore God sent him, by the hand of Gabriel, a reed of iron and a little bell, and the angel said to him, "God is pleased with thy humility, and He has sent thee this reed and this bell to assist thee in giving judgment. Place this reed in thy judgment-hall, and hang up the bell in the middle, and place the accuser on one side, and the accused on the other, and give sentence in favor of him who makes the bell to tinkle when he touches the reed."

David was highly pleased with his gift, and he gave such righteous judgment, that men feared, throughout the land, to do wrong to one another.

One day, two men came before David, and one said, "I left a goodly pearl in the charge of this man, and when I asked for it again, he denied it me."

But the other said, "I have returned it to him."

Then David bade each lay his hand on the reed, but the bell gave the same indication for both. Then David thought, "They both speak the truth, and yet that cannot be; the gift of God must err."

Then he bade the men try again, and the result was the same. However, he observed that the defendant, when he went up to the reed to lay his hand upon it, gave his walking staff to the plaintiff to hold, and this he did each time, so that David's suspicion was awakened, and he took the staff, and examined it, and found that it was hollow, and the stolen pearl was concealed in the handle. Thus the bell had given right judgment, for when the accused touched the reed, he had returned the pearl into the hand of the accuser; but David by his doubt in the reed displeased Him who gave it, and the reed and the bell were taken from him.

After that, David often gave wrong judgment till Solomon, his son, was of age to advise him.

One day, when Solomon was aged thirteen, there came two men before the king. The first said, "I sold a house and cellar to this man, and on digging in the cellar he found a treasure hidden there by my forefathers. I sold him the house and cellar but not the treasure. Bid him restore to me what he has found."

But the other said, "Not so. He sold me the house, the cellar, and all its contents."

Then King David said, "Let the treasure be divided, and let half go to one, and half go to the other."

But Solomon stood up and said to the plaintiff, "Hast thou not a son?" He said, "I have."

Then said Solomon to the defendant, "Hast thou not a daughter?" He answered, "I have."

"Then," said Solomon, "give thy daughter to the son of this man who sold thee the house, and let the treasure go as a marriage gift to thy daughter and his son" And all applauded this judgment.

On another occasion, a husbandman came before the judgment-seat to lay complaint against a herdsman, whose sheep had broken into his field, and had pastured on his young wheat,

Then King David said, "Let some of the sheep be given to the husbandman."

But Solomon stood up, and said, "Not so ; let the husbandman have the wool, and the milk of the flock, till the wheat is grown up again as it was before the sheep destroyed it."

And all wondered at his wisdom.

But the king's elders and councillors were filled with envy, because this child's opinion was preferred before theirs ; and they complained to King David.

Then David said, "Call an assembly of the people, and prove Solomon before them, whether he be learned in the Law, and whether he have understanding and wit."·

So the people were assembled, and the elders took council together how they might perplex him with hard questions. But or ever they asked him, he answered what they had devised, and they were greatly confounded, so that the people supposed this was a preconcerted scene arranged by the king. Then, when the elders were silenced, Solomon turned to their chief, and said, "I too will prove you with questions. What you have asked me have been trials of my learning, but what I will ask you shall put to proof the readiness of your wits. What is all, and what is nothing? What is something, and what is naught?"

The elder was silent ; he thought, but he knew not what was the answer. And all the people perplexed themselves to discover the riddle, but they could not. Then said Solomon, "God is all, and the world He made is as nothing before Him. The faithful is something, but the hypocrite is naught."

Thereupon he turned to a second, and he said : "What are most and what are fewest? What is the sweetest, and what is the bitterest?" But when the second could find no solution to these questions, Solomon answered, "Most men are unbelievers, the fewest have true faith. The sweetest thing is the possession of a virtuous wife, good children, and a competence ; the bitterest thing is to have a disreputable wife, disorderly children, and penury."

Then Solomon turned to a third elder and asked : "What is the most odious sight, and what is the most beautiful sight? What is the surest thing, and what is that which is most insecure?"

And when this elder also was unable to give an answer, Solomon interpreted his riddle once more, "The most odious sight is to see a righteous man fall away ; the most beautiful sight is to see a sinner repent. The surest thing is death, the most insecure thing is life." After that Solomon said to all the people, "Ye see that the oldest and the most learned men are not always the wisest. True wisdom comes not with years, nor is derived from books, but is a gift of God the All-wise."

Solomon by his words threw the whole assembly into astonishment, and all the heads of the people cried with one voice, "Praised be the Lord, who has given to our king a son who surpasses all in wisdom, and who is worthy to ascend the throne of his father David."

And David thanked God that He had given him such a wise son, and now he desired but one thing further of God, and that was to see him who was to be his companion in Paradise ; for to every man is allotted by God one man to be his friend and comrade in the Land of Bliss.

So David prayed to God, and his prayer was heard, and a voice fell from heaven and bade him confer the kingdom upon his son Solomon, and then to go forth, and the Lord would lead him to the place where his companion dwelt.

David therefore had his son Solomon crowned king, and then he went forth out of Jerusalem, and he was in pilgrim's garb, with a staff in his hand ; and he went from city to city, and from village to village, but he found not the man whom he sought. One day, after the lapse of many weeks, he drew near to a village upon the borders of the Mediterranean Sea, and alongside of him walked a poorly dressed man laden with a heavy bundle of fagots. This man was very old and reverend of aspect, and David watched him. He saw him dispose of his wood and then give half the money he had obtained by the sale of it to a poor person. After that he bought a piece of bread and retired from the town. As he went, there passed a blind woman, and the old man broke his bread in half, and gave one portion to the woman ; and he continued his course till he reached the mountains from which he had brought his load in the morning.

David thought, "This man well deserves to be my companion for eternity, for he is pious, charitable, and reverend of aspect : I must ask his name."

He went after the old man, and he found him in a cave among the rocks, which was lighted by a rent above. David stood without and heard the hermit pray, and read the Tora and the Psalms, till the sun went down. Then he lighted a lamp and began his evening prayers; and when they were finished, he drew forth the piece of bread, and ate the half of it.

David, who had not ventured to interrupt the devotions of the old hermit, now entered the cave and saluted him.

The hermit asked, "Who art thou? I have seen no man here before, save only Mata, son of Johanna, the companion destined to King David in Paradise."

David told his name, and asked after this Mata. But the aged man could give him no information of his whereabouts. "But," said he, "go over these mountains, and observe well what thou lightest upon, and it may be thou wilt find Mata."

David thanked him, and continued his search. For long it was profitless. He traversed the stony dales and the barren mountains, and saw no trace of human foot. At last, just as hope was abandoning him, on the summit of a rugged peak he saw a wet spot. Then he stood still in surprise. "How comes there to be a patch of soft and sloppy ground here?" he asked; "the topmost peak of a stony mountain is not the place where springs bubble up."

As he thus mused, an aged man came up the other side of the mountain. His eyes were depressed to the earth, so that he saw not David. And when he came to the wet patch, he stood still, and prayed with such fervor, that rivulets of tears flowed out of his eyes, and sank into the soil; and thus David learnt how it was that the mountain-top was wet.

Then David thought, "Surely this man, whose eyes are such copious fountains of tears, must be my companion in Paradise."

Yet he ventured not to interrupt him in his prayer, till he heard him ask, "O my God! pardon King David his sins, and save him from further trespass! for my sake be merciful to him, for Thou hast destined him to be my comrade for all eternity!"

Then David ran towards him, but the old man totttered and fell, and before the king reached him he was dead.

So David dug into the ground which had been moistened by the tears of Mata, and laid him there, and said the funeral prayer over him, and covered him with the earth, and then returned to Jerusalem.

And when he came into his harem, the Angel of Death stood there and greeted him with the words, " God has heard thy supplications ; now has thy life reached its end."

Then David said, " The Lord's will be done ! " and he fell down upon the ground, and expired.

Gabriel descended to comfort Solomon, and to give him a heavenly shroud in which to wrap David.   And all Israel followed the bier to Machpelah, where Solomon laid him by the side of Abraham and Joseph.[1]

It will doubtless interest the reader to have an English version of the Psalm supposed to have been composed by David after the slaying of Goliath, which is not included in the Psalter, as it is supposed to be apocryphal.

Psalm CLI. (*Pusillus eram*).

1. I was small among my brethren ; and growing up in my father's house, I kept my father's sheep.

2. My hands made the organ : and my fingers shaped the psaltery.

3. And who declared unto my Lord !   He, the Lord, He heard all things.

4. He sent His angel, and He took me from my father's sheep ; He anointed me in mercy with His unction.

5. Great and goodly are my brethren : but with them the Lord was not well pleased.

6. I went to meet the stranger : and he cursed me by all his idols.

7. But I smote off his head with his own drawn sword : and I blotted out the reproach of Israel.

This simple and beautiful psalm does not exist in Hebrew, but is found in Greek, in some psalters of the Septuagint version, headed " A Psalm of David when he had slain Goliath." S. Athanasius mentions it with praise, in his address to Marcellinus on the Interpretation of the Psalms, and in the Synopsis of Holy Scripture.   It was versified in Greek in A. D. 360, by Apollinarius Alexandrinus.[2]

The subjoined shield of David is given in a Hebrew book

---

[1] Weil. pp. 213–224.

[2] Greek text, and Latin translation in Fabricus ; Pseudigr. Vet. Test. t. ii. pp. 905–7.

15*

on the properties and medicaments of things. It is said to
be a certain protection against fire.   A cake of bread must be
made, and on it must be impressed the seal or shield of David,
having in the corner the word ‏ט' יר‏, and in the middle ‏אנ'רא‏
(Thou art mighty to everlasting, O Jehovah) ; and it must be

cast aside into the fire with the words of Psalm cvi. 30,
" *Then stood up Phinees and prayed ; and so the plague ceased ;*"
and also Exod. xii. 27, " *It is the sacrifice of the Lord's passover, who passed over the houses of the children of Israel*

in Egypt, when He smote the Egyptians, and delivered our homes."[1]

XXXVIII.

SOLOMON.[2]

I. HOW SOLOMON OBTAINED POWER.

AFTER Solomon had executed the last offices for his father, he rested in a dale betwixt Hebron and Jerusalem, and fell a-sleep. As he returned to himself, there stood before him eight angels, each with countless wings, diverse in kinds and col-ors ; and the angels bowed themselves before him three times.

"Who are ye?" asked Solomon, with eyes still closed.

" We are the angels ruling over the eight winds of heaven," was their reply. " God hath sent us to give thee dominion over ourselves and over the winds subject to us. They will storm and bluster, or breathe softly, at thy pleasure. At thy com-mand they will swoop down on earth, and bear thee over the highest mountains."

The greatest of the angels gave him a jewel inscribed with "God is Power and Greatness," and said, "When thou hast a command for us, then raise this stone towards heaven, and we shall appear before thee as thy servants."

When these angels had taken their departure, there appeared four more, of whom each was unlike the other. One was in fashion as a great whale, another as an eagle, the third as a lion, and the fourth as a serpent. And they said, " We are they who rule over all the creatures that move in the earth, and air, and water ; and God hath sent us to give thee domin-ion over all creatures, that they may serve thee and thy friends with all good, and fight against thine enemies with all their force."

The angel who ruled over the winged fowls extended to Solomon a precious stone, with the inscription, "Let all creatures praise the Lord !" and said, "By virtue of this stone, raised above thy head, canst thou call us to thy assistance, and to fulfil thy desire."

[1] סגולות ורפואית ; Amst. 1703.

[2] Solomon was twelve years old when he succeeded David. (Abulfeda, p. 43 ; Bartolocci, iv. p. 371.)

Solomon immediately ordered the angels to bring before him a pair of every living creature that moves in the water, flies in the air, and walks or glides or creeps on the earth.

The angels vanished, and in an instant they were before Solomon once more, and there were assembled in his sight pairs of every creature, from the elephant to the smallest fly.

Solomon conversed with the angels, and was instructed by them in the habits, virtues, and names of all living creatures ; he listened to the complaints of the beasts, birds, and fishes, and by his wisdom he rectified many evil customs among them.

He entertained himself longest with the birds, both on account of their beautiful speech, which he understood, and also because of the wise sentences which they uttered.

This is the signification of the cry of the peacock : " With what measure thou judgest others, thou shalt thyself be judged."

This is the song of the nightingale : " Contentment is the greatest happiness."

The turtle dove calls, " Better were it for some created things that they had never been created."

The peewit pipes, " He that hath no mercy, will not find mercy himself."

The bird syrdar cries, " Turn to the Lord, ye sinners ! "

The swallow screams, " Do good, and ye shall receive a reward."

This is the pelican's note : " Praise the Lord in heaven and earth."

The dove chants, " The fashion of this world passeth away, but God remaineth eternal."

The kata says, " Silence is the best safeguard."

The cry of the eagle is, " However long life may be, yet its inevitable term is death."

The croak of the raven is, " The further from man, the happier I."

The cock crows before the dawn and in the day, " Remember thy Creator, O thoughtless man ! "

Solomon chose the cock and the peewit to be his constant companions—the first because of its cry, and the second because it can see through the earth as through glass, and could therefore tell him where fountains of water were to be found.

After he had stroked the dove, he bade her dwell with her

young in the temple he was about to build to the honor of the
Most High.   This pair of doves, in a few years, multiplied to
such an extent, that all who sought the temple moved through
the quarter of the town it occupied under the shadow of the
wings of doves.

When Solomon was again alone, an angel appeared to him,
whose upper half was like to earth, and whose lower half was
like to water.   He bowed himself before the king, and said,
"I am created by God to do His will on the dry land and in
the watery sea.   Now, God has sent me to serve thee, and thou
canst rule over earth and water.   At thy command the highest
mountains will be made plain, and the level land will rise into
steep heights.   Rivers and seas will dry up, and the desert will
stream with water at thy command."   Then he gave to him a
precious stone, with the legend engraved thereon, "Heaven
and earth serve God."

Finally, an angel presented to him another stone, whereon
was cut, "There is no God save God, and Mohammed is the
messenger of God."

"By means of this stone," said the angel, "thou shalt
have dominion over the whole world of spirits, which is far
greater than that of men and beasts, and occupies the space
between earth and heaven.   One portion of the spirits is faithful, and praises the One only God; the other portion is unfaithful: some adore fire, others the sun, others worship the
planets, many revere winter.   The good spirits surround the
true believers among men, and protect them from all evil; the
evil spirits seek to injure them and deceive them."

Solomon asked to see the Jinns in their natural and original shape.   The angel shot like a column of flame into heav-
en, and shortly returned with the Satans and Jinns in great
hosts : and Solomon, though he had power over them, shuddered with disgust at their loathsome appearance.   He saw
men's heads attached to the necks of horses, whose feet were
those of an ass ; the wings of an eagle attached to the hump
of a dromedary ; the horns of a gazelle on the head of a peacock.[1]

2. HOW SOLOMON FEASTED ALL FLESH.

When Solomon returned home, he placed the four stones,
which the angels had given him, in a ring, so that he might at

------

[1] Weil, pp. 225–231 ; Eisenmenger, p. 440, etc.

any moment exercise his authority over the realms of spirits
and beasts, the earth, the winds and the sea.

His first care was to subject the Jinns. He made them all
appear before him, with the exception of the mighty Sachr,
who kept himself in concealment on an unknown island in
the ocean, and the great Eblis, the master of all evil spirits, to
whom God had promised complete liberty till the day of the
last judgment.

When all the demons were assembled, Solomon pressed his
seal upon their necks to mark them as his slaves. Then he
commanded all the male Jinns to collect every sort of material
for the construction of the temple he was about to build. He
bade also the female Jinns cook, bake, wash, weave, and carry
water ; and what they made, he distributed amongst the poor.
The meats they cooked were placed on tables which covered
an area of four square miles ; and daily thirty thousand portions of beef, as many portions of mutton, and very many birds
and fishes were devoured. The Jinns and devils sat at iron
tables, the poor at tables of wood, the heads of the people at
silver tables, the wise and pious at tables of gold ; and these
latter were served by Solomon in person.

One day, when all spirits, men, beasts, and birds rose satisfied from the tables, Solomon besought God to permit him to
feed to the full all created animals at once. God replied that
he demanded an impossibility. " But," said he, "try to-morrow what thou canst do to satisfy the dwellers of the sea."

On the morrow, accordingly, Solomon bade the Jinns lade
a hundred thousand camels and the same number of mules
with corn, and lead them to the sea-shore. He then cried to
the fishes and said : " Come, ye dwellers in the water, eat and
be satisfied ! "

Then came all manner of fishes to the surface of the water,
and Solomon cast the corn to them, and they ate and were
satisfied, and dived out of sight. But all at once a whale
lifted his head above the surface, and it was like a mountain.
Solomon bade the spirits pour one sack of corn after another
down the throat of the monster, till all the store was exhausted,
there remained not a single grain. But the whale cried, " Feed
me, Solomon ! feed me ! never have I suffered from hunger as
I have this day ! "

Solomon asked the whale if there were any more in the
deep like him. The fish answered : " There are of my race as

many as a thousand kinds, and the smallest is so large that thou wouldst seem in its belly to be but a sand-grain in the desert."

Solomon cast himself upon the earth, and began to weep, and prayed to God to pardon him for his presumption.

"My kingdom," called to him the Most High, "is far greater than thine. Stand up, and behold one creature over which no man has yet obtained the mastery."

Then the sea began to foam and toss, as though churned by the eight winds raging against it, and out of the tumbling brine rose the Leviathan, so great that it could easily have swallowed seven thousand whales such as that which Solomon had attempted to feed ; and the Leviathan cried, with a voice like the roar of thunder : " Praised be God, who by His mighty power preserves me from perishing by hunger." [1]

3. THE BUILDING OF THE TEMPLE. [2]

When Solomon returned from the sea-shore to Jerusalem, he heard the noise of the hammers, and saws, and axes of the Jinns who were engaged in the building of the temple ; and the noise was so great that the inhabitants of Jerusalem could not hear one another speak. Therefore he commanded the Jinns to cease from their work, and he asked them if there was no means whereby the metals and stones could be shaped and cut without making so much noise.

Then one of the spirits stepped forth and said : "The means is known only to the mighty Sachr, who has hitherto escaped your authority."

"Is it impossible to capture this Sachr ? " asked Solomon.

"Sachr," replied the Jinn, " is stronger than all the rest of us together, and he excels us in speed as he does in strength. However, I know that once every month he goes to drink of a fountain in the land of Hidjr ; by this, O king, thou mayest be able to bring him under thy sceptre."

Solomon, thereupon, commanded a Jinn to fly to Hidjr and to empty the well of water, and to fill it up with strong

[1] Weil, pp. 231–4.

[2] The story of the building of the temple, with the assistance of Schamir, has been already related by me in my "Curious Myths of the Middle Ages."

wine.   He bade other Jinns remain in ambush beside the well and watch the result.[1]

After some weeks, when Solomon was pacing his terrace before his palace, he saw a Jinn flying, swifter than the wind, from the direction of Hidjr, and he asked, "What news of Sachr?"

"Sachr lies drunk on the edge of the fountain," said the Jinn; and we have bound him with chains as thick as the pillars of the temple; nevertheless, he will snap them as the hair of a maiden, when he wakes from his drunken sleep."

Solomon instantly mounted the winged Jinn and bade him transport him to the well at Hidjr.   In less than an hour he stood beside the intoxicated demon.   He was not a moment too soon, for the fumes of the wine were passing off, and, if Sachr had opened his eyes, Solomon would have been unable to constrain him.   But now he pressed his signet upon the nape of his neck: Sachr uttered a cry so that the earth rocked on its foundations.

"Fear not," said Solomon, "mighty Jinn; I will restore thee to liberty if thou wilt tell me how I may without noise cut and shape the hardest metals."

"I myself know no means," answered the demon; "but the raven can tell thee how to do this.   Take the eggs out of the raven's nest and place a crystal cover upon them, and thou shalt see how the raven will break it."

Solomon followed the advice of Sachr.   A raven came, and fluttered some time round the cover, and seeing that she could not reach her eggs, she vanished, and returned shortly with a stone in her beak, named Samur or Schamir; and no sooner had she touched the crystal therewith, than it clave asunder.

"Whence hast thou this stone?" asked Solomon of the raven.

"It comes from a mountain in the far west," replied the bird.

Solomon commanded a Jinn to follow the raven to the mountain, and to bring him more of these stones.   Then

[1] The Rabbinic story and the Mussulman are precisely the same, with the difference that Benaiah, the son of Jehoiada, instead of the Jinns, lies in ambush and captures Sachr or Aschmedai (Asmodeus).   (Eisenmenger, i. 351–8.)   As I have given the Jewish version in my "Curious Myths of the Middle Ages," I give the Arab story here.

he released Sachr as he had promised.   When the chains were taken off him, he uttered a loud cry of joy, which in Solomon's ears, bore an ominous sound as of mocking laughter.

When the Jinn returned with the stone Schamir, Solomon mounted a Jinn and was borne back to Jerusalem, where he distributed the stones amongst the Jinns, and they were able to cut the rocks for the temple without noise.[1]

Solomon also made an ark of the covenant ten ells square, and he sought to bring it into the Holy of Holies that he had made ; and when he sought to bring the ark through the door of the temple, the door was ten ells wide.   Now, that was the width of the ark, and ten ells will not go through ten ells. Then, when Solomon saw that the ark would not pass through the door, he was ashamed and cried, " Lift up your heads, O ye gates, and the King of Glory shall come in!"   Then the gates tottered, and would have fallen on his head to punish what they supposed to be a blasphemy, for the doors thought that by "the King of Glory" he meant himself; and they cried to him in anger, "Who is the King of glory?" and he answered, "It is the Lord of Hosts, He is the King of Glory."   And because the doors were so zealous for the honor of God, the Lord promised them that they should never fall into the hands of the enemies of Israel.   Therefore, when the temple was burnt and the treasures were carried into Babylon, the gates sank into the earth and vanished.   And to this the prophet Jeremiah refers (Lament. ii. 9).[2]

Solomon also built him a palace, with great riches in gold, and silver, and precious stones, like no king that was before him.   Many of the halls had crystal floors, and crystal roofs. He had a fountain of liquid brass.[3]   He had also a carpet five hundred parasangs in length ; and whenever the carpet was spread, three hundred thrones of gold and silver were placed on it, and Solomon bade the birds of the air spread their wings over them for a shade.[4]   He built a throne for himself of sandal wood, encrusted with gold and precious stones.

4. THE TRAVELS OF SOLOMON.

Whilst the palace was being built, Solomon made a journey to Damascus.   The Jinn, on whose back he flew, carried him

[1] Weil, pp. 234–7 ; Talmud, Tract. Gittin. fol. 68, cols. 1, 2.
[2] Jalkut Schimoni, fol. 90, col. 4.   [3] Tabari, i. p. 435.
[4] Tabari, i. p. 436.

directly over the valley of ants, which is surrounded by such
crags and precipices, that no man had hitherto seen it.   The
king was much astonished to see such a host of ants under
him, which were as big as wolves, and which, on account of
their grey eyes and grey feet, looked from a distance like a
cloud.   The queen of the ants, who, till this moment, had not
seen a man, was filled with fear when she beheld Solomon,
and she cried to her host, " Hie to your holes, fly ! "

But God commanded her not to fear, and to summon all
her subjects, and to anoint Solomon king of all insects.   Solomon, who heard the words of God, and the answer of the
queen from a distance of many miles, borne to him upon the
wind, descended into the valley beside the queen.   Immediately the whole valley was filled with ants, as far as the eye
could see.

Solomon asked the queen, " Why didst thou fear me, being
surrounded with such a countless and mighty host ? "

" I fear God alone," answered the queen ; " If any danger
were to threaten my subjects, at a sign from me seven times as
many would instantly appear."

" Wherefore then didst thou command the ants to fly to
their holes when I appeared ? "

" Because I feared they would look with wonder and reverence on thee, and thereby for a moment forget their Creator."

" I am greater than thou," added the queen of the ants.

" How so ? " asked Solomon in surprise.

" Because thou hast a metal throne, but my throne is thy
hand, on which I now repose," said the ant.

" Before I leave thee, hast thou no word to say to me ? "

" I ask nothing of thee, but I give thee a piece of advice.
As long as thou livest, give not occasion to be ashamed of thy
name, which signifies *The blameless.*   Beware also never to give
the ring from thy finger, without saying first, ' In the name of
the God of all mercy.' "

Solomon exclaimed, " Lord !   Thy kingdom exceeds and
excels mine ! " and he bade farewell to the queen of the ants.[1]

After Solomon had visited Damascus, he returned another
way, so as not to disturb the ants in their pious contemplation.
As he returned, he heard a cry on the wind, " O God of Abraham, release me from life ! "   Solomon hastened in the direc-

<hr>

[1] Koran, Sura xxvii.; Tabari, i. c. xxviii.; Weil, pp. 237–9.

tion of the voice, and found a very aged man, who said he was more than three hundred years old, and that he had asked God to suffer him to live, till there arose a mighty prophet in the land.

"I am that prophet," said Solomon.   Then the Angel of Death caught away the old man's soul.

Solomon exclaimed, "Thou must have been beside me, to have acted with such speed, thou Angel of Death."

But the Angel answered, "Great is thy mistake.   Know that I stand on the shoulders of an angel, whose head reaches ten thousand years' journey above the seventh heaven, and whose feet are five hundred years' journey beneath the earth. He it is who tells me when I am to fetch a soul.   His eyes are ever fixed on the tree Sidrat Almuntaha, which bears as many leaves as there are living men in the world ; when a man is born, a new leaf buds out ; when a man is about to die, the leaf fades, and at his death, falls of ; and, when the leaf withers, I fly to fetch the soul, the name of which is inscribed upon the leaf."

"And what doest thou then ? "

"Gabriel accompanies me, as often as one of the believers dies ; his soul is wrapped in a green silk cloth, and is breathed into a green bird, which feeds in Paradise till the end of time. But the soul of the sinner is carried by me in a tarred cloth to the gates of hell, where it wanders in misery till the last day."

Then Solomon washed the body of the dead man, buried him, and prayed for his soul, that it might be eased of the pains it would have to undergo during its purgation by the angels Ankir and Munkir.[1]

This journey had so exhausted Solomon, that on his return to Jerusalem he ordered the Jinns to weave him stout silk carpets on which he and all his servants, his throne, tables, and kitchen could be accommodated.   When he wanted to go a journey, he ordered the winds to blow, and raise the carpet with all that was on it, and waft it whither he desired to travel.

One night, Abraham appeared to the king in a dream, and said to him : "God has given thee wisdom and power above every other child of man ; He has given thee dominion over the earth and over the winds ; He has suffered thee to build

---

[1] The Jews also believed in a purgatory ; see Bartolocci, i. 342.

a house to his honor ; thou hast power to speed on the back of Jinns or on the wings of the winds where thou listest ; now employ the gift of God, and visit the city of Jathrib (Medina), which will one day give shelter to the greatest of prophets ; also the city Mecca, in which he will be born, and the temple which I and my son Ishmael—peace be with him ! —rebuilt after the flood."

Next morning Solomon announced his intention to make a pilgrimage to Mecca, and bade every Israelite join in the expedition. The number of pilgrims was so great, that Solomon was obliged to have a new carpet woven by the Jinns of such vast size that it could serve the whole caravan, with the camels and oxen and sheep they destined for sacrifice. When ready to start, Solomon bade the Jinns and demons fly before the carpet ; his confidence in their integrity was so small, that he would not trust them out of his sight : for this reason also he drank invariably out of crystal goblets, that even when drinking he might keep his eyes upon them. The birds he ordered to fly in ranks above the carpet, to give shadow to the pilgrims with their wings.

When all was in readiness, and men, Jinns, beasts, and birds were assembled together, Solomon ordered the winds to descend and bear the carpet, with all upon it, into the air, and waft it to Medina.

When they approached this town Solomon made a sign, and the birds depressed their wings, and the winds abated, and the carpet sank lightly to the earth. But he suffered no man to step off the carpet, as Medina was then in the hands of idolaters. He alone went to the spot where afterwards Mohammed was to erect the first mosque—it was then a cemetery —and there he offered up his noon-day prayer. Then he returned to the carpet ; at a sign the birds spread their wings, the winds gathered force and lifted the carpet, and the whole caravan sailed through the air to Mecca, which was then under the power of the Djorhamides, who were worshippers of the One God, and preserved the Kaaba from desecration by idols.

Solomon, with all his company, entered the city, went in procession round the temple, performed the requisite ceremonies, and offered sacrifices brought for the purpose from Jerusalem. Then he preached a long sermon in the Kaaba, in which he prophesied the birth of Mohammed and the future glory of Mecca.

After three days, Solomon desired to return to Jerusalem, and he remounted his throne on the carpet, and all the pilgrims resumed their places.   When the birds spread their wings, and the carpet was again in motion, the king perceived one ray of sun which pierced the canopy of birds, and this proved to him that one of the birds had deserted its place.

He called to the eagle, and bade it go through the roll-call of the birds, and ascertain which was absent.

The eagle obeyed, and found that the peewit was missing. Solomon was inflamed with anger, especially as he needed the peewit during his journey over the desert, to discover for him the hidden wells and fountains.

" Soar aloft ! " exclaimed Solomon to the eagle, " and seek me this runaway, that I may strip him of his feathers and send him naked forth into the sun, to become the prey of the insects."

The eagle mounted aloft, till the earth was beneath him like a revolving bowl, and he looked in all directions, and at length he spied the peewit coming from the south,   The eagle would have grasped him in his talons, but the little bird implored him, by Solomon, to spare him till he had related his history to the king.

" Trust not in the protection of Solomon," said the eagle ; " thy mother shall bewail thee."   Then the eagle brought the culprit before the king, whose countenance was inflamed with anger, and who, with a frown, signed the runagate to be brought before his throne.[1]

The peewit trembled in every limb, and, in token of submission, let wings and tail droop to the ground.   As Solomon's face still expressed great anger, the bird exclaimed, " O king and prophet of God ! remember that thou also shalt stand before the judgment-throne of God ! "

" How canst thou excuse thine absence without my consent ? " asked the king.

" Sire I bring thee news of a land and a queen of which thou hast not even heard the name—the land of Sheba, and the queen, Balkis.

" These names are indeed strange to me.   Who told thee of them ? "

" A lapwing of that country whom I met in my course, to

---

[1] Targum Scheni Esther, fol. 401 tells the same of the moorcock.

whom I spoke of thy majesty, and the greatness of thy dominion, and wisdom, and power. Then he was astonished, and he related to me that thy name was unknown in his native land ; and he spake to me of his home and the wonders that are there, and he persuaded me to accompany him thither. And on the way he related to me the history of the Queen of Sheba, who commands an army generalled by twelve thousand officers."

Solomon bade the eagle release the peewit, and bade him relate what he had heard of Sheba and its queen.

5. THE HISTORY OF THE QUEEN OF SHEBA.

" Sheba," said the peewit, " is the name of the king who founded the kingdom ; it is also the name of the capital. Sheba was a worshipper of the sun, Eblis having drawn him from the true God, who sends rain from heaven, and covers the earth with plenty, and who reads the thoughts of men's hearts.

" A succession of kings followed Sheba : the last of the dynasty was Scharabel, a tyrant of such dissolute habits that every husband and father feared him. He had a vizir of such singular beauty that the daughters of the Jinns took pleasure in contemplating him, and frequently transformed themselves into gazelles that they might trot alongside of him as he walked, and gaze with admiration on his exquisite beauty. One of these Jinn damsels, Umeira by name, conceived for the vizir a violent passion, and forgetting the great distance which separates the race of the Jinns from that of mortals, she appeared to him one day as he was hunting, and offered him her hand, on condition that he should fly with her into her own land, and that he should never ask her origin. The vizir, dazzled by the marvellous beauty of Umeira, gladly yielded, and she transported him to an island in the midst of the ocean, where she married him. At the end of nine months she gave birth to a daughter, whom she named Balkis. The vizir, all this while, was ignorant of the nature of his bride, and one day forgot himself so far as to ask her to what race she belonged. No sooner had he asked the fatal question, than, with a wail of sorrow, she vanished forever from his sight.

" The vizir now left the island, and, regaining his native country, retired with his babe to a valley far from the capital, and there lived in seclusion.

" As Balkis grew up, her beauty became more striking, and was of such a superhuman nature, that her father became uneasy lest the fame of it should reach the dissolute monster then seated on the throne of Sheba, and lest his daughter should be ravished from his arms. He therefore redoubled his precautions to guard Balkis, keeping her much at home, and only allowing her to appear veiled in public. But these precautions were vain. Scharabel was in the habit of travelling about his empire in disguise, and making himself, by this means, personally acquainted with the condition of his estates.

" On one of these expeditions he appeared, dressed in rags, as a mendicant, at the door of the ex-vizir, and obtained a glimpse of Balkis, then thirteen years old, lovely as a houri ; she stepped out to give the beggar alms. At the same moment, the father hurried out towards his daughter. The eyes of the two men met ; a mutual recognition ensued. The vizir fell at the feet of his king, and entreated pardon, telling him all that had happened ; and Scharabel, who had fallen in love at first glance with Balkis, readily pardoned him, restored him to his place as grand vizir, and lodged him in a magnificent palace near Sheba.

" Installed there, the vizir was full of disquiet. His daughter observing this, inquired the cause, and received from her father the answer that he dreaded lest the tyrant should carry her off to his harem ; ' and,' said the unhappy man, ' I had rather see thee dead, Balkis, than in the power of this licentious monster."

" ' Do not fear for me, my father,' replied Balkis ; ' what thou dreadest shall not take place. Appear cheerful before the king. If he wishes to marry me, then ask him to give me a splendid wedding."

" A few days after, Scharabel sent to ask the hand of Balkis. The virgin replied that it should be his if he would solemnize the marriage with great pomp. To this the king agreed, and a magnificent banquet was prepared.

" After dinner, the vizir and all the company retired, leaving Balkis alone with the king. There were, however, four female slaves present, one singing, another harping, a third dancing, and a fourth pouring out wine for the king. Balkis took the goblet, and plied her royal bridegroom well, till he fell drunk upon the floor, and then, with a dagger, she stabbed him to the heart.

" She at once communicated with her father, and bade him send orders throughout the town that all the citizens were to bring their daughters before the king, that he might add the comely ones to his already extensive list of wives and concubines. He obeyed her, and the commotion in the town was prodigious. Parents gathered their friends, those who were officers in the army agitated amongst their soldiers, and the whole town rose up in revolt, and rushed furiously to the palace, determined on the death of the tyrant.

" Then Balkis cut off the head of the king, and showed it to the excited multitude from a window. A cry of joy rang through Sheba. The palace gates were thrown open, and Balkis was unanimously elected queen in the room of the murdered tyrant.

" From that hour she has governed Sheba with prudence, and has made the country prosperous. She sits to hear suits, and gives judgment on a throne of gold, robed in splendor. All prospers under her wise administration: but, alas! like her predecessors, she too is a worshipper of the sun."

When Solomon heard the story of the peewit, he wrote a letter and sealed it with his ring, gave it to the bird, and bade him carry it immediately to the Queen of Sheba.

The peewit flew like an arrow, and on the morrow appeared before Balkis, and gave her the missive. The queen broke the seal and read : " Solomon, son of David, and servant of the Most High God, to Balkis, queen of Sheba, sendeth greeting. In the name of the merciful and gracious God, peace be to those who walk in His ways. Do what I bid thee : submit immediately to my sceptre." [1]

[1] This is the letter according to Rabbinic authors : "Greeting to thee and to thine ; from me, King Solomon. It is known to thee that the holy, ever-blessed God has made me lord and king over the wild beasts and birds of heaven, and over the devils, and spirits, and ghosts of the night, and that all kings, from the rising to the down-setting of the sun, come and greet me. If thou also wilt come and salute me, then I will show thee great honor above all the kings that lie prostrate before me. But if thou wilt not come, and wilt not salute me, then will I send kings, and soldiers, and horsemen against thee. And if thou sayest in thine heart, ' Hath King Solomon kings, and soldiers, and horsemen ?' then know that the wild beasts are his kings, and soldiers, and horsemen. And if thou sayest, ' What, then, are his horsemen ?' know that the birds of heaven are his horsemen. His army are ghosts, and devils, and spectres of the night ; and they shall torment and slay you at night in your beds, and the wild beasts will rend you in the fields, and the birds will tear the flesh of you." This letter, the Jews say, was sent to the Queen of Sheba by a moorcock. (Targum Scheni: Esther, fol. 401, 440).

The queen, startled at the abrupt and peremptory command, read the letter to her council, and asked their advice.

They urged her to follow her own devices, and promised to agree to whatever she thought fit. She then said : " You know what disasters follow on war. The letter of Solomon is threatening ; I will send him a messenger, and propitiate him with gifts. If he accepts them, he is not above other kings ; if he rejects them, he is a prophet, and we must yield to his sway."

She then dressed five hundred boys as girls, and five hundred girls she equipped in boys' clothes. She collected, for presents, a thousand carpets of gold and silver tissue, a crown adorned with pearls and diamonds, and a great quantity of perfumes.

She also placed a pearl, a diamond cut through in zigzags, and a crystal goblet, in a box, and gave it to her chief ambassador.

Finally, she wrote a letter to Solomon, telling him that, if he was a prophet, he would be able to distinguish boys from girls in the train of the ambassadors, that he would be able to guess the contents of the box, pierce the pearl, thread the diamond, and fill the goblet with water which came neither from earth nor heaven. The chief nobles of Sheba were sent to bear the letter. Before they left, she said to them : " If Solomon receives you with arrogance, fear nothing ; pride is a sure token of weakness. If he receives you graciously, be careful—he is a prophet." The peewit, who had watched all these proceedings, and listened to the message and advice, now flew to Solomon and told him all.

The great king immediately ordered his Jinns to spread his carpet seven leagues long, leading from his throne towards Sheba. He then surrounded himself with gold and gems, and gathered all his courtiers and officers together, and prepared for the audience.

When the ambassadors of Sheba set their feet on the carpet—the end of which was beyond the range of vision— they were full of astonishment. This astonishment increased, and became terror, when they passed between ranks of demons, and Jinns, and nobles, and princes, and soldiers, extending for many miles.

When the leaders of the embassy reached the foot of the throne, Solomon received them with a gracious smile. Then they presented the letter of the queen. Solomon, without opening it, told them its contents, for it had been read by the peewit. They offered the box, and he said that in it were a pearl, a diamond, and a goblet. He next ordered his servants to bring silver ewers before the train of the ambassadors, that they might wash their hands after their journey. Solomon watched intently, and he picked out the boys from the girls at once ; for the boys dipped their hands only in the water, whilst the girls tucked up their sleeves to their shoulders and washed arms as well as hands.

Then the box was opened and the pearl produced. Solomon unclasped his pouch and drew forth Schamir, applied it to the pearl, and a hole was drilled through it immediately. Next he took the diamond. The hole pierced in it wound about, and a thread inserted in one end would not pass through to the other end. Solomon took a piece of silk, called to him a worm, put one end of the thread in its mouth and inserted it in the diamond. The worm crawled down the winding passage, and appeared at the other opening with the silk. In gratitude to the little creature, Solomon gave it for its food forever the mulberry-tree. Then he took the crystal goblet. He summoned to him a huge negro slave, bade him mount a wild horse and gallop it about the plain till it steamed with sweat. Then with ease, the monarch filled the chalice with water that neither came from earth or heaven.

Solomon, having accomplished these tasks, said to the ambassadors : "Take back your presents, I do not want them. Tell the queen what you have seen, and bid her submit to my rule."

When Balkis had heard the report of her servants, she saw that it was in vain for her to resist.

"Solomon," said she, "is a great prophet, and I must myself do him homage."

She accordingly hastened to prepare for her journey, and marched to King Solomon at the head of her twelve thousand generals, and all the armies they commanded. When she was a league from Solomon, the king hit upon a scheme. He called to him a demon, and bade him transport immediately from Sheba the throne of the queen, and set it beside his own. The Jinn replied that he would bring it before noon, but the king could not wait, for the queen would soon be there ; then Asaph, his vizir, said "Raise thine eyes, sire, to heaven, and before thou canst lower them the throne of Balkis will be here."

Asaph knew the ineffable name of God, and therefore was able to do what he said.

Solomon looked up, and before he looked down, Asaph had brought the throne.

As soon as Balkis appeared, Solomon asked her if she recognized the seat. She replied, " It is mine, if it is that which it was." A reply, which we are told, charmed Solomon.

Now the Jinns were envious of Balkis, and they sought to turn away the heart of Solomon away from her ; so they told him that she had hairy legs.[1]

Solomon, accordingly, was particularly curious to inspect her legs. He therefore directed the Jinns to lay down in front of the throne a pavement of crystal one hundred cubits square. Upon this pavement he ordered them to pour water, so that it might appear to be water.

In order to approach Solomon, Queen Balkis raised her petticoats, lest they should be wet in passing through what she supposed to be water of considerable depth. The first step, however, convinced her that the bottom was nearer the surface than she anticipated, and so she dropped her petti-coats, but not before the great king had seen that the Jinns had maligned her legs, and that the only blemish to her legs was three goat's hairs ; and these he was enabled to remove by a composition of arsenic and lime, which was the first de-pilatory preparation ever employed. This was one of the five arts introduced by Solomon into the world. The others were, the art of taking warm baths, the art of piercing pearls, the art of diving, and the art of melting copper.

The queen stepped gracefully towards the king, and bow-ing, offered him two wreaths of flowers, whereof one was nat-ural, the other artificial, asking him which he preferred. The sagacious Solomon seemed perplexed ; he who had written treatises on the herbs, "from the cedar to the hyssop," was nearly outwitted. A swarm of bees was fluttering outside a window. Solomon ordered the window to be opened, and the insects flew in, and settled immediately on the wreath of nat-ural flowers, not one approaching the artificial wreath.

" I will have the wreath the bees have chosen," said the king, triumphantly.

---

[1] According to another account, "that she had ass's legs " (Well, p. 267). Tabari says, "hairy legs" (i. p. 441).

Solomon took Balkis to be his wife, and she worshipped the true God. She gave him all her realm, but he returned it to her ; and when she went into her own land, she bore with her the fruit of her union with Solomon, and in the course of time bore a son, who is the ancestor of the kings of Abyssinia." [1]

6. SOLOMON'S ADVENTURE WITH THE APES.

On one of his journeys, Solomon passed through a valley which was inhabited by apes which dressed themselves like men, and lived in houses, and ate their food in a way wholly superior to other apes.

Solomon descended from his carpet and marched at the head of his soldiers into the valley. The apes assembled to resist him, but one of their elders stepped into the midst of them and said, " Let us rather submit and lay down our arms, for he who comes against us is a holy prophet."

Then three apes were chosen as ambassadors, and were sent to Solomon with overtures of peace.

Solomon asked them to what race they belonged.

The envoys replied, " We are of human origin, and of the race of Israel, and we are descended from those who, in spite of all warnings, have violated the Sabbath, and who have therefore, in punishment, been transformed by God into monkeys."

Solomon had compassion on the apes, and he gave them a letter on parchment, assuring to them undisturbed possession of their valley against all assault by men.

And in after days, in the time of the Calif Omar, some of his troops invaded this valley, and, with great amazement, beheld the apes stone a female which had been taken in adultery. And when they would conquer the valley, an aged ape came before them bearing a parchment letter. This they were unable to read ; so they sent it to the Calif Omar, who was also unable to decipher the writing; but a Jew at his court read it, and it was an assurance given to the apes against invasion by King Solomon.

Therefore Omar sent orders that they were to be left unmolested, and returned to them their parchment.[2]

<hr>

[1] Weil, pp. 246–267 ; Tabari, i. cc. 94, 95.   [2] Weil, pp. 267–9.

7. SOLOMON MARRIES THE DAUGHTER OF PHARAOH.

The throne of Solomon had four feet. It was of red ruby, and of the ruby were made four lions. None but Solomon could sit upon the throne. When Nebuchadnezzar came to Jerusalem and sought to ascend the throne, the lions rose and struck at him, and broke his legs. He was given remedies, and his legs were reset. No one after that ventured to sit on the throne.[1]

Djarada was the daughter of King Nubara, of an island in the Indian Sea, according to the Arabs; of King Pharaoh of Egypt, say the Jews.

Solomon marched against the king, on his carpet, with as many soldiers as it would accommodate; defeated him, and slew him with his own hand. In the palace of King Nubara Solomon found the Princess Djarada, who was more beautiful than all the ladies in Solomon's harem, surpassing even the beautiful Balkis.

Solomon made her mount the carpet, and he forced her, by threats of death, to share his faith and his couch. But Djarada saw in Solomon only the murderer of her father, and she recoiled from his embrace with loathing, and spent her nights and days in tears and sighs. Solomon hoped that time would heal these wounds and reconcile her to her fate; but as, after the expiration of a year, her sorrow showed no signs of abating, he asked her what he could do which might give her comfort. She replied that at home was a statue of her father, and that she desired greatly to have it in her chamber as a reminder of him whom she had lost. Solomon, moved with compassion, sent a Jinn for the statue, and it was set up in the apartment of Djarada. Djarada immediately prostrated herself before it, and offered incense and worship to the image; and this continued for forty days.

Then Asaph heard of it, and he ascended the pulpit in the temple and preached before the king and all the people. He declared how holy and pure had been the ancient prophets from Adam to David, how they had been preserved clean from all idolatry. Then he turned to Solomon, and praised his wisdom and piety during the first years of his reign; but he re-

---

[1] Tabari, i. c. xcvi. p. 448.

gretted that his latter conduct had not been as full of integrity as at first.

When Solomon heard this, he called Asaph to him, and asked him thus before all the people. Asaph answered, "Thou hast suffered thy passions to blind thee, so that idolatry is practised in thy palace."

Solomon hastened to the room of Djarada, and found her in prayer before the image of her departed father. Then he cried out, "We are the servants of God, and to Him shall we return." Then he broke the image and punished Djarada.

After that he put on him garments which had been woven and sewn by virgins, strewed ashes on his head, and went into the wilderness to bewail his sin. God forgave him, after that he had fasted and wept for forty days.[1]

Another sin that Solomon committed was this. He was very fond of horses. One day, when the hour of prayer approached, the horses of Saul were brought before him ; and when nine hundred had passed, Solomon looked up and saw that the hour of prayer was passed and he had forgotten to give glory to God. Then said Solomon, " I have cared for the things of this world, instead of thinking of my Lord ; " and he said, " Bring back the horses ; " and when they were brought back, he cut their throats.[2]

Some commentators on the Koran object that this was an act of injustice, for Solomon had sinned, not the horses ; and they explain away the passage by saying that he dedicated the horses to God, and that he did not kill them.[3]

8. HOW SOLOMON LOST AND RECOVERED HIS RING.

One day that Solomon retired to perform the necessary functions of nature, he placed his ring in the hand of Djarada ; for on such occasions he was wont to remove the ring from his finger. For the first time he forgot the advice of the queen of the ants, and gave no praise to God as he committed the signet to other hands.

Sachr, the mighty Jinn,[4] took advantage of this act of for-

---

[1] Weil, pp. 269–271 ; Tabari, pp. 450, 451.
[2] Koran, Sura xxxviii.   [3] Tabari, pp. 460, 461.
[4] In the Jewish legend, Asmodeus. In "Curiosities of Olden times" I have pointed out the connection between the story of the disgrace of Solomon and that of Nebuchadnezzar, Jovinian, Robert of Sicily, etc.

getfulness, and, assuming the form of Solomon, came to the Egyptian princess and asked her for the ring. She, nothing doubting, restored it to him; and Sachr went to the hall of audience, and ascended the throne.

When Solomon returned, he asked Djarada for the signet.

" I have already given it thee," said she ; and then, contemplating him with attention, she exclaimed, " This is not the king ! Solomon is in the judgment-hall ; thou art an impostor, an evil spirit who has assumed his shape for evil purposes."

Then Solomon was driven, at her cry, from the palace, and every one treated him as a fool or rogue. He begged from door to door, saying, " I, Solomon, was king in Jerusalem ! " but the people mocked him. For three years he was an outcast, because he had transgressed three precepts of the Law— " The king set over thee . . . shall not multiply horses to himself . . . neither shall he multiply wives to himself ; neither shall he greatly multiply to himself silver and gold." [1] And this is what befell him in that time. He went into the land of the Ammonites, and there he fell into great want ; but the master cook of the king's house took him to serve as scullion in the kitchen. After he had served for some time, he one day cooked some meats for the king ; and when the king tasted the meats Solomon had baked, he was well pleased, and sent for Solomon and asked him if he would be his head cook.

Then Solomon consented, and the king of the Ammonites dismissed the master cook, and placed Solomon in his room, and Solomon excelled greatly in cooking, and pleased the king more and more with the variety and excellence of his dishes every day.

Now it fell out that Naama, daughter of the king, saw Solomon from day to day, and she conceived an ardent passion for him, and she went to her mother and said, " I shall die of love, unless I am given the head cook to husband."

The queen was astonished and ashamed, and said, " There are kings and princes and nobles in Ammon ; take to you which you will." But Naama answered, " I will have none save the head cook."

Then the queen went and told the king, and he was exceeding wroth, and would have slain both Solomon and Naama ;

---

[1] Deut. xvii. 16 17.

but when the first fury of his anger was cooled down, he bade one of his servants take them, both Solomon and Naama, and conduct them into the desert, and there leave them to perish.[1] The command of the king was executed, and Solomon and Naama were left in the wilderness without food.. Then they wandered on till they came to the borders of the sea, and Solomon found some fishers, and he labored for them, and every day they gave him, in payment for his services, two fish.

Thus passed the time, till one day Solomon's wife, Naama, on cleaning one of the fishes, found in its belly a ring, and she brought it to her husband ; and behold ! it was his signet which he had put in the hands of Djarada, and which had been taken from her by subtlety by the evil spirit. And this was how he recovered it : on the ring was engraved the Incommunicable Name, and this the Jinn could not endure ; therefore he could not wear the signet, and he cast it into the sea, where the fish had swallowed it.

Now when Solomon recovered his ring, he was filled with joy, and the light returned to his eyes ; he went back to Jerusalem with great haste, and all the people recognized him, and bowed before him : and when the Evil Spirit saw Solomon, and that he had the signet upon his hand, he uttered a loud cry and fled. Solomon refused to see again Djarada, the author of his misfortune ; but he visited Queen Balkis every month, till the day of her death.[2]

When Balkis died, he had her body conveyed to Tadmor in the desert, the city she had built ; but her grave was known to none till the reign of the Calif Walid, when in consequence of a heavy rain, the walls of Tadmor fell. Then was found an iron sarcophagus which was sixty ells long and forty ells wide, which bore this inscription :—" Here lies the pious Balkis, queen of Sheba, wife of the prophet Solomon, son of David. She was converted to the true faith in the thirteenth year of the reign of Solomon ; she married him in the fourteenth, and died in the three-and-twentieth year of his reign."

The son of the Calif raised the lid of the coffin, and beheld a woman, as fresh as if she had only been lately buried.

He announced the fact to his father, and asked what should

---

[1] Emek Nammelek, fol. 14 ; Gittin, fol. 68, col. 2 ; Eisenmenger, i. pp. 358–60. The Anglo-Saxon story of Havelock the Dane bears a strong resemblance to this part of the story of Solomon.

[2] Eisenmenger, i. pp. 358–60 ; Weil, pp. 271–4 ; Tabari, c. 96.

be done with the sarcophagus. Walid ordered him to leave
it where it had been found, and to pile blocks of marble over
it, so that it might not again be disturbed by the hand of
man.[1]

Solomon, when he was again on the throne, placed a crown
on the head of Naama, and seated her beside him, and sent for
the king of Ammon. And when the king came, he was filled
with astonishment, and wondered how his daughter had escaped
from the desert and had found favor with the greatest of monarchs. Then said Solomon, "See! I was thy head-cook, and
this is thy daughter; bid her come to thee and kiss thee."
Then the king of Ammon kissed his daughter and returned,
glad of heart, to his own land.[2]

9. THE DEATH OF SOLOMON.

When Solomon had recovered his throne, he reigned twenty
years. His whole reign was forty years, and he lived in all
fifty-five years.[2] He spent these years in prosecuting the building of the temple. Towards the end of his life he often visited
the temple, and remained there one or two months plunged in
prayer, without leaving it. He took his nourishment in the
temple. He even remained a year thus; and when he was
standing, with bowed head, in an humble attitude before God,
no one ventured to approach him, man or Jinn; if a Jinn drew
near, fire fell from heaven and consumed him.

In the garden of Solomon grew every day an unknown tree.
Solomon asked it, "What is thy name, and what are thy virtues?" And the tree answered him, "I am called such and
such, and I serve such a purpose, either by my fruits, or by my
shadow, or by my fragrance."

Then Solomon transplanted it elsewhere; and if it were a
tree with medicinal properties, he wrote in books the kinds of
remedies for which it served. One day Solomon saw in his
garden a new tree, and he asked it, "What is thy name, and
what purpose dost thou serve?"

The tree replied, "I serve for the destruction of the temple.
Make of me a staff, whereon to lean."

Solomon said, "None can destroy the temple as long as I
am alive." Then he understood that the tree warned him that

<hr>

[1] Weil, p. 274.   [2] Eisenmenger, i. 361.   [3] Tabari, p. 454.

16*

he must shortly die.　He pulled up the tree, and of it he made a staff, and, when he prayed, he leaned on this staff to keep himself upright.

Solomon knew that the temple was not completed, and that if he died, and the Jinns knew of it, they would leave off building ; therefore he prayed, " O Lord ! grant that the event of my death may be hidden from the Jinns, that they may finish this temple."

God heard his prayer, that the temple might be completed, and that the Jinns might be humbled.　Solomon died in the temple, standing, leaning on his staff, with his head bowed in adoration.　And his soul was taken so gently from him by the Angel of Death, that the body remained standing ; and so it remained for a whole year, and those who saw him thought he was absorbed in prayer, and they ventured not to approach.

The Jinns worked night and day till the temple was finished.　Now, God had ordered, the same day that the soul left Solomon, a little white ant, which devours wood, to come up out of the earth under the staff, and to gnaw the inside of the staff.　She ate a little every day ; and as the staff was very strong and stout, she had not finished it till the end of the year. Then, when the temple was finished, at the same time the staff was eaten up, and it crumbled under the weight of Solomon, and the body fell.　Thus the Jinns knew that Solomon was dead.　Now, wherever the white ant eats wood, the void is filled up with clay and water by the Jinns ; and this they will continue to do till the day of the Resurrection, in gratitude to the little ant which announced to them the death of him who held them in bondage.　If the clay and the water are not inserted by the Jinns, whence can they come ?

The sages assembled and enclosed an ant in a box, with a piece of wood, for a night and a day ; then they compared the amount devoured in that time with the length of the staff, and thus they ascertained how long a time Solomon had been dead.[1]

---

[1] Koran, Sura xxxiv. ; Tabari, c. 97 ; Weil, p. 279.

XXXIX.

ELIJAH.

WHEN the prophet Elijah appeared, idolatry was general. God sent him to Balbek (Heliopolis), to persuade the inhabitants to renounce the worship of Baal, from whom the city took its name. Some say that Baal was the name of a woman, beautiful of countenance. The Israelites also adored Baal ; Elijah preached against idolatry ; and Ahab at first believed in him, and rejected Baal, but after a while relapsed. Then Elijah prayed, and God sent a famine on the land for three years, and many men died. None had bread save Elijah, and when any smelt the odor of bread, they said " Elijah hath passed this way ! "

One day Elijah came to the house of an old woman who had a son named Elisha. Both complained of hunger. Elijah gave them bread. It is said, likewise, that Elisha was paralytic, and that at the prayer of Elijah he was healed.

When the famine had lasted three years, Elijah went, accompanied by Elisha, before King Ahab, and he said :—
" For three years you have been without bread ; let your god Baal, if he can, satisfy your hunger. If he cannot, I will pray to Jehovah, and He will deliver you out of your distress, if you will consent to worship Him."

Ahab consented. Then Elijah ordered the idol of Baal to be taken out of the city, and the worshippers of Baal invoked the god, but their prayers remained unanswered. Then Elijah prayed, and immediately rain fell, and the earth brought forth green herb and corn.

Nevertheless, shortly after, the people returned to idolatry, and Elijah was weary of his life ; he consecrated Elisha to succeed him, and he prayed to God, "O Lord ! save me from this untoward generation." And God heard his cry, and He carried him away and gave him life till the day when Israfiel shall sound the trump of judgment.[1]

Both Jews and Mussulmans believe that Elijah is not dead, but that he lives, and appears at intervals. The Mussulmans have confused him with El Khoudr, and relate many wonderful stories of him. He is unquestionably the origin of the

[1] Tabari, i. c. 84.

Wandering Jew. His reappearances are mentioned in the
Talmud, and in later Jewish legends, as, for instance, in a
story told by Abraham Tendlau.[1] A poor Jew and his wife
were reduced to great necessity; the man had not clothes in
which to go forth and ask for work. Then his wife borrowed
for him clothes, and he entered the street seeking work. He
met a venerable man, who bade him use him as a slave. The
Jew engaged to build a palace for a prince with the assistance
of his slave, for ten thousand thalers. The mysterious stranger labored hard and angels assisted him, so that the mansion
was completed with astonishing rapidity. When the Jew had
received the money, the old man announced that he was Elijah, who had come to assist him, and vanished.

After the Arabs had captured the city of Elvan, Fadhilah,
at the head of three hundred horsemen, pitched his tents, late
in the evening, between two mountains. Fadhilah having begun his evening prayer with a loud voice, heard the words
" Allah akbar ! " (God is great !) repeated distinctly, and each
word of his prayer was followed in a similar manner. Fadhilah, not believing this to be an echo, was much astonished,
and cried out, " O thou ! whether thou art of the angel ranks,
or whether thou art of some other order of spirits, it is well,
the power of God be with thee ; but if thou art a man, then let
mine eyes light upon thee, that I may rejoice in thy presence
and society."

Scarcely had he spoken these words, before an aged man
with bald head stood before him, holding a staff in his hand,
and much resembling a dervish in appearance. After having
courteously saluted him, Fadhilah asked the old man who he
was. Thereupon the stranger answered, " Bassi Hadut Issa,
I am here by command of the Lord Jesus, who has left me in
this world, that I may live therein until He comes a second
time to earth. I wait for the Lord, who is the Fountain of
Happiness, and in obedience to his command I dwell beyond
the mountain."

When Fadhilah heard these words, he asked when the
Lord Jesus would appear ; and the old man replied that his
appearing would be at the end of the world.

But this only increased Fadhilah's curiosity, so that he inquired the signs of the approach of the end of all things ;

[1] Das Buch der Sagen und Legenden jüdischer Vorzeit, p. 45 ; Stuttgardt, 1845.

whereupon Zerib bar Elia gave him an account of the general social and moral dissolution which would be the climax of this world's history.[1]

"In the second year of Hezekiah," says the Rabbinic Sether Olam Rabba (c. 17), "Elijah disappeared, and he will not appear again till the Messiah come; then he will show himself once more; and he will again disappear till Gog and Magog show themselves. And all this time he writes the events and transactions that happen in each century.... Letters from Elijah were brought to King Joram seven years after Elijah had disappeared."

A prophecy ascribed to Elijah is preserved in the Gemara:[2] "The world will last six thousand years; it will lie desert for two thousand years; the Messiah will reign two thousand years; but, because of our iniquities which have superabounded, the years of the Messiah have passed away."

XL.

ISAIAH.

THE Book of the Ascension of Isaiah has reached us only in an Ethiopic version, which was published along with a translation by Archbishop Laurence, Oxford, 1819. Gieseler translated the book, and gave learned prolegomena, and notes, Göttingen, 1837; and Gfrorer has included it in his "Prophetæ Pseudepigraphi," Stuttgardt, 1840, pp. 1–55, with the Latin translation. It must have existed in Greek and Latin, for fragments of the Latin apocryphal book remain, and have been published by Cardinal Mai, in "Scriptorum Veterum Nova Collectio;" Romæ, 1824, t. III. ii. 238 et seq.: and it is very evident from these that they are versions of a Greek original, and not of the Ethiopic.

Whilst Isaiah was speaking to the king Hezekiah, he suddenly stopped, and his soul was borne away by an angel. He traversed the firmament, where he saw the strife of the angels and demons, waged between the earth and the moon. He entered the six heavens and admired their glory; then he penetrated into the seventh heaven, where he saw the Holy Trinity,

---

[1] Herbelot, Bibl. Orient., s. v. Zerib, iii. p. 607.
[2] Gemara, Avoda Sara, c. i. fol. 65.

and there the events of futurity were revealed to him. When he returned to himself, Isaiah related to Hezekiah all that he had seen and heard, except what concerned his son Manasseh.

This is the prophecy of Isaiah concerning Antichrist : "And when that time had passed, Berial, the great angel, the prince of this world, Berial will descend from his place in the form of a man ; an impious king, the murderer of his mother, a king of this world.

"And he will pluck up from amongst the twelve apostles the plant that they had planted, and it will fall into his hands.

"And all the powers of the world will do the will of the angel Berial, the impious king.

"At his word, the sun will shine in the darkness of the night, and the moon will appear at the eleventh hour.

"He will do all his pleasures ; he will ill-treat the Well-Beloved, and will say to him, Lo! I am God, and before me there is none other.

"And all the world will believe in him.

"And sacrifice will be offered to him, and a worship of adoration, saying, He alone is God, and there is none other.

"Then the greater number of those gathered together to receive the Well-Beloved will turn aside to Berial ;

"Who by his power will work miracles in the cities and in the country ;

"And everywhere shall a table be spread for him.

"His domination shall be for three years seven months and twenty-seven days." [1]

Only when Hezekiah was at the point of death, did Isaiah reveal to him what and how great would be the iniquities of his son. Then the king would have slain Manasseh : "I had rather," said he, "die without posterity, than leave behind me a son who should persecute the saints."

When the prophet saw that Hezekiah loved God more than his own son, he was glad, and he restrained the king, and said, "It is the will of God that he should live."

Manasseh reigned in the room of his father, and was a cruel tyrant. He worshipped idols, and sought to make Isaiah partake in his idolatry. And when he could not succeed, he sawed him asunder with a saw of wood.

"And whilst Isaiah was being cut asunder, Melekira stood

---

[1] Anabasticon, iv. 2–12.

up and accused him, and all the lying prophets were present,
and they showed great joy, and they mocked him.

" And Belial said to Isaiah ; ' Confess that all thou hast
said is false, and that the ways of Manasseh are good and just.

" ' Confess that the ways of Melekira, and of those that
are with him, are good.'

" He spake thus to him, as the saw entered into his flesh.

" But Isaiah was in an ecstasy, and his eyes were open,
and he looked upon the spectators of his passion.

" Then said Melekira to Isaiah : ' Confess what I shall say,
and I will change the heart of those who persecute thee, and
I will make Manasseh, and the heads of Judah, and his people,
and all Jerusalem worship thee.'

" Then Isaiah answered and said : ' Cursed art thou in all
that thou sayest, and in all thy power, and in all thy disciples !

" ' Thou canst do nothing against me ; all thou canst do is
to take from me this miserable life.'

" Then they seized the prophet, and they sawed him with
a saw of wood, Isaiah, son of Amos.

" And Manasseh and Melekira, and the lying prophets, and
the princes of Israel, and all the people, beheld his execution.

" Now before that the execution was accomplished, he said
to the prophets who had followed him : ' Fly to Tyre and
Sidon, for the Lord hath given the cup to me alone.'

" And whilst the saw cut into his flesh, Isaiah uttered no
complaint and shed no tears ; but he ceased not to commune
with the Holy Spirit till the saw had cloven him to the middle
of his body." [1]

In the Mishna [2] it is related that the Rabbi Simeon Ben
Azai found in Jerusalem (2d cent.) a genealogy, wherein it
was written that Manasseh killed Isaiah. Manasseh said to
Isaiah, " Moses, thy master, said, There shall no man see God
and live. [3] But thou hast said, I saw the Lord seated upon
His throne. [4] Moses said, What other nation is there so great,
that hath God so nigh unto them ? [5] But thou hast said, Seek
ye the Lord while He may be found." [6]

Isaiah thought, " If I excuse myself, I shall only increase
his guilt and not save myself ; " so he answered not a word,
but pronounced the Incommunicable Name, and a cedar-tree

<hr>

[1] Anabasticon, v. 1–14.   [2] Tract. Jebammoth, c. 4.
[3] Exod. xxxiii. 20.   [4] Isai. vi. 1.   [5] Deut. iv. 7.
[6] Isai. lv. 6.

opened, and he disappeared within it. Then Manasseh ordered, and they took the cedar, and sawed it into lengthways; and when the saw reached his mouth, he died.

XLI

JEREMIAH.

THE work entitled *De Vitis Prophetarum*, falsely attributed to S. Epiphanius, contains some apocryphal details concerning Jeremiah.   It is said that he was stoned at Taphens in Egypt, in a place where Pharaoh formerly lived.   He was held in great honor by the Egyptians, because of the service he had rendered them in taming the serpents and crocodiles.

The faithful who take a little dust from the spot where he died, are able to employ it as a remedy against the bites of serpents, and to drive away crocodiles.

The prophet announced to the priests and wise men of Egypt that when a virgin, who had borne a son, should set her foot on Egyptian soil, all the idols should fall.

Before the destruction of Jerusalem, he hid the ark of the covenant in a rock, which opened for the purpose, and closed upon it.   Then said he to the princes of the people and to the elders, "The Lord has gone up from Sinai, but He will come again with His sacred power.   And this shall be the token of His coming,—all nations shall bow before the Wood."

Then the prophet continued, "None of the priests and prophets shall open the ark, except Moses, the elect of God; and Aaron shall alone unfold the tables it contains.   At the Resurrection, the ark shall arise out of the rock first of all, and it shall be placed upon Mount Zion.   Then all the saints will go there and await the Lord, and they will put the enemy to flight who seeks their destruction."

Having said these words, he traced with his finger the name of God upon the rock, and the name remained graven there as if cut with iron.   Then a cloud descended upon the rock and hid it, and no man has seen it since.   It is in the desert, amongst the mountains, where are the tombs of Moses and Aaron.   At night a cloud of fire shines above the spot.

XLII.

EZEKIEL.

EZEKIEL, whom the Arabs call Kazquil, was the son of an aged couple, who had no children.   They prayed to God, and He gave them a son.

Ezekiel was a prophet, and he exhorted the men of Jerusalem to war, but they would not go forth to battle.   Then God sent a pestilence, and there died of them every day very many. So, fearing death, a million fled from the city, hoping to escape the pestilence, but the wrath of God overtook them, and they fell dead.

Then those who survived in the city went forth to bury them, but they were too numerous ; therefore they built a wall round the corpses, to protect them from the beasts of the field ; and thus they lay exposed to the heat and cold for many years, till the flesh had rotted off their bones.

Once the prophet Ezekiel came that way, and he saw this great multitude of dead and dry bones.   He prayed, and God restored them to life again, and they stood upon their feet a great army, and entered into the city, and lived out the rest of their days.   It is said that among the Jews there are, to this day, descendants of those who were resuscitated, and they may be recognized by the corpse-like odor they exhale.[1]

The Jews relate that a celebrated Rabbi found the greatest difficulty in comprehending the book of Ezekiel ; therefore his disciples prepared for him three hundred tuns of oil to feed his lamp whilst he studied at night the visions of the prophet.[2]

XLIII.

EZRA.

CYRUS, in the year 537 before Christ, put an end to the captivity of the Jews in Babylon, as had been foretold by Daniel ; and not only did he permit the Jews to return to Jerusalem, but he furnished them with the means of rebuilding their city

<hr>

[1] Tabari, i. c. 83.   [2] Bartolocci, i. p. 848.

and temple. The Oriental writers, to explain the motive of
Cyrus, say that his mother was a Jewess, and that he himself
was married to the Jewess Maschat, sister of Zerubabbel, a
granddaughter of the king Jehoiakim.

In 523 before Christ, Cambyses, having reigned a brief
time, was succeeded by Smerdis, the Magian, who is called, in
the Scriptures, Artaxerxes. He, being ill-disposed towards the
Jews, withdrew from them the gifts made by Cyrus, and arrested their work. Smerdis, however, reigned only two years,
and was succeeded by Darius Hystaspes, who continued the
work of Cyrus, by the hands of Ezra or Esdras, one of the instruments used by God to restore His people.

Ezra was the son of Seraiah, of the lineage of Aaron.

In the Koran [1] it is said that Ezra, passing through a village near Jerusalem, whose houses were ruined, exclaimed,
"Can God restore these waste places, and revive the inhabitants ?"

Then God made him die ; and he remained dead for one
hundred years. At the end of that time God revived him,
and he saw the village rebuilt and full of busy people.

The commentators on the Koran say that Ezra (Ozaïr),
when young, had been taken away captive by Nebuchadnezzar,
but that he was delivered miraculously from prison, and returned to Jerusalem, which he found in ruins. He halted at a
village, near the city, named Sair-Abad. Its houses were fall-
en and without inhabitants, but the fig-tree and vines remained
in the gardens. Ezra collected the fruit, and made himself a
little cell out of the fallen stones. And he kept near him the
ass on which he had ridden.

The holy man, on contemplating from his hermitage the
ruins of the holy city and the temple, wept bitterly before
the Lord, and said often with a tone rather of lament
than doubt, " How can the walls of Jerusalem ever be set up
again ? "

Then God bade him die, and hid him from the eyes of men,
in his cell, with all that he had about him, his fruit, his mat,
and his ass. At the close of a century God revived him, and
he found all as when he had died ; the ass standing, and the
fruit unwithered. Then Ezra saw the works that had been
executed in Jerusalem, how the walls were being set up, and

---

[1] Sura, ii.

the breaches repaired, and he said, "God is Almighty ; He can do whatsoever pleaseth him ! "

After his resurrection, he went into the holy city, and spent night and day in explaining to the people the Law, as he remembered it. But it had been forgotten by the Jews, and therefore they disregarded his instruction.

The Iman Thalebi says, that the Jews, to test the mission of Ezra, placed five pens in his hand, and with each he wrote at the same moment with like facility as if he held only one ; and he wrote all the Books of the Sacred Canon, as he drew them from his memory, without the assistance of a book.

The Jews, however, said amongst themselves, "How can we be sure that what Ezra has written is the true sacred text, since there is none amongst us who can bear witness ? "

Then one of them said, " I have heard say that my grandfather preserved a copy of the sacred books, and that they were hidden by him in a hollow rock, which he marked so that it might be recognized again."

They therefore sought the place which had been marked, and there they found a volume containing the Scriptures, which having been compared with what Ezra had written, it was found that the agreement was exact. Then the people, astonished at the miracle, cried out that Ezra was a god.[1]

At the time of carrying away into Babylon, the sacred fire had been cast into a well in the temple court. Ezra, having drawn some of the dirt out of the well, placed on it the wood of the sacrifice ; then the flame, which for a hundred and forty years had been extinguished, burst forth again out of the mire. When Ezra saw this wonder, he thrice drank of the dust out of the well ; and thus he imbibed the prophetic spirit, and the power of recomposing from memory the lost sacred books.[2]

---

[1] Herbelot, Bibliothèque Orientale, iii. p. 89.   [2] Abulfaraj, p. 57.

XLIV.

ZECHARIAH.

Sozomen[1] relates that the prophet Zechariah appeared to Colomeras, a farmer of the village of Chupher, in Palestine, and revealed to him his tomb ; and on excavations having been made on the spot, an ancient Hebrew book was discovered, which, however, was not regarded as canonical. Nicephoras repeats the story after Sozomen.[2]

---

[1] Hist. Eccles. lib. ix. cap. ult.　　　　[2] Ibid., lib. xiv. c. 8.